"WHO ARE THE HUNS?"

THE LAW OF NATIONS AND ITS BREAKERS

BY

DR. ERNST MÜLLER-MEININGEN
M. P.

WITH AN INTRODUCTION
BY THE TRANSLATOR

R. L. ORCHELLE

GEORG REIMER PUBLISHER
BERLIN 1915

G. E. STECHERT & Co. (ALFRED HAFNER)
151—155. W. 25th STREET NEW YORK

A FOREWORD.

The dispassionate historian of the future, of a future not far distant, striving with proper intellectual honesty to ascertain the truth that underlay and accompanied the titanic world war, will be forced to delve among mountains of material. But dead material is not and cannot be living evidence. Indeed, under the circumstances it may be said that the vast accumulations of printed news, reports, documents and what not are in many cases the absolute negation of evidence.

This war has produced not only a falsification of facts, of causes, of motives, of representations, on a scale never before approached in the history of the world, but it has produced the hypnosis and intoxication and even the persistent poisoning of entire peoples. The influences that were formerly confined to small, restricted circles have, through the monopolizing of the press and the cables by one party of belligerents, spread until they have created all-pervading mental atmospheres and climates, not only among the warring powers but among the neutral.

That truth is entirely relative has once more been proved in this tragedy of civilization. That falsehood may usurp its place and powers is appallingly evident. But it is no less apparent that the immortal vitality of truth will assert itself despite the most desperate and extensive attempts to slay, distort or smother it.

I believe that among the few reliable documents of the World War, which have been compiled during its progress, the conscientious historian cannot fail to yield a high place to this work by Dr. Ernst Müller-Meiningen, which is now given to the world in an English translation. Dr. Müller-Meiningen is not only a prominent personality of the Reichstag, in which he represents a Bavarian constituency, but he is likewise one of the most brilliant judicial minds of Germany, and a man of that incorruptible intellectual honesty which another German, Friedrich Nietzsche, lifted to the level of a great ideal. His work upon the world war and the breakdown of international law has been acclaimed as one of the most significant and authoritative in Germany—where the national thoroughness and love of exact truth have been nobly maintained through all the stress and distress of war—in sharp and luminous contrast to the *debâcle* of reason, justice and logic shown in the countries of her enemies, and also, alas, in many so-called neutral lands.

The original work, "Der Weltkrieg und der Zusammenbruch des Völkerrechts," of which this English edition is an abridgment, has passed into the third edition in Germany. Each successive edition has been carefully revised by the author and all necessary corrections made in the light of subsequent events and official testimony up to about July, 1915. All inaccuracies or doubtful statements have been eliminated in so far as this has been possible. Dates, names, places, when not forbidden by the military censorship, have been given, and where American or English sources have been quoted and the original texts were not available, these have been retranslated, as plainly marked, from the German translation.

The work is a tremendous and an incontrovertible indictment of the entire Entente in diplomacy, intrigue and warfare and at the same time a simple and logical justification of Germany's cause. It is not propaganda but protest, it is not even protest so much as an appeal to that sense of justice and sanity which, despite the terrible inroads made upon it by the violences and asperities of war, must remain the fundament of all civilization. It approaches the great question of international law and morality not so much from the viewpoint of the patriot, as from that of the jurist and the historian. And in those passages in which an added emphasis or feeling are encountered, Dr. Müller-Meiningen speaks rather as the inclusive humanitarian than the exclusive patriot.

The book possesses a special interest for us Americans. Its appeal is quiet, proud, almost unexpressed, and if we will only give ear to it, it cannot but redound to our intellectual and national advantage—provided the dissipation of erroneous conceptions and the destruction of false ideas insidiously inculcated into our minds, be considered an advantage by us.

As an American at present in Germany and one proud of the privilege of living in the midst of a great and noble people in the exalted hour of its destiny, the position of my own country has been a source of constant grief and much shame. These feelings are shared, I know, by all true Americans who understand the real motives behind this giant catastrophe to civilization and who have had the privilege of knowing the real Germany and the real German people. By them America is seen as a land helpless in the clutches of vast and evil forces, financial, journalistic and political, a people abandoned as a prey to those very influences that fetter and destroy all real freedom. They behold their native land, from the first an instrument in the hands of these evil elements, turned into a weapon of death against a friendly people struggling heroically for those very possessions, those priceless liberties for which the men of 1776 fought and died. They behold vainglorious, nay, bloodthirsty demagogues such as Roosevelt openly inciting with a fanaticism that amounts to delirium, the American populace to a war that would surpass in infamy and cowardice any that has ever been waged on this unhappy earth. They behold with amazement the patience, the dignity and the calm magnanimity of the German people in the face of these monumental wrongs.

Alas, no land ever had a more golden, a more splendid opportunity for rising in moral grandeur above the nations involved in the dire and tragic toils of war. No nation has ever flung away its glorious privilege more recklessly or for more ignoble and sordid ends. The great masses of our people, we know, are not to blame. But we must either confess that these lie helpless in the grasp of a tiny minority of financiers and politicians, and that our democracy is therefore a cruel and monumental failure, or that they are indifferent to the fate of half mankind. Have we not ventured to judge in the twilight of our ignorance? — and shall we not be judged in the cold, white light of History — implacable and just?

As an American I am able to speak with greater frankness to my countrymen than it is possible for Dr. Müller-Meiningen to do. And I hold the dissipation of error to be the duty of every true American, irrespective of his descent. To all those who hold intellectual integrity to be one of our noblest gifts and the realization of truth to be the most elevating function of the mind, I would commend the reading of the work of this German scholar in an open and hospitable spirit.

The vexed and murky question of Belgian neutrality, that cunning cry and device that won our sentimental American sympathies above all other pleas or principles, is revealed in its true aspects and relations. The growing rancor and bitterness of warfare on sea and land is proved to be the natural and inevitable result of England's disregard for the laws of nations and Germany's enforced retaliation by the means at her disposal. The fictitious and hysterical tales of those famous Belgian atrocities sown and shouted through the world by the millions of miry mouths and organs at command of the Allies, are opposed by countless and authentic instances of the most revolting cruelties perpetrated upon German soldiers and civilians under the impulse of that blind and fanatic hatred engendered by the press of London, Paris and St. Petersburg. For it is not only secret diplomacy which constitutes so terrible a danger to the welfare of all nations, but the still greater danger of a corrupt and vicious press such as that of Lord Northcliffe in London — a man who, even in the judgment of his own countrymen, must be held up to lasting infamy by mankind as one of the chief instruments in bringing about the gigantic disaster.

Since this book has been compiled, a still stronger and entirely non-partisan light has been thrown upon the roots of the great struggle by the publication of the correspondence of the Belgian Ministers in London, Paris and Berlin which, despite desperate attempts at silence and suppression, has been published in many neutral papers. The revelations and opinions of these Belgian diplomats have all the fascination of a portentous drama and prove once more that the Entente Powers are the living negations of all those things for which they are pretending to do battle. The latest proof of this is their lawless and uncalled-for outrage upon the rights of Greece. Once more actions speak louder than words.

The author's final indictment of those responsible for the great crime and conspiracy must sink like a flame into the hearts of all who are capable of sympathizing with the cause of a traduced, heroic and outraged people. There is a deathless and indestructible essence in truth which must at length leaven the great masses of falsehood, distorted fact and misrepresentation which have been heaped up to hide the causes and the consequences of this war. I am persuaded that this clear and conscientious work of Dr. Müller-Meiningen's will help to set the cause of Germany aright before the world of to-day as surely as history will set it aright before posterity.

Berlin, Oct. 25. 1915.

R. L. ORCHELLE.

CONTENTS.

PART ONE.

PART TWO.

Questions of Legality in Naval Warfare.

PART ONE.

Rules and Regulations of Warfare on Land.

CHAPTER I.

The Neutrality of Belgium.

Motto: If three confederate highwaymen lie in wait for a traveller whose business takes him through a forest, and pounce upon him from behind, is it the traveller whom we must arrest?
Frederick the Great, in his 'Apology for My Political Attitude'.

Let us openly confess to-day, we German fanatics for strict legality, that we were really alarmed when we heard of the violation of Belgian neutrality through the attack on Liège. To-day, in the light of ensuing events, there is no one, especially no German jurist, who is not filled with the deepest conviction that we could not have done otherwise! We were bound to take the course we did. In the name of all that is valid in history our right so to act was indisputable and absolute.

I recall the repeated debates of the Budget Commission of the Reichstag upon the neutrality of Belgium, especially with regard to the last great military measures. These discussions always resulted in a declaration by the German Imperial Government that it would never violate Belgian neutrality, except in the case of some other state first violating this neutrality, which would force the Government to ignore it on the score of military necessity.

One may now be permitted to mention the fact that this was for many years the point of view adopted by the Foreign Office in its private conferences. It was upon this standpoint that the Government based its action when, to the infinite surprise of the whole German people, from the Kaiser to the poorest workman, the forces of war were unleashed against us in a single night.

As England based her declaration of war entirely upon the breach of Belgian neutrality by the German army, this question of international law shall be threshed out at once.

I. The Vienna Congress of 1815 incorporated the Belgian territories with Holland by agreement of the latter and the four allied Great Powers, as the kingdom of the Netherlands. This created a barrier against new efforts by a restless France towards expansion in a northerly direction. When Belgium declared herself independent after the Revolution of 1830, this standpoint was recognized by the Powers, and the newly-established kingdom of Belgium was neutralised by the treaties of November the 15th, 1831. The course pursued towards Holland was dictated by the same political purpose as that towards Belgium. The resistance of Holland was broken by the armed intervention of France, and Belgium's new position was recognized by Holland in the Treaty concluded in London, April 19th, 1839.

On that day the two countries signed an agreement in which, in Article 7, it is stated:

"Belgium forms an independent and permanently neutral state. It is bound to observe the same neutrality towards all other states."

On the same day France, Austria, Great Britain, Prussia and Russia signed treaties both with Belgium and the Netherlands, in which the agreement between these two countries was inseparably incorporated. It is upon these treaties that the independence of Belgium is based.

The German Empire has now become the guarantor of Prussia.

As previously indicated, the kingdom of Belgium was originally founded by the other Great Powers as security against France. For various reasons, similarity of language, descent and so on, there was a gradual *rapprochement* of the Walloon Belgians towards France. We elders may recall that already in 1870 there were strong protests against the anti-German demonstrations on Belgian soil. Bismarck was even obliged on one occasion, as we may read in his "Reminiscences," to "throw cold water" on the fever that prevailed in Brussels in favor of everything French, which showed itself in the form of gross insults to the German refugees during the war. The manoeuverings of Paris and London to overthrow the neutrality of Belgium have become more and more determined ever since the Treaty of Frankfort. That these eternal machinations met with some success, and that Belgium allowed herself to be enmeshed in the Franco-British net, was plainly shown by the fortifications erected by Brialmont—in destroying which the German army has won such laurels.

A glance at the fortifications of Liège, Namur and above all, Antwerp, reveals the fact that the whole idea of the Brialmont fortifications was directed in the first place against Germany. A comparison with Holland tells heavily against Belgium. Holland would also have been drawn into this game of sham-neutrality, had the Dutch statesmen been no wiser than the Belgian. The fortifications at Flushing and Terneuzen at the mouth of the Scheldt prove that Holland took her neutrality seriously, above all in regard to the blockade of the Scheldt, a matter of the greatest political importance. Belgium, on the other hand was, as we now know, not only complacent, but had been well prepared for decades for a breach of her neutrality. It may justly be recalled at this juncture that Colonel Ducarmé once declared that France intended to annex Belgium on the strength of the speech made (1895) by the French Secretary of War, Zurlinden. Belgium has long been aware of France's intentions.

The existence of the Brialmont fortifications was a visible proof of that policy of Belgium which has perhaps cost her her very existence as a state.[1] Of course this *rapprochement* towards the two Great Powers was bound to become closer after the break-up of the old historic enmity between England and France and the formation between them of the Entente in 1902. The "Encircling Policy" of Edward VII. had to reckon upon Belgium as a base of operations. Against all these plottings and flatteries the young King Albert set up still less resistance

[1] In a pamphlet entitled "Bismarck and Belgium," Dr. Pius Dirr, Brussels, 1915, again points out that France in 1852 persistently entertained the project of annexing Belgium. Bismarck has given a direct proof of this in reference to Napoleon III. (1866 and 1869).

than the old King Leopold had done. The State was driven irresistibly forward along the crooked path of a one-sided anti-German policy.

II. The German Government had been perfectly aware for a long time of the existence of this state of things.[1] Therefore the formula—justly dictated by a legitimate feeling of distrust: "We will respect Belgian neutrality as long as other nations respect it." This could also have been worded: "We will respect Belgian neutrality if Belgium herself respects it."

One must realize all this, if one is rightly to estimate the attitude of Germany during those first days of August, 1914.

The German Government deserves all the more praise in that, in spite of all this evidence against Belgium, it nevertheless regarded the marching of German troops into Belgium during the night of the 3rd of August (according to the state of affairs as then understood) as objectionable and a breach of the agreement of 1839. It admitted this to be an "injustice" for which it promised full satisfaction and restoration of the *status quo ante*. This recognition seems all the greater since at that time the outrageous excesses committed by the Belgian population, particularly in Antwerp and Brussels, against German fugitives, were already known in Berlin, and these excesses proportionately increased, as soon as the entry of the German troops into Belgian territory became known.

The speech of the German Imperial Chancellor, von Bethmann Hollweg, was as follows, according to the shorthand report:

[1] The press also pointed with perfect justice to the Belgian legislative projects in 1905 concerning the extension of the harbor works and the defences of the town of Antwerp, and the motives thereof, as demonstrable proof that for ten years past England and Belgium had played their cards against Germany. It may be stated thus: "Antwerp is not only the metropolis of our commerce and navigation, but she is also destined to figure as the most important fortification in the country — a *rôle* which she never sought and of which no other town is envious. It is Antwerp which, in the event of war, must be the last bulwark of our independence and the last refuge of our nationality." The projected plans on the lower Scheldt were not carried out, as it was understood that Antwerp figured as an English bridge-head. After the declaration of war, England still made frantic endeavors to induce Holland to break her neutrality, so that the English army could advance through Antwerp and its safe retreat to the town be assured.

"Gentlemen, we are now in a state of necessity, and necessity knows no law. Our troops have occupied Luxemburg, perhaps they are already treading Belgian soil. Gentlemen, this is contrary to international law. It is true that the French Government has declared at Brussels that it is willing to respect the neutrality of Belgium if its enemies will do the same. But we knew that France was in readiness for an invasion. France could afford to wait, but we could not! A French attack upon our flank on the lower Rhine might have been fatal to us. We were thus forced to disregard the justifiable protest of the governments of Luxemburg and Belgium. This wrong —I speak quite openly,—which we hereby commit, we shall endeavor to make good as soon as our military purpose is attained. He who is threatened as we are threatened and is battling for all that is dearest to him, has the right to think of only one thing: how he is to hew his way through!" [1]

---

[1] In a speech in the German Reichstag on the 2nd of December, 1914, the German Imperial Chancellor, von Bethmann Hollweg, to a certain extent rectified his position of the 4th of August and at the same time supplemented and thoroughly illuminated it. He said, among other things:

"*The neutrality of Belgium, which England pretended to protect, was a mere mask.*

On the 2nd of August, at 7 o'clock in the evening, we communicated the fact in Brussels that the military plans of France were known to us, and that we were thereby compelled, for the sake of our own self-preservation, to march through Belgium. But as early as the afternoon of the 2nd of August, that is to say, before the least news of our *demarche* in Brussels was known or could have been known in London, England had promised France her support, and an unconditional support at that, in the case of an attack by the German fleet upon the French coast. Not a single word was mentioned with reference to Belgian neutrality.

"This fact is confirmed through the declaration made by Sir Edward Grey in the Commons on the 3rd of August, a declaration which, on account of the difficulties of telegraphic communication, was not known to me *in extenso* on the 4th of August. This fact is further confirmed through the Blue Book of the English Government itself. How then could England assert that it drew the sword because we had violated Belgian neutrality? (Laughter and cries of "hypocrisy!") And how could English statesmen, who must have been well-acquainted with all that went before, have the presumption to talk of Belgian neutrality?

When on the 4th of August, I spoke of the wrong that we had committed through our invasion of Belgium, it was not yet certain whether the government

The prolonged and vociferous applause of the whole house showed plainly that all the representatives of the German people—nay, the German nation itself, stood behind these words of the Chancellor.

From a strictly legal standpoint there is something like a contradiction in the Imperial Chancellor's words. But he was not speaking precisely as a jurist, or as a professor of international law, but as a politician, and as the spokesman of the German Empire. It was his intention at that time to hold out to Belgium a golden opportunity of resuming friendly relations, with the object of restraining and dissuading the Belgians from any act of war. At that time the Imperial Chan-

---

in Brussels would not, in the hour of need, determine to spare the country and withdraw under protest to Antwerp. You may remember that on behalf of our army leadership, I directed a new proposal to be made in this sense to the Belgian Government, after our occupation of Liège. It was necessary for military reasons to keep the possibility of such a development on the 4th of August in mind under all circumstances.

Even at that time there were various proofs of the guilt of the Belgian Government. Positive written proofs were not yet available for me, but the English statesmen were fully aware of these proofs. Now that the documents found in Brussels have been given full publicity through me, and the manner and degree in which Belgium had given up its neutrality in favor of England have been fully confirmed, there are two facts that must be proclaimed to the world.

Firstly, that when our troops entered Belgian territory on the night of the 3rd of August, they stood on the soil of a land which had long since discarded its neutrality: and secondly, that England did not declare war against us on account of Belgian neutrality, which she herself had long since rendered a dead letter, but because she believed that, in combination with two great military powers, she would be able to gain complete mastery over us. Since the 2nd of August, on which date England gave France her promise of co-operation in war, England ceased to be a neutral, and, in actual fact, stood ranged with our enemies. Her motive in basing her declaration of war of the 4th of August, on the violation of Belgian neutrality, was to mislead neutrals and also her own people as to the real motives of the war. It was a piece of bluff. Now that the Anglo-Belgian war-plan, with all its carefully-planned detail, lies open before us, the policy of English statesmen is for all time laid bare to the eyes of history. To this English diplomacy has added another stroke. England calls upon Japan to snatch from us heroic Kiao-Chow, thereby violating the neutrality of China. Has England taken any measures against this breach of neutrality? Has she shown in this instance her scrupulous consideration for neutral states?"

cellor was not fully informed of the evil part which the supposedly neutral state had played for so long, as we shall presently proceed to show. He therefore made a discrimination between the necessary state of self-defence against France and the necessary precautionary measures, which he defined as "illegalities," against Belgium. Of course his words, "France could wait, but we could not," gave his hearers plainly to understand that the co-operation of other powers with France was, under any circumstances, to be expected. He did not indicate whether the third power was to be Belgium herself or—England.

The speech of the Imperial Chancellor on the 4th of August was, therefore, undoubtedly dictated by diplomatic courtesy. In his opinion the Belgian Government and population were still open to influence—as by the open admission of the objective fact of a breach of neutrality by the advance of the German troops. Hence the admission of "the wrong that we are doing, for which we shall try to make amends." It was not the jurist who spoke thus, but the responsible politician, the statesman.

A few days sufficed to prove that neither the *bona fides* nor the goodwill that the Imperial Chancellor had anticipated had any existence in Belgium. Neither was there any sign of the good results which the Chancellor had hoped from his friendly advances. In fact, quite the contrary!

The development of affairs during the next few days (from the 4th to the 7th of August) also proved that it would have been sheer insanity to expect Germany to await the incursion of French or English troops into Belgium, in order to make good the advantage gained by our foes at the expense of streams of German soldiers' blood, and in order thereupon to plead a condition of necessity and defence before a court which from the very beginning, was hostile and partisan. This would, *in praxi*, have been the case, and the court would have been the forum of the English Government, which would have maintained a benevolent silence and uttered no word regarding a breach of neutrality—had France still more openly broken this neutrality than she had already done with the consent and according to the wishes of the English Government. Before what other court should Germany have accused herself? Possibly before the Hague Tribunal? After the French had stood in their thousands at Namur and Liège, a verdict such as this—delivered after many months—would scarcely have set the air a-tremble.

Germany acted according to the necessity of which she was conscious, and, as the further developments of military events have shown, in justifiable defence against Belgium, which had broken its own neutrality, as well as against France, guilty of the same breach of agreement.

The preservation of the German Empire, in view of the conditions described below, made it a matter of dire necessity temporarily to violate the duties of agreement in the matter of neutrality, which had passed from Prussia to the German Empire. And this even though Belgium had not broken the pact of neutrality with respect to the German Empire. The preservation of its own existence, its integrity, independence and position as a world power rendered it necessary that the German Empire should *in concreto*, adopt the legality of this condition of necessity.

It would already have sufficed that neutral Belgium had *tolerated* the mere threats of France against the existence of the German Empire, or the mere *neglect* of such negotiations as would have been necessary to obviate these threats on the part of France, in order to give Germany the right to protect herself against France and Belgium, even though this necessitated her violating the neutrality of the latter country.

Belgium, under the state of necessity imposed upon the German Empire would, like Luxemburg, have been fully entitled to demand complete compensation for the actions enjoined by this state of necessity—a right which was repeatedly and expressly acknowledged by Germany and which she has promptly and dutifully fulfilled in the case of Luxemburg. Germany was not obliged in this state of impending danger, first to establish by discussions this point of international law.

A state of necessity and defence demands deeds and not words. The compensation for damage committed was a matter for later and subsequent negotiations, both from the point of view of material and legal aspects, as applicable to the land whose neutrality had been broken.

Had not Belgium for more than a generation accustomed

itself to the idea of a struggle against Germany and devoted its entire military and other policy to this idea, it would have been able to gain complete compensation and an increase of its financial, economic and political position from the merely temporary disturbance of its neutrality, instead of annihilation and the ruin of its independence.

III. That Belgium itself was convinced that such a condition of necessity would immediately dissipate its stipulated neutrality, may be seen in the following:

As early as 1845, the "Revue Militaire Belge" published an article whose author does not in the least take Belgian neutrality seriously, and considers it to be a mere empty phrase. (Similar views are held by Frank, ("Muenchener Neueste Nachrichten" of the 20th of August.) It was all very well to proclaim this during peace but it became of itself null and void at the outbreak of war. Belgium, like every other state, would then be confronted by the question as to which party was to have its support.

The Belgian author Grandgagnage likewise declares that conditions are mightier than men, and that despite all treaties, Belgium, in case of war, would be the field in which European quarrels would be decided. Should Belgium seek to oppose them, it was to be foreseen that it would not only risk defeats, but might even be in danger of losing its independence.

The *Pandectes Belges*, (Vol. 68) contain several passages which, it is true, are opposed to such an interpretation. They nevertheless acknowledge in an unqualified manner two instances in which the neutrality of Belgium need not be observed: that is to say, the declaration of war by all the five guarantee powers and the non-observance of its neutrality by Belgium itself.

This Belgian view must undoubtedly be recognized as unobjectionable, both from the standpoint of the nation and that of international law.

Both instances, as we shall show, have been confirmed.

Firstly, the treaties of the 15th of November, 1831, regarding the neutralization of the Kingdom of Belgium, were signed by England, Austria, France, Prussia, Russia and Belgium. In 1871 Prussia was succeeded by the German Empire.

Thus, condition I. is fulfilled, namely that all signatory powers should be at war. At the beginning of August it was only England which *apparently* and formally stood outside the sphere of conflict.

However, it is of peculiar interest to observe what Professor Rivier, a celebrated Brussels *savant*, in his text-book of international law, (2nd edition, 1899, page 184) says regarding the state of necessity.

"A state is entitled to violate the sovereignty of a third state, should this be too weak to hinder the possibility of its territory from serving the attacking nation as a basis." One might almost believe that these words had been written in August 1914! We see that a state may violate a treaty of neutrality, when a subject of the treaty does not possess the power to prevent the enemy of the first state, that is to say, of the neutral state, from using its land as a basis of operations. This is the case in the present instance. Is there anyone who would venture to dispute the fact that Belgium was too weak to defend its territory against a French attack? Even though Belgium had the best intentions—(which of course, were lacking)—of asserting its sovereignty and neutrality, France would simply have overwhelmed it.

This fact in itself is in reality, the only moral excuse which Belgium could offer for the violation of its own neutrality. It was upon this assumption that the policy of Baron Lambermont, a policy which, unfortunately, was ignored by King Albert, was founded. Lambermont held that it was only necessary for the Belgian army to occupy the frontiers of the country in the defence of its neutrality; he held that it would be folly to take up arms against a stronger opponent. The new "Jungbluth tactics"—to take up a one-sided attitude—proved to be the ruin of King Albert.[1]

---

[1] In the Year Book of the d. V. R. I. 1127 there are published extracts from reports on the Belgian "Projets de Loi sur la Malice" (the Belgian Ministry, after the election of June 1912, had proposed an increase in the war footing of the army to 350 000 men) as follows:

"Il ne faut pas oublier que la neutralité de la Belgique a été proclamée non pas comme un bienfait pour la Belgique, mais exclusivement dans l'intérêt de l'équilibre européen ... "

We thus see that even authoritative Belgian legal experts have recognized that Belgian neutrality may be abrogated in the event of necessity, which would also be the case if Belgium would *in concreto* prove to be too weak to defend it with success. Of course in that country, one had reckoned that France would have urged the plea of necessity, against which neither Belgium nor England would have ventured to offer any objections.

This fact has been recognized by a number of influential English politicians, such as Ramsay Macdonald, Sir Arthur Ponsonby and others. They have not only conceded this point, but have because of it directly reproached Sir Edward Grey and his henchmen, Sir Francis Bertie and Sir Arthur Nicolson.

But of course, that which is right for one should naturally be just for the other. This is especially true in the case of a quick surprise attack on two fronts, made overnight, by two of the strongest of the Great Powers, as happened in the case of Germany. We repeat in the most emphatic manner, our declaration, based upon our absolute knowledge of essential conditions, and pledge our word, as every other Reichstag deputy could do, *that prior to July 31st no one in Germany had any thought of war.* No preparations for mobilization took place in Germany before the 1st of August. While Russia and France, as has now been proved, had for months been arming themselves for the great war which England had been preparing for years, Germany had no suspicion of the possibility of such complications and up to the 1st of August, still cherished the hope that it might be possible for her to pursue her way in peace.

There is an historical interest attached to the fact, which is expatiated upon in this report (I, 1129) that in the year 1840—that is to say, immediately after the treaty of the 19th of April, 1839—when the Oriental question had already once threatened to provoke a European war, France had communicated the following to the Belgian Government: Should this government (the Belgian) not be in a position to defend its integrity and its neutrality, France might find itself obliged, in the event of a war with Germany, to occupy Belgium.

This declaration vividly reminds one of the opinions which the English military attaché incautiously expressed to the Chief of the Belgian General Staff—as revealed through the publication of documents from the Belgian archives in the "Norddeutsche Allgemeine Zeitung".

As a proof of how heavily the burden of "extreme necessity" lay upon Germany and forced her to the breach of neutrality, one might cite the first proclamation of the German Government which clearly guaranteed Belgium complete damages and restoration of the complete freedom and independence of the country, as soon as the temporary military necessities had been met. See the Note which the German envoy von Below-Saleske, handed to the Belgian Minister of Foreign Affairs, Monsieur D'Avignon, on the 2nd of August, 1914. (Belgian Grey Book, No. 20, page 26.)

On the 4th of August, Germany delivered another note to Belgium, in which it gave notice that, "au besoin de la force des armes", it was forced to adopt certain measures of security which, in view of the French threats, had become necessary, ("indispensable"). Belgium, on its part, as soon as the Germans had marched over the frontier, had on the 4th of August, handed his passports to the German Minister. (Grey Book, No. 31 and 44. The answer of Belgium on the 3rd August, No. 22.) On the same day, King Albert of Belgium appealed to England for *diplomatic* intervention. (See English White Book, No. 153, and Grey Book, No. 25.)

The proclamation of the 12th of August, 1914, may also be cited for further important evidence, as follows:

..."The German Government deeply deplores the fact that, owing to the attitude of the Belgian Government towards Germany, a bloody conflict has taken place. Germany does not come as an enemy to Belgium. It is owing entirely to the pressure of circumstances, due to the military measures taken by France, that it has been brought to the serious conclusion to march into Belgium and to occupy Liège as a base for its further military operations. After the Belgian army had vindicated the honour of its arms by offering an heroic resistance to our large and superior army, the German Government *begs* his Majesty the King of Belgium, and the Belgian Government, to spare their country the further terrors of war. The German Government *is willing to make any compromise* with the Belgians, which may be compatible with its negotiations with France. Germany once more solemnly pledges its word that it has no intention of acquiring Belgian territory and that nothing could be farther from its purposes. Germany is still prepared to evacuate Belgium without delay as soon as the military situation permits of this."

The answer which the Belgian Government delivered to this on the 13th of August was in the nature of a curt refusal.[1] (See Belgian Grey Book.)

Is this the language of a greedy "militarism," hungering for world-power? Here the government of the victorious, most powerful military state of the world, *begs* the government of a small, impotent nation to call a halt to the farther terrors of warfare. Has there ever in the history of the world been a similar case of the making of such advances as border on the limits of self-respect? And this, despite the fact that one was pretty firmly convinced by the 12th of August of all that Belgium had brought about in the violation of its own neutrality! Not only are we conscious of a desire to make good every injustice, however trivial, but also of the state of absolute necessity which forced Germany to take measures against Belgium.

Of course, if the revelations of the "Frankfurter Zeitung" during the beginning of the month of October, 1914, regarding the personal attitude of King Albert toward the Triple Entente, revelations which moreover, are in perfect accordance with the views here expressed and perfectly confirm them,—be correct, it becomes clear that this continued insolent and haughty attitude of the Belgian Government must be looked upon as a mere result of the attitude of its king.

King Albert, according to these reports, had already concluded a sort of military convention with France and Eng-

[1] It is characteristic of the attitude of the Belgian Government, which was hostile from the very beginning, that this extraordinarily important proclamation to the Belgian people was completely suppressed—and that by public notices in the press and elsewhere, the false report was spread that Germany wished to compel Belgium to take arms against France and England under the Prussian command. This dishonest attitude also proves that the whole Belgian policy from the beginning had been so directed as to range itself on the side of the Triple Alliance, as the apparently stronger factor, through thick and thin. Even later, the Government perpetrated the most grievous wrong upon its own people by an attitude of the most unexampled untruthfulness.

land in the spring of 1914, and, as the representative of the Triple Entente, had undertaken to create a league among the neutral states of Europe in order completely to isolate Germany. This plan was wrecked by the resistance of Holland. Thereupon the King despatched a message to the King of England behind the back of the Belgian ministry, beseeching him to protect the neutrality of Belgium.

However this may be, one thing is absolutely certain. If ever there was a case in which one of the guarantors of Belgian neutrality was justified in abrogating this neutrality, it was in this instance.

The hypocrisy of the entire behavior of England and Belgium in this question of neutrality may, for example, be seen in the following characteristic Belgian expression of opinion:

In the "XXe Siècle" of Brussels, of August 20th, 1914, the leading article is a lecture given by the Abbé de Lannoy, before the "Faculté de Philosophie et Lettres de L'Institut St. Louis" in October 1913, that is to say, ten months before the outbreak of the war. The neutrality of Belgium is the subject of this lecture. After a general survey of the history of the development of this neutral state, the Abbé de Lannoy sought to make clear that to-day this neutrality was threatened only by Germany. This neutrality was first conceived as a protective measure against France in 1850, since England would under no conditions have permitted it to possess Antwerp: but now the positions were changed. *England would defend Antwerp against Germany.* Under these changed conditions, *Belgium had no longer any further interest in adhering to its neutrality*... In diplomatic parlance, Belgian neutrality will still remain a sort of formula to which everyone will appeal according to his immediate interests, and which everyone will interpret according to his own desire, until that day when tragic events will make clear that it was only a formula...."

"From this it appears that England could no longer confine herself to merely being the defender of our independence. *If England intends to defend us, it will not be as a guarantee power, but as a belligerent power.*"

De Lannoy, with prophetic vision, is thus able to foresee that England would in all events participate in the war, and *that the breach of Belgian neutrality was merely a prctext for engaging in the war.*

Therefore all Belgium was of the same opinion as the well-known Abbé and acted accordingly. On the other hand, similar views are expressed in the book of the American writer, Homer Lee,—"The Day of the Saxon," who declares that the neutrality of small states that lie between large ones, is a mere anomaly. Holland and Belgium were to become military annexes of Great Britain. Then England could be attacked only from the mouth of the Elbe, and Germany's expansion along the sea-coast would be impossible. Silvio Pietro Rivetta makes a very just observation upon this point: "No other nation has so frequently occupied neutral territory and broken its pledges, as England. Whenever a small neutral country lies between two large ones, it is extremely important to acquire possession of this state at the very beginning of the war, so that it does not fall into the hands of the enemy."

IV. If the question of legalisation through necessity, according to the foregoing exposition, is theoretically and in principle to be answered in the affirmative in favor of international law, so the concrete example is naturally decided only by the responsible authorities of that state which lays claim to the law of necessity, that is to say, in the case at hand the German army leaders in connection with the foreign policy of the German Empire. Any other solution is unthinkable. An appeal to a non-partisan court would be impossible for legal, and, above all, practical military reasons.

The state of necessity for Germany was based upon the following: that according to the views of the German army leadership, an irruption of French troops through Belgian territory into Germany was an immediate threat and that this irruption for Germany, involved in a world war, would have been fatal. Subsequent events have confirmed this view. This fact is of considerable significance.

More than once the Imperial Chancellor, von Bethmann Hollweg, declared: "We knew that the French plans of war contemplated a march through Belgium to attack the unprotected Rhine provinces!..." It was this fact which gave birth to the condition of necessity by virtue of which Germany had the right of ignoring the neutrality agreement of 1839. Germany is justified in making this appeal to necessity, not only with regard to a Belgium quite willing to act as a participant, but also with regard to the guarantee powers, one of which,—that is to say,—France, is naturally no longer entitled to be considered as such. He who does not wish to concede that Germany acted under a stress of necessity, must, as Miltner and others so justly point out, accept the monstrous doctrine that Germany should have first awaited the violation and then protested. And what then?

Not even the "Daily Mail" or the "Temps" could suppose that Germany would be so naively simple.[1]

V. In the first days of August, the German Government still adhered to the assumption, as proved by the speech of the Imperial Chancellor on the 4th August, that the Belgian Government was averse to a French penetration of Belgium in order to reach Germany. In the note which the German Chancellor sent to the German Minister in Brussels on the 2nd of August, he expresses his anxiety lest Belgium, in spite of the best intentions, should not be able to resist the French advance successfully without assistance. Germany must therefore anticipate the French attack.

According to the present situation, it is obvious that Belgium had no such intention. The French irruption into Germany was something that had already been agreed upon between France and

---

[1] The English conception of a state of necessity and self-defence may be shown by the classic example of the notorious onslaught made upon Copenhagen in 1807. This was made because, as the English declared, they feared that Denmark might possibly range itself on the side of Napoleon. Wellington at that time spoke the historic words: "Great Britain had only put into exercise that law of self-preservation, that needed no learned and intricate disquisitions to justify!"

That was sufficient for England in order to set the Danish capital in flames by a bombardment in the midst of peace — to reduce 300 houses to ashes and to drag away the whole Danish fleet. And only because Denmark did not break its neutrality! And to-day we have this English fanaticism regarding neutrality, although the justification of Germany is a hundred times stronger.

Belgium, as well as prepared for by military measures undertaken on both sides.

The facts and evidence in this direction are still accumulating. The entire official material which has been collected will be published at a later date.

Not only from considerations of a state of necessity, but also from another point of view, which had been foreseen, as shown above, by the "Pandectes belges," the proceeding of Germany against Belgium must be conceived as *fully justified and unobjectionable with regard to international law.*

In the passage from the "Pandectes belges" quoted above, it is declared that the violation of Belgium's neutrality by herself would automatically destroy it. Not the slightest objection can be urged against this. *Article 7 of the Agreement of 1839, Clause 2, which stipulates that Belgium is to observe the same neutrality towards all states, has been grossly violated by her.*

In common with France and England, she prepared military operations against the other guarantee powers of the agreement of 1839, that is to say against Prussia, and thereby against the whole German Empire and its ally, Austria. Thereby was the neutrality of Belgium destroyed. She has no right to make further demands upon the advantages of her neutrality.

Military and political facts furnish the most authentic confirmation of this. Among other things, Belgium, prior to the 4th of August, which was the day on which the German troops first crossed the frontier, that is to say, during the time from the 1st to the 3rd of August, had permitted numerous French military automobiles to proceed through Belgium towards the frontier, and French military airmen to fly above Belgian territory without hindering these breaches of neutrality, or even making any serious attempt to do so. It is further confirmed by a great number of witnesses that, as early as the afternoon of the 2nd of August, numerous French officers were officially on duty in Brussels. The 45th Regiment of French Infantry was despatched on the 31st July to Namur in military motors, as is attested by unprejudiced French witnesses. On the 2nd of August, French troops were stationed in the Belgian village of Erqueline.[1] (See French Yellow Book, Nos. 146 and 147: Violations of the frontier of Belgium and Germany through French troops on the 3rd August, 1914, as established by the German Ambassador in Paris, followed, of course, by refutation —146, 148, 149.)

According to declarations on oath before a protocol in the German courts, there were strong French detachments in Charleroi at the end of July. According to the "Norddeutsche Allgemeine Zeitung," a German gas-worker gave witness that Kerdavain, the Conseiller du Departement du Nord, officially acknowledged that 150 000 men were in Maubeuge on the 1st August, and the same number at Givet, in order to force a way into Germany through Belgium. (Onnaing on August 1st, 8 o'clock P. M.)

The methodical arming of the whole Belgian people with military rifles, converting them into *franc-tireurs*, as well as the preparations for resistance from the first village upon the frontier on, proved conclusively that the entire resistance against Germany had been organized and made ready, precisely as in France, where it had been officially propagated for some years.

It is also further established by the declarations of French prisoners that French officers were professionally active in Liège and Brussels some weeks before the outbreak of the war. Before the declaration of war, the Belgian soldiers were given prints of various French and British regiments, in order that they might thus be able to distinguish their future allies. An arsenal was discovered at Maubeuge containing—English ammunition, which had been stored up there long before the declaration of war! The denials of the English, in view of the revelations regarding the "Conventions," are absolutely not to be believed, and cannot furnish the slightest proof in refutation. France and Belgium had, on that day on which Sir Edward

---

[1] The "Norddeutsche Allgemeine Zeitung" of the 18th of January, demonstrates on a basis of sworn testimony that as early as the 24th July, 1914, some two companies of French infantry from Paris detrained at Erqueline. Countless witnesses under oath regarding the Belgian and French cruelties towards civil prisoners, confirm the opinion which prevails here that already in July all preparations for a common war against Germany had been settled between Belgium and France.

Grey thought himself able to play off the guarantee of Belgian neutrality officially as a trump card against Germany, already violated the so-called neutrality in every possible form.

Thus, through all her proceedings, of which more and more come to light, Belgium had broken her neutrality in the grossest manner, and had thereby herself annulled the contract of 1839.

VI. It is instructive to consider how the English Government itself to-day regards the question of a violation of the law of neutrality under necessity. The official edition of the rules of war, by Colonel Edwards and Professor Oppenheim, and published by order of His Majesty's Secretary of State for War for the guidance of officers of His Majesty's army, declares in article 468, page 101, Clause 3:

"However, should a belligerent violate neutral territory by marching troops across it and should the neutral power be unable or unwilling to resist this violation, then the other belligerent is entitled to attack the enemy in this territory." Lawrence, the most prominent English authority upon international law, designates in his "Principles of International Law," 1910, page 136, the occupation of Egypt as "justified by the vital interests of Great Britain." On page 69 he declares that "extreme necessity will justify a temporary violation of neutral territory." Other English authorities on international law, such as Hall, Edmonds and Oppenheim, are of the same opinion.

In the volume, "The Royal Navy, A history from the Earliest Time to the Present", we find the following:

"The (English) attack upon Copenhagen in 1807, (see above) was, without doubt, a wise and at all events, necessary measure. In times of general war, small weak nations that are not able to protect their own neutrality and might be used as tools by one of the stronger combatants, become sources of danger for the other belligerent. It is no more than wise if the opposed party should use the first opportunity to deprive these neutrals of their weapons which, though comparatively harmless in the hands of small and unambitious states, might, under the leadership of great and aggressive states, become most formidable." (*retranslation.*)

One of the collaborators in this book, Mr. Theodore Roosevelt, has now become one of the most frenetic of these "neutrality" fanatics.

Therefore, as soon as the French had crossed the Belgian frontier, the German Empire, even from an English point of view, was undoubtedly justified in moving troops into Belgium. This was what really happened. The country was not obliged to wait for this moment. Yet, in spite of all this, it did wait. When, in the first days of August, it saw that, on account of the toleration by Belgium of her violated neutrality, airmen, automobiles, single officers, and larger detachments of troops, would be bound to be followed by the French army, the German General Staff simply performed its duty. It had the right to choose the manner of defence, which, according to its opinion, was necessary to avert the immediate threatening and illegal attack of France, which had in effect, already occurred. This right was rendered the more apparent, since the neutral power of Belgium had proved to be "unable and unwilling" to defend itself against the French incursion and breach of neutrality and had in fact, of its own accord, surrendered it.

Thus Germany, even according to French, English and Belgian[1] authorities, was, both from a point of international law and military practice, justified in acting as she did.

VII. A great mass of facts still remains convincingly to substantiate our presentation of this long-prepared attack,

---

[1] In the "Pandectes Belges," 68, which we have already cited, I find on page 104, No. 34, the following remarkable statement regarding the Belgian conception of neutrality and the present German procedure:

"On peut se demander si dans ces deux hypothèses, la Belgique devrait attendre, l'arme au bras, l'attaque de son adversaire; s'il ne lui serait pas permis de prendre le devant et d'aller attaquer l'ennemi chez lui, alors que les préparatifs faits par ce dernier, ne laissent aucun doute sur son intention de nous envahir? Nous répondons, que cela lui serait permis, car dans le cas indiqué, l'attaque n'est qu'une forme de la légitime défense. Elle prévient l'aggression imminente. C'est la force employée pour éviter le préjudice irréparable que produirait l'attente." — Further, regarding the neutrality of Belgium, in the same work, No. 20:

"Au premier signal de la guerre tombe la neutralité" (Page 98); No. 23: "tous les engagements ne tarderaient;" No. 22: "conventions, qui ne deviennent définitivement obligatoires," see also Page 90, No. 137.

but of these we shall here quote only such as are publicly and personally vouched for by reputable witnesses.

These are documents of the greatest importance, not only on account of the false statement that the breach of Belgian neutrality by Germany was England's reason for her declaration of war, but also for the truth of the statement that England, from the very beginning, had intended to co-operate with France and Belgium. That England had made her calculations with both lands, and was bound to them by the 1st August either by compact or through the personal undertakings of the responsible leader of English foreign policy, is proved by the following facts and documents which complete and verify themselves. First of all, the Prime Minister, in a speech made in Cardiff at the beginning of October, revealed the fact that England, as early as 1912, had refused to declare its neutrality to Germany in case of a war. Let us first take the despatch of Sir Edward Grey to Ambassador Goschen on the 1st August, 1914. It says:

"He (the German Ambassador) asked me whether, if Germany gave a promise not to violate Belgium neutrality, we would engage to remain neutral.

I replied that I could not say that; our hands were still free, and we were considering what our attitude should be. All I could say was that our attitude would be determined largely by public opinion here, and that the neutrality of Belgium would appeal very strongly to public opinion here. I did not think that we could give a promise of neutrality on that condition alone.

The Ambassador pressed me as to whether I could not formulate conditions on which we would remain neutral. He even suggested that the integrity of France and her colonies might be guaranteed.

I said that I felt obliged to refuse definitely any promise to remain neutral on similar terms, and I could only say that we must keep our hands free."

(See No. 106, No. 85, 87, English White Book, and Blue Book.[1])

---

[1] The greatest Roumanian Teutophobe, Take Jonescu, declared that Prince Lichnowsky was firmly convinced, at least up to the 27th July, that

Let us take in addition to this, the representation of Ambassador Prince Lichnowsky, which appeared in the "Norddeutsche Allgemeine Zeitung" of September 4th, 1914, and gives a resumé of all the events from the 1st of August. Among other things we may here read: "In answer to my question whether he would give me a decisive answer regarding the neutrality of Great Britain if we should agree to respect Belgian neutrality, the Minister replied that *he was not able to do this.*[1]

Thirdly, we should add that Sir Edward Grey, on the 3rd August, declared in the House of Commons that as early as the afternoon of August 2nd, he had promised the French Ambassador the complete support of the English Fleet in the event of the German fleet attacking the French coasts or the French merchant marine. It was not until the night of the 3rd and 4th of August that the breach of Belgian neutrality by German troops occurred.

The German Government went to the utmost possible limits in order formally to assure the neutrality of England, as may be seen in a communication from Grey to Goschen. But invariably in vain. And this is perhaps the best proof that a plan of co-operation between the three states against Germany had been resolved upon and prepared for long beforehand.

VIII. In support of the correctness of this view one might quote much more evidence. This confirms us in the opinion that political difficulties of a domestic nature, above all, the civil war threatening on account of the question of Ulster, made it appear desirable to produce a feeling of unity in England through the provocation of a great continental war. This is publicly confirmed in an interesting interview with Senator Count Di San Martino, in the "Giornale d'Italia." Sir Edward Grey, on his part, acted in this way because of the ancient hate that he bore Germany. His policy had constantly taken its source from the fixed idea that Germany was the Alpha and

---

peace would not be disturbed. Even on the 28th he had advised him to continue his cure in Aix-les-Bains.

[1] See the formal and repeated assurance of Germany to England that Belgium's territory would remain inviolable if England were to remain neutral, and France respect this neutrality. (See White Book, No. 157.)

Omega of all obstacles with regard to England: Winston Churchill was his faithful henchman, the *enfant terrible* of the present unholy ministry.

An official document has been found at Tourcoing, near Lille in France. It is a poster, signed by the Burgomaster, Gustav Dron, a member of the French Senate, and it bears the date of the 1st of August, 1914. It is a proclamation addressed to the people with regard to the outbreak of the war. In this proclamation we find the following:

"England, our friend, has no thought of yielding up the dominion of the seas and the supremacy in world trade to German control. It was determined to put an end to this madness of armaments, which is ruining all the great nations of to-day."

This proclamation is of the utmost importance for the historian, for it proves that England was already determined on the 1st of August to take part in the war on the side of France and Russia.

"The Nation," an American pro-English weekly of considerable reputation, publishes certain interesting communications of its London correspondent, J. Ranken Towse.

Towse declares that since the 1st of August, that is, three days before the declaration of war, feverish military preparations were observed by him, such as the continuous transport of troops to the coast, and the requisition of horses, motors and motor-lorries. He further declares:

"It has now become obvious that preparations for the war had been made three months ago. I know for a certainty that several Naval Reserve officers had already been appointed to their ships at that period, and I am assured by a personality whom I regard as a responsible authority, that Lord Kitchener had, some weeks ago, made a secret trip to Belgium in order to confer with the Belgian General Staff with regard to our Expeditionary Corps."[1] (*retranslation.*)

[1] "The Daily Mail Year-Book for 1915" confirms in all details that England was the first of the warring states to have its fleet completely mobilized, as early as the 27th of July, before anyone in Germany thought of war, or a single man or horse stood ready. (See also "Freisinnige Zeitung," No. 2, 1915.)

IX If these facts, as attested by witnesses, are correct, the whole contemptible trickery of which Sir Edward Grey was guilty towards the unsuspicious representatives of the German Government, Ambassador Lichnowsky and the Imperial Chancellor Bethmann Hollweg, from the 1st to the 4th of August, becomes clear as day. This despicable jugglery with the representatives of a great power is certainly unparalleled in history for its absolute dishonesty.

But M. Sasonow and Sir Edward Grey would convince us that the "Marine Convention" which turned the heads of the All-Russian War Party, was an idea that existed only in the editorial office of the "'Berliner Tageblatt' and in the moon." They are unable, however, to dispute the evidence of the documents cited above—which are in accordance with the official English Blue Book—that within a few days, Grey at one time declared the question of Belgian neutrality as not decisive, and again, in answer to the assurance of the German Government that it would preserve this neutrality if England preserved hers, refused to agree to this. This, of course, was merely playing for time, so that, after the Germans had marched into Belgium, he might finally adopt the role of the protector of the right. Two days before this, however, Grey already had his declaration of war complete, since he declared the threatening of the French coasts and of the French merchant marine as a *casus belli*. This certainly is a true example of English double dealing. (See the English White Book, No. 123, 126 and the French Yellow Book, Nos. 144, 143.)

Of what the recognized leaders of English foreign policy are held to be capable, even in England, may be seen by the manifest of the English Independent Labour Party, issued in August, 1914. According to an undisputed press communication, the following sentiments were expressed:

The import of this is similar to a statement issued by Herr Erzberger, a member of the Reichstag, based upon a communication from an "absolutely reliable source," that on the 2nd of August, under the very eyes of the Antwerp police, a German steamer had been demolished and that Belgian troops had penetrated into German territory at Aix-la-Chapelle. ("Der Tag," October 7th. 1914.)

"Neither the Serbian Question nor that of Belgian Neutrality has plunged England into this terrible war. England is not fighting for oppressed nations or for Belgium's neutrality. If France had penetrated into Germany through Belgium, what man believes that England would therefore have declared war upon France?

Sir Edward Grey has made secret concessions behind the back of Parliament and the people. But when he was asked about them, he denied the existence of these concessions. And for that reason, our land is to-day confronted by universal ruin and the iron necessity of war.

Alliances and agreements have forced France into the bondage of despotic Russia, and now England is being dragged in by France. All this is now coming to light. The men who hold responsible posts must now be held to account. England has now placed itself in the service of Russia,—Russia, the most reactionary, the most corrupt and the most despotic power of Europe. If Russia's territorial desires are to be gratified and its Cossack dominion be extended, then civilization and democracy will incur the most serious danger. And it is for this that England has drawn the sword!" (*retranslation.*)

In a similar manner Keir Hardie and Clifford Allen in pamphlets in which they praise the honest confession of the German Imperial Chancellor, "Necessity knows no law," lay the entire blame at England's door. ("Daily Citizen.")[1]

---

[1] See also the exposition by Professor Sieper, in the "Berliner Tageblatt," (January 1915) regarding Asquith's exclamation, "No war! no war!" which prove that the Harmsworth press, Sir Edward Grey, Churchill, and the well-known ambassadorial *agents-provocateurs* (Sir F. Bertie, Cambon, Barrère, etc.) had driven the English nation, Parliament and the ministry ("These damned treaties have done it all") into this war.

The same clear judge of English conditions writes thus of Winston Churchill:

"The attitude of Winston Churchill is so repulsive for the reason that it is in shrieking antithesis to the former acts and speeches of this political renegade. He was present during May in 1906 at a reception at the Eighty Club, in honor of German visitors. Among the toasts was one that was devoted to "The Two Nations" and Winston Churchill was the speaker. He began his toast with the following words: "There are people who go about declaring that the German and English people hate one another. The prattle of these people—most of them fire-eating editors who are no longer capable of

X. Even the fanatic participation of the entire Belgian population in the war,—a population well armed with military rifles and abundantly supplied with ammunition from the first day on—is an indisputable proof of the fact that the passing through of French and, no doubt, English troops, through Belgium, and with it the surrender of Belgian neutrality, had been resolved upon. This is further confirmed by the hostile acts committed against German subjects before the declaration of war on Russia, and before the beginning of war with France, and three or four days before the German troops had stepped upon Belgian territory.

The shameful acts of cruelty committed in Brussels, Antwerp and other cities of Belgium, above all things, the demolition of German ships, especially the Lloyd steamer "Gneisenau," by Belgian gendarmes, as early as 9 o'clock on the 3rd of August, would alone have sufficed to justify before the whole world the entry of German troops into Belgium.

In a drastic communication of Bismarck's, dated 1870, the great Chancellor had threatened Belgium with an invasion by German troops, based upon acts of hostility which were comparatively mild. There is no doubt that on hearing of the Antwerp horrors of the 3rd and 4th of August, he would not have hesitated a moment to assume full responsibility for all consequences. Even from the point of view of the self-respect of the German Empire, there can be no question of "a wrong" on the part of the Germans.[1]

The whole world knows to-day that it is not fidelity to agreements nor to neutrality, which was the leading motive of

---

military service, may be dismissed with a smile by sensible folk, but their barking day after day, should nevertheless warn responsible men to be on guard."

The speaker then began to talk upon the economic rivalries of both lands: "Has there ever been a trade war which increased dividends by 6 d in the £? The first days after the mobilization the trade of a country will suffer more damage than could ever be compensated for by a successful war." And in conclusion he remarked: "Mother Earth has room for us all . ." (*retrans.*)

[1] See the Spanish newspaper, "El Debate," of the 4th of October, the opinions of the Bishop, Dr. Ruelsen-Zürich, in the "Augsburger Abend-Zeitung," the expositions of Houston Stewart Chamberlain in the "Internationale Monats-Schrift," Vol. 9, No. 1, Dr. Harris Aal, in the "Christiania Dagbladet," etc.

the declaration of war by England, but jealousy and a striving for the dominion of the world.[1] Egypt, India, South Africa, Ireland and Persia would have given the British people plenty of opportunity for interceding on behalf of freedom and justice. The one end in view here is the hoped-for destruction of German trade, of German industry and the threatening German naval programme.

And Belgium? It owes its ruin to the English policy by which it was blinded. In the face of this temptation, it should have insisted upon a strict adherence to its neutrality, or demanded its natural freedom of action, or else proclaimed openly to the world its inability to defend this neutrality against the Great Powers, and that the agreement of 1839 was therefore rendered null and void.

It owed it to itself and to the Guarantee Powers to clear up the situation either in one way or the other. But Belgium refused to adopt the first expedient, by means of which Switzerland and Holland worthily and out of their own resources preserved their neutrality, Holland especially going so far as to make it a punishable crime for its citizens to violate neutrality. But this splendid example of two really neutral nations was not followed by Belgium, nor did it attempt to release itself from the agreement of 1839. "It chose the wrong path and under the mask of neutrality, made common cause with the Triple Entente." (Miltner and others.)

Only ignorance or wilful calumny would venture after all this to accuse the German people of a violation of international law. German statesmen and German generals would have made themselves guilty in the eyes of history of the grossest neglect of duty had they not reckoned with the existing conditions.

But, as has been clearly proved in the foregoing, Germany was justified, through Belgium's violation of her own neutrality, and in accordance with the dictates of international law, in

---

[1] C. H. Norman, of the "National Labour Press" in April, 1915, declares: "The alleged reason for England's participation in the war, the violation of Belgian neutrality, was only a pretext. The real reason was the desire of England to destroy German progress.... Grey is the Autocrat of Great Britain... Parliament exercised no control whatsoever over the warlike cabinet... The actions of these men will call for a terrible retribution." (*retrans.*)

choosing Belgium as a base for her warlike operations, and in case of resistance, in making war upon the land itself.

This point is thoroughly understood and discussed by the famous thinker and playwright, George Bernard Shaw, in a letter written to the London "Nation" some time in February, 1915. Germany, said Mr. Shaw, in effect did not violate the neutrality of Belgium. What she did was something quite different. *She declared war upon her,* after having made her a perfectly justifiable offer, which she refused. In this brilliant letter, Mr. Shaw likewise annihilates with unerring aim several of the favorite misconceptions and prejudices of the English.

The German Government finally did everything in its power, even after these forcible but justifiable acts, to guarantee the integrity of Belgium's sovereignty and territory and to restore these as soon as the "state of necessity" had been done away with.

Even though yielding to "force majeure," had Belgium adopted the same attitude as that of the Grand Duchy of Luxemburg, it would have been spared the terrors of a modern war, and it would have had to complain as little of serious damage or alleged further violations of international law, as Luxemburg. This is proved by Germany's strict observance of Holland's neutrality. But as Belgium, fully aware of the international obligations it had disregarded, made one-sided and treacherous preparations in favor of the Triple Entente, it must bear all consequences of its foolish and unlawful attitude. In accordance with the desire of England, it had made itself, in the language of Lord Burleigh in the "Morning Post," "a counterscarp for Your Majesty's kingdom," and must therefore be treated as an English bridge-head.

The Revelations of the "Norddeutsche Allgemeine Zeitung" of the 12th of October:

The explanations above found an almost classic confirmation in their entirety in the revelations of the German Government as to the preliminaries of the Alliance between Belgium, France and England, published in the "Norddeutsche Allgemeine Zeitung" of the 12th of October. They read, literally:

"Through Sir Edward Grey's own declarations, the statement of the English Government that the violation of Belgian neutrality by Germany induced the participation of England in the present war is proved absolutely untenable. The pathetic moralistic indignation over the German invasion of Belgium, which was used by the English for the purpose of arousing sentiment against Germany in neutral lands, is given a new and peculiar illumination by certain documents which the German army authorities have discovered in the archives of the Belgian General Staff in Brussels.

It is proved by the contents of a portfolio which bears the inscription: "Intervention anglaise en Belgique," that as early as the year 1906, the despatch of an English expeditionary corps to Belgium had been decided upon in case of a German-French war. According to a letter written to the Belgian Minister of War, bearing the date of April 10th, 1906, the Chief of the Belgian General Staff, upon the repeated solicitation of the English Military Attaché, Lieutenant Colonel Barnardiston, in the course of frequent consultations worked out a plan regarding the common operations of an English expeditionary corps of 100 000 men in conjunction with the Belgian Army against Germany. The plan was approved by the Chief of the English General Staff, Major-General Grierson. The Belgian General Staff was given all information as to the strength and disposition of the English troop divisions, as well as the composition of the expeditionary corps, the points of disembarkation, an exact estimate of the time required for transportation, and the like.

On the basis of this information, the Belgian General Staff had prepared for the transport of the English troops into Belgian territory, as well as for their shelter and sustenance. This co-operation had been carefully worked out to the smallest details. For instance, a large number of interpreters and Belgian *gendarmes* were to be placed at the disposition of the English army, for which purpose the requisite cards were to be delivered. Even provision for the care of English wounded had already been thought of.

Dunkirk, Calais and Boulogne were intended as ports of disembarkation for the English troops. Thence they were to be transported by Belgian railways to their destination. This intentional disembarkation in French harbors and the transport through French territory proves that the Anglo-Belgian agreements had been preceded by similar ones made with the French General Staff. The three powers had thoroughly prepared the plans for the co-operation of the "allied armies," as they are called in the document. This is further confirmed by the discovery among the secret archives of a map showing the French line of march.

The document in question contains several observations of a special interest. In one passage the fact is mentioned that Lieutenant Major Barnardiston had noticed that at that time one could not count upon the support of Holland. He had further confidentially communicated the fact that the English Government had the intention of removing the base for the English supplies to Antwerp, as soon as the North Sea had been cleared of all German warships. Further, the English military attaché advised the establishment of a service of Belgian spies in the Rhine province.

The military material thus discovered is completed in a most significant manner by a report which was also found among the secret papers. This is the report of the Belgian Minister in Berlin, Baron Greindl, who had seen long years of service there and is addressed to the Belgian Foreign Minister. With great acuteness, Baron Greindl analyses the English offers, and reveals the hidden intention behind them. The Minister utters a most solemn warning as to the serious position in which Belgium would find herself were she to adopt a one-sided attitude in favor of the powers of the Entente.

In this very thorough-going report, which is dated the 23rd of December, 1911, and the complete publication of which has for the present been withheld, Baron Greindl declares that the plans of the Belgian General Staff for the defence of Belgian neutrality in a Franco-German war, as communicated to him, occupied themselves solely with the question as to what military measures were to be taken in case Germany violated Belgian neutrality. The hypothesis of a French attack upon Germany through Belgium nevertheless had just as much probability. The Minister then proceeds, literally, as follows:

"From the French side, the danger threatens not only to the south of Luxemburg. It threatens us along our whole common front. We are not reduced to mere assumptions for making this declaration. We have the most positive basis of proof.

The idea of an encircling movement from the north is, without doubt, a part of the combinations or arrangements of the Entente Cordiale. If this were not the case, then the plan of fortifying Flushing would not have called forth such howls in Paris and London. No one there thought of concealing the reasons for wishing to keep the Scheldt in an unfortified state. Behind this lay the purpose of being enabled without hindrance to transport an English garrison to Antwerp, and therefore the purpose of establishing a base of operations for an offensive in the direction of the Lower Rhine, and thus sweeping us along in the current, which would not, I think, have been difficult. Because, after the surrender of our national city of refuge, we would, through our own fault, have deprived ourselves of every possibility of resisting the demands of our doubtful protectors, after we had been so unwise as to permit them to enter.

The perfidious yet naif overtures of Major Barnardiston at the time the Entente Cordiale was concluded, have given us a plain indication of what was in the wind. After it had been proved that we were not to be frightened by the alleged danger that threatened us through the closing of the Scheldt, the plan was not given up but merely altered. The English auxiliary army was not to be landed on the Belgian coast, but in the nearest French sea-ports. This is also proved by the revelations of Captain Faber, against which no *dementi* has been issued, any more than against the reports of the newspapers which stated and in various points supplemented them.

The English army which was to land in Calais and Dunkirk, would not march along our borders towards Longwy in order to reach Germany. It would immediately penetrate our country from the north-west. It would thus secure the advantage of being able to enter into action at once, and to meet the Belgian army in a region in which we would not be supported by a fortress, if we should wish to risk a battle. It would also render it possible for this army to occupy provinces which are rich in all kinds of natural resources, and in all cases to hinder our mobilization, or to permit it only after we had formally pledged ourselves to carry out this mobilization only for the advantage of England and its allies.

It is urgently necessary to draw up a battle-plan for the Belgian army which also has regard to this eventuality. This is rendered necessary, not only by the interests of our military defence, but also through the conduct of our foreign policy in the case of war between Germany and France."

These expositions on the part of one who was without prejudice, establish in the most convincing manner the fact that the self-same England which now poses as the champion of Belgian neutrality, had determined to make Belgium adopt a one-sided partisanship in favor of the Entente Powers, and that, at one stage of the game, it had even considered the violation of the neutrality of Holland. From this we see further that the Belgian Government, by listening to the whisperings of the English Government, rendered itself guilty of a serious breach of the duties which appertain to it as a neutral power. The fulfilment of these duties would have necessitated that the Belgian Government in its plans of defence should also have foreseen the violation of Belgian neutrality by France, and that it should have taken measures in agreement with Germany for this event as it had already done with France and England.

The documents that have been discovered form written proofs of a fact which had been well-known in authoritative German circles long before the outbreak of the war, regarding the Belgian connivance with the powers of the Entente. They serve as a justification for our military procedure, and as a confirmation of the reports which had been made to the German army authorities regarding the intentions of the French. They may also serve to open the eyes of the Belgian people as to whom they may thank for the catastrophe which has now overtaken their unhappy land.

Unfortunately the warnings of Baron Greindl were of no avail. The young king was entirely in the hands of the Triple Alliance—and thus his fate and that of Belgium was sealed.

And what was the answer of England to these revelations

which stagger the whole world? An official English "scrap of paper" talks in an extraordinarily embarrassed manner of: "academic discussions regarding possible English help for Belgium."[1] Bernard Shaw says that the spineless Foreign Office limited itself to hiring street boys to put out their tongues at the Imperial Chancellor. This lamentable attempt to weaken the effect of the revelations of the 12th of October speaks for itself as something that thoroughly characterizes the dishonest political methods of England.[2]

Of course, academic recriminations would be too late at this period and would be little more than worthless in the face of English politics. Here deeds must speak and not words.

---

[1] The "Norddeutsche Allgemeine Zeitung" of the 6th of November, 1914, publishes a facsimile of a formula which bears the imprint of the English Ministry in Brussels, and the following text:

E. M. de l'armée anglaise ... je soussigné Dale Long, Attaché à l. E. M. réquisitionne ... 1914.

The "Norddeutsche Allgemeine Zeitung" thereupon remarks: "The whole packet of the formula printed above was found in the office of the English spy headquarters in Brussels. It was known long before the war that a certain Dale Long lived in Brussels and was spying on Germany in favor of England. It had also been possible to bring a number of his agents to trial. Nevertheless it could not be established with any certainty that Dale Long belonged to the English General Staff. But by means of the formula discovered, it appears that in case of war, Dale Long was to join the English General Staff and that he was entitled as a member of the English army, to make requisitions in Belgium. This authorization was confirmed by the English Minister in Brussels, as the seal proves. The finding of a whole packet of blank formulas of this sort proves further beyond all doubt that we have here to deal with a measure of mobilization—a measure which, without the consent of the Belgian Government, was simply unthinkable.

These formulas, naturally, date from a time prior to the beginning of hostilities and the declaration of war by England. They therefore form one of the exhibits for the charge that the co-operation of the English and Belgian troops had been prepared long beforehand.

[2] The effect of this revelation by the German Government was considerable, as proved by the opinions of the foreign press. I call special attention to an article in the "Nieuwe Courant" at the end of October, and an extremely interesting article in the "Neue Züricher Nachrichten" of the same time, which speaks plainly and proves that "the neutrality of Belgium was strangled by a conspiracy in 1908." It talks of its "disgust with English statecraft" which has "set itself up as the champion of neutrality." This regard for neutrality was proved by the English airmen on the 21st of November, 1914.

Deeds alone have any influence over these arrogant gentry. They have even the power of compelling them to act with naked egotism in every dealing with their allies.

One may, however, be thankful to the "Times" that it explained on the 12th of October that neutrality was a fatal gift to Belgium, and that the English and Belgian General Staffs (not only those of 1906, 1911, but those of 1914) could discuss military preparations only by means of a violation of Belgian neutrality.

That secret arrangements had in fact taken place and agreements been entered into and that these alone were sufficient to determine the conclusive breach of Belgium's neutrality, we believe the foregoing to have proved. It is also true that a state of necessity and defence had at the same time forced Germany so to act, as before God and her own rights as well as from the viewpoint of international law, she should and must have acted.[1]

The Revelations of the "Norddeutsche Allgemeine Zeitung" of the 24th of November, 1914.

In a fashion still more drastic than in the publications of the 12th of October, the new revelations which the German

[1] The way England and its powerful press regard the neutrality of small states, that is to say, with what lack of consideration the "perfida gens Britonum" deals with this neutrality, is proved in a most forceful manner by the Dutch "Allgemeen Handelsblad" in its sharp protest against an article in the "Saturday Review." In this article it was proposed that England should lease or purchase Zeeland, and give it to the Belgians. This should form the future boundary of Holland, as soon as there was talk of peace. The "Handelsblad" calls the attention of the British Minister at the Hague to the shameful insult offered to a neutral country, which was honestly endeavoring to perform its duty to all its neighbors, which was holding fast to its neutrality at the greatest cost to itself, and was certainly giving the British shipwrecked sailors and interned men not the slightest ground for complaint regarding the neutrality of Holland.

The newspaper then attacks that portion of the article in the "Saturday Review" which declares that in times of war, justice must yield to military law, that this was the right of the stronger, and declares: "When weekly journals, such as the "Saturday Review" talk like the most brutal militarists, we must come to the conclusion that all regard for international law is already shaken to its very centre."

Imperial Government issued just as the first German edition went to press reveal the entire one-sided and fraudulent game played by England and Belgium to use the latter country as a field of operations against Germany.

The "Norddeutsche Allgemeine Zeitung" of the 24th of November, 1914, in a polemical article directed against the replies of the Belgian and English Governments regarding the public revelations of the 12th of October, goes into fuller details, as follows:

"As may be seen by the foregoing outlined explanations, the English Government has from the very start refrained from attempting to dispute the established facts presented by the Imperial Government on the 12th of October. It has merely confined itself to an attempt to condone them. It is apparent that the English Government must have convinced itself that a denial of the facts in view of the overwhelming mass of the evidence on hand, would have been perilous as well as purposeless.

"The discovery of an English-Belgian military news service, which has in the meantime taken place, as well as the unearthing of war-maps of Belgium, issued from official English sources, offer renewed proofs that a **comprehensive military preparation** had been embodied in the Anglo-Belgian plan of war against Germany. There are facsimile reproductions of the text of the draft of the report made by General Ducarmé to the Belgian Minister of War on the 10th of April, 1906. This report ought certainly to be known to the Belgian Government, since the Belgian Minister in Berlin, Baron Greindl, especially mentions it in his report upon its contents, dated 23rd of December, 1911.

Should the Belgian Government have forgotten the existence of this document, its doubts may be dispelled by the following text of the report which was preserved in the archives of the Belgian Ministry of War in an envelope bearing the inscription: "Convention Anglo-Belge". It reveals the entire discussion carried on between General Ducarmé and Lieutenant-Colonel Barnardiston.

The Report of General Ducarmé

reads, translated into English, as follows: "Letter to the Minister with regard to the secret conversation."

The report, among other things, contains the following sentences:

"Lieutenant-Colonel Barnardiston communicated to me the anxiety of the General Staff of his country in view of the general political situation and the possibility of an early outbreak of war. An Expeditionary Corps, amounting in all to about 100 000 men, had been provided for the event of an attack upon Belgium. The Lieutenant-Colonel asked me how a measure of this sort would be interpreted by us? I replied that from a military point of view it could only be favorable, but that this question of intervention also concerned the political authority, and that it was my duty to acquaint the Minister of War of this as soon as possible. Barnardiston proceeded as follows:

"The landing of the English troops would take place on the French coast in the neighborhood of Dunkirk and Calais, and the movement of troops would be carried on as hurriedly as possible. The landing in Antwerp would require much more time, because larger transport ships were needed, and in addition to this, the security was much less.

After one had arrived at an agreement upon this point, there remained various other questions to regulate, such as transportation by railway, the question of requisitions to be made by an English army, and that of the Commander-in-Chief of the allied belligerent powers. He inquired if our arrangements were sufficient for the defence of the land during the time required to transport the English troops, a space of time which he estimated at ten days. I replied that the fortified places of Namur and Liège could not be taken in the turning of a hand, and that our field army of 100 000 men would be ready to attack in four days.

After Barnardiston had expressed his entire satisfaction with respect to my explanations, he laid special stress upon:

1. That our agreement was to remain absolutely secret.
2. That it was not to be binding upon the English Government.

3. That his Minister, the English General Staff, he and I, were to be the only parties to be informed of the arrangement.

4. That he did not know if the opinion of his Sovereign had been obtained beforehand.

In a discussion subsequent to this, Barnardiston once more returned to the question of the effectual strength of our field army, and insisted that no detachment be sent to Namur and Liège, since these places had sufficient garrisons. He begged me to turn my attention to the necessity of permitting the English army to take part in the preliminary arrangements with regard to any warlike actions. Finally he insisted upon the question of the chief command.

At another discussion, Lieutenant-Colonel Barnardiston and I tested the combined operations in the event of a German attack upon Antwerp, and under the assumption of a German march through our country in order to reach the Ardennes. The Colonel declared that he was entirely satisfied with the plans which I laid before him, and assured me of the consent of General Grierson, Chief of the English General Staff.

Several other questions of minor importance were also regulated, especially with regard to special offices, interpreters, gendarmes, maps, pictures of uniforms, special extracts of certain Belgian regulations to be translated into English, regulations with regard to customs-house duties, English shipment of supplies, the care of the wounded of the Allied armies, etc. No agreement was reached with regard to the influence the Government or the military authorities were to exert upon the press.

In the course of the discussion I had the opportunity of convincing the English military attaché that we would be willing as far as possible, to thwart the movements of the enemy and not to flee to Antwerp at the very beginning of things. Barnardiston, on his part, communicated to me that he had small hopes at the time of any support or intervention on the part of Holland. At the same time he told me that his Government intended to transfer the English base of supplies from the French coast to Antwerp as soon as the North Sea had been cleared of all German ships.

During all our discussions, the Colonel regularly acquainted me with the intimate communications which he had received regarding the military conditions of our Eastern neighbor (!). At the same time he emphasized the fact that it was an imperative necessity for Belgium to keep itself continually informed of all that went on in the neighboring Rhineland.[1]

This report of the Chief of the Belgian General Staff bears the following appendix. "When I met General Grierson during the manoeuvres of 1906, he assured me that the reorganization of the English Army would certainly ensure not only a successful landing of 150 000 men but also that by reason of this reorganization the action of the army would be able to take place in a much shorter time than one had assumed in the foregoing."

This document also bears the following marginal note. "L'entrée des Anglais en Belgique ne se ferait qu'après la violation de notre neutralité par l'Allemagne." The real connection between this document and the implied violation may be seen from a draft found in the Belgian Ministry of Foreign Affairs. This deals with the conversation of the successor of Lieutenant-Colonel Barnardiston, the English military attaché in Brussels,—Lieutenant-Colonel Bridge—with the Chief of the Belgian General Staff, General Jungbluth.

This document, which is dated the 23rd of April, and was apparently written in 1912, is from the hand of the Count Van der Straaten, a Director in the Belgian Ministry for Foreign Affairs. It bears the commentary, "Confidential." The English military attaché had expressed the wish to see General Jungbluth.

The gentlemen met on the 23rd of April. The Lieutenant-Colonel had told the General that England could send an army of 160 000 men to the Continent. This would consist of six

[1] The "Norddeutsche Allgemeine Zeitung" writes officially as follows; dated 21st of April, 1915. "The New York World," quoting certain newspapers, declares on the strength of an alleged expression of opinion by King Albert, that he himself had communicated the well-known discussions of General Ducarmé with Lieutenant-Colonel Barnardiston to the foreign military attachés in Brussels in 1906. Opposed to this report of the New York newspaper, we declare on a basis of the most authentic official information, that not one of the German military attachés who had been active in Brussels since 1905 had received any such communication.

divisions of infantry and eight brigades of cavalry. Everything was prepared. The English Government, during recent events, had determined upon an immediate landing on our soil, *even though we had not asked for any help.*

The General had objected that it would be necessary to obtain our consent for this. The military attaché had answered that he was aware of that, but that as he knew that we would not be able to prevent the Germans from marching through our country, England would, in any event, land troops in Belgium. So far as the place of landing was concerned, the military attaché expressed no clear opinion as to this point; merely declaring that the coast was a very long one, but the General knows that Mr. Bridges has made daily visits to Zeebrugge from Ostend during the Easter holidays. The General added that we were moreover quite capable of hindering the Germans from marching through Belgium."

The "Norddeutsche Allgemeine Zeitung" comments upon this:

"Here it is openly expressed that the English Government in case of a Franco-German war, had the intention of at once invading Belgium with its troops, that is to say, violating Belgian neutrality and doing precisely that which—after Germany in its justifiable self-defense, had anticipated the move,—it had used as a pretext for declaring war upon Germany.

With a cynicism absolutely unparalleled the English Government has made use of Germany's breach of Belgian neutrality in order to create feeling against Germany throughout the entire world, and to play itself off as the protector of small and weak nations. But with respect to the Belgian Government there is no doubt that its duty lay not only in rejecting the English insinuations in the most decisive manner, but in notifying the other signatory powers of the protocol of 1839, and in especial Germany, of the repeated English attempts to seduce it into a violation of the duties imposed upon it as a neutral power.

This was not done by the Belgian Government. It did, indeed, attempt to justify itself on the plea of duty for taking military measures in conjunction with the English General Staff based upon its alleged knowledge of the intention of Germany to invade Belgium. But it had never made the slightest attempt to make like preparations for the eventuality of an Anglo-French invasion of Belgium nor to discuss this matter with the German Government or with the proper military authorities in Germany, although it was well aware of the intentions of the Entente Powers in this connection—as proved by the material found.

The Belgian Government had already made up its mind to join the enemies of Germany and to make common cause with them. Since the system of vilification in vogue among our enemies compels them simply to lie away the existence of inconvenient facts, the Imperial Government has seen fit to publish facsimile copies of the documents in question and to bring them to the knowledge of the governments of the Neutral States." [1]

The document bears in a large bold hand the inscription "Convention Anglo-Belge." To say that all this was discussed and prepared for the event of an invasion on the part of Germany is to offer an objection of the most naive sort. The text of the paper, especially the part containing the observations of the English military attaché, is a direct contradiction of this statement.

The Documents and Proofs Substantiating the Belgian Betrayal.

These increase constantly in number and furnish the most damning evidence in an absolutely incontrovertible fashion.

1. On the 1st of December, 1914, the "Norddeutsche Allgemeine Zeitung" published the following official communication:

---

[1] A great controversy still rages about this highly-important document. Its existence is extremely unpleasant for England. Even Sir Edward Grey is forced to descend from his position of proud inaccessibility. Under the date of the 28th of January Wolff's Bureau officially repudiates the falsity of the representations made by the English Press Bureau in London. See the "Norddeutsche Allgemeine Zeitung" of the 28th of January 1915, also the English White Book, No. 105 with three appendices, also the letters exchanged between Paul Cambon and Sir Edward Grey on the 22nd and 23rd of November, 1912.

Evidence accumulates that England in conjunction with Belgium had, during times of peace, made the most complete preparations for war against Germany, not only in a diplomatic but also in a military way. Our troops recently seized a number of secret military hand-books descriptive of roads and rivers in Belgium and published by the British War Office. These bore the title:

BELGIUM.
ROAD AND RIVER AND BILLETING REPORTS,
Prepared by the General Staff,
War Office.

Four volumes of this hand-book lie before us. Of these Volume I was printed in 1912, Volume II in 1913, Volume III (in two parts) and Volume IV in 1914. They bear the imprint "Confidential," and the inscription, "This book is the property of H. B. M. Government and is intended for the personal information of ...., who is personally responsible for its safe custody. The contents are to be disclosed only to authorized persons."

These hand-books contain the most minute descriptions of the country with a special view to military reconnaisance. For instance, in Volume I, page 130, the highroad Nieuport—Dixmuiden—Ypres—Menin—Tourcoing—Tournai is discussed. The exact distances are given, as well as the most thorough details with regard to the network of connecting roads as to grades, bridges, cross-roads, telephone and telegraph connections, railway stations, including the length of the platforms and approaches, small gauge railways, oil-tanks, etc. It is invariably indicated whether the entire or only a part of the population speaks French.

As an example the tactical observations with regard to Dixmuiden are given verbally on page 151: "Dixmuiden would be difficult to capture from the north or south. The best position for defence towards the south would be west of the road and as far as the road of the railway embankment; east of the road there is a row of small hillocks. West of the road the line of fire is good for 1500 yards, to the east the outlook is hindered by trees. Two battalions would suffice for occupation." (*retrans.*)

It should be remarked, by the way, that the towers of

churches are usually mentioned as excellent posts of observation!

The entire course of the River Scheldt is described in the same detailed manner. These handy volumes thus form excellent guides for the leaders, General Staff officers and non-commissioned officers of every grade. A plan or survey of the houses available for troop quarterings, arranged according to parishes and villages, is also given, also a diagram of important landmarks for the use of flying-corps commanders. This book of memoranda, prepared in the most careful and comprehensive fashion, is supplemented by a map of the landing-places. It bears the inscription "Confidential" and the date July, 1914.

These military-topographical hand-books were not prepared shortly before nor during the war. On the contrary the material has been collected ever since 1909 by means of single and special investigations, as appears from remarks in some of the division of the work. The first volume was printed in 1912.

The leading threads of all this are centered in preparations for a campaign—preparations extending over five years, the thoroughness of which stands proved beyond all doubt.

2. The "Norddeutsche Allgemeine Zeitung" of December 14th writes thus in the matter of England's jugglery with the neutrality of Belgium:

"New and serious evidences of guilt have recently been discovered as to the complicity in crime of the English and the Belgians. Some time ago Grant Watson, a secretary of the English legation, was captured in Brussels. He had remained behind in the building of the British Ministry after the Ministry itself had been removed to Antwerp and later on to Havre. Grant Watson was recently caught in the act of attempting to destroy certain documents which he had been able to remove unobserved from the Ministry at the time of his capture. An examination of these papers resulted in the discovery that they were documents of a most private nature containing data relative to the mobilization of the Belgian army and the defense of Antwerp, dated 1913—14. Among these papers there were certain circular letters addressed to the most important Belgian headquarters and bearing the signature of the Belgian Minister of War and that of the Chief of the Belgian General Staff.

There was also a draft of the session of the Commission for the base of supplies at Antwerp, dated the 27th of May, 1913.

The fact that these papers were found in the English Legation is conclusive proof of the fact that the Belgian Government kept no military secrets from the English Government and that, moreover, both governments stood in close and permanent military relationship with each other. A written notice found among the papers, for the destruction of which the English secretary showed such concern, is of peculiar interest. The text of this reads as follows:

1. The French officers have received orders to join their divisions on the afternoon of the 27th of this month.

2. The stationmaster at Feignies received orders on the same day to send all available covered wagons, suitable for the purpose of transporting troops, in the direction of Maubeuge. Communicated through the Gendarmerie brigade in Frameries.

It should be remarked here that Feignies is a railway station on the line Maubeuge—Mons, about three kilometres from the Belgian frontier; Frameries is on the same line in Belgium, ten kilometres from the Belgian frontier. *It is to be seen from this notice that France had already taken its first measures for mobilization on the 27th of July, and that the English Legation was at once advised of this fact through Belgian authorities.*"

If still further proofs were necessary of the relationships that existed between England and Belgium, then this newly-discovered material provides a most valuable complement. It proves once more that Belgium had surrendered its neutrality in favor of the Entente, and that it had become an active member of the coalition that had been formed to combat the German Empire.

For England, Belgian neutrality meant in fact nothing more than a "scrap of paper," so far as this was in accordance with its interests. This it proceeded to set aside as soon as it served its purpose so to do. It is obvious that the English Government made use of the violation of Belgian neutrality by Germany really as a pretext in order to justify its war against us in the eyes of the world and the English people. It was a "neutrality" with which England did indeed proceed in a truly cynical manner, as proved by the use to which Antwerp was to be put in these plans. Even the neutrality of Holland would have meant nothing to England, if Germany had not anticipated England's move. Holland may be thankful to Germany in that it did not share the fate of Belgium. The treacherous politics of a country have never been more thoroughly unmasked than those of England in Belgium.

A complete espionage system in common against Germany! Without any formal alliance[1]*—an English habit, this—"a Convention," than which one cannot imagine one more powerful, is established between two nations. The publication of these disclosures confirms in the most dramatic manner all that has been elucidated in the foregoing with respect to the defence and the state of necessity of Germany.*

Will neutral countries still venture to doubt the authenticity of these documents concerning which Bernard Shaw declared that they had completely checkmated the English Foreign Office?

As to the attitude of England, and the true reasons for its declaration of war, see also Chapter 32. As to the final compulsion to enter the war, and the true obligations of England, obligations completely independent of Belgian neutrality, a certain clarity is imparted to English intentions by the English White or Blue Book, No. 105, appendix 1, with the significant letter of Sir Edward Grey of the 22nd of November, 1912, in his answer to Paul Cambon. See further the French Yellow Book, No. 63 and 66 and the English White Book, No. 89, and the report of Grey regarding his conversation with Lichnowsky on the 29th of July, 1914. Further, the intercepted report of the Belgian representative in St. Petersburg, M. de l'Escaille, of July 30th, 1914, which proves the incendiary effect of the English attitude in Greater Russian circles. Finally, the English Blue Book, No. 123. Also the essay by Secretary of State von Helfferich, "The Origin of the World War in the Light of the Publications of the Triple Alliance," and the well-

[1] The falsification of the correct date in the Appendix III, by the English and French Governments, one of the most remarkable acts in international intercourse, (see the essay in "Die Deutsche Eiche" January, 1915) proves how little serious attention is to be given to the defence of Sir Edward Grey in the English Parliament, 3rd of August, 1914.

substantiated proofs that England, long before the bringing-up of the Balkan question, had firmly determined, in spite of the greatest concessions by Germany with regard to Belgium and France, to participate in the war. There is also Bonar Law's letter to Asquith, of the 2nd of August, 1914. In this no word is said of Belgium, but only of the "support of France and Russia." This letter is written on the same day in which Sir Edward Grey made concessions to France which, quite independent of the question of Belgian neutrality, must inevitably have led to war. The splendid essay upon the previous history and the outbreak of the war in 1914, by Dr. Carl Strupp, "Zeitschrift für Völkerrecht," Vol. 8, pamphlet 2, page 111, should also be read.[1]

---

[1] Winston Churchill's statement that for five years, England had been provided with munitions for the war, and the fact that England had her navy in readiness before any other state, — whilst on the 26th of July, the German Fleet and Kaiser Wilhelm were still absent in Northern waters, proves that the Belgian question was a mere blind, and that England regarded the use of Belgium as a base of operations for the war for which she had so long prepared.

This point is also being gradually conceded under the pressure of public opinion by the most influential papers of England. See the articles in the "Times" and "Morning Post" on the birthday of King Albert, in April, 1915. The "Times" writes: "The chief reasons why England guaranteed the neutrality of Belgium and entered the Triple Alliance, were practical considerations of self-interest. We have already told our enemies that if they wish to have an acknowledgment of the fact that the preservation of the Balance of Power was one of the reasons why we began the war, they could have it." (*retrans.*)

The Socialist leader, Newbold, is still more frank: "England entered this war because foreign competition in the markets of the world had steadily grown more formidable. The Continental Powers that stand before the abyss are supported by us and lured into the war with promises. After the war, there will be many countries that will be deep in our debt, or that will require capital for the re-construction of their industries. Belgium will curse us. We defended Belgium because it guarded the mouth of the Rhine and the Scheldt. But where is our solicitude for Finland, the small Balkan states, Persia, Egypt and the Boers?" (*retranslation.*)

Lord Haldane has also, as is well-known, confessed that he was not certain as to whether England could remain neutral, even though the neutrality of Belgium had been respected by Germany (End of March, 1915). Houston Stewart Chamberlain in his "Kriegs-Aufsätze," writes thus of his Fatherland: "England wanted the war, and from the very beginning it was

CHAPTER II.

Mobilization and the Morality of Nations.

The right of mobilization at such times as may appear necessary for purposes of state is a right which is naturally enjoyed by every sovereign power. A neighboring state, of course, has also the right to meet measures of mobilization by similar measures. The political and international responsibility for the consequences must be borne by that country which is first to begin a movement for mobilization, and which forces the other to resort to measures of defence and necessity. The formal declaration of war does not reveal the aggressor. The occasion of a war is seldom the real cause. The apparent aggressor is frequently as justified in his action as the defender. It is for this reason that modern international law has rejected the examination of the *jus ad bellum* as maintained by Grotius and others. Naturally every state also enjoys the right of demanding an explanation with regard to the threatening measures of mobilization undertaken by another. In the event of its not receiving this, no course is left to it save a declaration of war or the sufferance of a continued and humiliating threat which may finally, despite all, lead to war.

The mobilization which Russia began against Germany without the slightest justification—the matter of the date is a subject of contention, since some declare it to have begun in May, others at the end of July—was in the mere nature of things, morally improper, treacherous and dishonorable.

According to the indisputable despatches of the German White Book, the Russian Minister of War, on the 27th of July 1914, gave *his word of honor* to the German military attaché that no order for mobilization had been issued,—"no reservist has been called up and no horse requisitioned."

---

the driving power. England succeeded in estranging Russia from Germany. England has kept on inciting France without intermission. It was a handful of men who in cold blood, and for the furtherance of purely material interests, determined upon this step some years ago. The primary instigator was King Edward VII, the intellectual element was furnished by a soulless and crafty diplomat, who honored the ancient English principle that lies and hypocrisy were the best weapons in affairs of state."

On July 29, the Chief of the Russian General Staff in the most solemn manner pledged his word of honor that mobilization had not yet taken place—that all reports to the contrary were false.

But on July 30th, the Czar confessed to the Kaiser, that the military measures which had come into force had been determined upon more than 5 days before, that is, at the very latest, on July 25th (German White Book, Appendix 23a). The Czar pretended to be desirous for peace and as late as noon on the 31st of July gave his solemn promise that so long as negotiations were proceeding with Austria-Hungary, through the mediation of the German Emperor, the Russian troops would undertake no provocative action. This mediation itself had been requested by the Czar! In spite of this the Czar had issued an order for the *mobilization of the entire Russian* army only a few hours before.

On the 1st of August, that is, before the expiration of the Russian ultimatum and before the declaration of war, the Russians had already begun their hostilities—after setting fire to some of their frontier garrison buildings on the 30th of July. Kohler is therefore entirely justified when he exclaims, in retrospect upon this fact: "This procedure is not that of a civilized people, but mere barbaric scoundrelism." ("Deutsche Juristen-Zeitung" 1914, page 1014.)

Thus did the "Czar of Peace" proceed. There exists not only international law, but international morality—which forms, in fact, the basis for international law. All the pompous phrases as to "humanity," "human nature," "public conscience," etc., are mere empty words when the most primitive rules of human decency, honesty, honor and integrity are trodden underfoot—as has happened in the case of the Czar and his government—the aggressors in this world war, and the protectors of the Serajevo assassins and of every wanton violation of the law of nations.

A war-beginning such as this was in itself a negation of all the valid moral laws that subsist between civilized peoples, as well as of every international principle.

The Commander-in-Chief of the German Army refrained on his part from mobilization until after the expiration of the period set by the ultimatum—still hoping to receive an assuring explanation with regard to the Russian demobilization.

He waited so long, because of his love of peace, that Russia was enabled to take advantage of the preparations it had been making for weeks and indeed months, to make a sudden irruption into East Prussia. He waited until the very last moment, to the very limits entailed by the fulfilment of his duty towards his own land!

Russia's treacherous and cowardly manner of procedure was one with that of the French Government. This government refused to declare to the German Ambassador that France considered itself in a state of war with Germany. By means of vague excuses it sought to gain time, although its mobilization had already been under way for some time. This attitude of France, which was going "to do that which its interests demanded," was quite in accordance with the treacherous attitude of Belgium, which, as has already been demonstrated in the foregoing, had made all preparations for action in common with France and England to attack the German Empire without the slightest intimation.

Of all our enemies England alone declared formal war upon Germany on the evening of August 4 th. Yes, it even went so far as to declare war upon Austria-Hungary on the 12th of August, a declaration with *retroactive* effect, which, as Kohler declares, is something absolutely unique in international law. It is an act which only England could have committed, an act which will have the strangest consequences as a precedent for the operation of piracy, especially in the field of civilian rights. Truly a self-imposed declaration of bankruptcy in the face of all international law and all its honest endeavors!

This form of declaration of war, to be sure, is at the same time the one open and honorable action on the part of England, whose further political demeanor formed a worthy conclusion to the encircling policy which for over a period of twelve years it had been carrying out against Germany.

If today the hate of the German people is directed first of all towards that land to which they are related in a racial and cultural sense, it is Sir Edward Grey and his colleagues who must be blamed by reason of their political and illegal acts and their unheard of means and ends in war, — for the destruction of precious values of civilization which entire generations will not suffice to restore.[1]

CHAPTER III.

Violation of the Congo Acts. The Colonial War.

Chapter III of the Congo Acts of February 23th, 1885, (General Acts of the Berlin Conference) which was signed by Germany, Belgium, France, England and Russia as well as other states, deals with the neutrality of the territory nominally included in the district of the Congo Basin.

These districts are carefully described in Article I. The whole of East Africa and other parts of the German colonial possessions are included (a third of the Cameroons, in especial New Cameroon); England is represented by British East Africa, the Uganda Protectorate, a small part of North Rhodesia (see, in supplementation, the memorial of the German Government of March 1915 with regard to the negotiations relative to the neutralization of the Congo Basin, in which proof is brought forward that the German Government had done all in its power in order to preserve the African colonies from war).

Germany, with the aid of the American Government who were especially interested during 1884—85 in the question of neutralizing all colonies lying within the Free Trade zone, had endeavored to procure the acceptance of this measure. But its efforts were frustrated by the opposition offered by the countries of the Triple Alliance, England, France and Belgium.[2]

[1] See an article by Brantschaninow upon the Russian-English preliminaries and their pernicious influence upon Russia and its declaration of war in the "Nowoe Zweno" of the 11th of July, 1914 ("Wiener Allgemeine Zeitung" of the 10th of October, 1914) and the familiar expression of the former President of the Duma, Gutschkow, upon the "Approach of the Pan-European War," as well as the remark of Ramsay Macdonald: "A war of the diplomats, made by half-a-dozen of them."

[2] See also the author's article upon "England's Guilty Share in our Colonial War," in the "Frankfurter Zeitung," 1st Morgenblatt, March 21st, 1915.

Article 10 stipulates that in order to obtain a new security for trade and industry and to ensure the preservation of peace and the furtherance of civilization in the lands in question, the contracting powers pledge themselves to respect this neutrality, "so long as the powers which exercise rights of sovereignty and protection over this district make use of the right to declare themselves neutral, and to fulfil the obligations of neutrality."

This purely theoretical declaration of neutrality is then succeeded by its practical interpretation in Articles 11 and 12.

In case of one of the powers being involved in war as laid down in Article 10, the other signatories pledge themselves to use their best efforts to the end that the territory of this power which may be included in the Free Trade zone, in accordance with the common agreement of this power and the other party or parties among the belligerent signatories, is to be placed under the laws of neutrality for the duration of the war, and is to be regarded as though belonging to a non-belligerent power. The belligerent parties *would therefore be called upon from this date onward, to refrain from extending their hostilities to the neutralized territories*, and from using these as a basis for warlike operations. In cases of serious differences of opinion, the signatory powers promise to avail themselves of the mediation of one or more friendly powers ere making use of the force of arms. A procedure based upon courts of arbitration is provided for.

The purpose of these provisions of the Congo Convention is beyond doubt, and for obvious reasons is based upon a desire to avoid the possibility of an eventual war between the Great Powers from affecting the "Congo district," as under the protection of the Congo Convention.

The powers which were to fulfil the function of mediators would naturally be those which were not involved in the war, yet were signatories of the Agreement, that is to say, Denmark, Spain, the United States of America, Italy, the Netherlands, Sweden and Norway. The blame for the non-compliance with the Congo Acts is not to be ascribed to these neutral states, but to those which hungered to achieve swift and cheap victories on African soil, and immediately began hostilities in neutralized territory after a gross violation of the pledges they had made—that is, England and Belgium—both signatories to the Convention "in the Name of Almighty God!"

England, as may easily be proved, at once began to conduct an aggressive war against Germany in East Africa, and it is therefore upon her head that the fearful responsibility must fall for the consequences which the subjugated peoples will inevitably derive from the actions of a so-called civilized Great Power.[1] For the charge made in the first German edition of this work—to the effect that England alone was to be charged with this abominable blood-guilt and with the betrayal of the race, has now been conclusively proved by the publication of the Belgian Grey Book and the German memorial mentioned in the foregoing.

In No. 57 Belgium expresses the hope that the war would not be extended to Central Africa. France at first appears to be in agreement with this. (No. 59 and 61.) France requests Spain to propose an agreement based upon the Congo Acts of neutralization. (Grey Book, No. 61.) England thereupon declared that it could not agree to this (see No. 75), and France naturally follows this lead (No. 74 and 75), withdrawing its proposal to Spain, which could do nothing without the consent of England. Secretary of State Solf is therefore entirely in the right in declaring, in an interview, that England, France and Belgium *are alone responsible for setting Africa ablaze with the war.*

At the beginning of August, some days after the outbreak of war on the continent and shortly before the declaration of war by England, the Paris newspapers printed a despatch dated London, the impressive tone of which plainly bespoke its official origin. The British Government,—according to

---

[1]) See also the declarations made on the 15th of December, 1885, by the representative of the United States of America, Mr. Kasson, who prophetically describes the effect which would follow upon a breach of the neutralization of the Congo. See the "Koloniale Rundschau," 1914, page 454, as well as the revelations of the Mr. E. D. Morel in the August number of the "African Mail" (reprinted in "The Catholic," a Swiss paper) in which this gentleman utters a warning as to the terrible consequences that would follow the extension of the war to these districts.

this communication from London,—in accordance with the agreement with Japan, would prove that it was *capable of and determined upon striking a mortal blow at Germany through its colonies.*

These explanations openly reveal the chief motive of English politics, the defeat of the competitor in commerce and the rival upon the seas—no matter at what price—even though it be the betrayal of all racial instincts and all the sentiments of civilization.[1]

This act on the part of the English Government, so contrary to all sound statesmanship and common sense,—an act that could only call forth the contempt of thinking men,—perpetrated against the German protectorates, is likewise, so far as German East Africa and parts of the Cameroons are concerned, a gross violation of the international agreement in regard to the Congo.

Relying upon Article II of the Congo Acts, and in order to avoid all appearance of threatening any neighboring and alien territory, Germany had constantly striven to keep its military forces in German East Africa merely as large as appeared necessary in order to maintain its authority in the territory of the protectorate. This faith in the common agreement has been shamefully abused, since England used its enormous ascendancy in the neighboring British protectorates in order

---

[1] Professor Adolf Harnack recently published an article in the "Tägliche Rundschau" which was a translation made of an article which had appeared on August 3rd, 1912, in an English weekly called "John Bull" which boasts of a circulation of a million copies. This article attempted to prove that war with Germany was inevitable, and the sooner it began, the better. The article comprised the following six headings:

1. Shall we wait until the income tax amounts to 1 shilling, 6 pence in the pound?
2. Shall we wait until the smouldering industrial revolution, of which all our strikes give warning announcement, has burst forth into flame?
3. Unloose the dogs of war!
4. The mastery of the seas belongs to us forever. No other nation shall dare to challenge our supremacy.
5. Man is a savage animal, and there is no place for the tame under present circumstances.
6. The war with Germany is much more important than the war between the yellow and the white man will be. *(retranslation)*

to make war upon German East Africa, though this lay well within the Free Trade zone.

This has now been thoroughly and indisputably established by the aforesaid memorial of the German Government. Let me recall the attack made upon the steamer "Hermann von Wissmann" by the English governmental steamer, "Gwendolin" on Lake Nyassa on August 25th, the bombardment of Dar-es-Salaam and similar heroic feats! The natural consequence of this was that Germany was also forced to begin military operations —at first purely defensive.

The brutal and unworthy methods by which this war has been carried on by England and France, are shown by a series of reliable and unpartisan and neutral reports, which, at the same time, confirm the fact that hostilities were begun by these nations. No respect was paid to German private property; the white civilian population of the colonies, men, women and children, were dragged off as prisoners of war and maltreated under the scornful laughter of the incited black inhabitants, and kept captive in districts which were simply ruinous to the health of these poor and unfortunate victims.

The day shall yet come upon which we shall exact retribution for those things, exact it from those criminals that befoul us with the words "Huns and barbarians"—and then introduce a system of war into Africa which is nothing less than a disgrace for every human being that boasts a white skin,—as Dr. Solf so justly remarks.

The English Government had begun its hostilities against the Government of the Cameroons, as proved by the official report of the Governor of that colony, as early as the end of July. As shown by the evidence given by subjects of neutral states, published by the Imperial Colonial Office in January 1915, the English carried on in the most shameless manner at Luederitzbucht. The whole civil population was separated and dragged as prisoners of war into the notorious concentration camps of Cape Colony. Everything was plundered. Even the dwelling of the British Consul Müller and his library were destroyed.

The English in German East Africa committed gross violations of the law of nations in that they attacked the Staff

Surgeon Dr. Schumacher as he was conducting a transport of wounded men, and shot him in spite of the sign of the Geneva Cross. (Report of the Government of the 7th and 6th of October.)

The English acted with special vileness in the Cameroons (see, for example, "Die Freisinnige Zeitung," No. 31, 1915) and also in Duala according to the reports of members of the Baptist Mission in the Cameroons. This report sums up these various outrages as follows:

"The English are doing everything to ruin the colony in an economic sense. They fell upon us in overpowering numbers, cut us off from all communication with the outer world, and by means of force, treachery, and lies, captured all the whites, soldiers, government officials, planters, missionaries, even the subjects of neutral states, whom, deprived of all means, they transported with wives and children, out of the country to become prisoners of war.

"Yes, England, the rich, was not ashamed of depriving these people of their money, merely now and then, in favored cases, making an exception to the extent of 100 Marks per person. Some were left without a single penny, and many who were arrested upon the streets, did not even possess the most elementary necessities. All work is suspended, all future development has been ruined. The respect for the white man is gone, negroes have been permitted to command them and war upon them, and have seen us as prisoners. Our parishes are left without missionaries in the hands of black assistants, and will have the greatest difficulty in making both ends meet, for Christian England did not even spare the work of missionaries!"

After attacking and plundering the station of Nyamtang, the English attempted to induce a missionary, and one of a neutral country at that, to utter false testimony against the Germans on the score of alleged "atrocities." This missionary, Wolf by name, relates:

"After we had arrived at Duala, I was asked to appear before the Chief Commando and requested to write down something with regard to the "cruelties" of the Germans. I refused and was dismissed. Soon afterwards I received a second invitation. I was again asked to comply with the demand previously made. After I had agreed to write down all that I had seen, I was once more permitted to go. The contents of the paper which I handed in, dealt with the shameless treatment to which we and other missionaries had been subjected.

"Hereupon I once more received a notice to appear, and was given a sharp warning that my report was an accusation against the English and French soldiers and cast suspicion upon the entire commando. They even had the rank audacity to go a step farther and to promise to release me from imprisonment, should I venture to meet their wishes and send in a report upon "Cruelties Committed by the German Troops!" Naturally I could not agree to this. Then, under the accusation that I had, as an American citizen, violated the neutrality of my country, and helped the German Government in its purposes, my wife and I were transported to England as prisoners of war. Even there I was charged with a violation of neutrality and deprived of my liberty."

It is with "atrocity stories" obtained by such fraudulent and forcible means as this, that public opinion in America is fed.

Other American missionaries relate similar stories.

At Duala the French and English took a direct part in the vile robberies perpetrated by the natives. The Germans (civilians, men, women and children) were escorted by the military through the most frequented streets, and then, amidst the ridicule, abuse and threats of the negroes, taken to the harbor.

Conditions during the long sea-voyage were deplorable. Everyone suffered. The French were especially brutal towards the civil prisoners in Dahomey. They were driven along by negroes who prodded them with the butts of their rifles. This humiliation of white men before the colored troops and the natives calls to heaven for judgment.

The most glaring violations of international law and breaches of faith were committed in this murderous war, such as the bombardment of Dar-es-Salaam, an absolutely unprotected town, by English cruisers, as Governor Schnee describes in detail in his report of February 13th, 1915.

From Togo too there are reports to the effect that wherever the French troops appeared, the most shameless plunderings ensued. "All plantations east of the Atakyama railway were looted. ("The Maltreatment of the Germans in West Africa;" see also the "Koloniale Rundschau," 1915, Number 2, page 115.)

As every one who is conversant with conditions well knows, this offensive undertaken by the English and French against the German colonies is, in a political sense, extremely unwise, and of course, *entirely superfluous*, for both the French and the English are aware that this war will be decided on the battlefields of Russia and France, and not in Southwest Africa, East Africa or the Cameroons. All these Ghurkhas, Basutos, Kaffirs and Hereros that have been incited against us shall one day become our avengers, even as the Japanese.[1] [2]

[1] In the first German edition of this book we published the letter of General Beyers' in which he gives his reasons for resigning the chief command. Herewith we publish the proclamation issued by Beyers and Dewet on the 28th of October, 1914. It forms the most telling answer to the hypocrisy of Botha,—a very noble-spirited sort of person!—whose excessive adulation of Germany in 1902 still echoes in our ears:

"All the burghers of the Union are hereby notified that, after the government of the Union had resolved upon the conquest of German South-west Africa and after this resolve, based upon incorrect reports and statements, had been confirmed by the Members of Parliament of the South African Party, and after the godless attack upon German South-west Africa and upon a people which had never harmed us but had wished us well at all times, had been protested against,—and after the right of the public to continue its protests had been prevented by the proclamation of martial law,—we now, arms in hand, make protest against this so dangerous principle which the Government intends to carry out against the views and the will of the people.

Since we are convinced that our people would be plunged into the greatest misfortune and misery and that we would incur the curse of God, and since our protest is not intended to bring about the shedding of our brothers' blood but rather to avoid this, and in no sense to assume an aggressive attitude,—we hereby call upon all burghers to summon all their energies and to use their influence against the conquest of German South-west Africa, and to refuse to permit themselves to be used by the government and to fight by force of arms.

(signed) Dewet, Beyers.
Generals of the Protesting Burghers,

Steenbokfontein, October 28, 1914. (*retranslation*)

Equally characteristic is a passage in the interesting negotiations that took place in the South African parliament over the question of war with Germany. One of the speakers in this assembly (Fichardt) pointed out a typical English forgery He declared: "The Germans are supposed to have

As may be seen from the official German report that has been cited above, England was firmly determined from the beginning of the war to unloose this struggle in our colonies as well. Even during the middle of July, that is to say while profound peace still prevailed, the English had already prepared for their warlike operations against Togo, by transporting great quantities of ammunition and money into the hinterland of the Gold Coast under the pretense that their frontiers were threatened by two rebellious Togo chieftains!

The truth was, of course, that preparations were made for an attack upon Togo from the west. And on the 23rd of July, as attested by the Imperial Resident in Garua, (North Cameroons) the German mails were opened in Yola (British Nigeria) and the open letters sent to the representative of the British Niger Company at Garua!

All this is conclusive proof of the indisputable fact that long before the outbreak of the war in Europe, measures had been taken in the British colonies of West Africa for carrying on a universal colonial war.

CHAPTER IV.

The Employment of Barbarous and Warlike Tribes in a European War.

There exists, unfortunately, no express law against the employment of such savage hordes. They are not directly con-

begun the war through an attack upon Nakob in the Cape Colony. This place was formerly to be found upon no English map. Now, according to the new railway map submitted to Parliament, it lies in English territory."

(retranslation)

Fichardt declared that when the map was held against the light, it was plain to see that the name Nakob had first been marked in German territory, and had then been erased!

[1] See Conan Doyle's annihilating pamphlet upon the "Crimes of the Congo" committed by Belgium, which was published in 1909. England out of purely political grounds had suspended the Congo League and its agitations, in order to cooperate with Belgium. (See "Koloniale Rundschau" 1915, Number 1, page 5.) And now Conan Doyle is one of the most fanatic of British Teutophobes.

sidered in the Rules and Regulations of Warfare by Land.[1] But there is no doubt that an indirect law *does* exist. Not only outward observances are imposed upon belligerents and their volunteers by Article I, but inner duties as well. The most serious and important duty imposed upon them is that of observing the spirit as well as the letter of rules and customs of warfare.

After the experiences of the past hundred years, all men know that all these tribes—Turcos, Ghurkas, and negroes of all kinds, have never adhered to the rules and regulations of the Geneva Convention. How much less would they care for the conclusions of the Hague Peace Conference of 1899 and 1907!

Even now countless instances have proved that all the rules of Article 23 of the Laws of Warfare by Land, (such as

[1] In the first German edition I recalled a speech by Pitt. I will now call attention to another speech which the venerable Pitt delivered in the Commons in 1778. In this he declared with warning voice that such revolting principles contradict both religion and humanity. He appealed to their honor to preserve the dignity of their ancestors. He appealed to the spirit and the humanity of his country, he invoked the genius of their constitution..... He protested against the letting loose of merciless cannibals who thirsted after the blood of men, women and children!.... They were terrible hell-hounds of the wilderness! "Hell-hounds!" he repeated. Spain loosed its bloodhounds in order to destroy the unhappy tribes of America and now the English were going to exceed this example of Spanish cruelty!.... He cried to the Lords that he was old and feeble and no longer capable of speaking further, but his feelings and his opposition were too strong to permit him to say less than this. He would have been unable to find rest within his bed that night, he would have been unable to lay his head upon his pillow, had he not aired his horror against principles so monstrous, so degenerate as these.

Edward Engel in his "History of English Literature" states that this speech is to be found "in all English school-readers."

The cowardly and trembling degenerates of the present day, those worthies of the mighty mouth *à la* Churchill, must also have forgotten the famous epistle of Edmund Burke to the British Colonies, written in 1777; in which he declared that the colonies would have found it difficult to believe that the English had planned to set upon them all those tribes of savages and cannibals in which all traces of human nature had been expunged by ignorance and barbarity. They did not hold that all things were justified in war.

Today these epigones are fighting in common with hordes, compared to which the old Red Indians were men of honor, and there is no crime, even that of the vilest assassination, which they do not condone and regard as proper!

treacherous murder or mutilation, the slaughter of defenseless enemies, the refusal of pardon, the abuse of military insignia, uniforms, robbery, theft, etc.) have been ignored by this colored riff-raff.

There is therefore only an apparent gap in the laws of the nations as applicable to these instances. The employment of savage subject nations as auxiliaries, whose customs *make it certain* that they are bound to ignore and disregard the rules of warfare as established between civilized peoples and the most ancient customs thereof, is in reality a gross transgression of the agreements of 1899 and 1907! But what regard is paid today to international law by England, that land which proclaims itself "the defender of treaties" or in France, the self-styled "grande nation?" [1]

It is to be hoped that these rascals will be put among the Englishmen and Frenchmen as prisoners of war. When this proposal was made in Germany, in order to cool the enthusiasm of the French and British, there were renewed indignant yells about the "barbarism" of the Germans. It is difficult to say whether one ought to laugh—or, giving way to another human function to which an appeal is here made—to weep bitter tears!

These wild tribes are good enough to serve the English purpose in being let loose upon honest German troops and in committing the most horrible cruelties upon them, as was the case in 1870. And yet these "comrades-in-arms" over whom the French women gush, and whom the French and English press flatter by describing them as "terrible," are, of course, not good enough to be fellow-prisoners in the internment camps—*that* is something that is just a trifle too "barbaric" for the pioneers

---

[1] That all these miserable tribes are fighting for England against their will is easily understood, so far as Mohammedans are concerned since the proclamation of the "Holy War." But that the Hindoos are of the same mind is proved by the following announcement of the Hindoo Committee of San Francisco in the American newspapers:

"England has compelled the Indian princes to contribute vast sums to the costs of war. It has forced the native soldiers to take up arms against Germany. It is a lie that India feels any enthusiasm for England's cause; and only the barbaric measures of war prevent the Indian people from expressing their real sympathy for the German nation."

of culture on the banks of the Thames and the Seine. No, let them all be shut up together—Mongols and Ghurkas, Frenchmen and Cossacks, Englishmen and Moroccans, Niggers of the Soudan and Australians. Those who would share the glories of the war against us, should also share our enforced hospitality! "Birds of a feather"—let them "flock together,"[1] [2]

[1] The natural cruelty of the savage auxiliary tribes is, of course, not sufficient. They must be incited to a frenzy by all manner of lies. When the Indian troops arrived in France, they were told that the Germans were in the habit of cutting off the breasts of women! ("Neue Züricher Zeitung," October 16, 1914.)

[2] An interesting document regarding the treatment of Indians in the English army has fallen into the hands of the Germans. It demonstrates to what a level an unscrupulous nation can descend, a nation which is capable of driving such poor wretched colored folk to the slaughter-house, folk who in their hearts feel only hatred for their oppressors and who battle against the Germans merely because they are commanded to do so.

In a retranslation of the German text this reads as follows:

Confidential. No. 3/3 (A)

Headquarters, Indian Army Corps.

Dated, October 22nd, 1914.

Memorandum for the conduct of officers of the Indian Army Corps.

1. According to the provisions of the Indian Army Law Paragraph § 45a; physical chastisement may be recognized as a law by a court-martial in all cases in which any military person in active service subject to this law, from a sergeant-lieutenant downwards, has contravened it. But upon the basis of the compiled commands of the Indian Army Corps such judgments can only be carried out against those who have been found guilty of:
   a) serious wrongs perpetrated upon the persons and property of the inhabitants of the country, according to § 41 of the Indian Army Law;
   b) Breaking into a house for the purpose of robbery, or robbing, either according to (a) or according to § 25 (j) of the same law;
   c) Robbery when acting as sentry or when mounting guard, etc., according to § 26 (c) of the Indian Army Law;
   d) dishonorable behavior, according to § 31 of the Indian Army Law;
2. ....
3. Physical punishment upon grounds of § 24 (2) of the Indian Army Law shall be limited to such cases in which persons have been guilty of acts in contravention of the clauses cited above (I).
4. Physical chastisement must not be carried out in the presence of British or other European troops or civilians.
5. According to the views of the Commandant of the Army Corps, robbery in this country is to be very severely punished; the punishment decreed is therefore not to be less than the major penalty.

A Swiss paper that is rather pro-French in its sympathies, speaks of "a blow levelled at the heart of all Europe," in fact of "a wanton attempt at racial suicide"—against which the "spirit of humanity of Switzerland" rises in protest.[1] And why are Herr Hodler, Herr Karl Spitteler and Jacques Dalcroze silent in the face of all this?

CHAPTER V.

The Violation of the Neutrality of the Suez Canal.

Hamburg shipping circles communicated on the 23rd of August that the Egyptian harbor of Port Said at the entrance to the Suez Canal was immediately occupied by English troops after the Egyptian declaration of war. These troops at once proceeded to render the German steamers in Port Said useless by taking away parts of the machinery. Especial attention in this respect was paid to the "Derfflinger," a steamer of the North German Lloyd.

Commenting upon this, the "Norddeutsche Allgemeine Zeitung" remarked: "This act, of course, occasions us no surprise. It is distinctly English. Nevertheless the attention of the whole world should be directed to the manner in which

6. A copy of this order should be in the possession of every British officer of artillery and of the Indian formations. A copy should be on hand at every court-martial which is held in the Army Corps under the Indian military law.

W. E. O'Leary, Colonel.
Substitute General-adjutant
Indian Army Corps.

Not only the reports and bulletins of German troops, but also many documents of the enemy which fell into German hands, furnish the most incontrovertible proof of the cruel manner in which many French villages were looted by these colored Englishmen. The secret order for officers cited above goes to prove what stringent measures were necessary to repel the lawlessness of these semi-savage allies.

[1] One of the greatest of ethnological authorities, Sven Hedin, declares (see pages 185 *et seq.*) that the use of these Indians in warfare is a "crime against culture, civilization and Christianity" and "the very top and summit of cruelty."

Great Britain, with a cold, cynical smile, simply thrusts the solemn agreements regarding the Suez Canal, so often ratified by international agreement, into the waste-paper basket *as soon as they become inconvenient to her.*"

We may add that at the same time the German coal depot at this port, the property of a Hamburg firm, was locked up, so that German ships might no longer be able to coal—hostile acts of the worst imaginable kind!

A case still more crass, even though it occurred after the declaration of war, is furnished by the acts committed against the two steamers of the Hamburg-American Line, the "Istria" and the "Sudmark." From the legal representative of the Hamburg-American Line I received the following information, dated Alexandria, the 22nd of October, 1914:

"I have in the meantime discovered that the steamers which had been lying at Port Said and at Suez, were captured in the following original and "legal" manner. On the 13th inst. divisions of Egyptian Police appeared aboard all German and Austrian steamers at Port Said and Suez, under the command of an officer who declared to the Captains that no one would be permitted to leave the ships and that these would be forced to quit the harbor. The Captains naturally refused to obey, whereupon the Egyptian port authorities put men aboard, supplied the vessels with coal and provisions for 7 days and thus sent the vessels out of the port on the 15th and 16th, flying the German flag.

A few miles from Port Said the English cruiser "Warrior" was awaiting them, and it is easily to be understood that her Captain, on seeing such a number of enemy vessels, should at once make efforts "legally" to "capture" them, and take them to Alexandria. The Captain of the "Warrior" observed all the regulations with the most painful meticulosity, and on reaching Alexandria the steamers were handed over to a Prize Court.

The agent of the Hamburg-American Line in justifiable anger remarks as follows with regard to this farce in connection with international law: "The facts cited above might suffice for a game for children, or if you prefer, a comedy in the style of Nestroy—but in order to establish international rights this ridiculous travesty is altogether insufficient."

But such is British "correctness" which strains at a gnat yet swallows a camel.

We have here to deal with a breach of the Treaty of October 29th, 1888, with respect to the Suez Canal, opened in 1869. (See the literature on this subject in Liszt's "International Law," Page 209, *et seq.*) The Agreement was based upon the negotiations at the Paris Conference in 1885, which had been approved of and signed by all the Great Powers, including Turkey, Spain and the Netherlands. According to this the maritime Suez Canal (originally a private enterprise) was to remain free and open in peace as well as in war to every merchant or war vessel without regard to the nationality of the flag it bore. The Powers agreed and pledged themselves that they would do nothing to prejudice the free operations of the Canal even in time of war. The rights of blockade were not *to be exercised nor was any hostile action to be taken against vessels at anchor there.* (See Article 1 and 3, 4 of the Agreement, see also Liszt Page 210, Ullmann on International Law, Page 342 *et seq.*)

In times of war belligerents were not to be permitted to disembark troops nor unload munitions nor other materials of war. Belligerents, in fact, were not to be permitted to send any vessels into the harbors of Port Said or Suez. (Article 7.)

But not only the acts against German ships which have just been described, but the entire procedure of the English troops, constitute, as the "Norddeutsche Allgemeine Zeitung" so clearly points out, "a real English breach of agreement." England, in spite of the clear and conclusive stipulations of Articles 4 and 5, simply regards the Suez Canal and all its appointments as English property, going so far as to fortify the Canal and making it the base for warlike operations.

It is true, as pointed out by Triepel and others, that England signed the Treaty with the very elastic reservation that it would be bound by its conditions only as these were compatible with the temporary exceptional conditions of Egypt, and in so far as these did not hinder the freedom of action of the British troops during the occupation.

In the meantime England by its agreement with France, as signed on the 8th of April, 1904, formally accepted all the essential points of the Suez Canal Convention, thus annulling the afore-mentioned reservation, this declaration not applying only to France, but also to all the other Powers—to whom the terms of the Anglo-French agreement were communicated. The terms that apply to the regulations of war in regard to the Suez Canal are therefore in every sense absolutely valid.

Ships of every nationality as well as their cargoes, are to enjoy the right of entry in all ports, as well as exit from them, also the right to traverse the Canal without incurring the danger of seizure or delay—provided that they pursue their courses in the usual way and without any undue delay. All ships are entitled to coal at the bunkers and to secure other supplies in so far as these are necessary for their voyage, etc.

Finally, it is contended that Article 13 (which, according to British interpretations, permits England to undertake warlike movements in Egyptian territory) was to be interpreted in accordance with the Suez Canal Convention. If any significance at all is to be attached to this, then as Triepel and others rightly declare, it can only mean that no hostile act whatsoever is to be undertaken in the Canal or its entrance harbors, or within a distance of three sea-miles of its ports, since this is expressly forbidden in the terms of the Convention.

Not even the "Times" would venture to deny that the acts which England,—land of sacrosanct treaties!—committed in this instance against German steamers, were hostile acts. By taking away parts of the machinery of these vessels, as is customary in acts of war, and by means of seizing or locking the coal depots of the Germans, England had broken the most important clauses of the Suez Canal Acts, and must acknowledge the full force of these violations.

The International Commission, to be sure, which was to supervise the carrying-out of the Suez Canal Agreement of October 29, 1888, was superseded by Article 8 of the Second Anglo-French Agreement of April 8th, 1904, so that England might be able to exert force in place of equity. (See also von Liszt, International Law, 6th edition, 1910, page 209.) But the mere removal of the International Commission does not in the least affect the rights which all nations are entitled to claim for their ships in the Suez Canal and its entrance ports.

England has not only treated Egypt like subject territory and ordered its mobilization despite the protests of the Khedive, putting aside the Egyptian officers and troops, but it has also made of the neutral Suez Canal a basis for its entire warlike enterprises. It has simply thrown the entire agreement of the Suez Canal Treaty into the waste-paper basket.

The British Government expressly condoned all the measures taken by the so-called "Egyptian Government," especially those by which "enemy vessels which had lain sufficiently long in the harbors of the Canal and were suspected of not wishing to depart in order to avoid capture," were to be ordered to leave the Suez Canal at once, the excuse being that the Canal was not meant to serve this purpose. This noble nation went so far as to make seizure of the German post upon an Italian steamer going to East Asia, and to burn it at Suez, in order to prevent the truth as to the conditions of war from reaching that part of the world.

The entire procedure of England is in violation of all the terms of the Suez Acts of 1888, and destroys the neutrality and internationality of that waterway. And yet King George in a proclamation of the 10th of September announces: "Great Britain and My entire realm regard the absolute respect to be paid to to Our pledged word in treaties as a common heritage!" [1] Through this act on England's part the entire validity of the Suez Canal Treaty ceases to exist for every nation in the world. No Power, after this breach of faith on England's part, need

[1] In sarcastic words the Imperial Chancellor of Germany has declared that the selfsame England which had acquired its enormous colonial empire by the exercise of brute force and cold-blooded egoism, was now pretending to guard the freedom of the world against the Germans.

"In the name of freedom Great Britain strangled the independence of the Boer Republics at the close of the last century, in the name of freedom it laid Egypt in chains after committing the basest breach of faith. And in the name of the same blessing England is robbing those Malay States of India that still enjoy some measure of freedom, one after the other, of their rights to their own existence. And surely it must have been their love for the freedom of the world that induced Englishmen to cut the German cable and thus suppress the truth concerning the war throughout the greater part of the globe." The Chancellor might also have spoken of Ireland and Persia and other victims of England's humanitarian principles.

trouble itself further about the declaration of the neutrality of the Suez Canal.

We trust that these deeds will yet cause the British Empire to suffer in a grievous degree precisely in those spots where it is most easy to wound. At all events this wanton action in respect to the Suez Canal Acts is a telling example of the worth England places upon international compacts. This is something which Germany must under no circumstances forget at the conclusion of peace. Germany, Austria-Hungary and Turkey (for which last country the terms of the Agreement of 1888 have no validity) must not forget, in the event of Turkey being forced to defend her possessions on the Red Sea, that the judgment of the great Bonaparte at the beginning of the 19th century regarding the importance of Egypt, still applies to the British Empire of today. England is well aware that the most precarious point in its *imperium* lies in Egypt.

This fact will and must determine the attitude of all states which are resolved to make an end of the world-power of Britain, so that a permanent peace may be secured and Europe be saved from the intrigues of this most dangerous of the disturbers of peace.

Let Egypt be made free of the enforced rule of Britain and the key to India is in our hands! *One of the many achievements of this war must be the unconditional assurance that the Suez Canal is to remain neutral. Since all international law is to England a mere inconvenient hand-cuff which it must needs shake off, real international rights can be enforced against England only after England has been defeated!* [1]

[1] My honored friend, von Liszt, touching upon this point, the justice of which he affirms, has induced me to express my opinion of the "Central European Union of States." This I shall do in another place. I will merely say that I am an enthusiastic supporter of such a union—from the North Cape unto Tripoli, from Flushing to Asia Minor—but I am pessimistic as to whether we possess the grand statesman, who after the ordeal of the conclusion of a mighty peace treaty, would have sufficient strength to create so gigantic a work. He who is able to form a union such as this will be accounted for all time one of the greatest figures in European history. But in order to form unions at least two parties are invariably necessary!

CHAPTER VI.

The Breach of Chinese Neutrality by Japan and England's Assault upon Kiao-Chau.

"War, Trade and Piracy,—
A trinity inseparable."

The Japanese *Chargé d'Affaires* at Berlin, acting upon the orders of his government, handed a Note to the Foreign Office on the 19th of August, 1914, which, making reference to the Anglo-Japanese Alliance, demanded the immediate withdrawal of German warships from Chinese or Japanese waters, or the dismantling of these ships, as well as the unconditional surrender of the entire leased territory of Kiao-Chau to the Japanese authorities. These demands were to be accepted unconditionally by the 23rd of August.

Germany made the proper answer to this insolent demand, unique in the history of the laws of nations—namely, no answer at all. Hereupon Japan and England began their warlike operations against the German leased territory.

This "policy of the vulture" (for Japan had from the very beginning looked upon Kiao-Chau as booty ready to fall into its hands)[1] had nothing whatsoever to do with the Anglo-Japanese Alliance. On the contrary the whole shamelessness of the Japanese attitude—of the serpent which we, under the influence of an amazing short-sightedness, had nurtured at our bosoms, may be seen in the very text of the treaty. In the introduction to the Anglo-Japanese Treaty of Alliance,[2] the goal of the compact is given as follows:

---

[1] The Japanese newspaper "Yomiuri" declared that it was "utterly incompatible with the laws of the ancient Japanese code of honor for Japan to make such demands upon Germany, which now found itself in the dire necessity of war.... It was entirely contradictory to the ideals of Japanese chivalry, and was doubly dishonorable, since it meant an attack upon one's own teacher, to whom, in accordance with the law of Confucius, all reverence and gratitude were due." Only a "financial Alliance" was able to overcome the repugnance of a number of the Japanese Ministers towards acting upon the request which England made of Japan on the 7th of August.

[2] One of the best-known authorities upon India and one of England's

1. The consolidation and maintenance of peace in the regions of East Asia and India.

2. *The preservation of the common interests of all powers in China through the assurance of the independence and integrity of the Chinese Empire and the principle of equal opportunity in China for the trade and commerce of all nations.*

3. The maintenance of the territorial rights of the contracting parties in the regions of East Asia and India and the defense of their special interests in the said regions.

The most important articles of the terms of the Alliance declare in detail:

Article 1. It is agreed that when, according to the opinion either of Japan or Great Britain, any of the aforesaid rights and interests should happen to be jeopardised, both governments shall openly and freely communicate the same to each other and take common counsel as to the measures which are to be taken in order to guard their threatened rights or interests.

Article 2. *Should one of the contracting parties by reason of an unprovoked attack or a non-aggressive action, wherever this may take place, on the part of any power, be drawn into war, made necessary by the defense of its territorial rights or its special interests as mentioned above, the other contracting party must immediately come to the assistance of its ally, conduct the war in common with it, and conclude peace on the basis of a mutual understanding.*

We see therefore that the *Casus foederis* (Bündnisfall) is only established in the event of the territorial rights being endangered, that is to say, in the event of an aggressive action by Germany against England, or in case of the jeopardizing of the independence and integrity of the Chinese Empire and the principle of the Open Door in China.

All this, of course, has not the slightest application to the case at issue in which England aggressively declared war against Germany. From the very beginning Germany made it prefectly clear—and Japan could have had the most formal assurance

---

most famous jurists, Henry Lanner Milne, declares in view of the dangers that threaten India by reason of its Japanese policy:

"Every European power which enters into an alliance with yellow peoples against a European power, commits treason against the entire human race."

in the shortest possible time had it desired anything of the sort—that Germany cherished not the slightest aggressive intentions against either England or China—least, of all, naturally, against Japan. The Japanese *Chargé d'Affaires* was at once informed that in the event of Japanese neutrality, the German squadron in East Asia would refrain from any hostile action in the waters there.

The most remarkable thing, however, was the intimation that Germany was threatening the independence and integrity of the Chinese Empire and the principle of the Open Door, and thereby imperilling the peace of East Asia and the territorial rights of other nations in East Asia. Japan and England resemble each other in their policies and in their skill in converting the most villainous and scoundrelly acts into something ethically correct, nay, even something magnanimous and noble!

Let any man consider and estimate the relative military strength of both sides in East Asia, and then—let us still keep our patience and our calmness!—judge the shamelessness of this wanton trifling with the rights of nations of which Japan has been guilty—an act that seems almost like a mockery of Germany and the entire world. And Germany had never once thought of ignoring the territorial rights of the contracting parties in the regions of East Asia or of India—and had made this perfectly clear on more than one occasion.[1] But England, according to her own official declaration, also longed "to strike a deadly blow" at Germany in the matter of her colonies. This, and this alone is the truth—and not the rank invention that

[1] Dr. Carson Chany, a prominent Chinese journalist, in a flaming protest now declares that the present policy of Japan and its 20 demands made upon China, is an act of aggression hitherto unheard of in the history of the world and directed against a people who are living in absolute peace with Japan. Chany is entirely in the right, when he says:

"Although the Japanese demands were first directed against China, their contents are such that their realization will cause all other states to be involved. The policy hitherto maintained by these in Asia was based upon the principle of the integrity and independence of China, and that of the open door. This was expressly confirmed in the agreement between Japan and France in July, 1907, in the notes exchanged between the United States and Japan in November, 1908, and in the revised treaty of alliance between England and Japan in July, 1911." (*retranslation*)

Germany was threatening the trade relationships in the East of Asia.

Of a state of defense or necessity on the part of Japan there is no trace—no trace of an iron compulsion to break its neutrality! Its policy is merely that of a corsair bent upon conquest.

Kiao-Chau was leased to Germany by China in the year 1898, just as Wei-Hai-Wei was leased to England and Port Arthur to Russia. A number of facts which are embodied in the essential nature of these respective contracts of leasehold, must be taken into consideration in order to form a clear judgment upon the relationships of the various Powers to each other with regard to these territories. The Colonial projects of Germany and the concurrent interests affecting the standing of the other participating powers must not be ignored in this matter. In any case Kiao-Chau *did not pass into the complete possession of Germany.*

According to Article 2 of the Agreement of March 6, 1898, China surrenders this district to Germany "only upon terms of lease, fixed at present at a period of 99 years." And according to Article 3, "the Chinese Government during this term of lease will not exercise its rights of sovreignty, but leave these to Germany." The natives did not become German subjects. Should Germany at any time express a wish to surrender the Bay of Kiao-Chau to China ere the termination of the lease, China pledges itself to grant Germany a more suitable place. (Article 5.) There is no condition of China's dependence upon Germany established by this, since China merely granted the exercise of German authority upon Chinese soil only by means of a general right of representation.

As Dr. Hatschek correctly points out ("Deutsche Juristen-Zeitung," 1915, page 366 *et seq.*) the English form of lease was the one here adopted, analogous to that entered into between China and England with regard to Wei-Hai-Wei. The lessee enjoys, according to this, a legal right in the matter of the leasehold, so that any disturbance directed against his possession by the party leasing the land or by a third party, may be protested against by a suit at law. This right of suit, dating from the time of Henry the Eighth, is likewise to be applied should the lessor without or against the will of the lessee, sign over the lease to a third party before its expiration. This eventuality is met for Germany as against China in Article 5 of the terms of Agreement. Only Germany is given the right of withdrawing from the lease before the expiration of the 99 years, and not China. Thus China, in consenting to the cession of Kiao-Chau at this time, commits a breach of contract. China must first await the results of the peace negotiations between Germany and Japan before it has the right to cede Kiao-Chau to Japan.

China may give its consent to the assignment only after the conclusion of peace, when Germany would in reality surrender the leasehold to Japan. Hatschezk calls attention to a very interesting precedent in the Treaty of Portsmouth, in which Article 5 proceeded in precisely the same manner to cede Port Arthur to Japan. Therefore, the contract of lease between Germany and China still continues in force as before, and China can only evade it as it would evade a contract made under all the stipulations of private and international law.

China has never made any objection to the exercise by Germany of the latter's legitimate rights according to the treaty, nor has it ever demanded the intervention of another power because of any violation of the terms of the treaty. The contrary, in fact, was true. And now comes Japan, and seizes upon foreign, neutralized Chinese territory —under the hollow allegation that it wishes to return it to China!

Japan, a nation that had ratified and signed all the terms of the Hague Convention, has flung these aside with an indifference which indicates plainly enough what the world may expect in the future on the part of this East Asiatic power. We need merely mention its violation of Article 3 with regard to the commencement of hostilities, or Article 5, regarding the rights of neutral powers and persons in the event of war by land, or Article 13, dealing with the same rights in war by sea. The fact that England appears upon the scene as the inciter of Japan, completes the picture of the complete moral bankruptcy of the white race in the face of the yellow and the black, and apparently the no less complete destruction of all international law.[1]

All further actions undertaken in East Asia are an uninterrupted series of violations of the law of nations, committed both on the part of England and of Japan, and not only against Germany, but also against China, which is by right even today the owner of the land and of all those inherent and sovereign rights which it did not cede to Germany as its authorised agent, as stipulated in the treaty,—rights which for this reason it can only negotiate with Germany.

China, of course, would have been obliged, according to Article 5 of the Hague Conference (Fifth Session) to which China was a party in 1910, to use forcible measures in order to

---

[1] It appears from the comprehensive parliamentary reports of the "Deutsche Japan-Post" that Japan determined upon the campaign against Kiau-Chau only after the express demand for this had been made by England. The Foreign Minister of Japan, Baron Kato, said in relation to this:

"Japan has neither the wish nor the inclination to be involved in the present war; it was merely of the conviction that it was its duty to remain true to the alliance; and to fortify its principles by making peace in the Far East a still greater certainty than before, and by protecting the special interests of the two allied powers."

Several speakers in the Japanese Diet objected to this declaration on the part of the Minister, many of them in the sharpest manner. The Deputy Matsuda, for instance, declared that according to the text of the Anglo-Japanese alliance, *Japan was under no circumstances obliged to fulfil the terms of the agreement so long as the territorial integrity and special interests of England in East Asia did not require such protection.* He demanded exact information as to whether Germany in any way threatened the permanent peace in East Asia, or had injured the special interests of England in that sphere. Dr. Tomizu went so far as to ask the Minister whether the diplomacy of Japan was so much under the influence of the English Government that the Foreign Office at Tokio was to be regarded as a mere branch of the English Foreign Office? The answer to this question was made only during a secret session.

Another statement of peculiar importance made by Minister Kato during the deliberations of the Budget Commission, deals with the intention of Japan *not* to restore Kiao-Chau to China. This evasion was expressed as follows: he had merely inserted the clause relative to the return of Kiao-Chau to China in the ultimatum to Germany, because he had fancied that the insertion of this clause would prove advantageous to Japan. But the clause was to be valid only in case no war ensued. This is true Japanese trickery—patterned after the genuine "English model." The Jap in his diplomatic dishonesty is truly worthy of his master!

keep Japan and England from committing this breach of neutrality. But the two Great Powers which violated the inviolability of Chinese territory, were well aware of the present impotence of the Chinese Empire, and so instead of *right* merely made use of *brutal might*.

It is a hollow and ghastly mockery of the most elementary justice and of all the laws that bind the nations, that a Great Power should have the presumption to deceive the world with the pretense that it takes away the territory of a country against the will of the very country that had granted the land to the other by a legal compact—in order, as it alleges, to restore it to the original owner—but in reality to deprive him of it in the very midst of peace!

And one of the crassest features of the entire affair consists in the spectacle of a nation, a civilized nation which pretends that treaties are held "sacred" by it, and alleges that it proclaimed war against Germany merely because of this sanctity of treaties,—as solemnly announced by King George of England at the beginning of August,—of such a nation treading the law of nations and the rights of formal compacts into the dust. The prophesy, as expressed by the author in the first German edition of this work,—that Japan would see that the moment had arrived for solving the entire Chinese problem without consulting the chief interests of that nation now immersed in its own folly, and for solving it purely in its own interests, has been fulfilled far more swiftly that he had himself imagined. Japan is now out for the entire spoils. Count Okuma, according to the Japanese Colonial Journal, ("No-chih") let the cat out of the bag, when he declared, in Tokio:

"Japan is not concerned only with putting an end to the ambitious plans of Russia and Germany; it also wishes to keep England and the United States from putting a finger into the Chinese pie...... The alliance with England limits Japan's influence in North China: and Japan was concerned in this to guarantee the inviolability of China. But this can be done only if Japan is able to extend its influence over southern China. The way things lie, Japan will be forced to break off its friendly relations with a certain power. Japan does not fear to engage in war with one or two of the strongest European powers."

According to a communication in the "Novoie Vremia," Count Okuma expressed himself as follows in the newspaper "Kokumin," in January, 1915:

"Japan has more important duties than to concern itself with the fate of the unimportant German colonies. Its duty consists in this: to open the eyes of Europe as to the real significance of Japan. The Pacific Ocean already lies within the sphere of Japanese influence. The Japanese may now bring the prestige of their realm to a high degree of development. An unarmed peace is no real peace."

We are here concerned only with the secondary question of the political influence which Great Britain's betrayal of the white race, unique in the history of the world, will exert upon all race consciousness and all concepts of Caucasian civilization.

The political effects both for England and the United States, which unfortunately entirely misinterpret their neutrality in this direction, permitting it to grow into an incomprehensible and dangerous weakness and pernicious passivity,[1] may perhaps prove terrible.

England is at present behaving towards Japan like a hysterical gambler at *Va-Banque.* Not only her influence in China, but also her position in India is being destroyed. Australia, New Zealand and Canada are faced with the most serious questions as to their destiny, as a result of the concessions to Japan. Russia, also, as well as England and the United States of North America, will one day curse the "statesmen" who set Japan in the saddle as the heir of Western European civilization.

Australia and other English colonies, who do not yet regard Mr. Rudyard Kipling's myth of "The White Man's Burden" as one of the conventional English lies, will one day revenge themselves for this high treason on the part of the motherland. *Exoriare aliquis nostris ex ossibus ultor!*

"And China also will clearly perceive before long that the 'life and death struggle' which is impending for that huge

[1] See the vigorous judgment of an American judge in the first German edition, page 90, Note 1, in regard to the attitude of the United States. In any event we shall have to free ourselves from that phrase, "The Yellow Peril," and suchlike sentimentalities, which have only injured us in the past.

empire against Japan, Russia and England can no longer be postponed. May it not fail to seize the happy hour."

Thus we wrote in our first edition. Time has justified us, just as we believed it would. The avenger of American greed and short-sightedness, of English meanness and craft, arises already in the person of Japan. Of course, at first, China will have much to suffer, on account of her military impotence.

Germany, especially, cannot be sufficiently warned against the transplantation of obscure race-theories into the domain of practical politics (China, Turkey). After this bankruptcy of European civilization, we shall henceforth estimate the nations only according to their political and moral worth.

CHAPTER VII.

The Use of Dum-Dum Bullets and the Like.

At the end of August, the following official announcement appeared:

"Our armies took from captured French and English thousands of infantry cartridges, which had the points of the bullets deeply hollowed out. Many of the cartridges were still in their original wrappings, bearing the label of the manufacturer. The mechanical manufacture of these bullets is proved beyond question both by the number and description of bullets found. In Fort Longwy a machine for this purpose was discovered. These cartridges were also issued direct to the troops by the Army Supply Headquarters. English officers, prisoners of war, have declared on their word of honor that their revolver ammunition was issued to them in this form. The wounds sustained by our soldiers show the devastating effect of these Dum-Dum bullets. While France and England, in gross violation of the Geneva Convention, allow projectiles to be employed whose use is characteristic of barbaric warfare, Germany preserves every detail of international law. In the whole of the German army not one Dum-Dum bullet is to be found."

At the same time it was also established that the Russians as well as the Servians continually used Dum-Dum bullets. On the 30th of August, at the examination of 62 captured Russian officers and 6378 men on an exercise ground in Silesia, large numbers of such bullets were found. ("Schlesische Zeitung.")

The bullets in their original French and English wrappings were sent to Germany in great quantities, and are at present to be seen (September) in the editorial offices of the leading German papers, (for example, the "Münchener Neueste Nachrichten.") Hence there can be no doubt as to the existence of these bullets, and as to their having actually been used.[1] Medical opinions substantiate the frightful barbaric effects of the kind of warfare indulged in by the alleged "Civilized nations." (see below)

The abuse gradually attained such dimensions that the Kaiser felt himself obliged, on the 8th of September, to address a protest to the United States in the form of a telegram to President Wilson. This telegram, of the greatest interest from the point of view of international law, was as follows:

"I consider it my duty, Mr. President, to acquaint you, as the foremost representative of the principles of humanity, with the fact that after the capture of the French fortress of Longwy, my troops found thousands of Dum-Dum bullets hidden there, in a certain factory belonging to the government. Bullets of the same kind were found upon the dead and wounded, and upon the prisoners, including the British troops. You are aware that these projectiles cause terrible wounds and suffering and that their use is strictly forbidden by the recognized principles of international law. I therefore address to you a solemn protest

[1] Furthermore, Privy Councillor Pays, a University professor, in a speech delivered a short time ago to German army doctors in the field (in Northern France) showed by means of X-ray photographs, the exact position of the various parts of a burst projectile in the body; and demonstrated conclusively that the wounds were caused by a special kind of Dum-Dum bullet, which the English had used at Lille. They looked like ordinary cartridges. The bullet had a jacket like others, under this an aluminium point, and then a special kind of leaden core. This would spilt on coming in contact with a bone, tearing the tissues and inflicting frightful wounds. (From the war-correspondent Dr. Oskar Bongard.)

against this kind of warfare, which, thanks to the methods of our opponents, has become the most barbarous known to history." [1]

The full confirmation of the Imperial reproach is shown in the following document:

Two English officers at present in German hands have in

---

[1] The following notes on the nature of these projectiles are taken from the Bavarian Military Museum:

"The genuine Dum-Dum bullet is of English origin; it is called after the cartridge factory of the same name at Calcutta, and was first used in India. The jacket reached only to the beginning of the egg-shaped point, and was in part furnished with lengthwise grooves. This first variety did not prove satisfactory. So a projectile with a hollow point was adopted. This was given a thinner jacket and only the base of the forward hollow was lined with an alloy of copper, tin and nickel. Used in the battle of Omdurman (Soudan Campaign, 1898). The frequent mushrooming of the lead core through the jacket remaining stuck in the riflings, led to the adoption of a harder lead core (with a greater proportion of antimony alloy, M/95).

This kind of Dum-Dum projectile has not been employed by the French in the present campaign, but a bullet subsequently hollowed out. For this purpose the old type M/98 and M/03 with a jacket of nickel-plate and a core of hard lead were used. By means of machines, and (as the rough work on some of the examples before us shows) sometimes by hand, the point of the projectile was removed and the bullet drilled out to a depth of 6 mm and a diameter of 5 mm.

This alteration naturally led to a considerable diminution of the trajectory and the power of penetration, but in contrast to the modern slender and polished French bullet with its penetrating copper point, it is able to inflict wounds which are a disgrace to all modern civilization. That this projectile, contrary to international law, had full official sanction is shown by the package now in the hands of the Munich Military Museum which bears the stamp:

ETUIS MEL B^{90} MEL POUDRE BF AM MEL

A VIS 1914 8 CARTOUCHES DE STAND M^{LE} 1906 LOT 121

the course of an official examination made statements as to the use of Dum-Dum projectiles in the English army. These were Colonel Gordon of the Gordon Highlanders, Adjutant to the King of England, and Lieutenant-Colonel Neish of the First Gordon Highlanders.

"As regards revolver ammunition, the bullet as issued was a flat-nosed one. The first time I had ever seen this bullet was during this summer at annual practice.

I make above statement in writing at the request of Baron von Lersner, as a summary of answers I gave him to verbal questions he asked me.

TORGAU. J. W. Neish, Lt. Col.
19 September 14. 1st Gordon Highlanders.

When I was taken prisoner at Bertry at 3 A. M. on 27 Aug., I had in my possession only 3 pointed revolver bullets. I had borrowed them from a brother officer. I had no flat-nosed bullet in my possession, as the ones I had issued to me I had buried. I do not remember when, but it was certainly several days before we commenced fighting in the vicinity of Mons on 23 Aug.

TORGAU J. W. Neish, Lt. Col.
19 Sept. 14 1st Gordon Highlanders.
(Written in my presence.)

Geschrieben in meiner Gegenwart.

Frhr. von Lersner. Frhr. v. Berchheim.
Lt. d. Res.-Husar. 7. Lt. d. R. 2. G. Drag.

I was issued at Plymouth with revolver ammunition—it was flat-nosed—as I was in doubt about it being correct ammunition and being unable to obtain any definite information from superior authority concerning the matter, I put my revolver ammunition in the ground four days before Mons (23rd Aug.) engagement which was the first time I met the German army. At the same time I placed my revolver in my heavy baggage and never carried it again.

The revolver ammunition was of the same pattern as issued

to me and the other officers of the Gordon Highlanders in June last to fire their annual revolver course."

(Written in my presence.)
Geschrieben in
meiner Gegenwart.
Frhr. v. Lersner.
Lt. d. R. Hus. 7.
Frhr. v. Berchheim.
Lt. d. R. II G. Drag. Rgt.

W. E. Gordon, Colonel
Gordon Highlanders,
A.D.C. to the King.

In the middle of October a well-known war correspondent proved in the "Berliner Tageblatt" that even the machine-guns of the English used Dum-Dum projectiles. In the matter of a violation of international law they have excelled even the Russians.

These revelations naturally created a tremendous sensation all over the world, especially since the soldiers had been officially equipped in this manner.

President Poincaré has, without a shadow of proof, simply reversed the whole matter and declares that the Germans had used Dum-Dum projectiles. The old Russian espionage method! "Evil communications" have taught the "grande nation" many such "Hunnish practices!"

In a number of cases the usage was quite naively confessed.

A French officer of high standing, for instance, made the following communication to the Paris correspondent of the Dutch newspaper, the "Tijd." He said: "The talk about the use of Dum-Dum bullets probably arose from the fact that a staff-officer in the fortress of Longwy used to occupy himself with the study of the manufacture of new forms of cartridges. He had also found in a store-room of the fortress several cases of hollowed-out bullets, which were left over from the time when these were not yet forbidden by the Hague Peace Conference. It had been intended to render these fit for use by a process of filing by machinery. It was possible that some few packets of forbidden cartridges had unintentionally been served out to the French soldiers."

The point of view regarding the French projectile has also undergone a complete change. Professor Kirchner in the

"Münchener Medizinischen Wochenschrift" emphasizes the fact that the new French infantry projectile is a jacketted bullet and therefore by pinching off the point may very easily be converted into a kind of Dum-Dum projectile.

And from whence do the English revolver Dum-Dum bullets come? From "some few packets?" Yet quantities of them are at present in official possession in Germany, and may be inspected. And not only in Germany. The "Kölnische Zeitung" cites a despatch from Zürich:

"In the office of the German Embassy in Bern there are at present (end of September, 1914) some Dum-Dum projectiles which were found upon French and English soldiers. Some of these were handed over to the Swiss Federal Government for inspection. A military expert who had examined these cartridges declares in the Bern "Bund:" It is plain that the projectile in question is a typical Dum-Dum. The soft core is exposed at the tip, and upon contact with a harder body, the soft, heated lead must pour from the opening in the tip and spread itself, causing the well-known ragged wounds.

The English infantry projectile outwardly exactly resembles the German infantry projectile, only it is 4·5 mm longer. The German projectile has a case of nickel steel, into which the lead core is compressed. The English projectile has a point 10·5 mm in length, covered with aluminium and containing a lead core. It is 32·5 mm long, the aluminium core is 10·5 mm long, the lead core 22 mm long. Through this procedure the centre of gravity of the projectile is transferred so far to the rear, that upon the slightest impact it reverses upon itself, with a Dum-Dum effect. We thus see the corroboration of the statement that every English infantry projectile has the effect of a Dum-Dum.

From this we come to the following: The English rifle has a spring which, as the English soldier mockingly explains, serves as a "cigar-cutter." With this contrivance, he cuts off the point of the projectile and exposes the leaden core. A Proclamation by the Bavarian General von Hellingrath of the 30th of October, 1914, clearly characterizes the employment of these most fearful projectiles. He says:

"This is the crudest kind of warfare; this projectile was

intended for use against the wild beasts of Asia and Africa. Its use shows to what depths the "civilized people" of England have sunk."

The English manufacture these things on a wholesale scale.

Not quite so childish and naive as the confession in the "Tijd," is the declaration which was given semi-officially in the German press of the 14th of September:

"Under date of 14th September appears the communication that a captured English staff-officer—he was the same English Major Charles Alice Yates who afterwards escaped and killed himself—was shown some of the Dum-Dum projectiles which had been found upon an English soldier. He did not dispute that such projectiles were used in the English army. He added however: "One must shoot with the cartridges that one receives from the Government!" *Quod erat demonstrandum!* (See also the interesting communication of Burgomaster Merkt of Munich, "Münchener Neueste Nachrichten" of the 8th of November, 1914.)

The French and English infantry have subsequently employed still more frightful methods. Projectiles were found which were hollowed out to a depth of 5 mm at the point, and 2½ mm in diameter. This hollow was filled with phosphorous and the opening sealed up with paraffin.

In other examples two wires were soldered over the pointed end of the bullet and bent back. These bullets, as may be imagined, caused horrible wounds.

After a long interval, in the battles of April 1915, reports again came in from East and West regarding the use of Dum-Dum projectiles by the English and Russians. On this account the "Norddeutsche Allgemeine Zeitung" of the 3rd of May, 1915, in its official reply to the reproaches of Lord Kitchener, says:

"Anyone who officially supplies his troops with munition capable of inflicting such ghastly wounds as the English infantry projectile Number VII, should avoid all possible allusions to the Hague Agreement of the 18th of October, 1904."

CHAPTER VIII.

Treatment of Diplomatic Representatives by the Triple Entente Countries in Violation of International Law. Acts of Diplomatic Representatives of the Triple Entente in Violation of International Law.

The following was reported from Vienna on the 14th of August:

"The facts given below were brought to the attention of the Foreign Office through the American Ambassador. On the 13th of August the Austrian-Hungarian Vice-Consul Hoffinger who had been left in St. Petersburg by the Austrian-Hungarian Ambassador in order to guard the diplomatic archives and for whose safety the Russian Foreign Office had given its distinct guaranty, was arrested as a prisoner of war. The protest made against this flagrant breach of the law of nations by the American Embassy, which, as is known, had been entrusted with the protection of Austrian-Hungarian interests for the duration of the war, remained without result.

The Austrian-Hungarian Government therefore felt itself obliged to combat this forcible act on the part of the Russians, —which had already been preceded by the wanton arrest of a secretary of the Embassy, Herr Loster,—by resorting to the legitimate weapon of reprisals, and it is for this reason that the Russian secretary of the Embassy, M. Stolkowsky, who had been left behind in charge of the diplomatic archives, was arrested as a prisoner of war."

Breach of treaties, breach of the given word of honor, violations of the law of nations, violations of common penal law! Weapons such as these, abuses such as these, have wiped away the thin veneer of civilization from the very first day of war and even before that. The point of view of the Tartar and the Mongol has superseded at one blow all those agreements and compacts entered into at the Hague in 1899 and 1907. And let it not be forgotten that the prime mover in all this was the "Czar of Peace" himself, or rather some sudden and uncontrollable whim of this potentate whose power is dependent upon such countless factors.

The very fundamental principles of international law which had hitherto been held sacred in respect,—the inviolateness of the recognized representative of a belligerent power,—had been trampled upon by Russia.

On the 3rd of May, 1915, the "Norddeutsche Zeitung" issued a special supplement in the shape of a memorial upon the treatment of the German Consuls in Russia and the destruction of the German Embassy in St. Petersburg, which not only confirms everything that we revealed in the first edition of this book, but also presents a terrible picture of the barbarities of this Asiatic-Tartar state towards the German Consuls. These officials were treated "simply as common criminals." With the exception of the officials of the Consulate-General at St. Petersburg and Warsaw and the Consulate at Vladivostock, all officials of the Consulates were arrested and treated as ordinary criminals. The treatment of the women was no better. An actuary was condemned to break stones and perform other heavy labors. This memorial also exposes in the most drastic manner the baselessness of the Russian charges regarding the treatment of their officials in Germany. The clearest proofs are given that these charges are nothing more than sheer calumny and hypocritical phrases. There are complaints regarding internments of a few hours—internments of which the interned themselves said that they regarded them as "un très bon souvenir!"

It should be especially remarked that all the Consulate officials were deprived of their money without the granting of a receipt, that is, the money was simply *stolen*. On the other hand the Russian Consuls in Germany, many of whom used their official posts as a cloak for espionage, were treated in a most exemplary manner.

I shall not take into consideration such instances as the arrest of the German Consul and his family at Abo, and many other cases in which the unwritten laws of international customs were transgressed,—I will confine myself to that deed of shame which constitutes a blot upon all international law—the destruction of the German Embassy at St. Petersburg on the 4th of

August—a deed committed under the very eyes of the Russian authorities. The venerable German dragoman Kattner was stabbed to death by the infuriated mob. The memorial rightly describes this act as "a monstrous breach of international law for which there is no parallel since the murder of the ambassador at Rastadt."

I will let two eye-witnesses give their testimony. They have expressed themselves in the matter of these heinous acts and their word cannot be disputed and has, indeed, *not* been disputed.

An eye-witness of the wrecking of the German Embassy at St. Petersburg sent the following description to the "Kölnische Zeitung:"

"I reached St. Petersburg on Thursday, the 30th of July from the interior of Russia, but was not able to leave the city, owing to the mobilization which was already under way. The German Ambassador had left St. Petersburg on the 2nd of August early in the morning, and I was in constant contact with the Austrian-Hungarian and the American Embassies during this time.

"On Tuesday, August 4th, the mass of demonstrators had increased to a number such as I had not observed before. I saw the procession arrive at the square in front of the Cathedral of St. Isaac, and observed that there were about 100 people in its midst part of whom were armed with axes, crow-bars and other implements. A short address was given and then the word went round to destroy the German Embassy. I felt that everything must have been previously arranged and then carried out with the connivance of the police...."

A detailed description of the murder then followed.

Another witness also gives evidence which absolutely agrees with the above.

"The destruction of the German Embassy was a planned-out and deliberate act of violence by bands especially detailed for the purpose, and not the rash and spontaneous act of a drunken mob. During the time in which mounted policemen and gendarmes kept things in order in the square in which the Embassy is located, whole hordes of ruffians, armed with all the necessary implements, ladders, axes, knives and shears, had obtained an undisputed entrance to the *palais* of the Ambassador and had completed their work of devastation before the very eyes of the military and the people.

While these bands made havoc in the rooms of the Embassy, slaughtered the venerable Dragoman Kattner, demolished works of art, furniture, archives, etc., and set the building on fire—work which occupied several hours—*the gendarmes of the Czar mounted guard upon the square and saw to it that the traffic in front of the Embassy was not impeded! Not one of them showed the slightest inclination to enter the building or to interfere with the brutal work of these robbers and assassins who were numbered by hundreds.* Nor did they make a single move when the life-size portrait of the Kaiser was dragged out upon the street and given over to the fury of vandalism that possessed the mob that was waiting here."

This description which had been published in the "Frankfurter Kurier" and many other papers, has been fully confirmed by the official memorial just issued. All the magnificent works of art in the Embassy were destroyed in part or else stolen. Why do we hear no ward of protest in such cases as this from Mr. Ferdinand Hodler and his colleagues?

The memorial, among other things, also gives the following interesting details:

"The police that were stationed in the square remained entirely inactive, the same thing applies to the Chief of Police.. Court Councillor Kattner, a grey-haired old man, was not able to run fast enough and was killed by the mob in the most atrocious manner. Another gentleman who already lay prostrate under a hooligan armed with a knife, escaped with his life in a very wonderful way, for the electric lighting of the building went wrong just at this moment, whereupon the crowd, seized by an instant panic, suddenly fled...... Shortly before twelve o'clock a new mob broke into the Embassy and renewed the work of destruction. At a quarter to two the assault increased in violence. At a quarter to three the mob tried to fire the palace. It may have been that the police feared for the safety of the adjoining houses, for at last they took certain measures for interfering with the work of havoc.

The ease with which the police succeeded in clearing the

Embassy and the square is one clear proof of the criminal connivance of the government. As early as 11 o'clock the German officials had spoken with the American *chargé d'affaires* who declared that he had already asked the Foreign Office for protection. The Austrian-Hungarian Ambassador at 1 o'clock called the attention of M. Sasanoff to these unheard of proceedings on the part of the populace, but received the incredible answer: "Ils ont cassé quelques vitres." This frivolous remark is illuminated in the findings of the American Embassy: "The German Embassy was completely wrecked by the mob, not a single article of furniture being left undestroyed." This heroic act on the part of the Russian Government may best be characterized by the famous words of Roman Dmowski: "The Russian people have many good qualities, but the government is an Asiatic one."

The ambassadorial privileges and exemptions according to all universally accepted legal opinions, extend also to the other members of the embassies, especially the secretaries, dragomans, and others. The guaranty afforded by international law also covers the buildings of the embassy, and in particular the archives of the diplomatic mission in question—even in times of war. The buildings of the consulates and their archives are also to be held inviolate.

The wrecking of the Embassy, the murder of one of its officials, the arrest of the other, are not only serious crimes under the penal code, but are most flagrant examples of an outrageous trampling upon the law of nations. These shocking wrongs cry to heaven for vengeance. They almost cause one to despair of ever again restoring the respect of mankind for international law. It is through actions such as these that "civilized" Great Powers, and "Christian" states sink to the level of negro republics and African negro communities.

The outbreak of war between the state that sends the ambassador and the state that receives him, leads, it is true, to a suspension of diplomatic relations, but persons and property remain as before inviolable. Of course no belligerent state need tolerate the diplomatic mission of its opponent upon its own territory, it may also demand that its staff take its departure, but the immediate arrest of persons who have been left in legitimate charge of the inviolate records of the archives, is something that is *not* permitted.

The country that receives the embassy is also obliged to see that the building and offices of the embassy are taken care of under all conditions, and to punish in the severest manner all looting of the property of the foreign representatives as well as injury done to it. It is self-understood that full damages should be paid and the necessary apologies made, when such crimes have been perpetrated.

What did Russia do in the face of this wanton destruction, committed under the eyes of its police, and silently condoned by them?

According to the "Novoie Vremia" of the 20th of September, it appears that the riff-raff who were arrested during the plundering of the German Embassy were liberated again. The examining magistrate, according to this paper, had determined that these people had acted not from a desire for pillage, but from "noble patriotic motives!" It would not be too much to expect to hear that the ring-leaders of this typical act of Russian valor had been decorated with high orders.

CHAPTER IX.

A. Non-observances and Violations of Red Cross Rules on the Part of the Triple Entente States.

I. Innumerable outrageous acts have been committed against the law of nations, against German physicians, and wounded men, as well as against entire hospitals and sanitary corps in both theatres of the war. All these are breaches of the Geneva Convention.

From the mass of available material on hand, I shall merely select a few examples as proofs, and only such in which the witnesses are named and a testing of the circumstances rendered possible, or such as have already been confirmed by investigation, or cases in which the witnesses are known to be trustworthy:

1. A large hospital had been erected west of Metz and the Red Cross flag upon it was plainly visible from a great distance. The head of this hospital was Professor Dr. Seiser, a surgeon who had brought along his valuable instruments from Erlangen. Hundreds of wounded men had been brought to the hospital, among them many who were seriously wounded. As the French advanced toward this place they opened a merciless fire upon the hospital, in spite of the Red Cross flag (August 28, 1914). ...The French occupied the village and were thrown back after a few days. A terrible scene was revealed to the doctors and nurses. The whole hospital was nothing but a mass of ruins and ashes, in which all the seriously-wounded men had met their death and the entire equipment had been destroyed. ("Frankfurter Kurier.")

2. The "Berliner Tageblatt" reports as follows from Strassburg in Elsass under the date of August 25th:

In the hospital at Metz the Landwehrman Christofl, Lance-corporal Hain, and Bruno Lehmann, testified in a protocol that French soldiers had penetrated into a German field hospital on the evening of August 25th and stabbed the staff-surgeon to death. Many of the wounded sought to flee with the help of the Sanitary Corps, but were pursued by the Frenchmen and murdered along with the medical helpers. The hospital went up in flames.

3. The following has the sanction of official publication: Béthencourt, September 10th. Two automobiles with wounded men and flying the Red Cross flag were attacked in the woods of Domaniale by a French Cyclist Division in charge of an officer. The wounded and the drivers were butchered and then robbed. Only two of the men escaped, wounded. They reported these facts to the staff physician of their battalion, who communicated them to the Sanitary Corps at Condreville on the 9th of September.

4. In a session of the Baden Red Cross Society on the 5th of October the Chairman, General Limburger, reported, that the transport train of wounded which had been attacked near Valenciennes in September had, consisted of seven members of a Baden division of the Red Cross. These Red Cross men had not only been killed, but maltreated in the most horrible manner.

5. The diary of a Medical Corps Sergeant hailing from Greifswald, and a member of a Pommeranian field hospital, from which facts are quoted in the "Frankfurter Zeitung," (No. 314) fully confirms the official presentations,—though a few established instances will suffice:

6. Following the investigation made upon the report of a Landwehr Infantry Regiment to its superior officers regarding the attack upon the hospital in Aelbecke, 8 kilometres northeast of Tourcoing, the following official communication has been made:

"On Sunday, the 11th of October, between 1 and 2 o'clock in the afternoon, 18 to 20 Belgian cyclists appeared in Aelbecke under command of an officer. They forced their way into the hospital, which had been turned into a field "lazarett," and which bore the emblem of the Geneva Convention. They discharged several shots—some five or six—in the two wards in which lay some 40 seriously-wounded and a few lightly-wounded men. A sergeant of the Medical Corps who happened to be in one of the wards was drawn through a window and shot upon the street, despite the fact that he bore the armlet with the red cross. An armoured motor-car had accompanied the cyclists. The inhabitants did not take part in this attack These details have just been reported to me by sergeant-majors Grallinger and Engel of the 2nd Regiment of Heavy Cavalry, as well as by the Uhlans Pfeiffer and Schneider of the 2nd Bavarian Uhlan Regiment both of whom were lightly-wounded and had left the hospital at dark in order to call German troops to the scene."

7. During the beginning of September the following communication appeared in the press:

"During the fighting in Upper Elsass, a medical train consisting of some 50 men, most of them from Munich, which was attached to a munition transport was attacked in the neighborhood of Markirch and surrounded on the 27—28th of August."

According to the statements of individual sanitary officials who were able to escape, the pursuing infantry were able to rescue one or two of the wagons of the train. The majority of the Medical Corps Men and the physicians were captured by the French.

I have myself received the most authentic information by means of private letters regarding the capture of the Hospital men from Munich, letters from those who were most directly involved in the matter, such as Dr. Dax. These letters with their quiet and objective descriptions throw so typical and characteristic a light upon the fanaticism of the French people as well as on the conduct of the authorities, that I trust I may be permitted to quote certain passages from them. After the seizure of the hospital convoy, against which the Red Cross had been of no avail, the physicians and the men were forced everywhere to endure the most shameful insults from the mob.

Dr. Dax writes as follows of Gérardmer: "The ride was ghastly. The population was raving mad, especially the women. The names they called us: "Dogs," "Swine," "Murderers" and other terms of endearment simply deafened our ears"...... From another passage: "The railway journey was horrible. At every railway station the mob would come crowding up to the carriages and shriek at us and curse us as though we were the lowest of criminals. We were forced to close the windows, since these beasts spat into the compartments and flung all kinds of filth into them. It was fortunate that we had a strong guard—otherwise we would have been torn to pieces. Even the better class people did not hesitate to blackguard us and to cry out against our Kaiser as the one instigator of the war and to call him a murderer.

"It was only with the greatest difficulty that we were able to secure food during the journey, apart from the mouldy bread they gave us. The rations we had taken with us from Gérardmer consisted only of a ham sandwich and some wine. Our entry into Montbrisont was frightful. It is hard to believe that such beasts in human shape really exist. Eight of us men were put into an ambulance, the others were forced to go on foot. Once again the same terrible yells, curses, volleys of stones. An old hag made a slash at a soldier with a knife and injured his eye. Helmets and caps were torn from our heads. We halted in front of a school-house, when suddenly there was a loud crash and a stone flew through the window of the ambulance,—the pieces of glass striking Dr. May in the neck. I sat beside him. The French troops who accompanied us were hardly capable of maintaining order, nor had they any particular desire to do so. I could plainly see that they were always pleased whenever some billet found its mark.

"Our protests that we were physicians and that according to the Geneva Convention we were not to be treated as prisoners of war, was met with the eternal reply, accompanied by a shrug of the shoulders: "C'est la guerre!" We were even obliged to take off our Red Cross armlets. We now made a protest to the XIII French Army Corps against our being detained as prisoners, calling attention to the regulations of the Geneva Convention. For a long time we heard no word. They did not believe our declaration that we were doctors, since we were captured in connection with the munition supply column. They said that all German officers carried such armlets so that they might quickly put them on when in danger of being captured and thereby escape! We were nevertheless forced to administer to our German sick. It was horrible, there was almost nothing in the way of conveniences at hand.

There were several cases of viscereal haemorrhage, for which we could not even obtain special food, though we offered to pay for it. The French doctor, a fellow as ignorant as he was conceited, did not think this necessary. A man suffering from a severe inflammation of the lungs he declared to be only slightly ill,—that he was not suffering from inflammation of the lungs, but from catarrh! It was impossible to obtain bandages, etc."

Head Physican Dr. Dax remained in the hands of the French until the 19th of September, until, pursuant to the rules of the Geneva Convention, he was finally liberated. The shocking story of another member of the hospital corps we publish in another chapter of this book, also the full account by Staff Physician Dr. May in the "Münchener Neueste Nachrichten" of October 11th, 1914, morning issue).

8. An interview given by the wounded Prince Franz of Bavaria, ("Augsburger-Münchener Allgemeine Zeitung," of October 13) in which the Prince strives to be most tentatively objective in his descriptions, shows how the bandaging station of the Bavarians in a chateau which had been recognized as a hospital by the French the day before and spared, was put

under heavy artillery fire and completely destroyed. This was at Saarburg on the 29th of August. The passage in which the Prince describes this is so interesting and so completely refutes the atrocity stories of the French regarding the barbarism of the Germans, that I feel the need of quoting it here: "I rode to the scene of the fire. Uninterruptedly the wounded went by me in groups,—pictures of misery and human woe. I saw how men with shot wounds in their legs clasped one another, three or four abreast, and dragged themselves forward with their last remaining strength. Some literally crawled upon all fours. I must expressly state, in honor of the officers of my Medical Corps, that in spite of the unbroken heavy bombardment, they rescued all the wounded from the smoking, burning ruins, —gallantly supported by volunteers from a battalion that was resting nearby. They rescued all, including the wounded Frenchmen. *As I rode up to our wounded enemies, I found them overwhelmed with gratitude towards our German Medical Corps men.* A wounded French lieutenant of his own free will wrote down a declaration that the French had shot the chateau to pieces despite its being filled with wounded and marked with the sign of the Red Cross. The men as well as the officers of the Sanitary Corps succeeded by their heroism in transporting the wounded to places of safety in the very midst of the deluge of hostile shells."

This took place at Chateauville on August 29th, 1914.

In spite of much research we have so far been unable to discover a similar instance of magnanimous behavior on the part of our enemies towards wounded Germans. Yet we are and remain "barbarians" who murder "women and children" and old people and throw wounded men into the flames,—deeds with which we are charged in the lurid phrases of so-called investigation committees.

How numerous were the cases in which the Geneva Convention had been disregarded, especially in the matter of capturing German physicians and medical corps, is proved by the stereotyped reports of the Swiss papers regarding the return of German doctors from French captivity. On the 13th of October a company of Red Cross soldiers consisting of 70 persons with 18 military doctors among them, came through Basel after being released by the French. A few days later 160 men arrived at the same place.

We thus see that it is not a matter of individual cases, but of a remarkable and dangerous accumulation of many instances. The fact that these Medical Corps men were afterwards liberated deserves no special credit, since this was done only under the pressure of the threat of reprisals by the Germans. The principles of Red Cross Law which had formerly been regarded as sacrosanct, especially in connection with physicians, have been so negligently and indifferently observed by the French as almost to verge upon felony. Horrifying conditions prevailed, even according to the English papers.

The Imperial German Government felt itself obliged last October in view of the constantly increasing and shameful abuses of the law of nations to publish a formal memorial based upon the breaches of the Geneva Convention by French troops and *franc-tireurs*. The date upon which this paper was issued was October 20th. Though we have already quoted brief extracts from this, we nevertheless regard it as a document of such great contemporary importance that we feel constrained to give the entire text of this official communication, as it appeared in the "Reichsanzeiger."

"The rules and regulations of the Geneva Convention of July 6th, 1906, which had been designed to ease the lot of the wounded and the sick in the active armies and which had been ratified by Germany and France, have been violated in the most flagrant manner by French soldiers and *franc-tireurs*.

Among the great number of cases which have become known, only those which have been proved by sworn witnesses in a court of law or by official reports, are given in full in the appendix.

One of the main points of the Geneva Convention consists in the stipulation (which is at the same time one of the most fundamental principles of warfare), that all the sick and wounded of the hostile army are to be treated and cared for precisely like the sick and wounded of one's own army. (Art. 1. Clause 1.) This law has been trodden underfoot by the French troops and *franc-tireurs* in that they not only maltreated the German wounded that fell into their hands, but also robbed them, and in part even mutilated and murdered them in the most bestial manner.

For the mobile medical units of an army the Geneva Convention has provided special protection in articles 6 and 14.

In violation of these rules French troops have attacked German motor ambulances carrying wounded men (appendix 6). They have fired upon medical supply wagons (appendices 11 and 14) although plainly marked with the Red Cross. German field hospitals were also attacked, their contents looted and their personnel robbed (appendix 7).

In Appendix 1 Grenadier Hänseler of the 2nd Company of the 3rd Battalion of the Brigade of Guards (Ersatz) testifies as follows with respect to the happenings at the railway bridge across the Meurthe north of Rehainviller on the 5th of September, 1914:

"The French kicked those of our people who were lying on the ground, and when these gave signs of life through their groans or cries, I heard shots. I also received a kick but remained perfectly quiet. When darkness came I looked about for my comrades and could see that they must now be dead, though they had been merely lightly wounded in the morning."

Appendix 2. Franz Mevisen of the 4th Squadron of the Mounted Jäger Regiment No. 7, saw from his place of hiding southwest of Arlons on Belgian territory, on the 7th of September, how the French went about the battlefield and stabbed wounded German Jägers with lances. The night was a bright one and their actions plainly visible.

Appendix 3. Musketeer Theodor Mündel of the 9th Company of the Infantry Regiment No. 138, was wounded at Luneville on August 25th. A Frenchman who carried a sword and a revolver, asked a Lance-Corporal who was lying beside Mündel as to where he was wounded. The Lance-Corporal answered: in the foot. The Frenchman then shot him through the head. When the Frenchman returned Mündel himself received a blow upon the right temple from the butt-end of a rifle and across the left shoulder, although the wound from which he was already suffering was plainly evident through the quantity of blood that had soaked through the uniform.

Appendix 4. Musketeer Kampen of the 8th Company of

the Infantry Regiment No. 78 observed the following on the 29th of August in the neighborhood of Guise near St. Quentin. Some 50 French soldiers under the leadership of several officers were crossing the battlefield in a zig-zag course. They stabbed the wounded lying upon the ground with their bayonets, one of these wounded being only some ten paces from Kampen. When he cried for help, a French officer shot him in the mouth with his revolver. Kampen himself, who pretended to be dead, received some nine minor injuries from bayonet thrusts.

Appendix 5 contains the report of the Head Physicians Neumann and Grünfelder, both belonging to a regiment of Bavarian Pioneers, regarding the robbing and mutilation of German soldiers of the 35th Regiment of Landwehr at Orchies. The bodies that were found had been robbed of their boots and stockings and all means of identification.

One man had been shot from behind. He lay upon his back. One had his left ear cut smoothly off; his face was blue through death by suffocation. His mouth, nose and eyes had been stuffed full of saw-dust. His throat bore signs of strangulation. The ring-finger of another had been cut off at the joint. His abdomen bore four shotwounds fringed with powder-marks, a sure sign that the shots had been fired close at hand. Five other dead men showed signs of having been done to death by some blunt instrument. One had his eyes pierced out. From the facts established it was proved that a great number of these people had fallen unwounded into the hands of the enemy.

Appendix 6 deals with the attack upon motor-ambulances carrying the Red Cross flag near Béthencourt on September 8th. Wounded men and chauffeurs were murdered and robbed.

Appendix 7 contains reports of the Army doctor of the 2nd Army, according to which the field hospital of the 2nd Army Corps at Peronne had been looted of its supplies and its helpers carried off.

In Appendix 8 Father Bernhard Brinkmann of the Redemptorists, a Catholic Army Chaplain, testifies how he was led away by gendarmes at Trefols after the battle at Esternay on the 7th of September. He was thrust into a filthy prison without windows and left without any food. On the day following he was chained up with a band of French criminals and transported through the villages for several days in company with these, being constantly subjected to the jeers and insults of the populace. His watch, money, suspenders and Red Cross badge were taken away from him at the police-station, despite the fact that he had all necessary papers.

On the 11th of September he was examined by court-martial at Chateau-Thierry. Although he was given written permission to leave the following morning, this certificate was kept concealed from him and he was detained for three full days at the railway station. There he found some prisoners, nearly all of them wounded or sick men. The Frenchmen who came by would go through the pockets of the wounded and would take whatever they pleased, especially watches and money.

The wounded soldiers lay day and night upon the stone floor in an open shed in the rain and the storm. No attention was paid to the wounds of the men. Brinkmann also relates several revolting instances of brutality to which the hungry prisoners were subjected. All this points to that peculiar trait of sadistic cruelty in the French which was so noticeable during the Revolution and has since 1870 been stimulated by a vicious press, by chauvinstic plays and novels and other poisonous means.

Appendix 9 deals with a meeting between a German Hospital Corps and French troops at Wic, which wound up by Assistant Judge Eyles, the leader of the Hospitel Corps, being carried off by the Frenchmen.

Appendix 10 deals with the shooting of Chief Surgeon Dr. Stahmer of the 19th Regiment of Uhlans by French riflemen at Villers la Montagne. Dr. Stahmer was shot from the immediate vicinity though the Red Cross band upon his arm must have been plainly visible.

According to Appendix 11 a large sanitary wagon of the 2nd Battalion of the 123rd Regiment of Landwehr Infantry, flying the Re dCross flag, was fired upon by machine-guns as it left Günzbach on the 19th of August. The enemy was only some 400 meters away and as the weather was bright and clear the Red Cross emblem must have been quite conspicuous.

In Appendix 12 there is a report from the 6th Infantry, Division to the General Command of the 3rd Bavarian Army Corps to the effect that patrols of stretcher-bearers while searching the battlefield for the wounded, had been fired upon by French Infantry without any attention being paid to the badges of the Red Cross. This took place at Maixe on August 26th.

In Appendix 13 the head of the supply base at Valenciennes, Count Reichenbach, reports that he was attacked while transporting wounded in a region which was usually considered quite safe. His detachment consisted of thirteen volunteer male nurses and the attack was made by the civil population despite the visible Red Cross badges. Six men were killed and one injured.

On the 2nd of September stretcher-bearers and ambulances of the 2nd Sanitary Corps of the 10th Division of Infantry were furiously fired upon by the French near St. Remy, at a distance of not more that 50 metres. Several Frenchmen ran directly towards the wagon, shot three of the wounded men that were inside this, the corporal in charge of the wagon, the driver and the two horses. There were 8 dead and 9 seriously-wounded men in the company as a result.

Five ambulance men who had been left behind in Baccarat to take charge of the German and the French wounded who could not be moved, were brought by the French military authorities to Rambervillers on the 14th of September and were there treated as prisoners. A French gendarme took away their badges of neutrality. The doctor who brought in this report was taken into Switzerland from Rambervillers. But in spite of the pleas of the doctor in their behalf the five ambulance men were held back, the only explanation given being this: "ce ne sont plus vos hommes."

It is with indignation that the Imperial German Government brings to the attention of the public this revelation of the treatment to which German wounded, German Medical Corps formations and the German Medical personnel were subjected—a treatment that mocks at all the laws of humanity as well as those of the nations. It hereby makes a formal protest against these unheard-of violations of those international agreements entered into by all civilized countries."

I have merely made a short extract from the original German memorial which consists of 79 large pages of print.

The original lies before me and I should be glad to place it at the disposal of neutrals with the approval of the government. Here we find a mass of legal exhibits and protocols, especially those of German doctors and medical corps men. There is a crushing amount of evidence to prove that the French troops systematically maltreated the German sanitary units that fell into their hands in outrageous violation of the Geneva Convention of the 6th of July, 1906. The articles that are especially called into question here are Nos. 6, 14 and 9.

This entire official document is an exposure of the most amazing kind, laying bare the incredible brutalities, the outrageous tortures and the deliberate assassinations to which the German Red Cross doctors, soldiers and nurses were subjected by the French military and civil authorities. Every instance is borne out with dates, names and facts plainly given, as well as the places in which the atrocities occurred. The beautiful emblem of the Red Cross, the symbol of humanity, of mercy and help for the helpless, was wantonly disregarded. Men occupied in the merciful and humanitarian errands of alleviating the woes and agony of their comrades or even of the enemy, were seized, imprisoned, insulted, robbed, starved and slain in cold blood. In appendix 23 one may read how a German Army Doctor was shot from his horse, killed as he lay on the ground, after which his eyes were gouged out with sticks. Wounded men in ambulances were shot to death at a distance of a few steps. There were no such excuses for these barbarous acts as those justly afforded a German artillery company forced to dislodge a French battery that had sheltered itself close to a French bandaging station. The French seemed to be deliberately bent upon annihilating not only the material but also the men of the German Red Cross.

Robbery was rife. Field-glasses, electric pocket lamps, photographs, underwear, decorations, cutlery, watches, cuff-buttons and money were seized and stolen. Nor did various French officers refrain from casting a further blot upon the honor of their nation by taking part in these robberies. The transportation of these prisoners, prisoners in violation of every rule of civilized warfare, was conducted with the most revolting brutality. 40 to 50 men would be packed into a filthy cattle-truck where they were forced to remain for whole days without sufficient air, food or care. The cars were sealed with lead seals so that conditions approximated to incarceration in a dungeon. No permission was granted the wounded to leave the trucks, either to have their wounds attended to, or to fulfil the necessities of nature.

No conveniences were provided in the way of latrines and the unfortunate sick and wounded men were frequently forced to undergo the degradation of exposing themselves to the public. Or where special places were provided these were in so foul a state as to make infection of the wounds almost certain. The treatment of women nurses was little better and turns the boasted French claims to chivalry and courtesy into a thing for the world to mock at. German volunteer sisters and nurses were exposed to the most inhuman treatment. Their trunks were forced, turned topsy-turvy and pillaged. Their feminine delicacy and honor were so little respected that sentries were set to watch them even in the rooms where they slept and dressed themselves. Most shameful of all to relate, these poor women were put to the dire necessity of satisfying the needs of nature in the broad light of day.

With that we leave these glaring evidences of the kind of civilization that prevails among the people whose habitual expression for the Germans is either "les boches," or "les barbares!" The unprejudiced observer is invited to note, in contrast to the French spirit and the French methods, those that prevail in the land of the ruthless Teutonic barbarians.

We do not, of course, desire to lose ourselves in glittering or in unsavory generalities. We concede that there are chivalrous men among our enemies who, it is to be hoped, regret these things as much as we do. But these cases of "frightfulness" (a term much applied to alleged cases of German misdeeds) are so numerous as to preclude all possibility of their being mere exceptions. On the contrary it must be confirmed that there exists in great masses of the population and the armies of the Triple Entente a state of incredible brutalization which imposes upon us the *duty of making the sharpest reprisals*. Conditions such as these make it plain that those in authority have been entirely negligent of their duty.

We grant that war is war. But in the foregoing cases we have to deal not with unintentional or unavoidable bombardment of hospitals, ambulances, sanitary columns, etc., but with deliberate and calculated trespasses against the fundamental laws for the conduct of modern warfare, open breaches which finally resolved themselves into a system. This system reached its height in the shameful verdicts delivered against German military doctors for robbery, base accusations of which the press of our enemies made much capital.

The chief blame for this is to be attributed to the deliberate vilification of the German army and the campaign of hatred waged against it. The French and English military authorities did not scruple to make official announcements to the effect that the Germans murdered their prisoners and the wounded of the enemy in the cruellest fashion. Therefore the terrible responsibility for all these horrors does not rest upon the heads of these deluded fanatics, but upon those of the unscrupulous persons who incited them.

II. Cruelties against members of the Red Cross and against prisoners of war naturally fall into the same category. The following items of news are most pertinent in this connection:

1. Dr. Stengel, a physician at Lahr in Baden, who was captured at Mülhausen during the fighting there on the 19th of August whilst performing his duties, was detained until the 7th of September in violation of the rules of the Geneva Conference. He was then permitted to return home by way of Switzerland. He describes with indignation the unworthy treatment to which the captured German officers and men were subjected. The fanatical population indulged in orgies of abuse directed against the defenseless German soldiers.

2. An Austrian Chief Engineer named Christen who had been interned at Toul, reports as follows:

"The ambulances brought up a great many wounded, among them 16 seriously-wounded Germans. The people and the soldiers behaved towards these poor injured men in the most contemptible manner. They reviled them with torrents of abuse and let them lie for three hours in the burning sun. I attempted to cool one of these unfortunates by fanning him with my handkerchief—but an officer thrust me back with his sword."

It would be senseless to aver that such cases as the foregoing were common to all French troops. But no excuse can be found for them under the conventional plea of "exceptions." The charges against the French for maltreatment of the wounded are legion, and their substantiation is complete.

This is confirmed by an uncommonly objective writer, a *French* contributor to the Danish paper "Politiken." He writes of what he had himself seen in repeated visits to French military hospitals:

"The French are accused of killing the wounded and so far as the care of wounded prisoners of war is concerned, showing the utmost negligence. If this were not so, why should it have been necessary for the government to issue a manifesto in which the point is emphasised that the wounded enemy is to be given the same humane treatment as a son of *la patrie*?

After a savage battle between the Prussian Guards and the notorious Turcos, one of the latter was given the order to guard the tent in which the wounded German soldiers had been placed. When the doctors were making their rounds and came to this tent guarded by the Turco, he motioned them away, and said reassuringly in his mongrel French: "Pe-malad-ici". (No sick men here.) A French doctor discovered that in his blind rage the Turco had cold-bloodedly cut the throats of all the wounded men that had been entrusted to his care! Could one seriously believe that a negro would pay any attention to the international laws of the Geneva Convention?

During one of my visits to the military hospitals, I myself spoke with a colored soldier who stood at the entrance to one of the sheds to which the Germans had been brought. He was a Senegalese with a broad, animal-like nose. "It would be much better to kill them all," he remarked, as he made a significant movement across with his hand across his throat, "instead of nursing them and giving them food. They are only barbarians!" This, undeniably, was a most remarkable statement to hear from the lips of a semi-savage!

Even reputable French newspapers have done all that lay in their power to induce the government to refuse humane treatment to the German prisoners. This terrible condition of things as well as the disregard of all the laws of humanity towards the wounded, in addition to the serious lack of supplies under which the faulty organization of the French Red Cross suffers, have caused many well-known Frenchmen, among them Albert de Mun, Gustave Hervé, and Clémenceau to make the most violent criticisms in their newspapers, criticisms based upon incontrovertible proofs."

This report by an absolutely unpartisan writer has a particular value in that it shows what a *dolus eventualis* had from the very beginning existed through the use of these colored ruffians of Turcos by the French Government. This government was well aware that these savage hordes do not care a pin about the rules of the Geneva Convention nor the "Regulations of Warfare by Land," but burn and murder for the sheer lust of it—and the more treacherous and cowardly the murder the more they glory in it. We are indeed pleased to see from the foregoing that M. Clémenceau has been forced to draw the bow a little more lightly, and we do not hesitate to do him the honor of thinking that the reproaches levelled against him have not been without effect.

But it is not only the Turcos who demean themselves in so barbarous a manner,—the infection spreads to the widest circles of the army and the people. A most terrible scene is republished in the Chicago "Evening News" from the "Daily Mail." It is the statement of a French abbé,—surely a very reliable witness!—regarding the treatment of the German prisoners during the bombardment of Rheims cathedral.

"Blows from fists and canes hailed down upon the wounded Germans. The raging mass heaved about us like an angry sea; I have never seen anything more terrible. Faces distorted with rage stared into mine. A wounded man who fell exhausted, was torn away by the mob and flung upon the pavement. Immediately the insane crowd fell upon him with kicks; several jumped upon his body. I pushed my way through the crowd, and succeeded in dragging away the German. He could no longer speak, but thanked me with his eyes.

"Can't you help me?" I cried to a French officer.

He merely gave me a cold glance. He then looked at the wriggling multitude and, shrugging his shoulders, remarked: "You will never reach the City Hall."

The brave priest rescued the wounded at the peril of his own life.

Additional weight is given to the foregoing statements by the proclamation issued by the French Minister of War during the middle of September. In this the order goes forth that the German wounded are to be treated with all care. "This is an imperative duty conditioned by the laws of nations, the rules of the Geneva Convention and the instincts of humanity. The Minister expresses himself as convinced that our doctors and Medical Corps will perform their duty towards the German wounded with all due devotion, and declares that he will instantly dismiss from duty all who in any way violate the established humanitarian rules of the Geneva Code in their behavior towards the wounded or towards prisoners."

The German press was entirely justified in seeing in this self-understood and obvious manifesto of the French Minister of War a confession that up to the time it was made, the French army had been lacking in those things which are here designated as emanating from the "instincts of humanity." It was not necessary for the *German* military authorities to recall the terms of the Geneva Convention, especially in a form so threatening as the above.

Although the Austrian Red Cross presented a strong petition to the International Committee at Geneva, imploring it to take measures against these abuses, and the Committee in turn requested all the warring states not to forget the stipulations of Article 25 which requires commanders to see that the rules of the Geneva Convention are observed, this was an entirely superfluous admonition so far as the German Army authorities were concerned. Its whole immense staff of physicians were already observing all the obligations of the Geneva Convention. Respect for the Red Cross of Geneva is bred in the flesh and bone of the German soldier. With him any outrage upon it is unthinkable.

Since we are concerned with an objective investigation of the truth, we are glad to affirm that the accusations levelled against French physicians for breaches of duty have, so far as proved instances are concerned, not been very numerous. [1] The French doctors may in general be said to compete with their German colleagues in their faithfulness to duty and in their sense of humanity.

The conditions vary in the different "lazaretts," and personal factors as well as the spirit of locality also play a great part in all this.

We must, on the other hand, enter an energetic protest against the slander which seeks to asperse German doctors, soldiers and commanders with committing breaches of the

[1] An official report of the Head Doctor of a Medical Corps throws a peculiar light upon the willingness of the French to help the wounded. The doctor reports as follows:

The first detachment of the Medical Reserve Corps (the second had been established at Epéhy and there detained) received an order on the evening of August 28th to go and erect a main bandaging station at Rocquigny. There were 250 wounded French and 2 wounded Germans there, apart from several hundred dead French and some 20 dead Germans. Our men began their work about seven o'clock in the evening, collecting the wounded French and transporting them to the village of Rocquigny which lay at a distance of some 2 kilometres. Since no other room was available they were put into the church there. But we were first forced to make an energetic presentation of the case to the village priest who was not willing to surrender the church for this purpose.

The care of the wounded Frenchmen in the church was consigned to three French military surgeons in uniform who were present in this place. They immediately protested against this, declaring that it was we, the victors, who were obliged to look after all the wounded. The next morning we discovered that not less than seven French military doctors were present in the village. Four of them, among these the oldest in rank, had kept themselves concealed during the night, as well as some nine-tenths of their men—who suddenly popped up during the next morning to the number of some twenty.

The parish priest, who had been requested during the night to prepare, with the aid of the inhabitants, something for the refreshment of the French wounded, though it be only coffee, immediately demanded to know who was to pay for this? His obvious duty as a priest and as a human being towards his helpless countrymen had first to be firmly impressed upon him ere he would move a finger in their behalf.

The crying abuses in the French Red Cross Service have frequently been alluded to in the French press, in the most drastic terms, especially by Gustave Hervé, and the above is merely another confirmation of these.

Geneva Convention.[1] It is *not* "six of one and half-a-dozen of the other." In order to sift truth to the bottom I adopted the following system. I am indebted to the courtesy of several neutral (Swiss) persons for whole stacks of French and English newspapers. As soon as I come across a particularly glaring instance of alleged German malfeasance, I make it a point to write to the German Headquarters or to the Chief of the Field Medical Service, sending him the paper in question and a request for light upon the subject. Sooner or later I always receive an answer to these. For instance, certain terrific descriptions of German field hospitals in the "Echo de Paris," (October, 1914) among which were charges concerning the field hospital at Ram-l'Etape. All the documents lie before me. I wish merely to declare the following: The malicious charges

---

[1] The manner in which such calumnies arise and the manner in which they are refuted is strikingly shown in the following story:

The "Gazette de Lausanne" of Colonel Secretan, who is also a Member of the National Parliament, recently published a correspondence describing the transport of a group of French ambulance troops near the French frontier. These soldiers, who had been conveyed to Germany along with prisoners of war, and who had then, in accordance with international law, been liberated, were transferred at Leopoldhöhe near Basel into the hands of the Swiss frontier-guards for further transport to their homes. The "Gazette de Lausanne" wrote as follows: "The doctors of this detachment of the French Red Cross declared that the Germans had deprived them of everything,—their instruments, their watches, their rings and their cash."

In contradiction of the slander circulated by this Swiss paper the Swiss General Staff publishes the report of the Local Commando at Basel regarding the passage of this body of French ambulance soldiers. The report states: "The officers wore their decorations, the Cross of the Legion d'Honneur, their watches, and had retained their pocket-books. They were abundantly supplied with money. I saw a number who had several rolls of 100 franc notes and I myself changed quite a number of 50 franc notes for them. They also made use of the money-changer's office at the railway station. The best proof that the French officers were not robbed by the Germans, as has been charged, lies in the fact that many of them ordered champagne for refreshment in the restaurant of the railway station,—as I myself am able to affirm."

So here we have the very opposite of what had been stated. And this is about the way all inquiries made with regard to the conduct of our German troops finally end, that is, wherever a definite charge has been made. It may assuredly be said that the German military authorities observe all the rules of the Geneva Convention in the most conscientious manner.

made against the German doctors *have not been confirmed in a single instance*. On the contrary it was the German physicians who were forced to cleanse the Augean stables of French mismanagement.

The same thing applies to the English military leadership, and its accusations against the Germans. A peculiar light is thrown upon these things by the "Daily Telegraph" of March 20th under the heading of "Comfort at the Front."

"The King yesterday inspected a contrivance which has been invented for supplying warm drinks to the troops at the front, and expressed his complete satisfaction with what he had seen.

The contrivance in question is a motor field kitchen which is to be sent to the French theatre of war as soon as possible. The wagons rest upon a strong substructure, and have the appearance of motor ambulances, which are designed to act in conjunction with the Red Cross. For this reason they also bear the sign of the Red Cross. The intention is to advance them as far as possible to the line of trenches in order that the soldiers who come from the firing-line there or go to it, may be supplied with hot tea, coffee, cocoa, and beef broth.

The permanent crew of each wagon consists of a preacher of the Salvation Army and a chauffeur. The inner equipment has a compartment in which all the objects necessary for the Holy Communion are kept;—a portable altar, a chalice, a surplice and other things." (*retranslation*)

The English misuse the sign of the Red Cross in order to protect their military operations. It may be sufficient to indicate that this characteristic English invention of a field kitchen with arrangements for giving the Holy Communion can deceive no one.

B. A Few Neutral Opinions with Regard to the Conduct of the German Troops Towards Wounded and Captured Enemies.

Sufficient evidence as to the way in which the Germans behave towards the wounded of their enemies is presented in the countless reports made by doctors of neutral states who have hastened to the theatre of war. Let us cite a few of these many examples:

1. One of two Norwegian physicians who had visited German field hospitals, Dr. Mathiesen by name, describes his impressions in the papers of his country. He was received everywhere in Germany in the most friendly manner; the journey was made without a single hitch; the feeling at Berlin was superb. There was only one opinion: Germany *must* conquer. He visited three hospitals in one of which he found 150 Frenchmen, 150 Russians as well as several hundred Germans. Each nationality was kept separate. It was a pleasure to observe the order and the cleanliness that prevailed in everything. "I rejoice to be able to say that the wounded of the enemy were given the same painstaking care as that devoted to the German wounded."

2. A Norwegian physician by the name of Holmboe, writes as follows in the "Aftenposten" some time during the middle of October. He had seen some 25 military hospitals. "The prisoners, whether they be Frenchmen or Belgians, Russians or Englishmen, were treated like princes and not the slightest difference made between them and the Germans. The "Liebesgaben" (love-gifts) which come pouring into the hospitals are equally divided between the Germans and their enemies. There are no modern hospitals that are better equipped. Instruments, food and all accessories are of the very best."

3. Innumerable letters written by French, English and Russian prisoners, all absolutely uninfluenced by the authorities,—(the "Frankfurter Zeitung" published a very interesting selection from these last October)—usually contain these stereotyped words: "We are treated as finely as though we were at home.... All that they told us there is pure stuff and nonsense.... We hope that the Germans are being as well treated by us as we by them."

4. A member of the Swiss Federal Council, Deputy Walther, addressed a letter to General Gaede of the 14th Army Corps at Freiburg in Breisgau under date of the 18th of October: In this he writes, in part:

"We have had the most valuable experiences, and stand amazed at the results of German power and German unity.

The sense of order and the foresight that prevails everywhere are magnificent. The joy and the spirit of devotion with which every sacrifice is made are simply wonderful. It has given us special pleasure to observe how excellently the numerous French wounded were nursed and taken care of. All the Frenchmen to whom we spoke gladly and thankfully acknowledged that they had been treated in every respect precisely like the German wounded. All that the Germans received they too shared. The doctors and the attendants showed them only kindness and friendliness.

All these expressions on the part of the wounded, so in consonance with our own experiences, have affected us in a most sympathetic manner. As the representative of a neutral state, I am impelled, your Excellency, to express to you my esteem for this true magnanimity which evidences itself in relation to the wounded enemies of your country.

I have written today to my friend, Deputy Ador at Geneva, the President of the International Bureau of the Red Cross, and described to him my impressions during my visit to the hospital at Freiburg. I am convinced that Ador will do everything possible to correct false impressions and to see that the German wounded in enemy countries are afforded similar treatment." [1]

5. Dr. Thorson, a Danish Head-Physician, has this to say in the "Berlingske Tidende:"

"Every wounded man, whether friend or foe, is treated in the same manner. He is transported and bandaged and brought to the hospitals in specially furnished trains. No difference whatsoever is made. This is the simple truth. The German Red Cross, the Red Cross helpers, doctors as well as soldiers, the means of transport, the hospital attendants, the ambulances, the bandaging stations and the sanitary trains are simply ideal. With the permission of the German authorities I visited all the larger hospitals at Cologne, Aachen (Aix-la-Chapelle) and Berlin in which lay Russian, French, Belgian and English

[1] See also the descriptions of Pierre Maurice, a Swiss, in the anti-German "Journal de Genève," of the hospitals at Munich and the splendid way in which the French wounded were received. "Münchener Neueste Nachrichten," No. 96, morning edition.

wounded." He concludes with these words: "If the treatment of the wounded among Germany's opponents in any way approaches this, humanity may well be proud of having attained to such a level of civilization."

The twelve Swiss Army Surgeons who paid visits to the hospitals at Karlsruhe, Mannheim and Heidelberg during the spring of 1915, sent a vote of thanks to the Red Cross of Baden. In this the medical gentlemen declare that they had learned a great deal through their inspection of the various arrangements. They had obtained the impression that all Baden, in fact that all Germany, the State as well as the private individual, the high and the humble, were all working in a spirit of inspiring unity in order to alleviate the lot of the wounded, be they friend or foe.

A number of Norwegian and Swedish doctors expressed themselves in a similarly enthusiastic manner. A vast number of letters from American nurses published in various papers, might be appended: From the "Literary Digest" of June 19th, New York, we take the following:

"The Germans have already won world-wide admiration for the efficiency and skill with which they prepared for war and have since managed it.... There is one branch in which they are said to excel that is not so generally known, and that is in the field-hospital. We know that the modern method of fighting taxes the most efficient hospitals to the utmost, and we also are aware that the field-hospital today, in all armies engaged, is something far ahead of anything known in any former war. But, it is claimed by Herbert Corey in the "New York Globe," German skill in the work of saving the shattered lives that drift back on the ebb-tide of every engagement is far superior, even, to that of most of the other armies. In the German hospitals, it might well be said, amputation is a forgotten barbarity.... Consequently, they are mending the bodies of from 50 to 60 per cent. of the injured that come in to them, and steadily increasing their percentage."

Compare this acknowledgment paid to the treatment we accord our enemies with the evidence in the official memorial of the German Government respecting the breaches of the Geneva Convention by French troops, and one at once realizes the tremendous difference between German deeds and French or English platitudes about "humanity" and "civilization."[1]

Still more characteristic than the universal and hysterical delirium in which the French people committed untold cruelties upon hapless wounded men during the first few months of the war, is the brutal behavior of the population towards the seriously-wounded prisoners of exchange in the spring of 1915. One of many neutral utterances upon these abuses is that of the "St. Gallener Tageblatt." A prominent member of the Swiss Red Cross Society expresses himself thus in this journal:

"I have described the dignified and splendid behavior of the German public during the departure of the French prisoners at Konstanz. I would that I might say the same of the French public at Lyons. I do not wish to deal with details in this place. But I may well say that during the departure of the train at the station I saw scenes which were among the most ugly and revolting that I have ever come across, and I have spent many years abroad in the world. I do not wish to blame the incited mob, nor the women and girls, nor the men and boys who in word and cry and attitude abused the Germans, showing no regard even for cripples,—no, the entire blame for all this is to be laid at the doors of an unscrupulous, maniacal Parisian press."

---

[1] On October 23rd the report given below was made from Darmstadt: "The French wounded in the Reserve Hospital of the Darmstadt Municipal Hall desire to give a voluntary expression of their gratitude for the excellent care and attention that have been shown them. They would like to see that every wounded German soldier who has been dismissed from the hospital as healed, is given a certificate specially written by one of the Frenchmen and bearing the official stamp of the hospital, so that in case he be taken prisoner, he may show this paper and thus be accorded as good treatment in France as the French receive at the hands of the Germans. The text of this certificate is as follows:

"Should the bearer of this card be wounded or taken prisoner, we hope that he will be as well treated and taken care of as we have been in the Municipal Hall at Darmstadt." (signatures.) The French press may easily ascertain the truth of this communication, which may also be confirmed from a number of other German cities. (See the open letter of the French prisoners at Münster in Wurtemberg, October 26th, 1914, to the Minister of War; also that of the prisoners at Weimar in the "Frankfurter Zeitung," No. 319, 1914).

It is significant that these grateful French prisoners should have thought it necessary that the German soldier fallen into French hands should be provided with some security for insuring good treatment!

Further details as to the treatment of prisoners of war in Germany are given in Chapter 14 of the original edition, especially in connection with the concentration camps of the English and the "Gefangenenlager" of the Germans.

CHAPTER X.

Franc-Tireur Warfare and the Maltreatment of the Defenseless Before and After the Declaration of War. Also the Imprisonment of Civilians.

Franc-tireur Warfare.

1. From the very first day of the beginning of hostilities the so-called *franc-tireur* warfare was waged in the bloodiest and most fanatical fashion against the German army in France and Belgium. By this is meant not only the war carried on by the so-called irregular troops but the participation of the whole native population, man, woman and child. It would be superfluous to cite all the details in this place, for these alone would suffice to fill a large volume. Thousands, yes, tens of thousands of our German warriors are witnesses to confirm this wanton violation of the international rules made to govern warfare on land—especially those in Articles 1 and 2 of the "Rules and Regulations of War on Land," as determined by their adoption on October 18th, 1907.

Every letter sent home to people in Germany by their relatives in the field is filled with indignant complaints. The "hysteria of war," to be sure, may play a great part in these, just as it does in the gossip of the trenches. He who would judge things in a purely objective light will be forced to exercise considerable scepticism in various places. And yet despite all this, there is a terrible quantity of the most ghastly evidence. Here, too, we can presume to give only a few choice specimens of typical examples as a basis for our expositions. [1]

[1] See also the pamphlet published by the "Deutsche Verlagsanstalt" in Stuttgart, under the title of "Franc-tireur Warfare in Belgium. Confessions of the Belgian Press," with 4 illustrations. In this it is made clear how the Belgian newspapers pursued a systematic course of incitement of the populace and how in effect the *franc-tireur* war was carried out along definite lines.

In consequence of the constant and serious complaints on the part of the army, the German Government saw itself obliged, some time during the middle of August, to issue emphatic and official warnings to France and Belgium and to call attention to the treatment accorded the Germans who had been expelled from France as well as to the fact that the civil population had shot at and committed acts of cruelty upon German Medical Corps troops and German wounded.

"The mob in Antwerp has destroyed German property in the most barbarous fashion and slaughtered women and children in the most bestial manner."

"Germany, in the face of the whole civilized world, demands retribution for the blood of these innocent people, for every act of that war carried on by Belgium in mockery of all civilization. Should the war hereafter assume a particularly harsh and cruel character, the fault must be laid at the doors of France and Belgium."

The lawless attitude of the Belgian population towards the German troops has found a worthy parallel in that of the Russian. During the night of the 14th and 15th August the German troops entering Kalisch were again fired upon from ambush. "This is the third attack of this kind that has occurred upon our eastern front. Here too, we regret to say, we must mourn the loss of brave men, for two were slain, and 20 to 30 wounded. There is not the slightest doubt that this attack was due to a regularly-planned onslaught by the non-military population, and there is every reason to believe that these bands, as was the case in France and Belgium, stand in close connection with the government." (official.)

As these bestial acts were constantly on the increase, especially in Belgium and France, the Kaiser uttered a formal protest against this *franc-tireur* warfare in that same telegraphic note in which he called the attention of President Wilson to the use of Dum-Dum bullets. The date of this was the 8th of September, 1914, and the words of Emperor Wilhelm were as follows:

"Not only did they make use of these cruel weapons, but the Belgian Government had openly encouraged the participation of the Belgian civil populace in the fight and carefully prepared it for this end for a long time. The cruelties which were committed upon wounded soldiers, doctors and nurses in this guerilla warfare (physicians were murdered and hospitals attacked by rifle-fire) even by women and priests, were of such a nature that my generals were finally forced to resort to the most severe measures in order to punish the guilty and to intimidate a blood-thirsty population from continuing its dastardly and murderous deeds.

Several villages and even the ancient city of Louvain with the exception of the beautiful Town Hall were destroyed[1] through the necessity of protecting my troops and assuring them some measure of self-defense. My heart bleeds when I realize that such measures should have become unavoidable and when I think of the innumerable innocent people who have lost their homes in consequence of the barbarous behavior of these criminals.

Wilhelm, I. R.

The Imperial Chancellor in his communication to the representatives of the "United Press" and the "Associated Press," also alludes to the systematic nature of the *franc-tireur* campaign in Belgium. Herr von Bethmann Hollweg writes:

"The fact that Belgian girls have put out the eyes of wounded men upon the battlefield is kept secret from you. The officials of Belgian cities have invited our officers to meals and then *shot them whilst seated at the table.* The civil population in violation of all international law was incited to attack our troops in the back by all manner of inhuman weapons after having received them in a spirit of assumed friendliness. Belgian women cut the throats of sleeping German soldiers in the quarters they themselves had offered the men."

And this lawless and inhuman method of carrying on war in Belgium was repeated in village after village as the German troops entered French territory. There was obviously a central-

[1] This sincere, manly and justifiable note of the Emperor was subjected to the foulest abuse and misinterpretation in England, and by journalistic reverperation, by certain newspapers of the United States. The full extent of the injury sustained by Louvain had not at that time been ascertained, but as has been subsequently proved, only a portion of the town had succumbed to the flames, the spread of which had been heroically fought by the German troops, to whose efforts the saving of the historic Town Hall was also due.

ized method of procedure organized and carefully prepared for secretly by the state in both countries. This is nowhere more conspicuous and evident than in the attack upon the Germans which occurred in the Belgian university town of Louvain. The use made of this affair in order to organize a most shameful and atrocious international campaign of falsehood against Germany, a campaign embellished with the most incredible tales of robbery and murder in order to embitter the whole world against Germany, is notorious.

Here, too, I will burden the reader with only a few short remarks relative to this case, for the official investigation has furnished the most detailed and complete information upon the subject. This campaign of vilification was rendered all the easier of execution inasmuch as the German-American cable, without the slightest provocation and merely to afford an unimpeded control of public opinion in other countries, had been cut in the most lawless fashion by England.

The preliminary official reports were couched in these words:

"The 40 witnesses who have so far testified under oath have already beyond a shadow of doubt established the fact that on the 25th of August a red rocket was fired into the skies from the houses that stood opposite and to the left and right of the railway station at Louvain. This red rocket was the signal for the immediate discharge of a green rocket. As the luminous spheres of both rockets threw their light over the railway station and the vicinity, a fierce volley of bullets was fired from the upper windows of the houses in the Rue de la Gare and partly from the roofs of these houses, upon the German troops who stood unsuspectingly in front of the station and in the streets. A dozen non-commissioned officers and men as well as several horses were wounded, some seriously, others slightly, before the Germans found time to return the fire."

The official memorial upon Louvain which has just been published, has an introduction in which a summary is given after the separate facts have been thoroughly discussed:

"According to this it must have been a case of an attack for which preparations had been carefully made, and which persisted for several days with the greatest stubbornness. The very duration of this revolt against the German military rule precludes all thought of a mere unpremeditated act on the part of excited individuals. The conduct and control of the murderous outbreak must have lain in the hands of some one in high authority. There is every indication that some official organization had the strings in its hands.

Louvain was the headquarters of the Chief of the so-called *Garde civique*. Shortly before the revolt this man was still frequenting the city. The movement began with the sending of young and undisciplined men to Louvain. They were furnished with no distinct badges and they concealed themselves in the houses in company with the soldiers who had converted themselves into civilians so that they might at the proper moment fire upon the apparently retreating German troops. The Belgian Government itself has never ventured to speak of the fact that regular divisions of Belgian troops took part in these acts. We have to deal here with the treacherous acts of *franc-tireurs*, who had been given a hearty welcome by the people of Louvain and then concealed in their houses.

The shameful acts of the *Garde civique* may in this classic instance of Louvain be pilloried before the whole civilized world. Whoever does honor to the authentic investigations of the German Government concerning what happened at Louvain,—an investigation based not upon the declarations of frantic and for the most part badly-educated persons by examiners who were equally excited,—but upon thorough investigations undertaken in all quiet, will be able to judge how much value is to be placed upon similar accusations against German troops on the part of the Belgians."

As to details, let us quote merely the following from the government memorial:

"The populace attacked the troops. In its fury it even fired upon doctors, soldiers of the Medical Corps, upon the sick and the wounded that were under the shelter of the Red Cross flag. So little did these people regard the rules of the Geneva Convention that they even shot from houses which bore the Red Cross flag, and discharged bullets against a hospital. The use of explosives and bombs is also established in various cases, as well as the pouring of hot tar upon the German troops.

Several persons also permitted themselves to perpetrate cruel mutilations upon the wounded German soldiers. Landwehrmann Mehlow had an ear cut off whilst he lay unconscious upon the street.

Landwehrmann Hoos found the corpse of a German soldier in the cellar of a house. The abdomen had been cut open with a sharp knife and the entrails were protruding.

In order to oppose these brutal attacks our German troops were forced to adopt energetic counter-measures. In accordance with the warnings given, the persons who had taken part in the attack were shot and the houses from which the shots had been fired, were set aflame. It was impossible to avoid the flames from these houses from setting fire to others, from which reason certain streets were destroyed. It was also owing to this that the cathedral was damaged. The further spread of the flames was prevented by the German troops who under the leadership of their officers took up the battle with the flames in the most self-sacrificing spirit. It is to them that thanks are due that only a small portion of the town, namely the section between the railway station and the Town Hall Square, suffered from the flames. Thanks to the endeavors of our troops it was possible to preserve the magnificent Town Hall. The Memorial contains appendices which furnish complete proofs of all these statements.

II. The assumption that these *franc-tireur* battles in France and Belgium were due not to a few fanatics, but to organisation and action on a great scale prepared long beforehand by the French and Belgian Governments, is proved not only by the quantities of military rifles and other weapons with the best of ammunition that were used, but also by the systematic glorification of this lawless method of conducting war which was carried on by the press of Belgium and France before and after the beginning of the war.

A well-known French military writer has been advocating *franc-tireur* warfare for France and Belgium for many years and has given great publicity to his ideas in a pamphlet. A family magazine by the name of "La vie illustrée" of November 1905, also defended the practice. It is an ancient institution among the French, something with which our troops became familiar in the year 1870. Even now Lothringen and the entire frontier districts of the Vosges have become, as at that time, the scenes of such combats.

An excellent illustration as to the opinion regarding Belgian *franc-tireur* warfare that prevailed in England and France, is furnished by the illustrations published in a number of periodicals. *Franc-tireur* fighting is not only conceded in these without the least scruple, but it is even lauded as heroic. There is, for instance, an illustration which was published in "The Sphere" of London on the 22nd of August, 1914, which shows a woman surrounded by her children and in the act of shooting through an opening in the door upon Uhlans in the street. There is a description under the picture meant to enlighten the reader of this "home magazine" as to the activities of this *franc-tireuse.*

Still more characteristic is the inscription which was appended to an illustration in "The Graphic:" "Belgian Women Kneel at the Bier of a Dying Belgian Soldier." Then, expatiating upon the "services" of these Belgian women, the paper remarks: "They repelled many an attack by Uhlans and at Herstal they put 2000 Germans *hors de combat* by means of boiling water."[1]

A French newspaper "L'Avenir Reims," confirms these abominations in an article upon the heroic defence made by the women of Herstal. This journal comments as follows: "The city was naturally quite empty of all men capable of bearing arms when the Germans entered, but the women, who were for the most part workers in the great arms factories, had sworn to prevent the Germans from seizing the various works. They therefore armed themselves with revolvers and with anything that might serve as a weapon. They repelled the attacks of the Uhlans more than once, and when their ammunition was used up, they barricaded themselves in their houses and from there poured boiling water upon the Germans who entered. It is

[1] H. G. Wells, who had always been one of the most enthusiastic admirers of Germany, only to become a foaming Teutophobe, and the chief agitator of the "Times," comes out quite openly with regard to *Franc-tireur* warfare: "Germans who invade England should not be fought, but lynched.—Hang the officers, shoot the men."

said that some 3000 Germans were rendered incapable of fighting by this means. Old men and children also took part in this defence."

All these facts and descriptions furnish the clearest proof that we have to deal here with systematic, long-prepared violations of international law, violations which justified the German soldiers in resorting to the most severe measures of reprisals and which annulled all claim the guilty ones might make upon the Rules and Regulations of Warfare on Land, or upon the consideration of humanity.

Whosoever desires to fire upon our soldiers, or do battle with them, might follow the example of our two million German volunteers, who do not adopt the cowardly methods of these assassins and shoot unsuspecting men from ambush, or strangle the helpless wounded, stab out their eyes or cut off their ears and noses, but meet the enemy in the open field and in honorable battle.

In order to approximate correctly the gravity of this lawless procedure on the part of the two governments, it is necessary to examine somewhat more closely the motives of the governments in the conclusions to the 4th Agreement of the 2nd Peace Conference of October 18th, 1907. These agreements as to the Rules and Regulations of Warfare by Land of October 18th 1907 (R.G.Bl. 1910, Page 107) were, as has been repeatedly emphasized, concluded and ratified by nearly all the 44 governments of the earth, these naturally including all the belligerent powers engaged in the present war. The slight reservations made by some of the nations are of no particular weight so far as the points in question here are concerned. Montenegro and Servia through their ratification of the corresponding resolutions of the Hague Peace Conference, have acknowledged the validity of the same principles.

In the introductions to these two important international agreements we may read these words:

"In accordance with the views of the high contracting parties, those regulations whose acceptance has been inspired by the wish to alleviate the afflictions of war so far as this is rendered possible by military necessity, are to serve the belligerents as a general guide of conduct for their demeanor to one another and to the population."

"It would, nevertheless, not be possible to arrive at a conclusion at this time with regard to all the cases that might eventually arise in practice.

"On the other hand it would be contrary to the intentions of the contracting parties to leave to the arbitrary judgment of a military commander the decision in those cases for which no written rules exist.

"Until such time as a more perfect book of the laws that govern war can be compiled, the contracting parties deem it advisable to establish the general rule that in all such cases as may not be met by the rules included in the accepted agreement, the populations and the belligerents are to remain under the shelter and the control of the principles of common law, as determined *by the customs prevailing among civilized peoples, by the laws of humanity and the dictates of the public conscience.*"

They make plain that Articles 1 and 2 of the accepted resolutions are to be interpreted in this sense. (Clause by Marten.)[1]

III. The "Regulation of the Laws and Customs of War by Land" is concluded as an Annex to the convention. The first section deals with the belligerents, and defines these in Chapter 1.

The literal text of this article, 1 to 3, is as follows:

The laws, rights, and duties of war apply not only to armies but also to militia and volunteer Corps fulfilling the following conditions:

1. To be commanded by a person responsible for his subordinates;

2. To have a fixed distinctive emblem recognizable at a distance;

3. To carry arms openly and

4. To conduct their operations in accordance with the laws and customs of war.

In countries where militia or volunteer corps constitute

---

[1] Regarding the significance of this clause both from the positive and the negative side, the reader is advised to consult the "Zeitschrift für Völkerrecht," page 86 *et seq.* Meurer also gives his resumé in this: "The Marten clause was rigidly observed by the Germans. The Belgians have shamefully violated the Ordinances of Warfare by Land as laid down at the Hague Conference; and are also to be held responsible for the destruction of Louvain."

an army, or form part of it, they are included under the denomination of "army."

A new idea was embodied in Article 2 in the year 1907, as expressed in the following:

"The inhabitants of a territory which has not been occupied, who, on the approach of the enemy, spontaneously take up arms to resist the invading troops *without having had time to organize themselves in accordance with Article 1, shall be regarded as belligerents if they carry arms openly and if they respect the laws and customs of war.*"

The *franc-tireurs* of France and Belgium and their accomplices were not "commanded by a person responsible for his subordinates." Their governments had simply thrust weapons into their hands as though they were so many robber bands and bid them do murder. A "citizen army" with responsible heads has never been proved as existing for these *franc-tireurs* and their methods in war. Even the *Garde civique*, which we have discussed in another place, was devoid of such command, and by no means fulfilled the other conditions of Article 1, inasmuch as it made a system of changing into civilian dress when in danger.[1]

The *franc-tireurs* with whom we have here to deal also carry no "fixed, distinctive emblem recognizable at a distance." On the contrary, they sought in every way to appear as harmless civilians. They showed a decided preference for shooting down stray soldiers who by reason of their wounds or for other causes, had been left behind, and their methods of murder were varied. Attempts were made to assassinate men by putting poison in their coffee, as reported in an undisputed semi-official despatch concerning an attempt against the life of a Prussian Major-general. They seldom carried their arms openly and their "operations" were all conducted without paying the slightest attention to the rules and usages of war.

[1] The English war-correspondent, Philip Gibbs in the "Daily Chronicle," clearly describes such an "heroic deed" by a Belgian civilian. He met a Uhlan who had lost himself, and, giving a "friendly answer" to his enquiry as to the way, at the same time, "through his pocket," shot the Uhlan with a revolver. "The lance now ornaments his cottage," says the Englishman, enthusiastic over this murderous coward. See also the brochure cited above "*Franc-tireur* warfare in Belgium, Confessions of the Belgian Press."

IV. I would merely cite a few more examples in connection with the official stipulations above:

The Berlin "Klinische Wochenschrift" of the middle of September, 1914, speaks of three atrocities which had been committed upon German physicians in France and Belgium. As may be seen from this, Dr. Max Stamer was shot by a *franc-tireur*, the Red Cross Surgeon Dr. Gottschalk became the victim of a treacherous attack by Belgian inhabitants, and the Staff Physician Dr. D. Xylander, as is expressly and emphatically stated, was shot in the most cowardly manner whilst performing his duty as a consulting expert on hygiene.

The German Medical Corps were forced to suffer terribly at the hands of these miscreants for whom, of course, the entire Geneva Convention simply did not exist. There is no connection between patriotism and murder of this sort. We know fully how to honor the feelings of those Belgians and Frenchmen who defend their country. But it is nothing less than a desecration of the holiest possessions of man to mention the love of one's country or to speak of courage in connection with abominations that violate all the canons of humanity.

The "Rules and Regulations of Warfare by Land" show how a people that wishes to defend its natal soil by force of arms from the attacks of an enemy is to conduct itself. It must carry its arms openly and observe all humane rules, especially those that deal with the defenseless. Should it permit itself to do the contrary, then—and we repeat this advisedly—then there is no punishment that can be too severe for combatting in the interests of mankind such a degradation of the code of war.

The manner in which these bands carried on and the ill-repute in which they stood is apparent from a peculiarly tragic case, that of the young artist Paul Hain of Munich, who was 23 years of age. He was a member of a Volunteer Motor Corps and as such had frequent occasion to be a witness of the cruel results of the warfare practised by these blood-hounds. It happened that one night in September Hain met with an accident to the engine of his motor. Seeing a band of *franc-tireurs* approaching, Hain shot himself rather than fall into their hands. It is likewise a fact that the German soldiers frequently carry poison upon their persons in order to avoid falling alive into the hands of these miscreants. This is well-known and not merely a yarn of the trenches.

The official report regarding the gruesome cases of mutilation at Orchies which have already been mentioned in a previous chapter, was published on the 30th of September.

V. A government which even goes so far as to incite to the limits of fanaticism the members of its regular army must bear the entire blood-guilt which must inevitably be the consequence of self-understood methods of reprisals within the rights of the international code of war (such as the burning of villages, etc.) and even of such as may exceed these. For reprisals form the permissible negation of international law. They who obviously violate the law of nations have no right to appeal to it,—on the contrary, their violation of it releases their opponents from its observance. This is the essential nature of reprisals.

Civilized states who proceed in the manner described above, and organize a form of warfare such as this, or tolerate it without taking the severest measures to repress it, renounce all right to being treated otherwise than one would treat robber-bands in Albania or in Mexico. Men like Villa and Carranza are in the same category as the French and Belgian guerillas. The states who tolerate such methods of warfare, or favor and support them, are responsible, according to Article 1 of the Convention of July 29th, 1899 and of Article 3 of the Convention of October 18th, 1907, for all damage which befalls the Germans —either civil or military—through the action of the *franc-tireurs*.

VI. Even without the emphatic confirmation of Colonel Beresford, [1] every private in the German, French, Belgian,

---

[1] A very interesting letter from Colonel E. E. de la Poer Beresford (formerly military attaché in St. Petersburg) to the "Times" and directed against Lloyd George and his "incendiary murderers" may be quoted from:

"I honestly wish that the civilian population may be enlightened upon the following points: The view prevails in the Russian, the French and the German armies that civilians and persons in civilian clothing are not entitled —no matter for what reason, be it through rage, patriotism or despair—to

English and Russian army knows that the participation of private citizens in warfare is rigidly forbidden and that it is punishable by shooting and by the destruction of the offending person's property through fire.

This opinion leads the "Eclair" to indulge in a fit of tempestuous rage: "Ere the all-too-courageous Frenchmen be disciplined one should remember that those Mayors who render useful services in hunting down pernicious animals or in combating conflagrations or national plagues are decorated with the Order of the Legion d'Honneur." The paper proceeds in this strain: "This is not the moment for discouraging the courageous, namely those that dwell near the frontier. In the face of an invasion every man must be more or less of a soldier. At least that is what our fathers thought." The article closes with the observation: "A regulation such as this would certainly be conceived as an unintelligent abuse of judicial power by the majority of Frenchmen."

Such is the opinion that prevails in France even to-day (the Spring of 1915) with respect to the warfare of the *franc-tireurs!* It is only the most rigorous severity that will suffice in such cases to protect soldiers against these wanton crimes.

I. Belgium.[1]

In order that all the evidence of Belgian acts of violence against Germans may be given the most unqualified credence and guarantee of good faith, the Imperial Commissioner to whom the task of examination has been assigned, had all the given facts confirmed under oath, in all cases where material proofs and original "exhibits" were not to be procured. A great number of these official protocols now lie before me in their formal transcripts.

I shall merely give a small selection from these since the entire number would suffice to make a comprehensive volume.

---

fire upon the soldiers and officers of an invading hostile army;—and that persons guilty of such crimes (in the military sense) are to be punished ruthlessly by death, and in specific instances, with the burning-down of the houses from which the shots have been fired. *Dura lex, sed lex!*" (*Retranslation.*)

[1] See the pamphlet by Richard Grasshoff, entitled "Belgien's Schuld," published by Georg Reimer, Berlin.

From this enormous amount of data I shall select only the most reliable and sworn declarations. As to other instances at Antwerp see page 150 of the original German edition. These cases are also of great importance in connection with the neutrality of Belgium, since some of them occurred before the 4th of August.

Belgium, to be sure, must bear the heaviest burden of guilt, especially Mons, Brussels and Antwerp.

1. Witness August St. said: "There was a young German married woman in our company, who had been confined two days before. She was quite exhausted, wept, and called continually for her husband. She was but poorly clad, *for she had been dragged straight from her bed......*"

2. Dorothea Melbo, single, a governess, testified under oath to the following, concerning Brussels: "There was a man led in, about 40—45 years of age, as near as I can say. At the same moment there was an outcry, and gendarmes took hold of the man and were leading him out handcuffed. While he was being led out, I saw that blood was running from his head on to his neck, which I supposed to be the consequence of a blow which he had received from a gendarme's club. I had just before observed this club in the hand of a gendarme. We saw from the window of the room in which we were held prisoners, that the handcuffed man was stood up against a wall. Immediately afterwards he fell, riddled with bullets, whereupon the crowd of Belgians assembled at the railway station broke into loud jubilations. On our asking the reason for the shooting, a station-official informed us that the condemned German *had carried a revolver.* In the course of the morning five or six other Germans were shot in the station."

3. Master-brewer Otto Emil Richard Sch. (on oath) made a statement regarding the frightful ill-treatment to which he was subjected in Mons: "Besides a number of slight wounds on the head and swollen bruises on the body I received a blow on the left eye and the bone of the nose through which the sight of the left eye has been injured, probably for life; I also sustained a heavy and dangerous kick upon the stomach."

His martyrdom was continued in Brussels. He went on: "The police-commissioner declared that I was a spy, and struck me with a rubber pipe which contained a heavy tube, on the back of the head. He struck me several times, till I had a number of fast-bleeding wounds and the pipe flew in pieces. He said: "Maintenant je vais vous montrer, comme il faut traiter un Allemand en Belgique." During all this two policemen stood near me, revolver in hand and a Garde civique with fixed bayonet. I bore the blows quietly and only exclaimed "Shame!" whereupon the Commissioner remarked: 'Ce malin est bien dur.'

"From here I was taken, with both hands handcuffed, by motor to the police barracks "Porte du Hal." As I got in and out, the mob pushed me, struck me and spat upon me.

"In the barracks I had once more to undergo an examination as at the station. A fat sergeant struck me several times on the nose with his fist. Other officials compelled me to wipe up my blood from the floor. I was obliged to stand still for two hours-and-a-half with my face to the wall." (Witness was in captivity until the 2nd of September.)

4. Margarethe Johanna, wife of R. (on oath):

"I saw in the Rue Creterie (in Liège) early on the morning of the 5th of August, how a child of scarcely two years lay on the ground and was trampled on by the Belgian soldiers. They said in French: "The Prussian ought to be destroyed." The child cried; whether it died of the ill-treatment or not, I do not know, for we went on. Bystanders told us that the child had been thrown from the window of a house."

5. The wife of a head-waiter, Albert Sch. (on oath), after repeated reminders that she was on oath persisted in this story:

"I saw on the 6th of August, a German torn back and forth on the pavement in front of the Bourse in Brussels by policemen, who finally struck off his head. They carried the head about on the point of their swords and all the people rejoiced."

On a repeated examination she gave an even closer description of the foregoing.

6. Friedrich Sch. (sworn statement): "In the German Café "Hansa," 56 Canal des Brasseurs, Antwerp, the mob broke open the doors and windows, threw all the furniture out into the

street and wrecked it. On the second story of the same house there lived a German captain, who shot twice in the air to bring the police to the rescue. Thereupon the mob swarmed into the house, threw a five-year-old boy from the second story into the street, and dragged three women from the same house, dressed only in a single garment, into the street by the hair and beat them. Directly after, the people near me wrecked a great window, about 3 m. high and 2 m. broad, with the leg of a table."

Witness told of the plundering of a German tobacconist's. "The police witnessed the doings of the populace, indeed, I saw policemen appropriate some of the cigars which had been thrown into the street.....

On the way to the station I saw a man who was known to be a German, stabbed by the mob."

7. Wilhelm K., Captain of the steamer A. of the Hamburg-America Line: "On the morning of the 3rd of August, 1914, I was told that I was not to leave Belgian waters, on pain of having my ship sunk. This injunction was given me by a Belgian major. On my arrival in Antwerp, the greater part of my wireless apparatus was destroyed by an officer of Engineers and some gendarmes, who threw it overboard"..... On the evening of the 4th of August, the witness saw great numbers of the populace with monstrous tumult, demolish the windows, doors and furniture in all the German houses by the harbor, and ill-treat the owners of these households in the most brutal fashion. "We saw through our field-glasses from on board the ship, that the young German girls from these houses were dragged along the pavement by the hair, after all the clothes had been torn from their bodies. The cries of pain and fear of these girls and women lasted at least an hour and a half, without the police interfering. At last, after midnight, two policemen appeared, who, however, did not interfere, but merely looked on.

"On the 6th of August, to the accompaniment of outrageous insults ("German dogs have no word of honor," "Scoundrel") the remains of the telegraphic apparatus on board was wrecked with a hammer."

8. Sch., Merchant: "I have seen how the mob robbed the houses of the Germans and destroyed everything, while the

garde civique looked carelessly on, and themselves took part in the work of destruction and ill-treatment. I saw the *garde civique* bayonet a young man who was afterwards taken away, severely wounded, by the Red Cross ambulance."

9. Witness L....: Merchant: "On the 3rd of August, I was obliged to go to Ghent on business. I had already been treated as a spy in Brussels, because I once asked a Brussels police-commissioner what the French officers, who had already been here in Brussels nearly four weeks, were doing here. In Ghent stones were thrown at me, and a shot grazed my leg. A police official struck me in the face as I tried to take his number..... When we were taking refuge in a circus in the evening, to the number of between 3—400 persons, I discovered that all my jewellery had been stolen. This could only have been done by the officials at the police-station. (1 wedding-ring, 3 seal-rings, 1 gold bracelet, 1 gold necklace and 1 brooch.)

I saw a woman, who was packing, thrown out of a house into the street by four men, and trampled underfoot."

10. The iron-turner Kr.: "On the 2nd of August I witnessed the following occurrence: The crowd was shouting that 10,000 Germans had been taken prisoner. Thereupon a man of the people declared that one ought not to believe such news. They yelled that he was a German spy and must be killed. The people then rushed upon the man, who had spoken in perfect French, and literally trampled him to pulp..... Every shop which bore the notice "Man spricht deutsch!" was demolished." The witness gave the names of 6 such establishments. The following evidence is important for the question of neutrality.

"On Sunday, the 26th of July, the Lord Mayor of London was in Brussels: on this occasion a great military review was held in Etterbeek. One regiment went by in dust-grey uniforms.

"On Wednesday, the 29th of July, therefore before the mobilization, I myself saw a French officer in an automobile with a civilian and two soldiers, at the Bourse. The French officer made a speech from the automobile to the crowd at the Bourse whereupon he was lifted from the car and carried shoulder-high with shouts of '*Vive la France!*' "

11. Brutal ill-treatment by Belgian police was reported

by the merchant Wilhelm L. (Imperial Government Report of 3rd of December 1914—4th of January 1915) in Antwerp. He swore upon oath that as early as the 2nd of August 1914, a mob plundered and destroyed German cafés, and that with his own eyes he saw German girls dragged along the whole length of the street by their hair. He also gave evidence that as early as July, French officers of an Engineer corps visited the forts in the company of Belgian officers. He told of the murder of several German sailors and women. Witness Elizabetha R. (Lower Court of Schwerin, 13th January, 1915) gave witness on oath to horrible ill-treatment in Antwerp.

12. Eugen Sch. believed the principal blame for the bitter feeling against, and molestation of, the Germans could be attributed to the Burgomaster de Vos. On the 3rd of August, while everything was still quiet, he caused a public proclamation to be issued to the effect that the Germans had broken their word and marched into Limburg. At the same time he caused the alarm to be sounded, to call out the citizen watch.

The proclamation certainly contained no direct incitement to commit outrages against the Germans, but certain turns of speech such as: "Our native city is in danger," and so on nevertheless caused a great outburst of feeling against them.

As Director Sch. on the afternoon of the 3rd of August, went to his office, he saw 6 to 8 Flemings set about a German sailor with rubber clubs and pieces of iron and leave him lying half-dead. Shortly after in an inn he saw a German dock-laborer stabbed by a Belgian. Close by there was a police-station. The police however did not show themselves.

13. Katherina H. whose home is in Anzing, declared: "On the 2nd of August this year, in the evening, everything in the German inns "Hamburger Buffet," "Adlershof," "Kaiserhof," "Deutscher Kaiser," "Berliner Rangen," "Stadt Dortmund," "Bremer Küche," and "Imperial" was broken to bits.

The German hotels, Braun, Weber and Germania, in the neighborhood of the railway-station, were stormed by the mob, and everything stolen..... On the way to the station, in the main street from the station to the town, witness saw a little girl, 10 to 12 years of age, thrown from the upper story of a house into the street. The child fell upon the pavement quite close to her. The police and the military did not attempt to interfere with the excesses of the mob.

14. Miss B. deposed: "My father, Otto B. for over 25 years a contributor to the "Berliner Tageblatt," and well-known as an author not only in Germany but also abroad, was for the last 2 years domiciled in Brussels." On suspicion of espionage and on account of his connection with the "Berliner Tageblatt," they were both interned. Here everything of any value was taken from them. "I do not know what became of my father." ... She touchingly described their reunion in captivity:

"He was changed beyond recognition, haggard, dressed in thin cotton underwear without socks, with only slippers on his feet and trembling with cold. His face plainly showed the traces of recent fearful ill-treatment. The whole left side of the face and nose had become green and blue from the blows he had received. Over the eyes and on the brow were great abrasions. He was unwashed and in a shocking state of neglect and exhaustion. He knew me, inquired after relatives, and began to weep bitterly. He complained like a little child.

I communicated the result of my visit to the American consul. He replied *that this was the 4th or 5th case of the kind. It seemed as if they wished to drive the prisoners insane through ill-treatment.* In spite of the seriously ailing condition of my father, he was again put in a cell, and I discovered from the authorities that he had already eaten nothing for eight days, and also that he had been confined in a padded cell.

Six weeks ago a healthy, mentally alert man, my father is to-day broken in body and spirit, his mind seriously affected, with only slight and short intervals of clarity." (See the details of this case, 1st Edition p. 151.)

The innumerable reports of the German papers are one in their complete accord with the official bulletins as to the attitude of the Antwerp police being one of complete passivity. Witnesses declare that police officials stood in the immediate vicinity with "smiling mien, and without raising a finger to interfere." A number of Belgian gendarmes were directly concerned in the acts of brutality aboard the "Gneisenau" in the harbor.

The legal adviser of a large German firm in Antwerp, who is personally known to the "Kölnische Zeitung," describes the *desecration of graves.* This gentleman may be believed when he says that his "heart seemed seized with a hideous cramp" at the sight of such things. He, too, writes of the cruelties, the maltreatment, the looting, the murders: "And the police, the *garde civique* who were supposed to protect us? These, to a great extent, *themselves participated in the robberies.* We saw the watchmen up on the galleries, watching the gulls in the most absorbed fashion, just as though what was going on did not in the least concern them. They simply *did not wish to see anything.*"

"The "Maasbode" of Rotterdam wrote at that time: "If things are to go on in this way, in two days no citizen of Antwerp will be safe in his own house. Yesterday and to-night the surburban villas of the Germans who had been driven out were looted and set on fire. To-morrow it will be the villas of Belgians who have fled the city or been enrolled in the army."

I have purposely cited more numerous instances of this reign of terror in Antwerp in order to contrast them with the behavior of the Germans after the fall of that city.

II. France.

Conditions in France were little better.

The Munich actor Max Stehbeck, who had sent an exhibit to the Exhibition of Cities in Lyon, writes thus in the "Münchener Neueste Nachrichten" and avers that he is able to confirm all he says upon oath:

"The refugees took up their residence in the Hotel Bordeaux, but they could have no hope of being allowed to remain there in peace, since a furious crowd in front of the house continued to cry out against the Germans. On another day the hotel proprietor insisted that the Germans should leave the house, as he feared that it would be set on fire.

The proprietor of the Hippodrome, Eder, as he left the German Relief Society, was beaten till blood flowed. A much worse fate befell a young dancing-master, who was thrown to the ground and trampled upon, so that his ribs were driven in; he is presumably dead.... The journey, in cattle-trucks. was to Thiers, near Clermont-Ferrand... It was worst in St. Etienne, where women stormed the car with broomsticks and knives.

In Thiers the prisoners, among whom there were also some Austrians, were confined in a large market-hall, in which swine had been kept. About 800 Germans and Austrians were jammed together in this place.... As the issue of milk to the young children was refused, several died during the eleventh day of imprisonment in the Gymnasium. A new infant arrival upon the scene was greeted by the unfeeling doctor with the words: 'Still another dirty German!' The child died the next day."

Sufferings still more atrocious than those of Herr Stehbeck were endured by the wife of a head-waiter, Gertrud Serito, as attested in a sworn protocol before the "Society for the Germans in Foreign Lands" (Verein für das Deutschtum im Auslande). She describes the brutalities that befell her during the journey from Paris to Brussels, at Brussels itself and during the trip from Brussels to the German frontier.

I select the following choice and typical bits out of the mass of sworn testimony that lies before me in connection with what happened in France.

J...., a male nurse, after having been duly sworn, declares as follows: "On the way to the Gare St. Lazare on the 3rd of August, I witnessed how a German of about 45 years who apparently had no very perfect command of the French tongue, and had asked the soldier for information, was stabbed by him in the eye with a bayonet. The eye ran out and it was necessary to take the injured man to a neighboring apothecary's."

On August 4th I went to the Gare du Nord. The station was blocked by the military. The vestibule and waiting rooms were filled with Germans who were anxious to return home, The corridors rang with the cries: "*A bas les Allemands! A Berlin!*" Whoever was recognized as a German was struck with clubs, thrown to the ground and kicked.

At Mons I went to the railway station, accompanied by the conductor of a German orchestra at Ostende. The conductor was known in Mons and was attacked by a number of half-grown youths (some 15 to 20) who hurled him to the ground, kicked him in the face, and other parts of the body, until several officers rescued him from their hands. His violin which he carried with him in a case and which he valued at some 1200 Marks, was smashed to fragments by the mob. A considerable number of Germans had gathered at the railway station; they too had been roughly handled and their faces and ears were bleeding....

There were some 2000 civil prisoners at Bruges, most of whom had injuries about the head, or the ribs or other parts of the body, and complained of pain.

Shocking brutalities of the French against women seriously ill or pregnant are described under oath by the witness Berta W., in the District Court at Oberkich on January 2nd, 1915. A Frenchwoman, wife of a German, tells of the terrible lack of food for civil prisoners, in testimony given at the District Court at Elberfeld on January 19th, 1915. The fury of the mob is depicted by a female witness in the District Court at Wiesbaden on December 4th, 1914. Johann H., a Head Maltster (District Court at Mülhausen in Elsass, December 4th, 1914) in complete agreement with numerous other witnesses, reports in detail the brutal and studied ill-treatment meted out to the civil prisoners at the end of August, after the French had captured Mülhausen. A female witness under oath describes how civil prisoners were locked up together with syphilitics of the worst form and how the defenceless were maltreated (District Court, Berlin, Central Division, 92.)

Similar brutalities took place in every part of France, north and south, east and west. Prostitutes were appointed to watch respectable women, typhus and summer cholera resulted from confinement in the most unspeakable holes—infinitely worse than the worst of German prisons. Wherever a criminal intention was not at the root of these things, it was a criminal lack of system. The police, as frequently attested by the witnesses, took no steps to stop the excesses, the throwing of stones, etc., but took an evident pleasure in these. There are accounts of the shocking conditions that prevailed in the concentration camp at d'Avrillé, which must have outdone the notorious

Boer concentration Camps of Kitchener. Mongazon was no better.

Recruiting for the French Foreign Legion was also carried on among these tortured men, as stated on oath by most of the witnesses. This recruiting was undertaken chiefly because it promised to be successful since it meant release to the prisoners in these hot-beds of disease.

Various witnesses give testimony relative to the injuries inflicted upon Germans by the mob in Oran which had been incited by the soldiers—one of these, Julius Bock, a merchant from Hamburg, dying from the effects. A female witness testified before the Lower Court at Ludwigslust as to the conditions in the prisoners' camp at Sebdous—which appear to be similar to those other witnesses relate of the camps in France. Another witness at Bremen, initialled M, has the like story to relate.

Anna W. a school-teacher, has many things to relate of the concentration camp at Rodez, and of the tragic conditions that prevail there, in a sworn statement made at the District Court at Karlsruhe on January 8th, 1915. (The prefect declared: "If some of them would die, it would not matter, for there are plenty of them left.")

Direct violation by French soldiers committed under the threat of a revolver is substantiated by the governess M. B. at the Würzburg courts on January 13th, 1915, and includes revolting accounts of the lootings and the libidinousness of French soldiers.

III. England.

That conditions in England following upon the first few days after the war were not much better than in France and Belgium appears from the thorough-going investigations undertaken by the German Government. They constitute a disgrace for England, a nullification of those very qualities upon which Englishmen had most prided themselves. We shall proceed to furnish a few specific proofs:

During the examinations carried on by the Imperial Commissioner to ascertain the facts regarding excesses committed against Germans in foreign countries, a German lady, resident in London, was examined under oath with respect to the murder of a German by the mob. The official documents in the case give the following details:

"On the evening of the 5th of August, about 11 o'clock, I went alone down Piccadilly, and saw two well-dressed German-speaking gentlemen taking leave of one another near Appendrodt's German restaurant. They were two young men, between 25—30 years of age, I should say. Hundreds of people stood in the street, and they had formed themselves into two queues one on either side, waiting for the motors carrying people from the theater which traverse this street in great numbers. It had in fact become the custom with the public in the first days after the outbreak of war to hold up the motors traversing the favorite after-theater route through Piccadilly and question the occupants as to their nationality. Whenever a motor showed no flag or bore no sign of its nationality, the crowd struck with sticks at the occupants, who mostly belonged to better-class commercial circles. In Piccadilly, therefore, at the time the incident occurred, the crowd were in a very excited state. As the two Germans above-mentioned took leave of one another, some persons standing near observed them and recognized them as Germans. With the cry, "They are Germans!" "Down with the Germans," "Kill the Germans!" the mob rushed upon the two unhappy men. One of the two succeeded in escaping, the other was thrown to the ground and trodden upon. There was such a crush that it was impossible for him to have been beaten, since to my thinking, no one could lift a hand. The young man was simply knocked down and trodden upon by the nearest persons. The people kept up this ill-treatment until the German showed no signs of life. I know for certain that during the whole occurrence a policeman stood not more than 3 yards off, and witnessed the illtreatment without stirring. At last, when the German no longer moved, he told the persons standing near that they must pick the man up and carry him away. Several people lifted up the lifeless body and carried it off, I do not know where. Some Englishmen, who took pity upon the German, endeavored to make the mob cease their rough treatment. The great crowd, however, made a stand against them, and, as I myself saw, some of these Englishmen were also beaten by the infuriated crowd."

IV.

Conditions in France to-day, as proved by the descriptions of the unfortunate Germans who had been returned as seriously wounded, have improved but little. The brutalized mob there has sunk too low to give one any hope of seeing it recover from its hysteria. A Swiss divine, Zimmerli by name, who had been deputized by neutral states to inspect the French prisoners' camps and hospitals, writes as follows regarding the feeling there:

"The same absence of discipline showed itself in the intellectual life of the French, whereby that hate blazed high which had for decades been implanted in the souls of the children against everything German. Already in December I could hear and comprehend the motive of the wild howling of the populace which expressed its feelings in the word "boches!," "boches!." The significance of this expression lies in the fact that its meaning is one which would never enter the head of a self-respecting, clean-minded man. It is established with certainty through unimpeachable witnesses, that things did not by a long way stop at these hysterical outbursts, but that on the contrary the German and Austrian refugees from France met with the most brutal insults and molestation by the way, indeed, in some cases with such ill-treatment as proved fatal. The civil prisoners coming back from France have given detailed statements on oath which afford a sad glimpse into the unbridled license and madness of French Chauvinism. The complete obliteration of the Germans from the face of Europe was their wish and goal! People in France were fully aware through the correspondent of the "Matin" in Germany, of the good-will of the Germans towards the French. But the "Matin" used these facts only as a new cause for mockery and contempt, and forbade in the name of the French nation all mercy and compunction in this war. "These Germans are so stupid!"—these words best indicate the Frenchman's mockery of the German's good-nature. A Frenchman however said to me: "As we drive the ape from his primeval world, so the criminal German rabble must vanish from Europe!"

Compare to this the calmness, the dignity, the deep compassion which the entire German nation displays towards its wounded enemies.

V.

The responsibility and the blame for all these atrocities and all this destruction must be placed at the doors of the French, English and Belgian authorities. For the most part these things happened with the knowledge and even the consent of the police. At the very least the police have rendered themselves culpable by not taking the proper steps for protecting the defenseless Germans and are responsible for all that these people suffered. The conditions upon which peace is to be concluded must make provision for damages for all those acts of havoc that took place 8 to 10 days before the war, and subsequently.

Let us for a moment compare these bestial and wanton perversities with the few noisy incidents which occurred before the declaration of war at Berlin and Munich. In the latter city, I regret to say, a few windows in a café were broken and several foreigners were forced to seek the protection of the police, though they had in nowise been injured. But these excesses of the crowd, which were condemned by the entire German press, are mere child's play in comparison with such heinous cruelties as those in question,—even though the foreign press ventured to describe them as cruel excesses. We have in part been witnesses of these incidents and are able to confirm in the most conscientious manner all that has been stated. There are numerous and reliable witnesses.

Since German public opinion as an undivided whole stood opposed to these passionate demonstrations of the crowd, all such excesses disappeared from the very day of the declaration of war. The sober dignity and seriousness of the German people gave ample assurance that no subject of an enemy state would suffer molestation.

In substantiation of this I would merely like to recall that a large number of British subjects (45) left Berlin as late as the end of September. They sent the following letter to the "Vossische Zeitung:"

"Pray permit us herewith to express our heartiest thanks to the railway and police officials for the trouble which they have taken on our account, and for the friendly and chivalrous treatment which we have received from them. We should like to say that our joy in returning home is only clouded by the thought of the many dear and good friends whom we must leave behind. Let us further declare that it is our intention to do our utmost to spread the truth in England as to the real position of things."[1]

Countless formal notices and announcements by neutrals —Scandinavians, Roumanians, and Americans,—as well as the Berlin representatives of the press of the entire world, have been preserved in Berlin, exposing the lies of the London press and its accomplices in Rome, Turin, New York, etc. with respect to alleged atrocities. Of course this occurred only after public opinion had already been prejudiced to the disadvantage of Germany.

We gladly concede that after the first outbreaks in England, the Germans there were apparently left fairly unmolested until October—so far as the insane fear of Zeppelins and spies permitted the English to leave them alone. Towards the middle of October "pogroms" against harmless German waiters and other German subjects began to take place—actions which the respectable portion of the English press stigmatized as *a disgrace for the entire nation.* The degraded and vulgar "Evening News" was the chief and most violent inciter of the uneducated mob against helpless German employees, in fact this Harmsworth organ has well merited the title of "gutter sheet" along with the nauseous and despicable "Daily Express."

I am constantly forced to declare: Where do those preachers

[1] According to the "Frankfurter Zeitung," the committee of the 600 Russian citizens who were allowed to leave Leipzig in October for their native land, published a message of thanks which contained the following words: "All the authorities have shown the nicest appreciation of our position, so that we have received still further proofs of the height to which German civilization has attained. We shall do our utmost to see that the facts of our excellent treatment and the great-heartedness of the German people shall be made known abroad."

and moralists who wax indignant upon the subject of international law—where are *they* hiding in the face of all these enormities, all these breaches of the Geneva Convention—acts which would shame the average negro? Here is a real opportunity for them to tear their hair in frenzy and assail the heavens with curses long and loud. No word is heard from these gentry. Of course, the instances mentioned deal only with "Germans, old men, women and children!"

CHAPTER XI.

Unlawful and Inhumane Methods of Conducting War Practised by the Hostile Armies and the Governments of the Triple Entente and Belgium.

"And it is with such riff-raff as this that I am forced to fight!"
Frederick the Great, August 25, 1758.

It is not to be wondered at that the *franc-tireurs* and the population committed so vast a number of lawless acts against the German army when one observes that the belligerent armies themselves were guilty of all sorts of wanton breaches of the law of nations. Here, too, the mass of available material is so great that only a few instances can be given. This great body of evidence is being sifted by a special Imperial Commission as well as by another special body under the auspices of the Ministry of War.

So we confine ourselves to a few particularly crass instances, since the accumulation of facts would alone suffice to fill a large folio.

I. Treatment of Prisoners. Treatment of Germans in Violation of International Law. Exemplary Treatment of Prisoners in Germany.

The treatment of prisoners by Belgians and Frenchmen has already been touched upon in the preceding chapter. According to Article 4 of the much quoted Convention of the year 1907, with which the Convention of 1899 is in entire agreement, thus making it applicable to all the countries engaged in the war, all prisoners of war are subject to the power of the enemy country, but *not to the power of the persons or the divisions by whom they have been made prisoners.*

"*They must be humanely treated.*"

"All their personal belongings, except arms, horses, and military papers, remain their property.

"Prisoners of war ... cannot be confined except as an indispensable measure of safety and only while the circumstances which necessitate the measure continue to exist;" (Art. 4)—that is to say, only temporarily.

According to Article 7, "prisoners of war shall be treated as regards board, lodging, and clothing on the same footing *as the troops of the Government which captured them.*

"The State may utilize the labor of prisoners of war according to their rank and aptitude, officers excepted. The tasks shall not be excessive and shall have no connection with the operations of the war.

"Prisoners may be authorized to work for the public service, for private persons, or on their own account." (Article 6.)

"The Government into whose hands prisoners of war have fallen is charged with their maintenance."

All these humane regulations, which,—as I by personal observation am able to confirm,—have been most conscientiously fulfilled in Germany, have been disregarded and ignored in France.

According to unanimous reports from Belgium, England, France and Russia all prisoners, yes, even those that were captured in violation of international law,—Germans not liable to military duty, inclusive of women and children,—were in many cases subjected to extraordinarily harsh treatment. A memorial of the German Government consisting of 56 large pages of print, which lies before me, contains a vast amount of preliminary matter in connection with the treatment of German prisoners in French hands,—treatment in distinct violation of the Geneva Convention of July 6th, 1906, and of the Hague Conference of October 18th, 1907.

Herr Kristen, an Austrian Chief Engineer who had been released from French imprisonment towards the close of September, 1914, has some very interesting facts to relate:

"When I first observed, in the course of my professional journeys, that great masses of troops were being assembled in the Vosges, I called to mind the prophecy of Jaurès, that there would soon be war. This was on the 18th of July. Suddenly, on the 21st of July, a state of war was proclaimed. On the afternoon of the 24th of July I received my papers with a command to leave France. However, travelling by train was already forbidden to civilians. In the afternoon I was arrested, and, together with 179 Germans, Austrians and Hungarians, confined in a cellar. The next morning we were taken under guard to Toul. On the way through the city the populace pelted us with stones, gravel and dirt. In the evening we were put in an ice-cellar to sleep on straw. At Toul, from the 2nd of August on, we were compelled with blows to dig trenches and fortifications and erect barbed wire. The trenches, which had a breadth of 1.30 metres were covered with barbed wire.

Among our number there was a certain Paul Schambach, business manager of the German wool-factory of Schlumberger in Belfort, who had about him 80,000 francs belonging to his firm.

When he complained of the seizure of the money, he was taken behind a citadel and obliged to dig his own grave. He was then shot out of hand. On the 10th of August we heard the thunder of cannon, and shrapnel spattered on the roof. During the next few days we were particularly roughly handled and badly fed. We had to give up all our money, which in my case alone amounted to 800 francs in wages, and 28,000 francs in paper securities."

The "Berliner Morgenpost" publishes the following cry of distress from German prisoners of war in France under the date of September 14:

Report of a German doctor:

"I beg you to make known the unbelievable brutality with which the German prisoners of war were treated in France. I declare to you on my word as a physician, that no person, however healthy, could endure such treatment for more than 8 days without collapsing. I can state these facts with the greater assurance, since I was myself a prisoner of war in Brest."
Armin H. Strobel, M. D. Berlin.

An issue of the "Petit Marseillais" which appeared about the end of September gives an account of how the first German prisoners were brought to Marseilles at night. The prisoners, who were few in number, were brought from the station to their place of internment in wagons with windows fastened down. The account proceeds as follows:

"The crowd grows; loud cries, mostly from women, increase in volume and become a tumult. Now stones fly thicker and thicker till a perfect hail falls rattling over the transport wagon. The weak escort is no longer in a position to protect the Germans. The crowd breaks through and sets about us with sticks, etc."

A non-commissioned officer of the Sanitary Corps by name of Frank, hailing from Cologne, who had been released from imprisonment and happened to be at Freiburg in Breisgau, gave the following testimony on the 18th of October and is willing to substantiate it at any time under oath. Frank was taken to the Artillery practice ground at Clermont-Ferrand as a prisoner. He was accompanied by some twenty officers. He describes the conditions, giving a careful attention to detail:

... "Whatever the prisoners themselves possessed was taken from them. The pain and privation suffered by these men absolutely cry to heaven.

A sergeant had command of the prisoners. He was entirely devoid of all human feeling. To take but one example:

Dr. B., a non-commissioned officer, was ill, and a French doctor had given him permission to buy tea. The sergeant noticed the sentry attempting to hand over the tea to the non-commissioned officer. He took the tea away from the sentry and gave Dr. B. a blow with his fist in the stomach, so that he fell over backwards. He likewise punished him with 5 days solitary confinement (water and a piece of bread daily), The non-com. asked the Sergeant why he had been so severely punished? He had obtained permission from the doctor. The punishment was outrageous. Hereupon the French sergeant struck the prisoner's head against a flight of stone steps. A sentry at the same time belabored him with the butt-end of his rifle, until B. gave a heartrending cry of pain and lost consciousness.......

After this the non-com., without any examination was sentenced to 15 days solitary confinement and led off to prison. Eight days later the French sergeant reported his death. It is uncertain whether he was shot or died in consequence of the ill-treatment."

The wish expressed in the 1st Edition for a complete investigation of this "Case of Frank" will be fulfilled. A careful special memorial of the Prussian Ministry of War relating to this Frank Case on the grounds of sworn testimony, which lies before me, has revealed the full unreliability of the French Government, which sent a verbal note on the case to the American Ambassador on the 15th of December 1914, claiming that the affair was untrue. In a fashion as correct as it was individual, the memorial protested against the untruthfulness of the French Government, which did not hesitate to deceive the neutral countries, and to cover up the atrocious conditions proved as existing at Clermont-Ferrand.

We have already indicated in the foregoing the brutal treatment meted out to the German prisoners by the French mob. When these men were made prisoners, it happened at the same time that a Bavarian munition column was captured in a hollow road by French Alpine Chasseurs, that is to say by some of the crack troops of the French army.

After the negotiations with regard to the surrender had taken place between the Frenchmen and the captured German officers, these as well as the substitute officers and some twenty or thirty soldiers were locked up in a shed. During the serving-out of water at night, a light happened to be struck in the shed. The French without a word of warning began to fire into the shed. A captured Bavarian Captain was mortally wounded; he gave a loud cry: "My wife and children! Good-bye!" and fell over dead. Two other prisoners were wounded. The prisoners were forced to spend the whole night with the dead man, and the two wounded without being able to move a hand. Not a soul troubled itself about them, as they lay pent in the dark shed. Thus does the *grande nation* treat the prisoners and the wounded of its opponents! The testimony respecting this incident was given by one of the wounded men.

Inasmuch as they are most characteristic a few passages

from the statement made by the clergyman B., who had been taken prisoner in violation of Article 9 of the 2nd Geneva Convention, and who has already been mentioned in the foregoing, as quoted in the "Kölnische Zeitung" may not be inappropriate:

"I found that there were still about 38 German prisoners there. Finally (after 2 days) each of us received a piece of French biscuit which was, of course, as hard as stone. No water was given us. The prisoners asked for water. "No!" was the short and decisive answer of the stern-faced monsieur le Commandant. It was a sorry plight. Here on the floor, leaning against the walls of the prison, sat the poor captives. They were dying of thirst, for the weather was torrid and they had been forced to make tremendous marches. Opposite them, at a distance of not more than 4 yards, there was a well with water. French soldiers made use of this to refresh themselves and their horses. The Germans ask for a drink and their answer was the gruff refusal of the Commandant. When one of the soldiers rose and ventured to approach a full bucket, he was pushed back.

"When I made my request to be examined and dismissed to-day, I received a smiling, affirmative answer. I was soon to learn what this meant. About ten o'clock we were all forced to form into line, in fours, I as a Catholic priest in Catholic France at the head. Gendarmes surround us and the order was given: "Forward March!" We went past the French troops and were compelled to hear their ridicule and mockery..."

This reverend gentleman proceeds to describe the behavior of the dehumanized populace. It is the same story everywhere: derision, insults and acts of violence.

This priest was treated like a felon. After the fifth day of his captivity, the authorities at last consented to hold an examination. All his possessions, pocketknife, papers, linen, money, rosary and crucifix were taken from him, even his suspenders were torn from his clothes. The official Red Cross armlet, stamped by the authorities, was ripped from his sleeve. A mass of abuses of all international agreements! Not the slightest respect shown for those rules and regulations which all the civilized nations have pledged themselves to observe

These instances are not to be considered as mere exceptions. The cases that have already received publicity and which constitute in themselves an enormous body of evidence, prove that there had been a systematic goading on of the lowest instincts of the mob by means of the most impossible falsehoods. These went so far as to declare that the Germans murdered all their wounded and prisoners! These gross slanders explain why the French mob and the French soldiery became imbued with a spirit so inhuman that almost without exception *our* prisoners and to a large extent *our* wounded were maltreated in that country and why the laws that regulate these things were so persistently ignored.

That this charge is based upon fact is proved by its confirmation by the Bordeaux correspondent of the Italian Socialist paper, the "Avanti," who accuses the Paris "Matin" of deliberately and publicly demanding the murder of the German prisoners and by the circumstance that the censorship had stricken out the objections which the "Humanité" had made to such brutalities. According to the "Avanti" the passage in question, published by the "Matin," runs as follows: "No pity in the coming battles, should these miserable criminals against the laws of man fall into our hands! It is possible that Wilhelm the Second may have formed his bodyguard of them, *but they are only fit to be butchered like pigs.*" All France, the paper goes on to say, would utter an unceasing protest should it be lead to believe or to fear that it would be burdened with such prisoners. They are unworthy of pardon, *they should be slaughtered like wild animals.*

II. Regarding the Capture of Civilians.

The peculiar feature of this war consists in the fact that the main basis of all international law that has prevailed hitherto,—the segregation of non-combatants, that is, of peaceful citizens from the armies and their adjuncts, has been widely disregarded. It is upon this principle that the resolutions of the two Hague Conferences rest. (See Articles 1 to 3 of the 4th conference of 1907 and Articles 1 to 3 in connection with "armed force", Articles 22, 46 of the Rules of Warfare by Land.)

It appears as though the States of the Triple Entente

had agreed to ignore these principles from the very first day of the war. This systematized breach of the accredited laws of nations is of the most momentous significance and is bound to lead to a brutalization of the entire conduct of war.

The Author gives specific details in the original edition of the barbarous treatment to which civilians were subjected in Russia, England and France. See original German version, 3rd edition, page 191 *et seq.*, especially the descriptions of the condition of German civilians in English concentration camps.

A. The number of complaints which have been published in the press in connection with the maltreatment of prisoners of war is naturally exceeded by the reports concerning abuses of the usages of war in battle of which the Frenchmen, the Belgians, the Russians and the English have made themselves guilty with regard to our armies. The same accusations are made on the part of the Allies against our own troops. It must be conceded that elements enter into these questions which make an objective judgment and a thorough supervision of the various statements exceedingly difficult. The entire passionate sur-excitation of these participating in the battle, a state of mind which often amounts to pathological illusion, the frightful physical and psychological impressions and effects of modern warfare, especially where huge modern guns are used, etc., make it almost impossible for either side to judge its own actions or those of its opponents in a calm, judicial manner. A certain amount of scepticism is therefore most natural in connection with all battle reports. The actual and the merely imagined mingle in an inextricable confusion. The talk of the trenches riots luxuriantly in a mixture of truth and fiction.

Of course, exception must be made between these fantastic ideas of what is supposed to happen during the battle and detailed and special investigations made after the battle.

We shall also do our best when considering the following stories, to weed out all fantastic yarns from irresponsible soldiers' letters, whenever there is no way of ascertaining the truth. So far as we are now able to judge, it is upon such evidence that most of the nonsense of the French, Belgian and English press stories (things like the famous "bridge of the dead," etc.) is based, as well as the latest Belgian and French "Red

Books" of alleged atrocities, the pamphlet "Les crimes allemands" by Joseph Bédier, and similar publications. It is my intention to leave such things to care for themselves and to portray only such occurences as have been related in "cool blood" and the truth of which may be followed to its sources. At present some difficulty is encountered in this direction because of the military censorship which forbids the mention of places and troop divisions.

A great sensation was caused in Germany by the following communication under the date of September 6th. It appeared in all the newspapers and also received confirmation in another place from the Prussian Ministry of War. A *dementi*, so far as I am able to ascertain, was never made.

1. "The newspapers of Stettin relate hair-raising accounts of the bestialities of English troops as communicated to them from reliable sources (letters from citizens of Stettin now serving with the Red Cross). The writers expressly state that they desire these facts to be made known. The following is from the "Ostsee-Zeitung:"

A first Lieutenant made a speech to the assembled soldiers and to us, in the presence of the captured Englishmen. He said: "Comrades, repeat in your native towns all that I now tell you. These captured Englishmen have treated our troops in a barbarous fashion. They held up their hands, showed the white flag, and allowed our men to come within 50 meters. They then shot them down. The prisoners and wounded had their wounds torn open with clasp-knives and iron hooks, their throats cut with knives, and so on. Here are the scoundrels. Everything that I say is from official sources. Our brave fellows have to fight with such beasts as these."

A cry of rage and indignation went through our ranks, a snort of disgust at England's troops. Only iron discipline prevented us from falling upon these brutes."

2. From the private letter of a Prussian Major, the original of which is in the possession of the "Frankfurter Zeitung," we take the following unimpeachable and authenticated result of an official military examination:

"Yesterday I was commanded by my brigade to go to the field-hospital and to sit in judgment upon a Frenchman.

I found a lance-corporal, a man in the later thirties, who had been a soldier since 1895. He confessed without further ado that he had put out with his bayonet the eyes of two wounded German soldiers of the X. Army corps, which had taken the crossings of the Meuse some days before. Asked the reason for his deed, he replied quite calmly: "C'est une revanche comme toute autre." (That is also a form of revenge, like any other.) Therewith the man's guilt was established, and I announced this to the Brigade which immediately had him shot. This happened in X. on the evening of the 31st of August. The lance-corporal's name was E. B. He was caught in the act by the Red Cross men. He told them that he was acting on orders from his superiors. The German ambulance men stated, as witnesses, that the French lance-corporal had put out the eyes of about 30 wounded Germans."

After an interval of some months the English seem to have recommenced their illegal methods of warfare in the spring of 1915, as the following communications attest:

The "Weserzeitung" (reprinting the reports of eye-witnesses in other papers,) reports from the north-east of Neuve Chapelle on the 14th of March: "The English have again given thorough proof in this fight of what mean actions they could be capable. In their first attack they drove Sikhs and Ghurkas in front of them, apparently unarmed, and holding up their hands, as though they wished to give themselves up. Of course we did not shoot, so that they reached our trenches unmolested. In this manner the English storming-party, following close behind, was easily able to gain possession of our trenches. In a second attack these English brutes then used the prisoners captured in the morning, about one company strong, again as a shield, driving them in front. Those who would not go were struck dead with cudgels."

"The "Kölnische Zeitung" takes the following from the letter of a substitute officer who fought against the English at Neuve Chapelle, and writes from the front: "I will own that before I had stood in our fighting line I viewed all stories of English cruelty and meanness with the greatest distrust. Now I have been taught by my own experience, and I must affirm that our papers paint conditions pretty black, but not black enough by a long way. Here are two examples, for the accuracy of which I can myself vouch, because they were officially communicated to our division as a warning: 250 English, in German coats and helmets, beckoned a company of German soldiers to come closer so that they could let fly at them at short range. German prisoners were actually used as cover by the English." [1]

In many cases there is an obvious system that is followed. Again and again we hear that the English, at the command of their officers, hold up their hands during a German attack, thus giving the understood sign of surrender without further fighting. Then when the German troops advance to meet them, the English suddenly begin to fire upon them. The result of this has been that the salute of captured English officers is no longer returned, as an expression of contempt for this method of warfare.

There is here no question of a legitimate and permissible "ruse of war," according to Article 23, of the Rules and Regulations of Warfare by Land, but simply of the "treacherous murder" of an opponent. No more abominable and pusillanimous act can be conceived, and one would be entirely justified, according to international law, in refusing all pardon to the perpetrators of such deeds.

B. From the letters of countless eye-witnesses, whose credibility I would myself vouch for, I know that it was a common practice with the Belgians, the Russians and the French in Lothringen, to show the white flag, or raise their arms, only so that a treacherous volley might be poured into the unsuspecting Germans.

To what excesses the insolence of the Russians, for instance, will go in the abuse of the flag of the Geneva Con-

---

[1] On the 14th of December 1914, the following was received: On the 4th of December a German sentry who had been appointed to watch a barbed-wire entanglement was found dead, shot through the head, and with his ears cut off. The very next day, at the same place, an officer of the 165th Infantry regiment appeared before the German lines of defence, and asked to be taken with blindfolded eyes before the General in command. The French officer then declared that his division had no part in the perpetration of this cruel deed. The guilty man was to be shot on the same day, December 5th, in expiation of this crime. Bravo!—a little glimmer of light!

vention, is described by an eye-witness, the well-known war correspondent, Paul Lindenberg—censored by the Great General Staff. According to this the chests and wagons of the Russians, filled to the brim with shells and rifle cartridges, were all marked with the Red Cross! That is as much as to say: "Take care! —Wounded men here!"

"This kind of warfare," Lindenberg proceeds, "is quite in harmony with the order found upon a captured officer. This was placed at my disposal by the authorities, and the following is a faithful translation of the text:

"Order of the Regimental Head to the 221 Roslawski Regiment stationed at Tapiau. It has been repeatedly proved that the crafty enemy has abused the uses of the white flag. (N.B. This is a distinct misstatement, for there was not even an occasion for misusing the flag). I therefore give orders that his white flags are not to be trusted, nor taken any notice of, and to proceed with the battle in order to conquer him, or even annihilate him. The Commander of the 1st Army, Adjutant-General, General von Rennenkampf.

It must also be remarked that the Russians make use of Dum-dum bullets,—furthermore that celluloid strips (cellulose?) have been found upon many of the prisoners taken to-day;—one detachment of prisoners that went shambling by us consisted of not less than 3800 men. These strips had been given them by their officers so that they might set fire to houses on German territory. Those which we tested burned like tinder!"—thus writes Paul Lindenberg.

A military surgeon, writing in the "Post" from the eastern theatre of war, describes an unlawful use of the Red Cross emblem by the Russians. He recounts: "Among the trophies which the army of Rennenkampf has left in our hands, there are some 80 to 100 cars of a hospital train at the station of Wirballen. Only a few of the railway cars show any arrangement for seats. All the others, which were all marked with the Red Cross, were full of infantry and artillery ammunition. In two uncovered cars there were Russian field-guns."

In this case we know at least, that the disregard of the flag of the Geneva Convention as well as the white flag was approved officially by the Russians and systematically practised by them. [1]

The depths of degradation and brutality which have infected the widest, so-called cultured circles of Belgium, England and France, may be seen from a letter which fell into the hands of the Commander of the 1st Regiment of Marines after the fall of Antwerp. This letter is written to an English doctor, Richard Reading by name, a volunteer with the 4th Company of the Belgian "Corps Mitrailleuse," by his sister, Jane Reading. The letter is dated Birmingham, September 28, 1914. This gentle creature writes to her brother: "I would like to be a nurse, I am sure I could kill one or two Germans." A *nurse*! Let us hope that the letter is an invention. But no denial of its authenticity has been received, despite its wide circulation in Germany and in America. And the letter simply cried for refutation.

And we Germans? We are proud to nurse and to tend our wounded enemies as if they were our own. And though this is attested a thousand-fold by countless neutral witnesses and even by the wounded prisoners themselves, yet the ancient, weary and immortal lies persist, and we continue to remain the "barbarians"—upon whom those "defenders of civilization," the black, grinning, low-browed Turcos, may afford to look with disdain!

III. The Slaughter of Defenseless Prisoners in Particular.

The Rules and Regulations of Warfare by Land decree in the frequently-cited Article 23 of the Convention of October 18th, 1907, especially in clauses c and d, that it is specially forbidden "to kill or wound an enemy who, having laid down his arms, or having no longer means of defence, has surrendered at discretion."..... "Or to declare that no pardon will be given."

According to the principles which we have already enunciated we wish to be extremely careful with regard to all cases

---

[1] The results are shown, for instance, in the Army Orders of the 10th Russian Army of January 11, 1915, which go to prove that the robbing of the dead and of the wounded through the Medical Corps was quite in keeping with the official view of things. ("Norddeutsche Allgemeine Zeitung," No. 64, 1915.)

which may have been reported in a greater or lesser state of war hysteria. The German soldiers, as well as those of the Triple Entente, have retailed many such tales of the butchery of defenceless prisoners. (See, for instance, the "Braunschweiger Landeszeitung," No. 258, etc.) An elucidation, or objective proof, as experience has shown, is exceedingly difficult. And yet, after a thorough sifting and testing of all evidence, the following may be asserted:

So far as the slaughter of poor wounded or defenceless men is concerned, the colored troops of England and France have achieved the most. As already stated in Chapter 6, all humanitarian rules and international observances have not the slightest meaning for these wild men. But according to the express stipulation of Article 25 of the new Geneva Convention and Article 3 of the 4th Hague Convention of 1907, the chiefs in command of the English and French armies must be held wholly and solely responsible.[1]

From recent material and data to hand I select what is given below:

1. The following is the sworn statement of a neutral foreigner, an American, who was in the service of the English army.

State of Illinois, Cook County.

Robert F. Meyer, now living at 4050 Washington Boulevard, Chicago, Illinois, after he had duly taken the prescribed oath, testified as follows:

"That he was born on the 2nd of March, 1886 in Chicago, Illinois, that on the 10th of September, 1914, he had fraudulently allowed himself to be enlisted in Liverpool, England, in the 14th Company of the Grenadier Guards, under the name of Frederick Meyer. He was landed with his regiment in Ostend, Belgium, on the 17th of September, 1914. The witness under

[1] A drawing in the "London Illustrated News" shows how the Gurkhas attack the Germans in a trench and murder them with their broad knives ("kukris"). There is a description beneath the picture which explains that the Gurkhas attacked a trench of the Germans upon the right wing, surprised them and threw them into confusion with their notorious knives. After the battle many of them dragged the men they had killed back to the lines in order to show their British confrères how successful they had been.

What of Article 3 of the Convention of Geneva?

oath declared that on the 19th of September, 1914, he was wounded in the neck by a rifle-bullet during the fighting at Rheims and brought back to England to the Millbank Hospital, Rochester Road, London. He stayed there from his arrival on the 20th of September 1914 until the 25th of September 1914, and was then transferred to the Caterham Hospital, Surrey, England.

The witness said further that during his stay in Millbank Hospital, he saw wounded German soldiers, and that there were at least 8 cases of mutilation among these wounded men. These were the following: 3 had both eyes put out, 3 had lost their tongues, and 2 their ears.

The witness further stated that the above-named 8 persons also bore other wounds, which they had apparently received in battle, and that 4 of the mutilated men had told him that they had been mutilated by English soldiers.

"During my stay in Millbank Hospital I was with Thomas Perry of my regiment, who also saw the cases of which I speak."

(Signed) Robert F. Meyer.

Signed and sworn in my presence this day, the 14th of December, 1914.

(Signed.) D. C. Douglas, Notary Public.

2. On the 26th of December the 22-year old musketeer, Anton Raabe, of the 171st Infantry Regiment, died after suffering terrible agonies, in a Munich Hospital to which he had been brought on the 1st of September. Raabe, who came from Thuringia, was wounded at Lunéville on the 25th of August. His wound (a shrapnel bullet in the thigh) was not in itself mortal, but the barbarous treatment which the unfortunate man had undergone at the hands of French soldiery, had 4 months later, in spite of the most skilful and painstaking nursing and doctoring, led to his death. His comrades, obliged to retreat before the enemy's superior numbers, and unable to take him with them, had laid Raabe under a tree, after he had been wounded in the open field, so that he might have some protection from the pouring rain. Here, towards evening, he was found by French soldiers, who tore the uniform, stiff with the blood from his wound, off his body, and robbed him of his pocket-book. In answer to his plea for water, one of

the Frenchmen poured the contents of a field water-bottle over his face. They then dragged the unfortunate man for some distance over the rain-soaked field, and left him lying helpless. Raabe lay the whole night in the pouring rain in a dirty puddle, his serious wound without any bandage. The German Medical Corps found him in this condition on the following morning, and took him to the field-ambulance, from whence he was sent some days later in a hospital train to Munich.

IV. Compulsion to Commit Treason.

There is not a single basic rule of the existing law of nations, not a single usage of war sanctified by time, which has not been outraged by the soldiery, and in especial by the officers of the Triple Entente armies.

Article 44 of the Rules and Regulations of War by Land forbids the belligerents to force the population of occupied territory to give information with respect to the army of the other belligerent or of his means of defence. This, as is self-understood, is still more applicable to prisoners of war and most of all to captured officers. Articles 4, 6, etc., absolutely forbid the threatening of a war prisoner with death should he refuse to betray his army.

Any opposite course would constitute an act of great inhumanity. If one is not permitted to compel a prisoner to perform "tasks" which have "connection with the operations of war," (Article 6) it is to be conceived that a still stricter prohibition would be placed upon any attempt to make him break his oath and commit treason against his own army!

It is impossible to imagine a more shameful or a more insulting act towards the enemy, in fact the whole hostile army, than the insinuation of betrayal of one's own comrades. It is unthinkable among all honorable antagonists.

According to a report of the "Echo de Paris," dated August 28, even this shame was not spared to German officers. This monstrous attempt is described in that sheet, as follows:

"The German officer was led before General X.

"Lieutenant, your word of honor that you will not attempt to escape!"

He abruptly refused.

"You will not? Then you will be put into chains."

A fresh outburst of passion on the part of the German. The General, who, observing him, believed that under this mask of impudence and brutality, he detected the coward and the braggart, said coldly:

"Enough! I must have information. I have 10 or 12 questions to put to you. If you have not answered them within 5 minutes, I will have you shot at once."

The German answered with these words: "I have already deliberated, and I am ready to speak. But I would like to have the assurance that no one in Germany shall know of it."

And he spoke.....

This story was told me by Monsieur A. P. Lemercier, a Professor of Caen University, and an honorary Deacon of the Philosophical Faculty. He also told me the name of the French General."

If this story is true—and I have not heard a single word in refutation to this day—then it must be said to represent the very acme of baseness. Either the whole story is a lie—in which case we must set it among the millions of other lies concocted by the "holy" alliance,—or the story is *not* a lie. In that case all must have taken place as represented. A German officer, under the threat of death, was forced to give "information," —that is betray his army. Should this be true it constitutes an act which must inevitably extinguish the last spark of respect for the French in their conduct of the war.

What would be said were we to adopt this system with our thousands and thousands of French, English and Russian officer prisoners—and strive to force them to reveal all the military secrets of the Triple Entente? Reprisals such as this would do away with the last vestige of chivalry in this war, a war which already represents all the lowest instincts of the Tartar and the Hottentot!

I greatly regret that the German press paid so little attention to the incident which I have described in the foregoing, It is something so despicable that no judgment can be too severe for it—whether the tale be true or not. For even if it be untrue, as I assume it to be, for I have too high an opinion of the honor of our officer's corps to imagine that a knave of this sort would be found among them, even then the circulation of such a yarn is in itself a low and unworthy act. But if the account be true, then the vileness of the affair stains the reputation of the general in question as well as those that make capital out of it. For the cowardice of a single officer they barter the degradation of a system which meets the approval of a French commander of high standing, and *reflects upon his entire nation.* The German army authorities certainly have the best of reasons for endeavoring to clear up the case, and I trust that this may be done.

V. Other Various Breaches of the Rules of War by the Triple Alliance. (Premiums for Murder, for Espionage by Neutrals, the Utilization of Convicts, etc. The use of Civilians as Screens. The Recruiting of German Civil Prisoners of War in France for the Foreign Legion. Other Instances of Unlawful Weapons.)

War is a "bloody trade," it should nevertheless remain a "respectable trade." All nations which may be considered as affected by a modern war have ratified these conclusions at the two Hague Conferences, and that frequently in eloquent language, as in the introduction to the IVth Agreement of the 18th October, 1907.

The nations still lack a complete international code of war. The so-called Rules of Warfare by Land are merely intended as a sort of provisional regulation. For those fields to which no rules as yet apply, the general basis of common law is the determining factor. The general population and the combatants alike are to remain "under the protection and the control of the principles of Common Law, such as are customary *among civilized peoples* and according to the laws of humanity and the demands of the public conscience."

1. War should be "honest and open war" and not murderous assassination. This is not only an express stipulation of the rules of war, but a time-honored edict, perhaps the most fundamental principle in the war-code of civilized peoples. A perusal of this document will show how little attention is paid to the observance of these conditions to-day. Among the

oldest, but nevertheless most heinous of these breaches, I count the *incitement to assassination*.

A public offer of a large money premium by Great Britain for the destruction of German ships was recently announced. This means nothing less than the incitement to an illegal espionage on the part of neutrals, especially of neutral skippers. This creates, we perceive, an international method of procedure of a most peculiar nature, for the English fleet is certainly not in need of any such "premiums." To assume that the English fleet would require any such offer to induce it to search for and attack German ships, would be to cast an aspersion upon England's entire navy and its methods in war. The offering of this premium can only be considered as an inducement to neutrals; thus: Betray to us the position of German ships, so that it may be possible for us to surprise and overpower them under favorable circumstances. This inducement to a breach of neutrality by means of premiums may be easily apprehended to be in the highest degree an immoral act, and in distinct violation of the 13th Agreement of the 2nd Hague Conference, not to speak of all international ethics.

2. That one is justified in assuming that the English have the worst intentions and ends in view, is proved by the communication published in a neutral newspaper, the "Neue Zürcher Zeitung." The facts have been proved to be beyond all dispute.

"It was reported that a division of English Sappers had been captured by the Germans. On closer inspection, the troops proved to be liberated gaol-birds and negroes, the scum of the London slums. Each one of this gang had received thirty-five Pounds, and was then taken to France and let loose."

Is there any cause for wonder that military service in England is regarded as something of a disgrace?

"The English nation, regarded as a people, forms a most estimable unit of human beings in relation to each other, but regarded as a State in relation to others, it is the most pernicious, high-handed and domineering of any in the world!" says Kant.

The attempt to bribe Adler Christensen, the Norwegian

servant of the Irish leader, Sir Roger Casement, to murder his master, or deliver him as a prisoner to England, is in the manner of its execution, one of the most scoundrelly plots which have been hatched in the last hundred years. M. de C. Findlay, the Minister of Great Britain, acting under the instructions of his Government, hereby committed a most barefaced violation of international law. How the English Government, in a neutral state, was able to guarantee immunity to a hired assassin and betrayer of his benefactor, together with transportation, if he so desired, to the United States, will be a matter for later investigation. In any case, this atrocious crime, which must cause the English Government to be despised by every decent person, shows such an extreme degree of unscrupulousness and high-handed treatment of neutral nations, that even the greatest Anglophiles among them must have their eyes opened.

It may be perceived that there is a plenitude of vile schemes made use of in this gigantic struggle, schemes such as no other war in the history of the world has in any manner approached.[1]

3. Special attention must be devoted to the utilisation of women and children as shields against bullets, an act which is in distinct violation of international law, and in particular favor with the Russians.

The "Norddeutsche Allgemeine Zeitung" of the 14th November, 1914, writes officially as follows:

"A particularly gross example of barbaric warfare has recently been given by the Russians at Tomaszow in Poland. Official enquiries with regard to the report that the Russians had driven enemy civilians before them as protection against

[1] The English "silver bullets" which were to have assisted this assassination seem to have exerted their evil effects elsewhere, and not only with the so-called neutral press. A similar case to that of Sir Roger Casement is afforded by the announcement in the "Kölnische Zeitung" during the middle of February, of the monstrous attempt to bribe the Captain of a Dutch steamer. This man was offered ten thousand pounds if he would sink his ship and declare that it had been done by the Germans. Upon a similar moral plane are certain advertisements in the London "Times," according to the "Basler Anzeiger" of the 22nd February, 1915, as for example: "Someone requiring a loan" offers as security the killing of eight Germans, and there are basenesses similarly vile, such as reveal the deep moral decay of England

bullets and in order to make it impossible for our troops to fire, led to the following evidence. The Cavalry regiment of Landwehr, No. .., reported as follows to Headquarters on the 31st October: "That the battalion of Landwehr which was to support the cavalry regiment had to take up a position at Tomaszow on the south bank of the Piliza, on the 29th October, during a rear-guard action. The men then observed that the Russians who were coming up from a northerly direction were driving before them numbers of the inhabitants of Tomaszow, among them women and children, along the main road, just as they had already done in Kipanen and Sendrowen, near Willenberg, in East Prussia. This was to shield themselves against the fire of our troops. As strong Russian divisions sought to protect themselves in this manner, and approached to within four hundred metres behind these living shields, our men were at last forced to shoot, whereby it was not possible to avoid wounding some of these civilians."

From the Austrian War Press Bureau, Vienna, March 9th, (Wolff's Agency) it is reported:

"A Russian *parliamentaire* appeared this afternoon before the fortified position north of Radworna, who bore word from the Russian commander that to-morrow forenoon some fifteen hundred Jewish families which had been assembled during the day at Kamiona and Tysmieniczany would be transported across the Russian lines into those of the Austrians and Hungarians. As the Jewish families feared that they would be shot at by the Austrians, the *parliamentaire* had appeared to give due warning. By means of this unheard-of brutal action, the enemy was enabled to drive thousands of non-combatants whom he had deprived of food and shelter, like a herd of cattle before his lines, so that without danger to himself he might approach the Austrian positions. The carrying-out of this villainous intention remained unaccomplished at the last moment, inasmuch as the end in view was so obvious as to be immediately perceived."

This shield formed by the bodies of poor women and innocent children may well be stigmatized as one of the primal blots upon the conduct of war. To the same category belongs the alleged trick of the English of protecting themselves and their fleet against aerial attack by placing German wounded and prisoners, among them some civilians, upon ships in Portsmouth and other places. According to an Amsterdam communication of the 25th January, 1915, Lieutenant Atherstane-Robbs declared that over twelve hundred (including two hundred wounded) were used in this manner as a protective shield. An exact confirmation of the *intention,* which naturally would be the very apex of dastardliness, is in my opinion, not likely to be forthcoming, serious as the suspicion may be.

VI. Concerning the Recruiting Among German Civil Prisoners in France, in Particular for the Foreign Legion:

That mockery of all modern social reform, the French Foreign Legion, is an institution which cries for reform at the conclusion of peace.

German civil prisoners who have returned to their country from France, have given abundant testimony to the effect that in those concentration camps in which Germans and Austrians of military age were confined, all sorts of attempts were made both by persuasion and by threats to induce the young men to join the Foreign Legion. It is charged that the miserable food, the wretched housing and the brutal treatment were all devoted toward one end, that is to say, to making conditions in the camps so intolerable to the young prisoners that they would choose service in the Foreign Legion as the lesser of two evils.

A number of sworn declarations are now available with respect to this recruiting for the Foreign Legion, from which it appears that these efforts of the French authorities have, unfortunately not been entirely in vain.

There is not the slightest doubt that both from the standpoint of international law (Articles 4—7 of the Regulations and Laws of the War on Land) as well as from that of ordinary morals, recruiting such as this, carried on under the pressure of force and persuasion, constitutes a peculiarly base violation of the laws of the nations. It is in fact a greater wrong than the violation of the two analogous articles, 44 and 45 of the laws of land warfare which are designed to protect free populations from the oppression of the enemy, since the confinement of civilians is in itself a trespass upon the rights of civilians as laid down in the international code.

CHAPTER XII.

Russian Atrocities in East Prussia.

"Russia is the greatest danger to the Peace of Europe."

Sir Edward Grey in the Spring of 1914.

A. A veritable mockery of all conventions that exist between civilized nations, all laws and customs, even those that are held most venerable and inviolate in war, not to mention all considerations of humanity, is afforded by the attitude of the allies of the two Western Powers. These nations which riot in orgies of hollow phrases regarding liberty and righteousness and strive to horrify the world with the acts of the barbarian Germans through the utterances of Messieurs Huysmann, Vandervelde *e tutti quanti*,—gentlemen who appear to have forgotten all their former remarks concerning the "Blood-stained Czar," and "the most hideous despotism the world has ever seen," for which potentate and power they are now content to act as helpers and as commercial travellers,—are silent where they were once indignant. Even in the furtive and falsified proclamations of the International Bureau of Social Democracy their spokesmen dare utter no word in criticism of this arch-enemy of all liberty and all justice.

Thousands of Social Democrats, the comrades of these remarkable "democrats" *à la* Sembat, Guesde and their like, now withering in the dungeons of Russia, will learn with mixed emotions of the attitude assumed by their confreres who dare utter no word of protest against Russia's manner of making war, and whose Chauvinism could scarcely be exceeded by the most feudal of the Royalists and Bonapartists. It is a veritable *collapse of the entire structure of Socialistic Internationalism.*

The monstrous acts perpetrated by the Russians from the 10th of August to the beginning of September, until the great Field Marshall General von Hindenburg and his brave troops drove them into the swamps of the Masurian Lakes, shall not be presented in detail here. The official reports with regard to these atrocities are being published and will present a complete picture of these Hunnish cruelties, in particular those committed by the Cossack hordes. A few specimen cases are nevertheless given below.

We would like to say that we make no attempt to generalize over the specific instances that we produce. We are aware that even in East Prussia there were single instances of well-disciplined Russian troops conducting themselves in a proper manner and that their officers sometimes gave warning of the shameful outrages committed by those that followed them, and were sincerely concerned as to the doings of the Cossack ruffians. But these, unfortunately, were exceptions. The average Russian troops, especially the Cossacks as a whole, showed to even greater disadvantage when compared with these exemplary few. And month by month the character of the Russian soldiery grew from bad to worse.

An official communication of the middle of September contains the following:

"The continuation of the investigations instituted by the authorities with regard to the devastations by the Russian troops in East Prussia, has now taken the form of a thoroughgoing examination of the inhabitants of the destroyed places, in so far as these may still be alive.

These examinations have proved beyond all possible doubt that the local authorities had urged the inhabitants of these places to maintain the utmost quiet and to offer no resistance in the face of the invasion of the Russians. There has not been a single instance in which the people of East Prussia permitted themselves to make a *franc-tireur* onslaught upon the Russians.

Unmindful of the quiet demeanor of the East Prussians, the Russian commanders issued orders for the destruction and burning-down of all villages whose inhabitants proved too poor to pay the contributions levied. According to the information at present to hand 25 large villages were destroyed in this manner, twice as many heavily damaged and partially destroyed.

In the governmental district of Gumbinnen we have so far ascertained that 360 inhabitants were murdered. An exact record of the complete number of victims of the Russian soldiery can be made only at a later period."

This report was delivered at a meeting of the East Prussian members of the Reichstag and the Upper House at the end of October, with the remark that not less than a thousand civilians in East Prussia had been murdered without the slightest provocation by the Russian soldiery.

The damage to furniture alone amounts to over 20 million marks; the entire contents of 80,000 homes were destroyed. The descriptions of certain places (as for instance, Lyck, Gerdauen, Abschwangen, Tapiau, Soldau, Domnau, Uderwangen and others) are altogether gruesome.

Apart from this, the *franc-tireur* warfare which was waged in various parts of Russia,—it was, for instance, conducted with great cruelty in certain districts, such as Kalish—was here and there replaced by another and more subtle method of warfare, concerning which we have a report from the Commander-in-Chief of the German Army in Russian Poland during the end of December. In this there is an appeal to the Polish inhabitants of the country:

"The Muscovite robbers who have plundered this land and dragged its inhabitants to Siberia, are now fleeing before the liberators of the Polish nation, that is to say, the German and Austro-Hungarian army. Though already in flight, the Muscovites heap one dastardly deed upon another. Agents and spies creep into the houses of peaceable Polish citizens, where they treacherously murder German and Austrian soldiers," etc.

This was all done with the obvious intention of inciting the German and Austrian troops to reprisals, and thus giving occasion to the inhabitants for committing acts of violence against the allies!

This manner of *franc-tireur* warfare is naturally in still greater opposition to international law than the Belgian and the French. It is the procedure of hired assassins.

Rolf Brandt, war correspondent of the "Augsburger-Münchener Abendzeitung," continuing his descriptions as an eye-witness, writes as follows about the middle of September, 1914:

"East Prussia is free. It has been cleansed of robbers and murderers. I wrote in my last report that so much had been proved that little more remained to say. The glaring fact remains that there is scarcely one dastardly deed of which the Russian soldiers in East Prussia have not been guilty.

"I was able to convince myself through the testimony of my own eyes of facts which Europeans would easily have held to be impossible. In order fully to describe the conduct of the Russians, it would be necessary for our rich German language to invent new words; our stock is wholly inadequate to designate these brutalities and bestialities. We Europeans and Germans found it hitherto impossible to imagine such things."

Like most correspondents sent to the Eastern field of war, the correspondent of the "Vossische Zeitung" relates the following details of Russian barbarities from a report communicated by Army Headquarters:

"Two days after the battle at Zorothowo, I found upon the road that runs between Guttstadt and Seeburg a troop of some twenty-one recruits, who had been attacked by Cossacks the day before. Either a leg or an arm had been hacked from each of them, and they had then been left lying upon the highroad. A policeman who had accompanied the recruits lay upon the road. He had been so fettered, with hands bound upon his back, that he was forced to assume a kneeling position. His ears and nose had been cut off. I had these mutilated men carried to Guttstadt by some civilians, but had no time to look after them further.

(signed) von Tiedemann,
1st Lieutenant of Reserves, Cuirassier Regiment, No. 5."[1]

At the beginning of October, the representative of the "Nieuwe Rotterdamsche Courant," wrote to his paper:

[1] Two further official communications from Army Headquarters are at hand from the same source, as follows:

"Private August Kurz, of the 5th Company of the Landwehr Infantry Regiment, Nr. 19, and Private Hermann Fanseweh of the 1st Company Ersatz, 152, declare upon oath that they first saw eleven, and the second nine corpses of women with breasts cut off and abdomens ripped up, in the woods at Grodtken." War hysteria?

It is reported from Heinrichswalde, a small town in the Lowlands:

"The Russian Captain of Horse ordered all inhabitants, including the women and children, to assemble in an open space. In the immediate vicinity

"In the Southern part of East Prussia the population has been pacified and has returned home, in so far as dwellings still exist. Important towns, such as Ortelsburg, have been burnt down to an extent of 70 %. The most ghastly deeds of shame were perpetrated by the Russians without the least cause," and so on.

In the "Allgemenen Handelsblad" a Dutch correspondent writes, in April 1915: "In the face of all this unnecessary cruelty, one unconsciously clenches one's fist."

The war correspondent of the "Vossische Zeitung" in the eastern theatre of war, telegraphs: "Here are two outrageous facts, which have been communicated to me from a reliable source (September 12th, 1914):

1. The Russian Generalissimo Rennenkampf, has given orders that a "specially smart" company was to search out all foresters of the Rominter Heide, and to shoot them.

2. General Martos has commanded that all villages occupied by Russian troops are to be burnt and all male inhabitants shot, even though these may not have taken part in the fighting or refused to give up provisions."

Thus the bestial propensities of this soldiery extend even to its highest commander.

---

of burning houses, half-scorched by the heat of the flames, these wretched people awaited their fate. Then the order went forth that all inhabitants, without exception, were to be shot. No reason was given. Hearing this terrible decree, the entire community of Heinrichswalde fell upon its knees and begged for mercy. Little children cried: "Dear God, do not shoot us dead." The parson opened negotiations with the Captain. Finally this officer permitted the women and children to leave. The executions were to be confined to the men. For two hours longer the parson used his best endeavors to persuade the officer, quite disregarding the brutal action of this man, who did not hesitate to pluck the reverend churchman by the beard. At last the Russian gave way. He nevertheless demanded that at least one should suffer death for all the rest. An old school-teacher offered himself. The Captain remarked:

"Well, since you are so brave, I will not take advantage of you," and allowed the old man to live; but the people were not to go unpunished, declared the Captain. They were therefore forced to bare their persons and to lie down upon the ground, old und young, rich and poor, aristocrat and commoner, and were beaten with knouts, some of them so severely that it was necessary to carry the unfortunate men from the spot. The Captain himself placed his foot upon the neck of these unhappy men, while a soldier held them by the feet and a third struck them with the knout."

The representatives of the Czar were also signatories to that agreement of the 18th October, 1907, pledging themselves to fulfil "the laws and customs established by civilized peoples and the usages of humanity, and the demands of the public conscience!"

Yes, the Czar is proud to be the originator of all those resolutions at the Hague, which his blood-stained vassals from the highest general downward now trample into the dust.

Not soldiers, not their legitimate enemies, no, but defenceless women, children and old men were murdered in masses by these ruffians. The orders issued by Rennenkampf and Martos are nothing less than a complete negation of all international law. They are the public proclamation of ordinary massacre.

A proof—a wireless message, intercepted on the 25th August, 1914, twelve o'clock noon.

General Postowski to the Commander of the 1st Army Corps: "I beg you immediately to forward to the 21st Division and the staff of the 23rd Army Corps. 7. 13 a. m. To Bek. . . (context missing). The officer in command to send out a company under energetic leadership with the order to shoot all foresters without mercy."

We have also to deal with a systematic and customary robbery of the most brutal character. The soldiers, no doubt, were still further incited by the action of certain inhabitants, who even under force, refused to commit treason.

The regulations with regard to the levying of contributions appear, as has already been declared, to have been completely ignored.

No greater outrage has ever been committed against right and humanity! From the official investigations made upon the spot, it is conclusively proved that in all cases the atrocities of the Russians were perpetrated upon an absolutely peaceful German civilian population, which displayed not the slightest hostility towards the invasion and advance of the Russian troops, and offered no opposition whatever.

The German Kaiser, after the great victory of the Masurian Lakes on the 18th February, 1915, gives vent to his impressions in the following words:

"My joy over this magnificent success is lessened through the aspect of this once blooming strip of land, which has remained in the hands of the enemy during many weeks. Void of the least human feeling, in the senseless fury of his flight, he has burnt or destroyed almost the last house and the last barn. Our beautiful Masurian land is a waste. Things that can never be replaced are gone for ever, but I know that I voice the opinion of every German when I affirm that all that human power may perform will be done in order that new and fresh life may grow up out of the ruins."

The French Press, however, displays an unholy joy over these atrocities, as may be seen from a dispatch of the Havas Agency. In the "Zürcher Post" we may read:

"Petersburg, September 23rd.

The Russians are retreating from East Prussia in the best of order, taking with them all supplies and field ambulances. Everything that they were not able to carry away was set on fire. The Germans were unable to obtain even a pound of flour!"

France as the unqualified admirer of Cossackdom and bloodthirsty Tartarism!

"Culture, whose tongue beslubbers every land
Now with the Devil makes a final stand,"

cries Mephistopheles in the witch's kitchen. Gambetta and Victor Hugo, the great Napoleon and all the heroes of history would bury their heads in shame over these degenerates.

B. In the face of the horrible atrocities of which we give details in this and in the following chapters, and which scarcely comprise a thousandth part of what happened, one is now able to appreciate the following political estimate of Russia as an opponent:

"On England lies the chief guilt; against England therefore as is always the case with near neighbors, the hate of the masses is still directed, no less because of her brutality, hypocrisy and her betrayal of the interests of Europe. But this opposition is entirely a political one, and may again be set aside. Against this, we have the great historical background, the centre of gravity of a great national historical process, the combat of the Occident with Russian barbarism. For centuries there can be no reconciliation between these two. From Peter the Great and Catherine the Second down to Alexander, all attempts to bring Russia into the family of European states and under the influence of European culture, have been failures, utter and complete. This is a fact which should not be overlooked at the conclusion of peace with Russia, if the Central Powers do not wish to be crushed by the hundreds of millions that the future will bring forth. Here the word must hold good: *Divide et impera!*"

Sven Hedin gives a description of the days of the Russian occupation in Memel, in a telegram from Königsberg to the "Aftenbladet." He arrived at Memel on the 26th of March, on the day after the Russians had withdrawn. The corpses of peaceful citizens still lay in the places where they had been butchered. Hedin spoke with a number of severely-wounded civilians.

Among these was a twelve-year-old boy, who had been struck on the head by the butt of a rifle, and a second Burgermeister, who had received numerous thrusts of a bayonet through the body. The father of a young girl who had died from the effects of outrage described the tortures of his daughter. The mother out of grief had poisoned herself with arsenic, whilst the father in his desperation had severed an artery in his wrist, but had been rescued in time by a physician.

A school-teacher of eighty-two years was shot dead without the slightest provocation. Many similar cases that occurred in the city and district of Memel might be cited. 458 persons were carried off, among them 189 women, and 100 children. Further, 63 persons were killed and 43 wounded, 14 women and girls were outraged.

As we may now see from the comprehensive picture obtained of the damage inflicted upon the Province of East Prussia, the following facts are clear:

"So far as has now been confirmed, 1620 civilians were killed by the Russians in the Province and 433 wounded. Figures as to violations and rape cannot be given with exactitude. According to reports up to the present the Russians carried off 5419 men, 2587 women and 2719 children. A large proportion of the adults were aged folk. The people who were thus dragged off frequently lost either their lives or their health. 7 cities, 75 villages, and 56 estates were either wholly or partially destroyed in the district of Königsberg; 10 cities, 292 villages, and 97 estates in the district of Allenstein; 7 cities, 205 villages and 83 estates in the district of Gumbinnen. The total number of buildings destroyed amounts to 33 553. Of these about one-third were dwelling-houses. The furniture of some 100 000 homes has been completely demolished, and in an equal number either partially stolen or destroyed.

In that fifth of the province occupied during the winter by the enemy, there was scarcely a single piece of live stock left after the enemy had been driven out. In all the border districts all the farming implements and machines were either stolen or destroyed. Most of the mills, tile-works, distilleries and dairies were systematically destroyed."

CHAPTER XIII.

Jewish Pogroms and Other Russian Atrocities in Poland, Galicia, the Caucasus, etc.

I. 1. Naturally enough, the dehumanized Russian soldiery whose worthy leaders have the impudence to prate of violations of international law, carried on their abominable practices not only in East Prussia, but wherever they were able to drive their "steam-roller," in their own land as well as that of others.

Terrible are the charges brought by Dr. Arthur Levy, D. D. of Lodz, in a letter to the "American Hebrew," written on the 24th December, 1914. We are able to publish only extracts from this. (See, for example, "Münchener Neueste Nachrichten," 21, 1915.) Dr. Levy, among other things, writes as follows:

"In Radom, the Russians hanged three innocent Jews without a trial and without a sentence. Among them was a man, the son of the famous Alexander Rabbe, who was famous throughout all Poland, a man who was reverenced by the entire community as a saint, and who spent his days sitting before the Talmud, plunged in pious meditation, a modest, self-effacing man, who did not trouble himself with the affairs of this world. . . The pogroms of earlier times are as nothing compared to the frenzied destruction of Jewish life and Jewish homes which accompanies the Russian army throughout all Poland, now wallowing forward, now backward, and ever accompanying it like a threatening shadow. Pogroms have taken place in more than 215 villages, and so far there is no sign of an end to the terrors. . . ."

On the Day of Atonement in Staschew eleven Jews were hanged in the synagogues in their gowns and tallises.

Two of the most highly-esteemed Jews in Kladowa were hanged one evening on the balconies of their own houses just at the hour when the Jews were leaving the Synagogue. The wife of one of these unfortunates was forced to fetch the rope herself. The corpses were ordered to be left hanging thus for twenty-four hours and the Jews of the neighborhood were not permitted to close their window shutters, so that they were forced to endure this terrible sight in front of their eyes. On the breast of the dead men a placard had been fastened, bearing the inscription: "Hanged, because they would not give change for a three-rouble piece."

In Schidlowice Jewish girls who had been outraged threw themselves into the Pilicier Pool, unable to endure their shame.

In Ostrowice the Cossacks demanded the surrender of the Rabbi Zaddik-Kalischer, who was to be hanged, because he was alleged to have favored the Austrians. The real truth was that, in company with the Polish priests, he had gone to meet the Austrian and German troops, as he had already done in the case of the Russian, in order to implore merciful treatment for the inhabitants.

In Klescew 150 Jews were arrested as spies and dragged off to Warsaw.

In Zyrardov, Pruschkov, Bialabrzeg, Ivangorod, Grodzisk, Skierniewice and many other places, the entire Jewish popufation was driven from the town.

In Lowicz, two young Jews by name of Sandberg and Fränkel, who came from Zgierz, were arrested for alleged espionage, and were hanged after one had been previously mutilated.

The same fate befell the worthy wheat merchant, Moses

Lipschitz, because he had done business with Germany—before the war.

In Bechava (Government of Lublin) 78 Jews were hanged on one day in October because of "espionage."

In Kramostav (Government of Lublin) many houses were reduced to ashes. Two hundred Jewish families, most of them with their women and children, perished.

In Lodz, 15 000 petty merchants were robbed of all their possessions and reduced to beggary. Many women from Lodz wished to visit their husbands in the hospitals at Petersburg and Moscow. This was forbidden them, because these cities were not within the pale of settlement.

In Zdunska-Wola, all the women and girls were violated. Even a woman on the third day after childbirth. Children of five and six years were not spared.

A woman whose husband was at the front died from the effects of rape. Soon after this the man returned home wounded. He found his child motherless and his wife violated to death by a "comrade."

2. Professor Georg Brandes has an article in the "Göteborgs Handels-Tidning" regarding outrageous cases of anti-semitic persecutions and their victims in Poland:

"In these cases all the edicts of immunity which had been passed for the benefit of the Jews during the war, had been broken in the most flagrant manner. Jewish nurses are denied the right to serve in the hospitals and lazarettes in the district of Semstvo. The expulsions of the Jews from the larger cities of Russia continue as before. . . In Moscow, a wounded Russian soldier who had suffered the amputation of a leg, was commanded by the police to leave Moscow immediately after the operation. His statement that his home was occupied by the enemy and that therefore he was not able to reach it, was of no avail. He was permitted to leave his leg in "Holy Moscow," but his other members he was forced to shelter elsewhere."

3. Prince Paul Dolgorukov writes indignantly as follows in the "Russkya Wjedomosti," a Moscow newspaper:

"According to the prevailing laws, a Jew must not be found beyond the pale of his settlement. Thousands of wounded Jews are now scattered all over Russia. Their relations, however, may not even visit them for a short time and close their dying eyes, because they have not the "right of habitation." Such services of love are possible only through a violation of the law!"

Similar reports exist concerning the terrible Jewish pogroms in the Naprzod of Crácow.

4. The Austro-Hungarian Press Headquarters reports as follows upon Russian atrocities against the Jews:

"As proved by official investigations, the Russians after the occupations of Galizisch-Dolhopole, shot one inhabitant and crucified a second on two firs which had grown together. They mounted guard before this martyred man for three days ere he died. A Jewess lying ill in bed was literally butchered and her husband shot.

In Dichtinez, the Russians burnt down 42 houses, including all the houses of the Jews, the public school and the town hall. The occupants of the houses were driven out almost naked, etc."

The truth of all these portrayals is shown by the following:

The journal "L'Humanité" published a call of the Jewish proletarian Socialist organization in Russia, the "Bund," addressed to the civilized world. According to this, most unheard of Jewish persecutions have taken place in Russia since the outbreak of the war. This address tells of Jewish persecutions in the military zone and of pogroms in Poland, even in Lodz; of mass expulsions, and emphasizes the fact that on the slightest pretext the Jews were summoned before a military court and condemned either to death or to hard labor.

The address closes with an appeal to the civilized nations to remind Czarism that even in times of war the conscience of civilized peoples would find words to condemn these disgraceful acts. "L'Humanité" adds that this account is the most striking "*dementi* for the reports of a certain press, which declared that the Jews have been promised political equality by the Czar. There had been no change in Russia's domestic policy since the beginning of the war."

A leading article in the "Novy Woschod" gives us a glance into the various afflictions that have befallen the Jews during the first six months of war, and declares, among other things:

"Hundreds of innocent Jews have been condemned to death; tens of thousands have been hounded from their native place; countless pogroms have taken place, and what is worst of all, a dense atmosphere of pogroms has been created. . . . (At this point the Censor performed his work) and during all this time Jewish blood flowed daily upon the battlefield for the benefit of its torturers."

But all this eloquence does not alter the fact that Messieurs Viviani and Sembat, Guesde, and their colleagues have grovelled disgustingly at the feet of Czarism. It does not prevent them from giving fanatical support to the Nationalists of this stripe, thus degrading themselves to the level of mere myrmidons of a Czarism such as this.

II. Not only the Jews were thus bestially tortured. Here is a proof of this: the war correspondent of the "Neue Freie Presse," the well-known author, Roda Roda, repeats the description which was given to him by the Catholic father of Limona, Canon Ledarski, in the Latin tongue, regarding the excesses committed by the animal-like Cossacks. The priest said that the Russians had conducted themselves in his own house quite properly, and then proceeded as follows:

"Cossacki autem in urbe virgines nostras defloraverant, cibos furtim coegerunt, pauperam feminam judicam septuaginta annos natam coegerunt."

Immediately after the conquest of Lemberg in Galicia the Russians sent for the Metropolitan Eulogius, and proceeded to introduce the Orthodox belief by the most forcible means. (This, in spite of Article 46 of the Rules of Warfare on Land.)

The "Universul," a neutral Roumanian paper, in two long articles towards the end of March (27th and 28th), describes the atrocities in the Bukovina. This paper says that the officially published documents are in the highest degree a disgrace to the Russian army of occupation. A vast pyramid of shameful deeds, of robberies and burnings as well as brutal assaults upon Roumanian inhabitants, especially upon girls and women. (See the Austrian Red Book, published in April, with regard to the violations of international law by Russia.)

CHAPTER XIV.

The German Administration in Belgium. Reproaches as to Starvation, etc.

The "Münchener Neueste Nachrichten" reports semi-officially from the Hague as follows:

"With regard to the accusations made by the Belgian minister at the Hague the day after the fall of Antwerp, to the effect that Germany in violation of Article 43 of the Fourth Hague Convention, was exposing the population of this occupied country to the danger of starvation, I am apprised as follows from an official source. It is affirmed that the German Government had already communicated to the Dutch Government, in its note of the 15th August, that it would in no wise hinder the export of provisions from Holland to the civil population of Belgium; but would even facilitate this by having in readiness trains of cars.

The Dutch Government, in its Note of the 17th August, expressed to the German envoy its sympathy with this plan, but communicated further in its Note of the 3rd of October that the Belgian Government was of the opinion that the export of provisions would have to come from Germany and not from Holland. The Dutch Government further communicated the fact that the English and French Governments were opposed to the plan of exporting provisions, since hereby Holland would obviously give up its neutrality, and that Germany would in this manner receive more food for its own troops.

This is the edifying manner in which "the starvation policy" is waged against Germany, under the abuse of the term "neutrality." It was intended to force Germany herself to provide food for the civil population of the occupied portion of Belgian territory. This territory was occupied in accordance with the rules of war, based upon Articles 42 and 56 of the Hague Convention. Naturally there is here no question of a violation of the neutrality of Holland. In the whole agreement regarding the rights and duties of neutral powers and persons in the case of a war by land, there is no decision that could be thus interpreted.

Of course the fact that the territory in question is in the power of the Germans is something that can not be disputed. (Article 42.) After the legal power in Belgium had passed into the hands of the Germans, the German Government was obliged to make all requisite provision to restore public order and to re-establish and support the normal life of the populace, and this, in so far as the difficulties were not insurmountable, under the observation of the laws of the land. (Article 43.)

This, then, is the duty of Germany: to restore the administration, to maintain the laws, re-establish the police, the postal service and the railways of Belgium—in the interests of the inhabitants, as well as of the occupying forces. The re-establishment of the normal public life, the press, open meetings and the rights of society would naturally first have to be considered with regard to the needs of the victorious occupiers. This also applies to the eventual summoning of the Chamber of Deputies. The old form of government has been suspended, and the carrying-out of the laws of the country lies in the power of the occupying state.

The "observation of the laws of the land" applies only in so far as there is no insurmountable obstacle in the path of the occupying force. This is a commendation to the effect that the maintenance of the laws of the land, to an extent compatible with the interests of the occupying power, that is to say, primarily, its military interests, is to be enforced. But where the military interests demand it, the existing laws are automatically suspended.

This naturally applies first of all to the military laws of Belgium, for example, the laws of recruiting would have to be abrogated. Since recruiting for the army of the occupied country would be wholly incompatible with the military interests of the victors, and recruiting for the victorious army is expressly forbidden by Article 52.

Germany immediately took the most extensive steps to restore the statutes and their administration in Belgium as well as in part of Russian Poland, all in accordance with the prescribed order of things. A complete German administration had been created as early as August. Of course the carrying-out of the laws required the co-operation of the officials of the hostile country. Without this co-operation everything must proceed through the central offices of the provisional German Government.

The statement which the German Government required from the Belgian officials "that they would promise in accordance with the resolutions of the Second Hague Conference that they would resume their usual activities in a conscientious and faithful manner and undertake or tolerate nothing that would injure the German administration" is in strict accordance with international law and embodies the ratification of the agreement of the 18th October, 1907, in its most solemn form.

According to Article 44 the population is not obliged to give any information regarding the army and its means of defence. Private property, the honor and the rights of families, the lives of the citizens, their religious convictions and church observances must all be respected.

The occupying power shall "as far as possible" restore public order and the normal life of the people. This also includes the best possible provision of the country with the means of subsistence. When, however, the military leaders of the country in question, which in this concrete instance are England and France, hinder the provisioning of Belgium by means of a blockade investiture and all possible chicanery, such as diplomatic protests to Holland, it is obvious that the occupied land must bear the consequences of this policy, which is that of the still *de jure* existing Belgian Government. It is a *naiveté* that borders upon imbecility to suppose that Germany, which is to be starved out, is to send its supplies of goods and provisions into a hostile country which, in violation of all international law, had carried on a *franc-tireur* warfare for ever a month. This assumption is actually a little too much even for the patient German Michel, and his good-nature which had undergone so much strain in Belgium.

A notice, published semi-officially by Wolff's Agency on the 24th of November, 1914, denies with commendable directness any intention on our part to decrease our supplies for the benefit of the Belgians. An American-Spanish Committee, with branches in many cities has from the beginning delivered, and still continues to deliver sufficient supplies to the Belgians by way of London. This notice also plainly describes in detail the method of delivery. It is here made plain that the German Government had more than fulfilled its duty towards the Belgian population. Moreover, it appears to me that the Belgians had little reason to complain regarding the treatment meted out to them by the former Governor General, von der Goltz.[1]

With respect to their precious art-treasures, the Belgians will certainly fare no worse in the hands of the Germans than under their former government. We have not only refrained from seizing these art treasures, but have taken means to protect them from all possible damage. This is true of Louvain, in spite of the criminal acts and treacheries committed there; and of Malines, despite the intentions of the Belgians who shelled the town; and in Antwerp, despite our own heavy bombardment. In Bruges and Ghent the same scrupulous care was taken of the celebrated treasures of art, though these, as it appears, had in part been removed to London by the Belgians or the English.

The system of gross vilification of the German army instituted by the Belgian Government, is the only possible explanation of the insane flight of a large part of the Belgian population, especially from Western Belgium, to England, France and Holland.

The German Government did all that was possible to ameliorate the condition of the people and to recall the inhabitants in order that they might resume their orderly pursuits.

---

[1] Reuter on the 1st of January, 1915, published the following message dated from Washington. "The Belgian Minister delivered a protest to the Foreign Secretary against the requisitions made by the German military authorities in various Belgian cities. These are supposed up to now to amount to about 57 000 000 francs. The Minister declared that the goods have not been required for the army, but were requisitioned in violation of the terms of the Hague Convention. Among these goods are quantities of cotton, rubber, machinery, tools, metals, preserves, etc.

According to the Hague Convention, everything that is directly or indirectly required by the army, may be requisitioned."

When it comes to a stoppage of contraband of war, everything is supposed to be required for the army; but in the matter of requisitions our enemies do not hesitate to set the narrowest possible limits as to what is required for the needs of our army, in order that many necessary supplies may be withheld from it.

One proof of this is a speech made by the Belgian Deputy, M. Franck, at Rosendaal, in which he enjoined his hearers to return to their homes.

There is no doubt that the German Government is absolutely justified in refusing to support the riff-raff, the loafers who refuse to work, and lounge about the streets with hands in their pockets. It is indeed even the *duty* of the government to proceed thus, out of justice to its own people, which cannot in reason, be placed in a worse position than the Belgian mob.

Countless reports and official communications regarding the social and political, as well as the administrative and financial plans and preparations of the German Government, plainly attest the fact that all the duties imposed upon the occupying power by Article 43 of the "Rules of Warfare by Land" are being fulfilled in Belgium with the utmost thoroughness by the Imperial Government. The Belgian people will soon realize how shamefully they have been betrayed by their own government and by the original instigator of their misfortunes, England. They will soon realize the true significance of this so-called German "militarism."

German power of organization, conscientiousness, good faith, stand in place of that greed of power and tendency to oppression which they had been falsely taught to fear. The errors of the past will teach them to estimate rightly the prospects of the future, and will serve to warn them against committing any fresh follies.[1]

[1] Germany's support of the Belgian population is recognized by Mr. Herbert Hoover, Chairman of the Belgian Relief Committee, who returned to London after his trip through Belgium. The "Vaderland" cites the following passages from the report published by him:

"The German army of occupation gives much more assistance to the necessitous Belgians than might be reasonably expected from an army in time of war. The larger portion of Belgian territory is occupied by the Landsturm regiments, whose officers and troops, having been torn from their own domesticity, evidence much more sympathy than would many a professional soldier. Many officers have been actively and even enthusiastically engaged in distributing food supplies and other gifts. No customs duties whatsoever have been levied upon any of the food supplies brought into Belgium by the Commission. All contrary reports are mere inventions. The army of occupation observes the terms of the agreement in the most scrupulous fashion."

CHAPTER XV.

"Private Property in War" According to German and International Interpretations.

I. Our government has protested in the most energetic manner against the incendiarism, robberies and murderous deeds of the Russians, who in their invasion of our borders, rode rough-shod over unprotected villages and farms and totally destroyed them. Such proceedings in a war between civilized nations are, as already made clear in another chapter, absolutely unheard of. For the most important basis of the Law of Nations, the principle which is recognized by all civilized nations of to-day, is this,—that States, and not private persons, wage war upon one another.

All wanton damage done the country, all destruction of private property, all curtailment of the natural rights of the natives and their possessions, not rendered absolutely necessary by the needs of war, is an infraction of international law. (See Articles. 1, 46, 47, 53, 55.)

The soldiers of the hostile forces are even required, by the laws of war, (Article 23) to protect the persons as well as the possessions of the inhabitants of the country which they have invaded. The book issued by the German General Staff upon "Customs of War in Land Warfare," expressly emphasizes these points, and adds that it is nevertheless true that wars against savages and barbarians "have not been successfully waged in our day through the application of humanitarian and protective measures, and that one is unable to proceed against such enemies without destroying their crops, driving away their herds, seizing hostages and similar measures."

Our troops in this war have behaved according to the same principles as those in use in the war of 1870, in so far as the necessities of war permitted. They have in fact, neither destroyed hostile property, nor plundered, nor seized it, except in cases where this destruction or seizure was rendered inexorably necessary by the demands of war. It is of course understood by international law that even the most extensive disturbance, limitation and even imperilment of private property, is permitted when this is, for military reasons, unavoidable. It is often necessary, for example, for troops to cause a certain amount of unavoidable damage to the country. The carrying-on of war requires the razing of many houses or other buildings, the destruction of bridges, railways and telegraph stations.

The inhabitant is obliged to endure these things, and also the possible requisition of his house and possessions for the shelter and care of troops or of wounded, and also, if necessary, the use of his property as an observation point, defence or fortification. But it is absolutely forbidden to commit any purposeless destruction or devastation in the hostile country, and the German soldier who transgresses in this respect is treated as an ordinary criminal. Not the slightest damage may be wantonly committed by the private soldier, but the greatest damage may be inflicted upon private property by the express command of the General Staff, as appears from the following semi-official observations in the German press:

"In Louvain our soldiers, who had been betrayed in the most shameless manner, were able, despite this, to save not only the priceless Town Hall, but also to preserve all the churches and valuable architectural monuments. This was also the case in other places. Of course, where *franc-tireur* warfare has taken place, in violation of international law, neither persons nor property can remain immune. This also applies to cases where the inhabitants forcibly lock their doors against the invader. Bismarck once declared: "War is war. When the soldier freezes, he must warm himself, and if he is unable to find any other fuel, he must make use of mahogany furniture. One could hardly expect that the living bodies of our soldiers should be frozen to death in the open field in order that their last words to the French may be: 'We have spared your mahogany furniture'."

Fortunately, the French scarcely penetrated 20 kilometres into German territory. Their conduct in Lorraine, especially in Saarburg, as well as in Upper Alsace, demonstrates in the clearest manner, the kind of deeds of which this people would have been capable towards defenceless Germans and their property, in the event of a French victory. Certain witnesses from

Francophile Lorraine report having heard the following universal expression of opinion: "In three days the Frenchmen have made better Germans of us than the Germans were able to do in forty years." This is the way in which "La Grande Nation" behaved in the territory it coveted!

II. Very peculiar conceptions regarding justice, enemy property and international agreements appear to prevail in the England of to-day.

The English "pogroms" of last October, especially those against German barbers, waiters and bakers, proved plainly that the civilization of the English mob differed very little from that of the Russian. Shops were plundered and robbed. Poor, unfortunate Germans, employees who had lived and served in England for many years, were brutally maltreated. These scandalous scenes were repeated on a much larger scale, in Liverpool and other English cities, on the 8th of May and the following days, when the torpedoing of the *Lusitania* became known, and the gutter press foamed at the mouth.

But that the Russian sense of justice, stigmatized as corrupt beyond bounds by the opinion of the entire civilized world and especially by English public opinion, approximates closely to the English idea, may be seen from the following telegram, dated London, October 29th, and issued by Reuter:

"The police-magistrate at Deptford, on the 27th October liberated a soldier on the promise of future good behavior. He had been accused of having taken part in the outbreaks against the Germans and had been found by the police in the bedroom of one of the plundered houses in possession of a ring and watch which he had stolen."

Precisely *à la Russie.* (Moscow and Petersburg.)

III. The Russians, during their flight from East Prussia, frequently adopted the method of destroying great quantities of bread and flour by drenching them with petroleum, but they reckoned without their host. General von Hindenburg commanded that this bread which had been so wantonly destroyed, was to be given to the Russian prisoners to eat. This was one of those humorous touches which even this terrible war is not able entirely to eradicate.

(Translator's Note. It should perhaps be explained that

the consumption of petroleum-flavored bread involves no particular hardship to Russians, who have been known to slake their thirst during this war with quantities of benzine, wood alcohol and furniture polish.)

CHAPTER XVI.

Various Testimonies of Neutral and Enemy Witnesses as to the Conduct of German Troops.[1]

We give below the objective testimony of various neutral correspondents regarding the behavior of the German army and the German conduct of the war. These reports grow more numerous day by day, and furnish the best answer to the unjust attacks of the foreign press.

1. One proof that the attitude of the German troops, wherever war was waged between the contending armies, without introducing the guerilla warfare of the *franc-tireurs*, was exemplary, is demonstrated by the correspondent of the Dutch newspaper, "Algemeen Handelsblad" of the 21st of September, 1914. This gentleman had penetrated close to Soissons, on the day of the first battle in that neighborhood:

"It is astonishing how soon the scene changes when one crosses the Belgian frontier into France.

"In Belgium destruction is everywhere, smoking ruins, scarcely one undamaged house. Here, on the contrary, there is no sign of war, and no devastation. I have spoken here with Frenchmen of all classes of society, all of whom unanimously declared that the Germans neither plundered nor burned. They were all aware of the devastation in Belgium, but not through the newspapers, for the Germans themselves had told them of these things. They believe, however, that these soldiers committed these acts, rendered necessary by the

---

[1] See Sven Hedin's book, "A People in Arms" which is a brilliant defence of the honor of the German army by a neutral. The distinguished explorer declares upon his oath that he did not write a single line which diverged from the absolute truth, and that he describes nothing but what he has seen with his own eyes.

attitude of the Belgian population, entirely against their own will, for the speakers themselves had not been molested in the slightest degree."

2. The Italian author, Vittorio Ambrosini, who resides in London, and who, according to his own declaration, was asked to furnish Crown witnesses to give evidence of German atrocities, wrote as follows at the beginning of October:

"My first impression on reaching Brussels on the 20th of September, was one of astonishment, for everything appears so peaceful that one might imagine that the German soldiers were only there on a visit. They are all quiet and respectable people, who pay cash for everything. You may ask whomever you please, but you will find no one who has suffered at the hands of a German soldier. . . A walk through the city of Brussels will confirm the first impression as to the mild rule of the conquerors, and their strict discipline. . . It is possible that the Belgians are still permitted too many liberties. A man may do whatever he pleases here, so long as he does not injure the Germans."[1]

3. A member of the American Government Commission, sent on the cruiser "Tennessee" last September, to bring back the Americans from Germany, writes as follows to the German-American Committee:

"I spent more than four weeks in Germany, during which time I had the best opportunities for observing how the German people regarded the war which had been thrust upon them, and what a noble enthusiasm, combined with a quiet and essential earnestness, had seized upon the whole population. . . A people standing upon so high a plane of civilization, and

[1] It is interesting to note in what manner the same Italian author gives his opinion concerning the German troops in the "Stampa," towards the end of April, 1915. He says, among other things:

"They have organized themselves and welded themselves into a single unit. And this is the new thing that they discovered, this was their might, their power, their pride, and also their danger. On the day on which their growth had reached its apex, the primitive in them again gained the upper hand, though outwardly they remained Germans in their discipline, their organization and their power of adaptation. Thus in the middle of the Twentieth Century they have been able once more to invoke the sacred springtime of their race."

capable of so great and glowing an inspiration, can never be defeated. *These people are no barbarians, but men of the noblest sort.* This is proved by their treatment of prisoners and of wounded: "Here I know no difference between friend and foe, for to me they are all wounded men." Thus spoke the head of one of the great local hospitals, and I found the same magnanimous spirit prevailing in the whole empire.

"I feel most strongly compelled once more to declare that the behavior of the Germans made the strongest impression upon me. And I have met no American who had not the same feeling. They all considered themselves fortunate in such tremendous times as these to have enjoyed the hospitality of a land such as Germany. All Americans, who have been able to observe this great exaltation of the German people, are of the same opinion."[1]

These Americans differ from the official English attitude only because they had the opportunity of seeing the German people in those early August days, and of observing their profound enthusiasm and inspiring conduct during the first weeks of war. They did not depend for their judgments upon a shameless and lying press.

The anti-German "Gazetta del Popolo" published a letter from Belgium in the middle of last October, in which it is declared that the German army behaved in the most exemplary manner. . . All that had been written about so-called German cruelties was the rankest lying and invention. The population declared unanimously that the attitude of the Germans was most correct. Also the Paris correspondent of the "Corriere della Sera," who found himself "by accident" upon Belgian territory, and who could hardly be reckoned among the friends of the Germans, was full of praise for the exemplary bearing and demeanor of the German troops.

The correspondent of the "Matino," who had gone from

[1] See also the Open Letter of the war correspondent of the "Chicago Tribune," James O'Donnell Bennett, to Sir Arthur Conan Doyle, a German translation of which is published by G. Reimer, Berlin. Mr. Bennett was a witness to the finding of 60 000 dum-dum bullets at Maubeuge, and he has given splendid testimony to the character of the German army, just as Sven Hedin has done in his pamphlet.

Paris to Tournai, writes a letter, in which he draws a very engaging picture of the German troops passing through this city on their way towards Lille. (See also the testimony of Sven Hedin, that of the Belgian Van Op den Bosch in the "Kölnische Volks-Zeitung," No. 1078, 13th November, 1914: "German soldiers are as complaisant as possible," etc.)

Colonel Müller, of the Swiss Army, who accompanied the German troops, writes as follows in the "Neue Zürcher Zeitung:"

"The fresh and joyous soldierly spirit, the splendid comradeship, the decent behavior of the German soldiers in the field, must make a strong appeal to every attentive observer. Firm as a rock is the conviction and the faith of every man in ultimate victory. Troops informed by such a spirit and under the leadership of capable officers inspired by the highest sense of duty, such as the German, are assured of performing the most tremendous tasks. . . During my last days at the front, in constant communication with the officers, my regard for the soldierly thoroughness, for the high degree of education, the sound conception of duty, the glowing love for the Fatherland, and the amiable comradeship of the German officers' corps was immeasurably increased. A true and noble attitude of mind, and a spontaneous, soldierly gaiety soon enabled the stranger-guest to feel at home, and caused his heart to beat the more warmly."

Thus do objective critics estimate the qualities of the German soldier.

Colonel Müller has also something to say regarding the behavior of the German soldiers towards the enemy, when on the 11th January he states that the inhabitants had declared in his own hearing that the Germans had brought system and order into the methods of supplying them with the necessities of life, etc.

Even the Agence Havas reports on the 30th January: "Several military doctors, who had been detained in St. Quentin by the Germans, describe the condition of the city under German rule. The spirit of the population is excellent. With the exception of the usual war levy which the Germans have imposed, there have been no violations of the rights of property, and the same is true with regard to plundering. Not a single building has been destroyed or set on fire."

Still more interesting are the following official reports, following an investigation:

A Commission composed of Frenchmen of good standing arrived at Folembray on the 2nd of November. It was their duty to report upon the condition of those who had fallen prisoners into the hands of the Germans as well as to investigate the condition of the inhabitants in those portions of the country occupied by the invader.

The members of this commission were: Descambres, the Mayor of Chauny Soulier, a member of the Red Cross Society, of the Chamber of Commerce of Chauny and a Town Councillor; Comte de Brigode, the Mayor of Folembray, and M. Navarre, wine merchant and Assistant Deputy of Folembray.

The Commission itself selected the places where it wished to make its investigations. From the 2nd to the 7th November, it collected evidence in two towns and five villages. The investigations were conducted by Monsieur Descambres. Everywhere he made inquiries as to whether any acts of violence had occurred, or brutalities towards women and children, or incendiary acts and wanton destruction of property. These questions were always answered in the negative.

Further more, several prisoners were examined. It was proved that their treatment was good and humane. The Mayor of Chauny bore witness to the fact that wounded Frenchmen, upon being questioned, had invariably declared that they had been treated as carefully in the German hospitals as the Germans themselves.

Special and grateful recognition was given to the fact that the German military doctors also attended the necessitous population, and that the German troops were everywhere supplying the poor people with bread and soup. L'Eveque, the Mayor of Sinceny, was of the opinion that the poorer section of the population were, to a large extent, anxious that the war be prolonged "since they were now receiving everything from the German troops!"

Faits qui parlent! If one compares these reports with both of the so-called books of atrocities, one will recognize the fact that,—leaving on one side the enormous influence of lies and hysteria,—the fury of international *franc-tireur* warfare must inevitably lead to the most unhappy results.

In a report from Royon, the arch-chauvinistic "Petit Parisien" writes as follows:

"The city has not at all suffered under the rule of the enemy, and the ordinary life of the inhabitants is not interfered with. The Mayor, Senator Moel, is on the best of terms with the Commandant; the German officers see to it that the inhabitants want for nothing in the way of provisions."

We would add to this a purely objective remark which we have repeated more than once and would purposely emphasize. We would never presume to say that our troops are incapable of committing acts which cannot be foreseen. Our soldiers, as we declared in a former chapter, are not all angels. No sensible man would deny this. And passion is responsible for all excess.

It is possible that young men who had never perhaps drunk wine in their lives before, might have succumbed to drunkenness in the land of champagne, and carried on in a foolish manner. It is also possible that older troops, and even Landsturm, made reckless by being torn away from their wives and children, may have gone beyond permissible limits.

This and more, we are willing openly to acknowledge.

But what we do declare with the greatest emphasis is that such cases must be considered as *rare exceptions* and that where they become flagrant, they are punished in the most rigorous manner, and that the magnificent discipline of the German army immediately roots out such exceptional cases. Thus the committing of great, numerous and systematic excesses, contrary to civil or international law, is absolutely precluded. Our splendid officers' corps and the troops themselves are deeply concerned over such exceptional instances. The culprits are invariably severely punished.

Should such cases as must naturally occur in a war conducted in such a manner by our enemies, become more numerous, it is certain that the German leaders would not hesitate to issue a strict mandate against them. It has not yet been necessary to issue proclamations similar to those which have been rendered necessary in the French army. This is the best proof that excesses are of the rarest possible occurrence, and that it is unnecessary for the army authorities to take any general measures against them.[1]

CHAPTER XVII.

The "Spirit" of the Troops of the Triple Entente. Plundering and Destruction of Their Own Country's Property. Self-Mutilations. Verdicts Upon the Troops of the Triple Entente by Their Own Officers.

It is not to be wondered at that the Frenchmen, in many cases, acted like Russians and Huns when they reached German territory (that is, Elsass-Lothringen) and that they committed all sorts of depredations upon private property, in violation of all the laws of nations. They have proved in *their own country* that in the matter of unbridled license there was very little difference between them and the Cossacks—against whose atrocities the Russian officers were again and again forced to warn the inhabitants of East Prussia. Classic examples of this insubordination are the following *official* communications embodying strict warnings against the unruly conduct of the troops, as issued by the French Commands. The text of these, according to a translation in the "Norddeutsche Allgemeine Zeitung," is as follows:

1. "The First Army, General Staff, 1st Bureau, No. 790, August 26, 1914. Special Order, No. 9. The General Commandant of the First Army has been furnished by the town authorities of Rambervilliers with proof that acts of looting and violence had been committed by soldiers in this town. These acts are the more to be deplored and condemned inasmuch as they

[1] See also the very enthusiastic testimony regarding the exemplary behavior of the German army in the declaration of the American Committee of Investigation in Munich, dated October 10th, as well as the testimonial of eight well-known University professors at Barcelona, 21st November, 1914.

Further, see also the war diary of the Fleming, Steyn Steuvels, who in an extraordinarily direct manner, delivers his judgment upon the excellent attitude of the German soldiers.

were committed upon French territory. The General in Command of the 21st Army Corps will immediately conduct an examination in the matter and bring those who have been found guilty of these crimes to the notice of the courts-martial.

(signed) Du Bail.

Approved copies for communication to all corps and service divisions,—as proclaimed on the 28th of August, 1914. The Commanding General of the 14th Army Corps by order of the Chief of the General Staff.

(signed) Masselin."

2. Grand Headquarters of the Army of the East, General Staff, 1st Bureau, No. 3190, Headquarters 1. September 1914. I have received a report to the effect that bands of soldiers in our rear have looted and committed acts of violence against the populace. This crime is legally punishable by death. The swift action of the army courts will enable you to punish the evil-doers, as soon as they are apprehended, with all the speed consonant with due formality. But should the regular jurisdiction not be in a condition to prevent acts which, under the prevailing circumstances, are nothing less than attacks upon the nation itself, I beg to call your attention to the fact that Article 129 of the Code of Military Punishment empowers a superior officer to punish a subordinate in "cases of justifiable defense of himself or others, or of the formation of bands of deserters, or through the necessity ofpreventing looting and devastation."

It will be necessary from now on to put an end to these crimes by means of exemplary punishments, since their continuance would imperil the welfare of the army. You may therefore, without the slightest hesitation, and pursuant to the foregoing, adopt the most rigid measures, so that soldiers who roam about in bands and commit depredations, may be rounded up and obedience enforced. J. Joffre.

Authorized copy for execution to be sent to Monsieur the General in Command of the 2nd Army Corps. By Command of the Chief of the General Staff. Dessens (2).

3. A similar order was issued by General Macher of the 7th Division on the 18th of August, 1914, and contained grave

charges of insubordination. The following communication may also be added in the way of further official proof.

Nogeville, August 26, 1914.

4. Monsieur le Sous Prefect: The entire population stood in fear yesterday of a bombardment by the Germans, and fled. During the day the 59th Chasseurs à Pied, the 211th and 220th Regiments occupied the surrounding districts. As unbelievable things had occurred on the part of the French before the arrival of the 220th—as may be confirmed by the commander of this regiment and by M. Dantremepuits, Lieutenant of the R. V. P. of the Cattle Depot of the 6th Army Corps —as they were in part eye-witnesses of these unseemly happenings,—I wish to protest most energetically against these various plunderings and outrages. I will merely mention today that the flag was torn in pieces and flung into a corner, that the sentries were insulted, the cellars turned upside down, the necks of the chickens and rabbits wrung and the animals thrown into the garden, etc., and, in short, thievery and destruction were the order of the day. I demand that an investigation regarding all this be made as soon as possible. The population is very much excited over these things.

(signed) le Maire, Huret.

These documents establish in the most irrefutable manner the truth of the statements made by many witnesses, especially in the district occupied by the army of the Crown Prince, as well as that of the 6th Army, that the depredations which had been committed and usually attributed to the German soldiers, *were without exception the acts of French troops.* [1]

Colonel Müller of the Swiss Army states that the French, as soon as they discovered that even a tiny detachment of enemy forces was in possession of one of their villages, would proceed to destroy it with artillery without the slightest regard for the inhabitants or houses.

[1] The excellent behavior of the German troops in Belgium and the North of France, where the *franc-tireur* warfare had ceased, was acknowledged everywhere even by French and English newspapers. Statements by the town authorities of Florenville and other places, in which this was attested, were published (see the preceding chapters). Also Sven Hedin's popular edition of "A People in Arms," page 125: "Devastation by Germans is never the result of mere vandalism or lust for destruction."

A request for the despatch of supplies of food which had been sent by 14 French communes of the departements of Aisne and the Ardennes to Switzerland on the 28th of November, contains the following passage:

"For months the communities have been exploited by the troops in the most disquieting manner. Of late French troops have been reprovisioning themselves on an extensive scale in our communities. They even went so far as to pour away the wine which they could not carry off. Only the absolutely indispensible things were left to the inhabitants. Yes, even the abandoned houses were looted."

A large number of letters from combatants, French, Belgian and German, testify to the fact that in all those places in which no cruelties had been perpetrated against German troops, the behavior of our soldiers was exemplary[1] and that in comparison the French and Belgian soldiery plundered, burned and robbed, precisely in the manner of those under Napoleon 1st and Napoleon 3rd.

---

[1] The spirit of brutalization which prevails in the French and Belgian armies through the slanderous incitements of the press of the Triple Entente, is shown by a number of drastic letters which were found on dead or wounded French soldiers. A few particularly characteristic specimens have been published by a German author, Herr Georg Queri, in the "Münchener Neueste Nachrichten." The originals were discovered in the knapsack of a French soldier. They were written on August 20th, and addressed to the man's uncle and brothers. The following exact translation gives only a few passages from the letters, but these are typical of the spirit that inspires these men:

"Oh, how I long to march into Germany! I have made up my mind that I would look up the nearest jewellers in the first German city I reached and pick out a few pretty presents for myself. And before I leave the shop, I'll send a couple of blue beans through the skull of the jeweller — good French coin for which he need give no change."

The second epistle is couched in a similar vein and is addressed to the brother and sister of the writer:

"We are close to the frontier and a few more steps will see us in Alsace-Lorraine. Then quickly into Germany, so that I may purchase a few pretty souvenirs for you. For if I am lucky enough to be able to march thither, I must certainly get some pretty present — and instead of payment, I'll see that the shopkeeper gets a couple of solid balls in his brains. One must not have any pity with these monsters...."

Such displays of the spirit of "la grande nation" evoke only smiles of pity and disdain on the part of the "monsters."

A description of French soldiers as given by a French doctor of the 4th Company of the 6th Regiment of Pioneers, in a diary which was picked up by a German officer and submitted to a great German daily, confirms this charge. Here we may read:

"Thus we came to Attigny on the Aisne, where we found a relay of the Ambulance Corps to which we handed over our wounded. The look of things in Attigny is revolting. It is like madness,—the flight, and then, quite apart from this, and the most shameful feature of all,—the *plundering!*"

The looting and devastation of a number of the houses in Attigny are confirmed by the statements of officers of a high German command. The officers reached Attigny by motors at a time when not a single German soldier had as yet entered the place. The inhabitants declared that the French troops had conducted themselves like vandals; they were glad *that order was established with the coming of the Germans.*

"The soldiers broke down the doors, drank up all the wine, all the alcohol that they found, and even sacked the jewellers' shops. Our captain had a *sappeur* arrested just as he was in the act of pocketing a gold chain. The case was clear: court-martial—shot dead. These fellows are no longer human beings—they are mere savage animals."

"An infantry soldier of the XVII Corps, who was in the habit of running away in the most cowardly manner whenever it came to a fight, boasted that he had killed a wounded German soldier by kicking him to death. He wished to take his coat from him—the wounded man would not let go. As he had no strength left, he merely gave him a few kicks. It is disgusting."

This is the story of the French military doctor.

The "Augsburger-Münchener Abendzeitung" published the extremely interesting diary of a French officer, on the 19th and 20th of October. Its genuineness is made clear by the dates, the style, and the entire contents. I select two very characteristic entries:

"August 26th. Towards 8 o'clock we were once more conducted towards Ch. We discovered with joy that the enemy had retreated along the whole front last night.

Bitterness and disgust seize us when we see the terrible havoc committed by the Germans... The Germans conducted themselves like savages.

August 30th. To-day is Sunday. I was not able to attend Holy Mass. It is just 6 days since the Germans occupied Champenoux. The priest, an old man of 84 years, was forced to leave the village. There was no mass last Sunday, and there will be none to-day.

I am sorry to say that the looting of which I wrote on the 26th, was not done by the Germans, but by the French. What a disgrace for us! May God be merciful to us and help us to conquer ourselves, so that we may conquer our enemies."

In September there are similar, though more emphatic entries with regard to French plunderings.

If only all the shameless calumnies uttered against the German army might be so swiftly disposed of as was the case with this pious French officer! One might well say, "What a disgrace for the French army!" Such revolt against discipline, such disregard for the laws of nations, preclude in themselves all possibility of achieving a victory.

Here again we have the usual sequence of events: Charges against the German "vandals." A thorough investigation. Proof that the havoc is the work of the French soldiery. This was the case with the charges made by the "Echo de Paris" with respect to the Chateau Montmort Champaubert et Baye. Here it was proved by sworn witnesses that the vandalism of which the Germans had been accused had in reality been the work of French troops. (See the Memorial issued by the German Government, in which all accusations are completely repudiated on the testimony of a great number of sworn witnesses—Prince Ernest August and General von Emmich among them.)

During the reoccupation of Creil, excesses of such seriousness were committed by the English and French troops, that two men were condemned to death, several to life imprisonment, and a great number to heavy penal punishment (Middle of November). Nothing is more significant of the unmilitary spirit that pervades such wide circles of the French army, than the decree issued by the French Main Headquarters of the Army of the East and the Commander in Chief of the IV Army (beginning of January, 1915) in connection with the growing habit of self-mutilation among the soldiers.

"For some time," runs this notice, "a number of suspicious injuries among the men of various troop divisions, especially among the infantry, have been observed. It has been ascertained that these are nothing less than cases of voluntary mutilations committed for the sole purpose of escaping military duty."

In appendix 3 of this communication we find the following illuminating note: "By court-martial of the IV Army of the 18th of December 1914, the following men were found guilty of self-mutilation for the purpose of leaving the field of battle, and duly sentenced: One man each of the regiments 151, 34, 7, 149, 247, 336, 135, 88; of the Chasseurs 21, and two men each of the Colonial Regiment 24 and Chasseurs 19. The sentence was carried out on the 19th."

Equally damning is the following notice sent to the prefects and commanders of the 3rd Army zone:

"For some weeks the streets of Elbœuf and the neighboring parishes have, on certain days, been filled with drunkards. It has been ascertained that the secret sale of absinthe has never been interrupted, and that it is very easy to procure absinthe in bottles. The wounded men who go out for a walk on Sundays or holidays return to the hospital in a condition that borders on drunkenness."

On the 25th of March, 1915, this quaint official protocol was made public:

The Mayor of Roisy, Gustave Guillaume, and the *Garde Champêtre* of Roisy, Cyrille Romagny, testify as follows:

"The French Infantry Regiment No. 94 and the *Chasseurs à Pied*, No. 8, were quartered at Roisy from the 31st of August until the 2nd of September, 1914. Nearly all the inhabitants had left the parish a few days before. Only a few old men and ourselves remained. We have seen how the soldiers, in great numbers, penetrated into the houses in order to plunder them. They searched all the cupboards hoping to find money, and threw all the linen into disorder—so that finally the houses were completely looted. They took along linen for their personal use. Wines and provisions which were found in the houses or cellars were consumed or carried off. In consequence a great number of the soldiers became drunk. The homes of Messrs. Douttez, Barrois and Delonne were looted with a greater thoroughness than the others. In order to gain admission to the house of M. Douttez, the soldiers broke the windows, since the door had been locked. This house was almost completely sacked by the soldiers.

"Officers were standing in front of the house and were witnesses of the looting. To these I addressed myself, I, Gustave Guillaume, the Mayor of Roisy, in order to put a stop to this plundering. One of these officers answered me thus: "The owners should have remained at home." Another replied: "Rather for us than for the Germans." In the evening I addressed myself to the Commandant of the First Battalion of the 94th Infantry Regiment, Eugene Narbaroux, in order to forestall any further looting at night. He gave me some slight assurance, but the plundering continued in spite of this—the whole night and the following days.

"The troops left the parish on the 2nd of September, but despite this, several soldiers were left, possibly stragglers, who searched everywhere for money or valuables. As we two made the rounds we found a number of soldiers who were continuing the looting in the house of M. Douttez. In order to stop this, I, the Mayor of Roisy, clad in my mayoral scarf of office and with a revolver in my hand, demanded that they come down. Two of these soldiers escaped through a window in the first story, a third was seized and held by me. Owing to the lack of regular troops, I was forced to let him go—though I gave him a severe reprimand ere doing so."

The following letter expresses the opinion of an officer of high rank in the army of republican France, regarding the moral worth of the army, of French officialdom, and in fact of the entire French régime. He had gained much experience as a member in a Commission of Investigation in Morocco, and from these experiences he deduces the following damning testimony:

"When I had attained the end of my mission and cast a

glance backward, I discovered that under the protection of our arms and our flag, which stood for freedom, justice and honesty, there existed a most shameless system of brigandage. Fields, houses, persons, private property and public moneys—nothing was respected. As vultures follow up armies, so bands of adventurers, among them many of my subordinate officials, looted the land that had been entrusted to my honor. . . My written evidence against all this mismanagement was torn up, burnt and scattered to the winds; my legal witnesses were arrested by the dozen, locked up and banished.

After waiting two years, I now discover that all these crimes have gone unpunished, yes, that the perpetrators of these and their accomplices have been honored and rewarded. . .

Saint-Fargeau (Yonne) August, 1913. General Toutée."

Yet this is the nation which poses as the champion of civilization and dares to make false and abominable charges against the German Army!

The fate that would have befallen the German people and the German countryside at the hands of this undisciplined soldiery, is made clear by a large number of sworn examinations of French prisoners in German Courts, as published in the "Norddeutsche Allgemeine Zeitung" of the 20th of March, 1915. A feminine witness, for instance, declares, upon her oath:

"A sergeant who halted his horse directly in front of us, spoke about as follows:

"Nous avons un ordre du jour, du général, nous devons considérer l'Alsace comme pays ami et pas comme pays ennemi. Mais arrivés sur l'autre côté du Rhin, là nous pourrons jouer de revolver. Les femmes et les enfants en supporteront les conséquences."

In the following there is no question of the hysteria of war, but, as unanimously proved by a number of witnesses, of something issued as a command—as confessed by two French *Gardes Champêtres*:

"We have been commanded to conduct ourselves decently here in Alsace. But when we reach Germany and Berlin, they will all have to run the gauntlet"—here one made a gesture as though cutting off a head—and went on—"there we shall plaster the streets with the heads of children.'"

The expression may be the mere bombastic exaggeration of a soldier. But the mere number of similar utterances goes to prove that the French soldiers had received orders to use moderation in Elsass, but to carry on the war as recklessly and as cruelly as possible in Germany.

In contrast to the anxiety with which Rheims, Antwerp and other French and Belgian cities were protected, so far as military measures rendered this possible, let us quote the following, as republished in the "Norddeutsche Allgemeine Zeitung" of the 12th of November from the Amsterdam "Telegraaf."

"The inhabitants of Beerst, north of Dixmude, had a dismal experience. From Friday on, Belgian soldiers began to pile straw in the great and roomy church, and to pour petroleum over this. On Sunday they were forced to set fire to this venerable and beloved house of God. They felt the barbarousness of their action, so they declared to the villagers that the Germans would use the tower for observing their positions and for planting machine-guns upon it in order to shoot the inhabitants of Dixmude."

Discipline and subordination and immunity from the vilest forms of crime against property, do not seem to be much better in the English than in the Russian and French armies.

Evidence of this is furnished by the Order Book of a fallen English officer which was officially communicated to Wolff's Agency. In an Order of Day, we may read:

"Order of the Day.

of B. Coy. II Battalion Royal Scotch Fusiliers.

Since there have been many cases in which houses occupied by British troops have been plundered and much damage done, it must be recalled to mind that our troops are for the moment operating in the country of our allies."

The following passages from English Orders of the Day, are also very significant:

Order of the Day
of First Lieutenant Baird Smith, Commander of the Royal Scotch Fusiliers.

Terhand, 19. 10. 14.

Extract from the Army Order of the Day.

a) —
b) Straggling behind the troops.
d) Partial Civilian dress is strictly forbidden.
e) Insignia. The habit of the soldiers of giving away their regimental insignia is strictly forbidden.

Officers in charge of a commando must take the necessary steps in order to hinder any damage being done. If there should be any recurrence of the *already existing conditions*, the commanding General is to take the most rigid disciplinary measures.

(retranslation)

Such orders are the most infallible proof of the evil ways, of the "Hunnish manners" of our enemies—to adopt the language of the unspeakable "Daily Mail."

A soldiery whose character is thus estimated by its own commanders, as appears from the foregoing, and which finds itself in a very spacious glass-house, has no right to throw stones at an army whose magnificent military spirit in a struggle against overwhelming odds has already become a historical fact.

CHAPTER XVIII.

Ruses of War? Official Lies as a Means of Warfare. Misuse of the German Uniform.

"These strangers have lied away many of our honors and our victories, and every day they endeavor to cheat us of these—both the Englishmen and the French." E. M. Arndt.

By virtue of Article 24 of the Agreement of October 18, 1907, "ruses of war and the employment of measures necessary for obtaining information about the enemy and the country are considered permissible."

To such ruses, for instance, belongs the use of dummy guns placed in the open for the purpose of diverting artillery fire to the wrong spot. The approach towards the enemy lines by creeping between fallen soldiers, especially at night, though not quite beyond reproach, is also permitted. In order to deceive the enemy and cause him to believe that there are none but dead soldiers about, these men remain lying quietly among the dead, even letting patrols pass over them—a favorite trick of the French in Lothringen.

Among legitimate ruses of war may be mentioned primarily the placing in position of weapons, helmets, cook-pots, dummy batteries of machine-guns, etc., in order to mislead the enemy as to the position and number of the troops—also cries and commands in the language of the enemy. But it is not permitted to force or bribe enemy prisoners to reveal facts about their own men or disposition or lay of land—nor to foster betrayal or espionage by offering premiums. In short, all means, the effect of which cannot be controlled and which therefore must be held to be immoral and against the usages of war, are forbidden.

The falsification of despatches of the German General Staff and their circulation in foreign countries, has nothing whatsoever to do with such permissible ruses of war—as little as the forgeries and mutilations made of the German White Book and other official German documents, such as the speeches of the Kaiser, etc.

The actions of the French and English Governments, which did not hesitate to carry on a systematic and continuous falsification of these official despatches, and by means of the English monopoly of cable lines, to send them forth into the world in this mutilated form in order to arouse feeling against Germany —*is an undermining of the whole of that morality* which must form the basis for the entire code of international law.

An example: On September 10th, 1914, Wolff's Agency reported from the General Headquarters, that the right wing of the German army, after a successful battle, had been withdrawn, as the advance of fresh hostile forces had been announced. This official communication proceeded: "The enemy did not follow at any point. The booty of this battle has so far been announced as 50 guns and several thousand prisoners. The divisions of the army that are fighting west of Verdun are engaged in progressive battles." (See the "Norddeutsche Allgemeine Zeitung," No. 224, 1914.)

By means of changes and omissions this communication was converted into something that bore precisely the opposite meaning. Still more crass was the falsification of the apparent verbatim repetition of the German official report after the battle of Soissons. The most important passages, referring to the losses of the French, were suppressed in this. (Middle of January, 1915.)

One of the grossest swindles was the invention of a great English victory at La Bassée, though, according to a subsequent acknowledgment of the "Times," no such battle had taken place at that point. This unseemly attitude towards the German Government amounts to a deliberate deception of the neutral states —something that has been systematically carried on for months with the cooperation of the governments, in order to deluge the neutral lands with lies. The matter finally attained to such a condition of offensive crudeness that the Great General Staff of the German Army authorities felt compelled to issue the following official declaration on the 2nd of February:

"The French official bulletins regarding the events of the war have of late been full of the most monstrous statements, distorted to our disadvantage, and in many cases simply invented. . . The German Chief Army Command naturally refuse to enter into discussions respecting the details of such allegations. Everyone is able to test their worth for himself by a comparison with the official German communications.

Chief Army Command."

As might have been expected the Russian Government was guilty of even greater crudeness in the matter of false bulletins. At the time when Italy's entry into the world war was expected the dishonesty of these official *communiqués* began to assume monumental dimensions. The great Russian defeat at Gorlice and Tarnow (at the beginning of May, 1915) by which the Russians were thrown back some 150 to 200 kilometres and suffered a loss of almost 250 000 men, was presented in the Russian reports as a Russian victory and as an advantageous strategic move! And the same tactics were adopted, more or less, by the Allies in the West.

The General Headquarters reported officially as follows on April 28th, 1915:

"Our opponents have never adhered closely to the truth in their official *communiqués*. But now, day by day, these untruths assume greater dimensions."

This is substantiated by several peculiarly gross instances.

During April, 1915, the Lie Factory of the Allies worked under full pressure—after it was seen that instead of the French and English offensive, it was the German offensive that unexpectedly led the way to success.

A characteristic light is thrown upon the methods in vogue among Germany's enemies by the following passage taken from the official bulletin of the German General Headquarters, published the day after the defeat of the Entente troops at Mesnil. "The French prisoners that we captured here, we found to be in a lamentable state of mind. They trembled with fear, for they had been told by their officers that they would be shot as soon as they fell into German hands."

These are true Churchill tactics. It is by such means that the insanity of hate is engendered among the nations. Among such lies as these we must also place that shameless one of the "Corriere della Sera" which, obedient to the pressure put upon Italy during April, published the monstrous falsehood that the Russians were making reprisals because the Germans had cut out the tongue of a Russian scout (esploratore) who refused to betray his comrades! This cut-out tongue officiated first as the tongue of an officer, then as that of other persons,—a new *rôle* was constantly found for it. Then the Commander of the Northwest front, General Zilensky, some time in September accuses the German army of "poisoning" the wells with cholera Bacilli!—a lie repeated in South Africa.

Devastating Russian defeats, such as that in Galicia, with its 300 000 Russian prisoners (May-June, 1915) were falsified into "victories"—until even the "Novoie Vremya" attacked the Reuter Bureau. These lying reports were industriously circulated by the diplomacy of the Triple Entente, and given official sanction. The German bulletins were declared to be chiefly invented. Their veracity, nevertheless, has always been proved.

All those ghastly stories of the dead, or captured, or insane

Kaiser and Crown Prince, of revolution and starvation in Munich and Berlin, of the entry of the Russian troops in these cities, of the German Uhlans, who, "driven by hunger, kill, roast and eat Belgian children," are not to be conceived as jokes (see an instructive list of fairy-tales culled from the American press, in the "Münchener Neueste Nachrichten," of the 2nd of November, morning edition, also the "Münchener-Augsburger Abendzeitung" of the 9th of November, 1914) [1] but as melancholy examples of the self-defilement of nations which seek to make good their want of efficiency and their lack of success in war by a systematic campaign of lies. Such foul activities are doomed to be overtaken by evil and disaster. [2]

Among the permissible ruses of war there is no doubt that there exists none which permits the driving of the civil population in front of troops in order to prevent the enemy

---

[1] Even the "New York Herald," one of the most degraded and scurrilous of the Teutophobe organs of New York, mocks the lying reports of the American and enemy press concerning the acts of the German Crown Prince. This sheet writes as follows:

"Crown Prince Frederick William has become the will-o'-the-wisp of the great war. He has been murdered several times and also been killed in battle; he has died in two different hospitals, he has been wounded about once a week, his funeral procession has gone through the streets of Berlin at least twice, while the public stood with bared heads; he has been banished, he has been locked up in some distant royal castle, he has become a victim of insanity, he has suffered from fever, he has been publicly boxed upon the ears by the Kaiser, he has been given the chief command of the allied German armies in Poland, he has been deprived of his honors and rank and dismissed in disgrace. Many other things have happened to him since the 1st of August A brief chronological study of his career during the last eight months, composed of the despatches that have reached us from the European news bureaux, proves what a terrible worry he has become to the newspapers of the world."

The heading which the "New York Herald" gives to this horrible mess of falsehoods, is very fitting:

"The Crown Prince is dead, in disgrace, wounded, insane, leads an army in Poland and at the same time robs a chateau in France."

[2] See other details in the subsequent chapters. The maddest things, such as those published in the "Journal du Pas de Calais," I shall reserve for another place, The reading matter in the French and English papers which I have been receiving *via* Switzerland during the last few months has aroused in me not only a feeling of the profoundest disgust, but also of a sincere pity for these nations, so shamefully betrayed and so degraded in all the finer aspects of civilization. The condition of mind revealed is simply appalling.

from firing (see Articles 1, 2, and 46 of the Rules and Regulations of Warfare by Land). This was a method especially favored by the Russians (as, for instance, by the 1st Siberian Army Corps on the 18th of November, 1914) and frequently repeated by them.

Nor is it likely that permissible ruses of war include the wearing of German troop or officer uniforms by French and Belgian soldiers, as was the case in Lothringen, as well as Belgium,—as proved in particular by the letters of officers. Clad in these false uniforms, the enemy would shoot upon German troops from the rear or commit atrocities upon wounded men.

This is not only murder by assassination, which is forbidden by Article 23 (par. b) of the Agreement, but it is distinctly forbidden by Article 23 (par. f) "to make improper use of a flag of truce, of the national flag, or of the military insignia and uniform of the enemy, or of the distinctive badges of the Geneva Convention." Deception by means of trumpet signals, the battle-cries of the enemy (the "Hurrahs" of the Germans) are a different matter. These are ruses of war such as are comprehensible and self-understood.

The misuse of German uniforms is the more reprehensible, as it affords the opportunity of accusing German officers and soldiers of all sorts of atrocities.

CHAPTER XIX.

The Destruction and Misuse of Telegraph Cables.

Hand in hand with the misuse of the monopoly of the cables enjoyed by England, an advantage of which she made abundant use in disseminating false news to neutral countries, goes the lawless destruction of the German-American cable and other telegraphic connections,—acts absolutely contrary to international law. This cannot come under the head of a ruse of war. It is a moral outrage against all neutral countries. According to Article 54 of the Ordinances of War by Land, submarine cables may be destroyed or seized only in cases of absolute necessity. At the conclusion of peace they are to be returned to their owners and the damage made good. This proposal, to which England at first offered objections, was afterwards unanimously accepted upon the motion of Denmark.

There is no "absolute necessity" for the doing-away with all cables,—especially with the cable connections between neutral countries—at least in the estimation of nations which have been in the habit of conducting war honorably and with honest weapons as in accordance with the usages of civilized countries,—ere England made this the meanest war ever waged.

Soldierly nations have hitherto foreborne from using lies and deliberately false communications as "ruses of war" in order to carry on a systematic deception of neutral countries.

At all events the high contracting parties of the 1st and 2nd Peace Conference did not for a moment think it possible that a system such as this, so contrary to all the decency embodied in the laws of nations, all morality and public conscience, would be adopted in order to ensnare allies by means of falsehoods—a practise of which England in particular has been guilty—with the help of that cable-monopoly she acquired by forcible means.

How far this system of vilification—a system such as the world had never seen before, this slander of an honorable foe and his conduct of war,—extended, may be seen by glancing at the press of the United States, Italy, Greece, Brazil, Switzerland,—in fact, of all neutral countries. The most daring imagination would find it impossible to follow this torrent of calumny in all its ramifications, or to explain how it was possible to keep great nations and millions of contemporary human beings so completely in the dark regarding the real course of events in August, 1914, and the following months.

That this system of lies was in reality a formidable weapon is shown by the ill-natured attitude of a large part of the outside world towards Germany. This evidences itself not only in the usual commonplaces and platitudes regarding Germany's "reaction," and Germany's "militarism," but in alleged concrete instances of the "vandalism" and the "barbarism" of the German army. We shall exhibit a small crop of these things in our next chapter.

We do not pretend to claim that this system for the distribution of fairy-tales was *alone* responsible for the hatred and ill-will that was displayed against Germany. We are well aware that other ethical, historical and economic factors were here concerned,—all of which shall be discussed in another place. But one of the chief reasons was without doubt the unparalleled campaign of lies to which foreign countries succumbed during the first few months of war.

And, let it be said to their shame,—the so-called intellectual *élite* of France and Belgium took part in these unworthy attacks upon the German people. Apart from the frenzied attacks of such men as Maeterlinck, Bergson, Aulard, Verhaeren, Maurice Barrès, Hanotaux, etc., there were other poets, philosophers and historians who wrote without the slightest regard to the most rudimentary rules of exact logic or of authentic knowledge.

To what loathsome lengths of confiscation, suppression, and censorship of telegrams that sought to reveal the truth to other countries, Great Britain resorted, might be abundantly revealed by American newspaper correspondents, though most of them, in so far as they are still in Europe, dare not venture to speak out. Protests published by individuals were not of the slightest use. [1] Finally the "New York Evening Post," which, (after the "N. Y. Times,") is one of the "most representative American journals," protested in drastic terms against the systematic humbugging of the world by the English Censorship and the suppression of the true official German reports. The "British Press Bureau" is now commonly called "the British Suppress Bureau."

The "Sun" declares that "to see John Bull converted into an Ostrich is one of the most remarkable spectacles in history." The "Westliche Post" of St. Louis after bestowing warm praise upon the official German bulletins, speaks of the "manufacture of superlatives" among the Triple Entente Powers.

---

[1] The Scandinavian countries in especial have suffered heavily under this system. In spite of mutual agreements, England has determined to interrupt the American exports of cotton to Sweden, if possible, and that by means — of a cable blockade! For a long time past all correspondence by cable between American exporters of cotton and their Swedish customers has been simply flung into the waste paper basket by the English censor of telegrams.

Great Britain also infected its colonies in the most pernicious manner by means of this system.

"Permissible ruses of war?" No! If that were true let the greatest scoundrels command the armies of the future. Slander as a weapon of war, ignorance as a bond of alliance, and all the world a mad-house!

In this wise does that country to which "treaties" are "sacred" interpret solemn and accepted international agreements, such as the Rules and Regulations of War by Land! [1]

Does England really fear the truth—England that now goes humbly begging for help to all the neutral states, yes, even to savage tribes. Poor England!—upon whose possessions the sun never sets—even if the Truth does.

As to the effects of this snatching of the cable, let the reader consult the following chapter regarding the campaign of falsehood by the press of the Triple Entente." [2]

CHAPTER XX.

Further Details as to the Vendetta of Lies of the Press of the Triple Entente. A Method of Waging War Contrary to all International Law.[3] The French "Art of War."

1. In revenge for the establishment, step by step, of the incontrovertible proofs of the breach of agreements on the part

[1] It is self-evident that in the later course of the war Germany was forced to adopt measures of reprisal against England by cutting a number of enemy cables. This is in accordance with the old law that a breach of international rights forces the other contracting party to adopt similar measures. In any case the international laws relating to cables will not only require complete reformation and clearing up, but Germany must in the future see to it that her own cables span the entire globe, and that these communications are made secure at all costs—in order not to fall a victim for the second time to this subtle system of the wide-spread Lie.

[2] How completely Germany is sundered from telegraphic communication with the rest of the world, is shown by an article in "Electrical Engineering" (republished in the "Kölnische Zeitung") according to which not less than 11 German telegraph cables have been cut or interrupted.

[3] See the essay of the well-known criminologist Dr. Hans Gross-Graz,

of the armies of the Triple Entente with respect to the Hague Agreement, an attempt is made to fasten the same serious charge upon the Germans—by simply distorting the facts. He who knows the discipline of our troops, the sense of responsibility of the German officer and non-commissioned officer through the testimony of his own eyes, knows that 99% of these charges have about the same degree of truthfulness as the following yarn—a story which, with the maudlin outcry over Rheims cathedral, forms the *clou* of the counter-charges levelled against the Germans. It is also illuminating with regard to the value that may be placed upon the evidence of witnesses in a land permeated by the most insane fanaticism:

"On the 25th of September the "Westminster Gazette" published a story according to which the Germans had cut off the left breast of a nurse by name of Hume, who belonged to the Scottish Red Cross and lay ill in a hospital at Vilvorde in Belgium. She wrote a letter to her family in Dumfries, the text of which was printed by the "Westminster Gazette." It was related further: After she had written the letter the Germans also cut off her right breast, which caused her death. All this had happened because Nurse Hume had shot down a German soldier who had attacked a wounded man whom she was transporting.

This story, in view of its circumstancial detail, also made a tremendous impression in Holland—the more so as the declaration of the nurse had been witnessed by two Belgian priests as well as a parson in Hampshire and the Chairman of the Parish Council! An English journalist happened to make inquiries at 62 Trinity Street, Huddersfield, at the home of Nurse Hume. The supposedly dead nurse opened the door herself! She was fresh and healthy-looking; neither she nor any other nurse had been maltreated in any way. The whole story was a lie from beginning to end. (See a number of similar cases in Chapter XXI.)

A special Commission was now organized in London in

upon "Lies and War." In this, Gross comes to the conclusion that the entire action of the British people is, in its spirit of falsity, to be regarded as a "dolus, a crime," and not only as something "pathological." (See "Deutsche Juristen-Zeitung," 1915, Nos. 1 and 2, page 53 *et seq.*)

order to convict the infamous "Barbarians" once for all. A little later (towards the end of October, 1914), the fact was communicated to the English press that the sister of Grace Hume, an hysterical girl by name of Kate Hume, had been arrested. It now became clear that the whole affair had originated only in her imagination. All the documents had been forged. The "Times" in subdued tones announced:

"Kate Hume, a teacher in Hampshire, has been condemned to three months imprisonment for uttering forged documents. In view of her mental condition a suspension of punishment for two years was ordered, in the event of her good behavior."

The lie of this woman had gone through the entire world and, like all other infamies, had been slavishly believed. Once more there was no doubt as to the brutality of the Germans! But who took notice of the *exposure* of the disgraceful hoax? No one.

There was a similiar outcome to the affair of Mademoiselle de Brahandére, a woman of 40, at Courtrai, as tried before the German military court at that place. The entire series of charges against the German army proved to be a typical example of how the purest fabrications and horror-stories regarding German barbarism find their way abroad and are there received in all good faith. The defendant, like her brother, Dr. de Brahandére, confessed that everything was untrue. A story that resembles the Hume hoax is that communicated by one Parson Rapson to "The Methodist Recorder" on the strength of a story told him by a nurse named Sharp, another tale of horror, that was almost instantly repudiated,—all instances of typical feminine war-hysteria. The story of the shooting at Ternath (April 2nd, 1915) also turned out to be a mere invention.

Equally base are the falsifications and swindles of the "Matin," in the case of Dr. Fromlet and Dr. Reippt, two Swiss physicians, who are supposed to have held up the emperors of Germany and Austria to public obloquy. These two doctors have no existence in reality. The entire affair, like that of the Swiss "Postage-stamp Swindle," turned out to be a mere invention on the part of this low and incendiary sheet, itself a public menace. The same depth of vileness is attained by the atrocity story published in the "Matin" on the 22nd of October, regarding the shooting of a French veteran of the war of 1870. The Mayor of Thiancourt, M. Stef, declares in a protocol that everything stated in the "Matin" is pure "fake."

The same results were given after investigations following upon the accusations levelled against German doctors to the effect that they had treated English wounded at Rousselaere in an abominable fashion. The German Government made a full investigation of this tissue of lies and called four Belgian physicians of the place in question to the witness-bench,—Dr. Elie Delcroix, Dr. Emile Ameye, Dr. de Moine and Dr. Louis Scharlaken—as well as M. Jean Mahien, the Mayor of Rousselaere. All these gentlemen confessed under oath that this atrocity story had never come to their ears, and that, had there been even a slight rumour of this sort in the little town, they could not failed to have heard of it, in view of their prominent positions.

The physicians, who are themselves active under German leadership in attending to the care of the wounded, added that all the enemy wounded were treated exactly like the German, and that the German authorities had ordered that all were to be given the same attention.

There was as little basis for a story in the Paris "Journal" of the 16th of December in which there was a carefully detailed account of how Uhlans had burned wounded men in a barn at Ligny l'Abbeye. The Mayor and a great number of French witnesses testified under oath as to the utter falsity of this. All positive statements with exact dates were subjected to the most rigorous investigation. *The result proved to be the same in every case: a system of the most unscrupulous falsehood.* In the first edition of this work I have given a great number of idiotic fairy-tales (see page 300, *et seq.*) which I have gathered from the press of the Triple Entente.

The "Kreuzzeitung" (towards the end of October) has given an excellent example of the manner in which these "Hunnish" yarns originate, and are bandied about.

I received the following letter from a German-American who was living at the time at Bern, Switzerland.

"I heard a great number of horrible stories of "German cruelties" at the Hotel Beau Rivage and at other places on the Lake of Geneva.

Here is a specimen: A gentleman had driven in his auto from Paris to Bevey. On the way thither he counted between 200 to 400 girls and children who had fled out of Belgium and whose ears were supposed to have been cut off by the Germans. I was assured that this story was worthy of my belief because the gentleman in question was known to my informant and was also a friend of the person who had told my informant this interesting fairy-tale. Our conversation took place in a tailor's shop and "tout le monde" knew all about it. It seemed to be an easy task to investigate the truth of this story, so I obtained the name and address of Monsieur H. and looked him up. He was frightened when I told him the yarn and begged me to deny it everywhere! The origin of the fable was as follows: Before his departure from Paris the chauffeur of Monsieur H. had told him that a young girl was living in his "quartier" who, it was assumed, had come from Belgium and whose ears had been cut off by the Germans. He did not know whether or not his chauffeur had even seen this child. Such was the origin of this fantastic horror story.

Emil Ahlborn, Boston, U. S. A.

A similiar result was obtained in another case supposed to have taken place at Lörrach and investigated by an American (see "Norddeutsche Allgemeine Zeitung," October 9th, 1914, No. 246/14).

It would prove very illuminating if all tales of atrocities might be run to earth in the same way. By means of such degraded gossip, the effect of which is, of course, immeasurably increased by the hysteria of war, arise those innumerable calumnies which afterwards are sent broadcast all over the world.

II. The author in the earlier edition of his book proves that the various governments of the Entente are responsible for this campaign of lies, unparalleled in the history of the world, since it is they who give their official sanction to the press for the dissemination of these falsehoods. (See Page 302, *et seq.*)

The lack of veracity among the official military heads of the Triple Entente has become more painfully apparent from month to month. See, for example, the *resumé* of all the French official *communiqués* as republished by the German General Headquarters, under the date of January 24, 1915. These French reports comprised all the actions that had occurred from November, 1914 to January, 1915. The whole mass is permeated with falsehoods from beginning to end. It was published in German by the Chamber of Commerce of Paris and circulated in all German-speaking districts. But the maddest thing that has so far been achieved by military authorities is surely that French Army Order issued by the "Great General Headquarters" on the 8th of March, 1915, and signed, "Chief Army Command."

He who understands German conditions must simply ask in amazement whether this hodge-podge of half-true and fantastic "facts" and judgments of the "Grand quartier général deuxième bureau," is not meant to be an April fool joke. Such impossible fiction as this could be offered only to a despairing, wholly uneducated and hopelessly credulous people and army.

"Our victory is certain,"—such are the opening words of this proclamation,—so interesting from a national pathological point of view. "The French Army has now been fighting during seven months with the will to victory. From now on it will fight with the certitude of victory." This is followed by a rigamarole about the German losses, the "starving-out of Germany," the "defeats suffered by Germany's allies," the "crimes of the Germans," "the sufferings of the French prisoners,"—then details as to the "certain victory,"—all of which might be the emanation of a mad-house, but for its studied expression.

Let us merely quote one choice bit from the text: "We have seen in countless battles how the Germans systematically killed our wounded with the bayonet. The few who are taken prisoner are subjected to the most frightful brutality and tyranny in Germany. They die of hunger. Their food consists both mornings and evenings of a broth prepared from acorns; at noon they are given soup, and a mouldy loaf of bread for every five men."

The author of this book, as it happened, had an opportunity of inspecting a large, well-equipped German prisoners' camp on the very day on which this shameless bulletin was issued—

and was thus able to judge with his own eyes the falseness of this disgraceful statement and to estimate the profound corruption of mind by which it was inspired.

Again and again we are forced to ask ourselves: Why do all the neutral nations tolerate this unparalleled and monumental humbugging and deception without offering the slightest protest? Björn Björnson is absolutely right when, in an open letter to Georges Clémenceau, he speaks of "the inexhaustible garbage of calumny directed against the German people" to which the neutral newspapers succumb, and when he alludes to fantasies which "draw their sustenance from the sewers of Paris."

The German army authorities were forced to call repeated attention to similar "faked" stories of the French General Staff. The army order (1st Army) of General Dubail of the 5th of April, 1915, belongs to a similar category. It bristles with untruths, concocted to inflame the courage of the soldiers. Then there is the Order of the Day, dated March 2, 1915, with all its signs of a guilty conscience—which forbids all intercourse with comrades who are prisoners of war. It closes with the unbelievable statement: "In reality our prisoners in Germany are dying of hunger" (crèvent de faim). Anything!—everything in order to start hatred flaming anew!

III. There was complete cooperation in this work. The chief lie-organs of the French, and their tutors, the "Times" and "Daily Mail," do not merely feed each other with all this slanderous stuff—but also all the Francophile newspapers of neutral countries. It might prove an interesting, perhaps even grateful, task to make a register of all this idiocy, in order that one might see how much may be laid at the doors of these paragons among the civilized nations.

Great feats, in this respect were also achieved by a portion of the Italian press, especially the "Secolo," and the "Corriere della Sera." Follows an example: The Paris Correspondent of the paper repeats a description which, it is alleged, was written by a native of Luxemburg to the "Figaro." In this the writer gives an account of the fate that has overtaken his native land. Here we may read:

"The Germans seized the Grand Duchess, a pretty girl

of 20 years, and kept her a prisoner in a castle in the neighborhood of Nuremberg. The army of Luxemburg consists of 200 volunteers; the mighty German army deprived this body of its leader, despite its complete insignificance. The Commandant, Major van Dyck, and the officers, 10 in all, were shot and the soldiers transported as prisoners to Germany."

This nonsense was even denied officially by the Germans. And yet another leading Italian journal repeated this impossible rubbish! It was the same system by means of which the Italian people were hounded into the war. The English press, to be sure, used methods that were still more unspeakable. [1]

I wish to emphasize this fact: I am in no sense an Anglophobe. On the contrary—quite apart from many intimate personal relationships—I was, up to the 4th of August, a most unqualified admirer of English colonial work and English political systems. It is still painful for me to think to-day that the people of Shakespeare and Byron could sink so abysmally low as now to warrant only the hatred and contempt of all Germans. The English incendiary gutter press is chiefly responsible for this, and it is upon its head and those of the few well-known leading demagogues that the blood-guilt for this horrible war must fall.

Where hatred such as this is sown, a dragon's brood of inhuman barbarisms is sure to arise. The state of mind in England to-day is no whit better than that of France in its extreme fanatic excitation. This is shown by such verses as the following which appeared in the "Daily Graphic" of London on August 20th. This is a paper which is one of the favorite sheets of Christian England. The doggerel jingle reads:

"Down with the Germans, down with them all!
O Army and Navy, be sure of their fall!
Spare not one of them, those deceitful spies,
Cut out their tongues, pull out their eyes!
Down, down with them all!"

The consequences of such vicious agitation are merely an increased hate on the other side, and the firm resolve not to rest until the enemy is crushed to earth. Thus, in maniacal

---

[1] Sven Hedin, for instance, says: "The English press is one *systematic Lie*," and establishes this annihilating judgment beyond all refutation.

blindness and fury, the civilized nations of western Europe lacerate one another in their rage, until—too late—they will see that only criminal ignorance, lust for power, and the egotism of a few men have brought this unspeakable misery upon the peoples. And the fanaticism of this lust for lying infects one people after another, like some foul and contagious disease. Italy, a soil which offers a particularly good nourishment for the noxious weed, now leads this delirium of foaming calumny.

It is characteristic that even "L'Humanité" uttered a protest at the beginning of October against the shameful campaign of falsehood carried on by the "Matin" and the "Temps," and quoted several concrete examples.

"Spare us!" this paper cries;—"the families of our workmen are already suffering far too much. . . We would not add to their fears by creating new fears nor plunge them into the abyss of hatred and revenge. Now, in the hour when our comrades go forth to death in defense of the Fatherland, have at least the decency not to utter all these shameless lies. . . ."

IV. Extraordinarily significant, in fact, typical, is the following occurrence.

Lord Selborne, the Colonial Secretary in the last Conservative Ministry, published the following letter in the London "Times" under the date of September 12, 1914:

"On page 6 of your issue of to-day I read the following in a letter to the son of a London vicar from an officer now serving with our army in France: 'We have three girls here in our communication trenches who sought protection at our hands. One was naked, and all three had been outraged by the Germans.' And in another place: 'A poor girl has just arrived here both of whose breasts had been cut off. Fortunately I caught the officer of Uhlans in the act, and shot him with my rifle at a distance of 300 yards.'

"Permit me to remark that such statements as these cannot possibly be permitted to remain resting upon anonymous authority. The civilized world has the right to demand that names and all details be given. If the assertions are untrue, I am convinced that you will deeply regret having given them publicity in any form, and that you will partake of the feeling that our just cause has been seriously injured by such vilification of the German army. But if these things be true, then God and mankind shall judge. Would it not be possible for experienced jurists and judges, belonging to a neutral people, to hold an investigation under oath regarding charges such as these?" (*retranslation*)

Lord Selborne is to be applauded for his courage. We are able to meet here on common ground, and if the method he suggests were adopted, this madness and this slander would soon be put an end to. But the judges would have to be persons capable of forming an objective judgment—not creatures of the stamp of a d'Annunzio and other madmen. Lord Selborne is quite right and we must thank him for his frank protest. An end must be made of this devil's dance of lies.

All who know the quality of the German officer and the nature of the German people, know that the charges made are so monstrous as to call in question the honor of the entire body of German officers. We ourselves demand to be told the truth, the whole truth and nothing but the truth. There is not a soul in all Germany but knows that the German officer is incapable of such enormities even in times of war. But what we demand is an absolute and fearless clearing-up. Should a member of the German Army have conducted himself only in part as badly as our enemies have declared, he would have forfeited his life within twenty-four hours. But if the whole story, as we firmly believe, is merely another of those shameful lies with which this press attempts to blacken our name, surely the investigation or exposure of this disgrace of the nations must be given a chance for being cleared up before some international court!

It is not to be hoped, of course, that this yelling and filthy pack will change its tactics: reformations in opposition to one's essential nature are not possible. But we must seize upon specific and flagrant instances in order to show the world with what foul weapons this war is being waged against us. So far every accusation that has been examined in detail has ended with the complete discomfiture of the enemy. Let us merely recall such cases as that exposed as false by the Italian Deputy Leonardi—that of 16 Italian laborers being shot at Jarny. Let us not forget that atrocious story of the massacres at Magdeburg, which the "honorable" "Corriere della Sera," forced into a corner, republished in an obscure part of the paper. Nor must the case of Nurse Hume, already described, be forgotten.

V. Even in England the terrible danger that lurks in this unlimited vilification as a means of warfare is beginning to dawn upon the saner minds, as may be seen in the open letter of an English writer H. N. Brailsford in the "Daily News." Mr. Brailsford proves that the tale already criticised by Lord Selborne is simply on the very face of it impossible and incredible. He justly estimates the danger such slanders embody for the final conclusion of peace, and how difficult this is made through the propagation of such abominable yarns, the poison of which will tend to inoculate whole generations.

The following furnishes another characteristic case:

It is reported from Amsterdam under the date of the 26th of November: In Falmouth a "gentleman" by name of Samuel Phillips violated a little girl. The judge condemned this criminal to a punishment of 10 shillings and to 12/6d costs, under the stipulation that he would gallantly enter the English army and serve at the front. "Truth" which presents this case, calls attention to the indignation that has resulted in England regarding the deeds which the Germans were alleged to have committed, and goes on to say: "We need feel no wonder when the Germans declare that we are a nation of hypocrites."

This is a frank confession of the truth. We would confirm this fact: All that still remained of sympathy for England in Germany—(the vast amount of sympathy and admiration we used to cherish for the English people has been simply squandered and trodden underfoot by the official braggarts of the English Government) was finally destroyed because the English press, *without exercising the slightest discrimination or critical judgment*, simply trumpeted the most absurd and childish lies of the French press broadcast throughout the world, and deliberately embellished and intensified all that was mean and base in them.

This systematic campaign of falsehood, maintained by an abuse of the cable in violation of all international law, has called forth a hatred of England in Germany which is perhaps exceeded only by that now directed against the blackmailers on the banks of the Tiber. This feeling, so far as one may at present judge, seems to give an almost hopeless aspect to the possibilities of restoring amicable relations between the German and English people, relations that are absolutely necessary for the well-being of the community of nations. The anger of our people may be said to be aroused to a still greater degree by the ghastly miscarriages of justice in the English courts which are not ashamed (as in the case of Captain Falke, who was sentenced to six months' imprisonment for possessing a revolver and a camera) to stigmatize the entire German nation as a people without honor. (North London Police Court.) [1]

VI. The language of English war prayers as reported to us by Germans who have been permitted to return to their country, forms the very apex of pietistic hypocrisy. One of these official English war prayers, for example, runs in part, as follows:

"God, show Germany and its Kaiser how wrong it is to make an attack without having a just cause. Make it clear to them, that Thou canst not bless that which doth not originate in Thee, and convince them that all those who take the sword shall perish by the sword."

Another glories in such terms as the following:

"Lord God, now we have prayed for our own people, but true to the teachings of Christ, we would also pray for our enemies. Thou hast wrapped the spirit of the German Emperor in the night of insanity—Thou hast induced the German Crown Prince to commit suicide—now, O Lord, let Thy anger be sufficient, and once more be merciful to them."

Ought a sane man to laugh or weep at these displays?

But the abuse of the pulpit embodies a still greater danger. The most magnificent achievement in this line has been made by the ex-Jesuit Coube, one of the best-known preachers in the Church of the Madeleine at Paris. His audience was composed of the *élite* of Parisian society. And thus spoke this man of God:

---

[1] The original edition gives the text of foul aspersions upon the Kaiser, such as are almost unfit for the decency of print, and insults of the most unspeakable nature levelled against the German people—as communicated to "The Financial News," (page 311), also quotations of the most abominable coarseness from the "Figaro," and the "Matin," (page 314), also the "Gaulois," (page 312).

"The modern Attila has given his commands. He has proclaimed himself as the Scourge of God. No pity with the innocent little children—up, my Dragoons, and strangle them—such was his command. No pity for the honor of young women and girls—violate them! No pity with the holy office of the priests—shoot them! No pity for the museums—plunder them! No pity with monuments of art and historical buildings—bombard them! And these commands of Attila were carried out to the letter." Other passages in this charming sermon read as follows:

"Yea, the hour of vengeance nears. Yea, the savage beasts leap upon us, beasts more terrible than those of the amphitheatre. Nero may spur on his beasts as much as he pleases, and they may bellow never so loud, yet they shall be forced to give way and stain the soil with their blood."

The "Tijd," a newspaper of Holland, which could hardly he called pro-German and which has always been a warm defender of the Belgian cause, voices its indignation in the most withering terms over this monstrous abuse of the pulpit for the sake of inflaming ignoble passions.

He that murders women and children is a criminal of the deepest dye, but he who wantonly and light-heartedly casts such abominations into the hearts of the nations and breeds hatred and dissension there, is a still greater scoundrel.

VII. The disgusting polemics by means of which the Entente Powers seek to make good their defeats on water and on land, are laid bare in the following declaration of the middle of September, 1914:

"The undersigned American citizens who were present in Germany at the beginning of hostilities, hereby request the United Press to give the widest publicity to the following facts:

The reports originating from French and English sources to the effect that Americans have been badly treated by Germans are absolutely false.... All official German bulletins regarding the course of war have been reliable from every point of view, whereas the English, French and Belgian reports have been proved in nearly every instance to be false.

We are of the opinion that these false and distorted reports were sent to America with the express purpose of deceiving the American people and of arousing in them a prejudice against Germany."

This report is signed with the names of several hundred of the most influential citizens of the United States.

Sven Hedin, the celebrated Swedish explorer, who has himself inspected the fields of war, writes thus: "I should like to advise the neutral states to weigh the news of the war with the utmost detachment and critical judgment. Never before has the world had to struggle with such avalanches of lying reports as in this war. Germany is the object of calumny and of a systematic tissue of falsehood."[1]

VIII. We have nothing to add to these objective testimonials of neutral citizens as to German behavior and the German conduct of the war. But what shall one say to this typical and amusing bit of impudence from the "Temps," published sometime during the end of October. This paper in a leading article complains that: "Germany floods the world with news against which the short, matter-of-fact *communiqués* of our (that is to say, the French) Press Bureau cannot cope."

One might well say to an utterance such as this: "This is the very limit!" It is well-known that months went by ere the deeds of the German army were given a little of the credit that was due them.

IX. As is well known, a Commission for the investigation of "German atrocities" was established in Belgium as well as in France. Dr. Albert Moll, the First President of the Psychological Society in Berlin, expressed a very interesting opinion as to this: He justly criticises the unfortunate and unprofessional compilations of this commission, which revealed neither objectivity nor expert knowledge. He calls attention to the operation of a potent "mass hypnotism" on the part of the Belgians, such as made an objective judgment quite impossible. See the

---

[1] These worthy All-lies (to give them an American nick-name) do not even spare one another. According to the "Neuen Züricher Nachrichten," a Canadian illustrated paper by the name of "Courier" (November 28th, 1914) has the following under screaming head-lines: "All Belgian officers were bribed. German money bought them all, with the exception of General Leman, the heroic defender of Liege!"

following chapter with regard to this "Atrocity Commission" and its work.

The following points of view are also well taken:

"A rôle by no means small is played in the reports of the Belgian Committee of Investigation by the alleged violated girls and women. Whoever has had any experience in legal-psychological matters, is all too well aware how many such accusations are the products of an excited imagination. It frequently happens that girls and women build up all sorts of sexual happenings out of their fantasies, and then, coming in contact with some quite innocent man, compel him to defend himself against charges of immorality.

"As we have to contend with innumerable such cases even in times of peace, we are forced to adopt an attitude of the greatest distrust towards the report of this Belgian Committee of Investigation. It is well-known that hysterical women are peculiarly prone to accusations of this sort. It would be interesting to know whether the Belgian Commission called in the services of non-partisan, that is to say, non-Belgian nerve specialists? Should this not be the case the Belgian Commission has laid itself open to the charge of a serious sin of omission, for many hysterical women are disposed to make an immoral crime out of a harmless accidental contact. And is it a mere coincidence—that famous case in Belgium of Louise Lateau and her stigmata? It was in the Bois d'Haine near Charleroi that Louise Lateau cropped up in 1868 and excited the fancy of the entire world."

Dr. Moll calls attention in his expert review of the Belgian Report to the grave discrepancies in the testimony of individual witnesses and concludes with the observation that it is to be much regretted that the Belgian government should attempt to influence public opinion with such untrustworthy reports.

All that Dr. Moll says of the Belgian Committee of Investigation is still more applicable to the wordy statements of the French Commission—in so far as these have become known to us through the press.

It is unfortunate that the Germans waited for too long a period ere taking steps to refute in some degree the overwhelming slanders of the English, Belgian and French press. The so-called Investigation Committees, which by means of suggestive questions, were able to achieve the results desired, were not even supported by evidence taken on the spot by preliminary commissions. They all went to work and regarded the whole matter through the spectacles of national fanaticism. (See the following chapters, XXI and XXII.)

X. "Art," so-called, has also been debased for the foulest purposes of vilification in Belgium, England and France. The most pernicious products in this field are certain drawings by one Julien Felt, published by the Uitgave "Patria." They represent the most unimaginable and most horrible atrocities alleged to have been committed by German soldiers. The one thing they *do* prove, and that in the most revolting manner, is the systematic methods adopted by the Belgian Government for seducing its people into carrying on the *franc-tireur* warfare that plunged them into perdition.

Special efforts are made to influence the pious inhabitants of various districts by means of pictures which depict the German soldiers as blasphemers and violaters of churches. One large picture shows the interior of a church, in which drunken Germans, clad in the vestments of the priests, with a chalice in one hand and a wine bottle in the other, and their helmets on their heads, imitate the ceremonial of the mass, the while other German soldiers drive weeping Belgian women out of the church with the butt-ends of their muskets.

The following three flagrant examples are typical of the shameful abuse of the printed word and picture in order to cover our troops with obloquy.

1. The "Norddeutsche Allgemeine Zeitung" in a special edition of January 24, 1915, publishes a collection of photographs, which had been sent to an Argentine paper from Russian sources under the title of "German Barbarism," and "Graphic Historical Documents," and published by this paper. These pictures were in reality nothing more than pictures of pogroms, and therefore of *Russian* atrocities. And these were now to serve as "substantiations" of the lies levelled against the German army. The photographs represent murdered Jews, and not only were the features photographed, but also the Jewish prayer-book, the Talith, which was spread out upon nearly

all the corpses. . . One of the pictures dates from the Jewish Pogrom at Bialystock, in the year 1905, and is one of the illustrations in a book called, "The Last Russian Autocrat," on page 340. Two other pictures are of the Jewish Pogrom at Odessa in the year 1905, and are circulated in thousands throughout Russia.

2. Swedish newspapers about the end of December, 1914, pilloried another example of this unscrupulous method of conducting war. The popular Russian periodical "The Whole World" published a picture in a November issue, No. 45, which it had taken from a Berlin sporting paper. It represents the Kaiserin presentating a racing trophy to Lieutenants von Herder, von Egan-Krieger, and Prieger. The Russian paper gives a reproduction of this picture with the title: "German Robbers at Warsaw."

The text under the photograph is as follows: "Our artist, the photographer, succeeded in snapping a group of marauders, representatives of the German Army, at the moment when their hands were filled with stolen booty. . ."

"Lietopie Voiny" is a periodical that appears in Petersburg. No. 14 of this paper contains two pictures: "A Farmhouse in Poland Demolished by Germans" and "After the Retreat of the Germans." Both pictures are apparently drawn from nature by someone named Müller Petrow, in order to illustrate German atrocities. A courageous and highly-esteemed paper called "Kievlianin" of the 26th of January established the fact that the whole thing was a clumsy forgery. Both pictures had already appeared in the periodical "Lietopie Sobytiy," the first on the 1st of January, 1906, with the inscription: "The Demolition of a Farmhouse by Revolting Peasants;" the other on the 14th of January, 1906, with the inscription: "The Destruction of the Barricades in Moscow."

To this category also belongs an ingenious photograph of the Town Hall at Louvain which lies before me. The ruins of half-burnt houses, which were destroyed for the purpose of saving the Town Hall, have been so skilfully brought into the photograph that they appear to form a portion of the Town Hall itself.

Björn Björnson, in his well-known open letter to Georges

Clémenceau, expresses himself as follows with regard to this species of "art."

"Some days ago a Swiss returned from France, bringing with him a collection af drawings, picture postcards, and illustrated magazines. Some of them were merely stupid and tasteless. There was plenty of the same sort of thing here at the beginning of the war, but all these have now vanished But he also showed me some that were so viciously base, so foul and yet so deliberate in their perverse attacks upon Germany and its leaders, that only an imagination which draws its sustenance from the Paris sewers could have created them. This war has produced nothing more disgusting and horrible than these French drawings by eminent artists." [1]

Of course, if we wish to condemn all such expressions of a bestialized fanaticism, we shall, unfortunately, be forced to acknowledge that a few most regrettable excesses of the same sort occurred with us. These, however, were sharply censured by most of the German Press. I would recall, for example, the "Hate Poem" of Heinrich Vierordt, and similar products, which were the natural echoes to the howls of hate uttered by the great rabble of the French and English Press. But if these things have a psychological explanation, they are by no means excusable, when regarded from the view-point of superior German civilization and national seemliness. We deeply and honestly regret them. They form, to be sure, only a small and dwindling proportion in contrast to the splendid German newspapers and the vast body of serious literature, both of which sharply reject all extravagances. There is no support in Germany for such a creature as Horatio Bottomley of "John Bull."

[1] Our opponents do not utilize the Press alone; they have also recognized the powerful suggestive force of the Cinematograph, and make use of this for a systematic baiting of the Germans. The "Erste Internationale Film-Zeitung" in its issue of the 30th of January, 1915, and under the title of "Anti-German Films" gives the contents of one of these pieces which had been presented in Chicago. (See No. 85 of the "Freisinnige Zeitung," an article entitled: "The Cinematograph as one of the Great Powers.") The German Imperial Government might see to it that its propaganda in neutral countries will soon be reinforced by suitable films. As may be seen by "L'Action Française" of the 20th of April, 1915, it appears that the most gory atrocity films are all cooked up by actors. The Americans, however, accept them in all seriousness.

The "Norddeutsche Allgemeine Zeitung" had an article on the 6th of November with the heading "Away with Insulting Pictures." In words whose truth was everywhere recognized, the paper denounces this vulgar trash "as something not consistent with the dignity of the nation, something we might well leave to the English mob, the Parisian Apache and the Russian moujik." Such is the opinion of the overwhelming majority of the German people and the German press.

XI. In Johannes Scherr's beautiful book of colored pictures, depicting scenes in the time of Blücher, there is a passage quoted from the "Memoires" of the revolutionary Barrère, which might have been specially coined for application to the campaign of vilification which the Triple Entente wages against Germany:

"Slander is a power among those nations that are corrupt. She holds in her iron hand a poisoned pen. Her heart is of mud, and her head of bronze. She is without ears and hath no mercy. Dumb and full of malignity, she listens neither to facts nor to justifications."

The question of how such scandalous systems of unscrupulous slander may be forestalled in the future, is something that will have to occupy the serious attention ot the German people. Not only telegraphic communications must be assured in the future through the laying of German cables, but the psychological and material basis of our relations to foreign countries will require the most thorough investigation and reform. This, to be sure, is a question which has a close connection with the greatest demand we have to make of the future,—the complete reform of our German Diplomatic Service. This is to-day the most popular demand of the German people. That German Government which, in this respect, would place difficulties in the way of this universally-expressed desire on the part of the people, would commit a grave political error.

As to the rest, let us not overvalue during the duration of the war, all the work of enlightenment,—which usually comes too late. Let us trust to the iron besom of our victories. It is deeds that shall vindicate our good cause,—and these deeds shall speak so loudly and so plainly that the whole world shall hear. [1]

The enlightenment of foreign countries regarding the facts will, of course, be one of the greatest duties that will confront us during the equally important time that shall ensue after the conclusion of war.

Whom the gods would destroy, they first make blind. The Russian-French-English crusade of falsehood assumes more grotesque forms day by day. The difference between the attitude shown towards facts by Germany and that adopted by the Allies is clearly demonstrated by the fact that the German Headquarters publishes the English, French and Russian reports every day without abbreviation. On the other hand the army authorities of our opponents either wholly suppress the conscientious German reports, or falsify them, yes, they even suppress the bulletins of their allies, in case these are unfavorable. The German is able to stand a bit of bad news now and then; *the Frenchman, the Britisher and the Russian, like the neutral countries, must be systematically lied to!*

1. Under the date of June 9th, 1915, the "Norddeutsche Allgemeine Zeitung" writes as follows:

"'If this be madness, yet there's method in it.' These words of Polonius may well apply to the form and manner in which the English financial paper, "The Financial News," communicates to its readers the weekly report of the German Imperial Bank of May 15th and May 22nd.

The weekly report of May 15th is given in this sheet as follows:

"Immense Note Issue. No Gold.

Hopelessly Bankrupt Position of the German Reichsbank."

---

[1]) The reports of the most hostile press,—such as the "Times" and the "Bulletins de l'Armée de la République,"—prove the truth of these conjectures. Here we have the opinion of the highest officers and experts who, repudiating the gutter speech of the incendiary press, express their lofty esteem for the efficiency, the contempt of death and the behavior of the German soliders. As an English General declares: "The German soldier has no equal in the world." It is these men who save their own honor and ours, in thus opposing the calumnies of the aforesaid press.

"Amsterdam, May 18th. Below is given the report of the German Reichsbank of the 15th inst., edited by the "Financial News" in accordance with facts:

+ Add. — Subtract	Amount	Compared with previous Report	Amount in Corresponding Week Last Year
	Pounds	*Pounds*	*Pounds*
Total reserve in metal currency....	121 222 950	+ 132 550	83 723 550
Gold, etc. in this..................	Nothing	—	67 133 250

Reuter."

In reality the reported Gold reserve of the Imperial Bank on this day consisted of 2 376 150 000 marks = £ 118 808 000.

A lengthy article is devoted to the report of May 22nd, in which the figures are indeed correctly given, but with the following observations: "The figures are as wholly bogus as anything ever produced by the fraudulent managers of a swindling bank."

The attacks of the English mob upon defenceless Germans find a worthy corollary in this article. It merely proves that the public to which the sheet caters, considers it possible for a great Central Bank of Issue to falsify its status, and that they regard this as a reliable method of contention in times of war. We doubt, of course, that serious-minded English circles would give earnest consideration to such an article. As for the rest, we are quite content to have England under-estimate our economic strength in the same degree as that in which she under-estimated our military strength.

2. The English attempts at bribery,—as reported in the "Svenska Morgenbladet" of June 12th, 1915,—to induce neutral newspapers to publish defamatory articles against the German barbarians, reveal the source as well as the method of this vilest of all international crusades of calumny ever undertaken in human history.

That dawn is beginning to break in upon these beguiled and deluded peoples—what an awakening there will be!—is attested by the latest proceedings in the House of Commons, as well as by an article of Clemenceau's—and the three important items that follow:

In an article entitled "The Right to Truth," in the "Guerre Sociale" of June 8th, 1915, Hervé makes a stand against the manner in which the French people are kept in the dark about the war. He deplores the fact that the censors admit only news that is favorable for the Allies and unfavorable for the Central Powers, and objects especially to the suppression of the German, Austro-Hungarian and Turkish bulletins of the day. It would have been easy to avoid the surprise and consternation resulting upon the Fall of Przemysl. He could only shrug his shoulders when he saw how the French agencies published the most fantastic figures of German losses, and compared this with the fact that the French losses had been systematically concealed since the outbreak of war. Another great mistake was the form in which the French official bulletins were issued.

Hardly a day passed in which some serious set-back for the Germans, the capture of hostile trenches, houses and mills was not reported, but almost never was there an acknowledgment of French losses. "But the public was at last growing aware that the French losses must be heavy, and that the French were standing in almost the same spot as last November. By such means it would finally come to pass that no one would believe a word of the official reports, and thus the faith of the French people would be killed." [1]

[1] The „Norddeutsche Allgemeine Zeitung" of June 12th, published a supplement containing pictures from the French periodical "Miroir," taken originally from German periodicals and reproduced with false inscriptions. One illustration, "German Soldiers on the East Front take Bedding from their Quarters into the Trenches," appears in the "Miroir" with the description: "Plunderers in Alsace who are carrying off Bedding. The Soldiers Break into Houses in the Most Brutal Manner and Drag away, Without Permission, Blankets, Pillows and Mattresses."

On the 28th of February the same periodical published some six photographs with the title: "What Happens to Woollen Garments Stolen in France." Undoubtedly these are reproductions from photographs. By means of such pictures, unheard-of accusations are levelled against our troops to the effect that they had systematically robbed the peaceful population of France and Belgium, in order to carry off bedding, woollen goods and garments and send these to Germany where a carefully organized system for converting them to military purposes had been devised. The tags to the pictures are meant to convey the impression that looting had been scientifically organized amongst us Germans. Our boys, so eager to help, do not escape calumny in this. With the exception of the first, the illustrations are nothing more than photographs, taken during our "Empire Wool Week." Their publication in the "Miroir" gives one an idea of what weapons are considered permissible in France in order

According to English, French and Russian reports of victories, every village in Germany ought to be in the hands of its enemies long ere this![1] [2]

3. The "Norddeutsche Allgemeine Zeitung" in its issue of June 13, and under the caption of "Russian Atrocities," writes as follows:

"Since the beginning of the war, the Russians, by means of official declarations, articles in their own press and in that of their allies, have conducted a vicious campaign of slander against our troops. They have accused them of all manner of things, especially of cruelty towards Russians and of other violations of the terms of the Hague Conference and the Geneva Convention. This torrent of lies has taken on increased dimensions of late.

---

to incite an ignorant population against the German troops and the German soldiers, thus fomenting an ardor for war which but for such infamous methods, would have subsided long ago.

[1] A reader of the "Deutsche Tageszeitung" sends it a leaflet which was found in the cartridge-box of a dead Frenchman. The leaflet bears the inscription "grand quartier général 2. bureau," the date is also given, the 8th of March, 1915, and the heading: "Notre Victoire est certaine!"

The contents of this screed read as follows: "The German armies can no longer renew themselves; their losses exceed the number of three million men. Their recruits have only one gun to three men, their cannon are worn out. The capital of Turkey is threatened by French and English ships. Greece and Roumania are prepared to march against Germany. The Russians have not yet sent one-fifth of their available men into the field."

This is followed by all sorts of "news" regarding "German atrocities" in Belgium, and alleged cruelties towards French prisoners who are said to be dying of hunger. The conclusion takes the form of a demand that the Frenchman should vow rather to die, than fall into the hands of the Germans.

[2] As the "Neuen Züricher Nachrichten" (14th of June) communicates, a Swiss journalist with a commission from a large firm of publishers, recently travelled through Belgium with the consent of the German authorities and in company with two colleagues from other neutral lands. The party also enjoyed the protection of the American Belgian Relief Committee. The paper quotes as follows: "We should like to remark that we conducted investigations in various places where alleged German atrocities were supposed to have taken place. We used as our guide the official document issued by the French Government. In three places we found that persons with the names given did not exist. In the fourth place we found a man with the given name, but not his wife. Here, too, nothing was known about the atrocities alleged to have been committed by Germans."

Scarcely a day passes but similiar "fakes" of the press of the Triple Entente are exposed and refuted. But they are as the heads of the hydra!

It is difficult for the Germans to reply to these charges, since the Russians, in nearly all cases, prefer not to mention the place and time of the alleged violations of international law. When these points have been mentioned, investigation by the Germans has immediately followed. By means of their new tactics the Russians have the obvious intention of rendering futile all serious investigation of their charges, and of preventing the falseness of their statements from being exposed. This attitude of the Russians can be explained only by the fact that their charges have not the slightest foundation and are nothing more than lies which are intended to throw mud upon the honor of our troops from some safe coign of vantage."

Wherever no mention is made of place or date, the neutrals, for whom this "news" is chiefly intended, have the best reason for assuming that it is nothing but sheer invention.

The "Novoie Vremia" on the 8th of June, 1915, publishes an open letter to the Reuter Bureau, in which it accuses this news agency of reporting the bulletins of the Russian General Staff in a very sparse and unreliable manner. An example is given, as follows: When, according to official German reports it had been firmly established that the third and eighth Russian armies no longer existed and that the whole Carpathian Army had been annihilated, the "Reuter Rureau" contents itself with reporting harmless little battle episodes. This open letter addressed to Reuter, is no doubt, a concealed attack upon the Russian General Staff, which keeps secret the most important facts—since Reuter had in reality reported all the *communiqués* of the Russian General Staff up to the present time.

The Russian Moujik was to be *forced* to believe that the terrible defeat the Russians suffered in Galicia, with a loss of 300 000 prisoners and the surrender of all Galicia, was a Russian "victory." After a small town in East Prussia had been taken by storm, the Russian soldiers were stuffed with the lie that they had now captured Berlin and that the campaign was ended! This poor and brutalized people seems destined never to know the truth. Were it only to guess this, then the mighty revolution which would shatter this colossus of clay would follow as the day follows the night.

CHAPTER XXI.

A Few Remarks upon the French and Belgian "Books of Atrocities," and Similar Things. General Observations in Connection with the German Investigations.

I. I have procured the French so-called "Book of Atrocities" in the original, as well as most of the works of a similar tendency.

Les Atrocités Allemandes en France. Rapport présenté à M. le président du conseil par la commission instituée en vue de constater les actes commis par l'ennemi en violation du droit des gens (Decret du 23 sept. 1914). Prix 5 centimes.

This official document is printed in blood-red ink. It is with increasing astonishment and growing indignation that I have read this report of *Monsieur Georges Payelles, I. président de la cour des comptes,* of *Monsieur Armand Mollard, ministre plénipotentiare;* of *Monsieur Georges Maringer, conseiller d'état* and of *Monsieur Edmond Paillot, conseiller à la cour de cassation,* dated Paris, December 17th, 1914.

Never before in my life have I read anything more superficial or pretentious. Without furnishing the slightest proof, one ghastly story after another is retailed here. Every act of violence is supposed to be established, and the entire blame, without judgment and without discrimination, is simply shoved upon the shoulders of the German soldiers. The statements of women, of *demoiselle* A or *madame* X, play a certain part. Ancient yarns, such as that of the chateau de Baye, already refuted by the sworn testimony of *French witnesses,* are rewarmed and served up in this book. The Commission has made tremendous discoveries at this place, since the names of "I. K. Hoheit," and "Major von Ledebour" and "Graf Valdersee," and "Exzellenz," were found there. So the "Matin" has deemed the aforementioned worthy of being pilloried (pictorially *Au Pilori*) along with the Kaiser, the Crown Prince and others. The execution of every *franc-tireur* is depicted in the blackest and most frightful colors as simple murder. And, of course, it goes without saying that every red-handed *franc-tireur* is innocent as a lamb and pure as snow.

The Uhlans, of course, play a great rôle—*carboniser, piller, fusiller, violer, tuer*, and so on. Very often the atrocity fable degenerates into the grotesque, still more frequently into the burlesque. The big and the little are mingled in inextricable confusion: "*La chambre du baron de Baye était dans le plus grand* désordre . . . un bureau avait été fracturé; un commode Louis XVI et un bureau à cylindre du même style avaient été fouillés."

In this childish fashion the report proceeds. Let us compare such puerilities and petty slanders with, for instance, the open letter to Sir Arthur Conan Doyle by James O'Donnell Bennet, the captured correspondent of the "Chicago Tribune" (published by Georg Reimer, Berlin 1915), which furnishes a splendid testimonial for the German army and its behavior in hostile country. It is indeed exceedingly difficult to understand how a nation whose chief representative has uttered the phrase: "*c'est la guerre,*" could have permitted a report of this nature to be compiled by four men who make pretences to serious consideration. One is really forced to ask oneself whether M. le président, to whom the report was presented, felt no sense of shame in permitting such a piece of bungled work to be issued by the printing-office of the *Journaux officiels*.

I would request every jurist and every layman to read this wretched and claptrap "fake"—concocted from the gossip of hysterical old women and girls, of children and old men. They will be forced to agree with me that the moral and intellectual degradation of the French nation has never been proved so conclusively by any other contemporary document—as by this famous official report of the four members of the French "Atrocity Commission." But worse than that, one's faith in the sense of justice of a nation to which one ventures to submit such "proofs" of the "Hunnish" character of the German soldier, receives in turn a staggering blow. Inasmuch as only "Madame X" and "Monsieur X" are cited as witnesses, and not the violated, the outraged, the injured, etc., all confirmation is absolutely impossible. The whole plan and purpose of the report becomes obvious—the systematic and unrestrained vilification of our army in other lands.

Even in France this point of view regarding the "Atrocity Stories" is meeting with a growing recognition. The "Eclair" of Paris regrets that the French Government should have encouraged the discussion in the press as to what is to be done with the children of French women alleged to have been violated by German soldiers. The "Eclair "remarks:

"We believe that such instances are extremely rare. *Not a single authentic case has been made known to us.* We are of the opinion that all discussions of such things are entirely regrettable."

"L'Humanité" also takes up a strong position of protest.

The opinion of neutral-minded foreign countries as to this deluge of French atrocity tales, is shown by the following: The "Basler Nachrichten" of March 28th, 1915, contains an article by Professor Wernle of the University of Basel, dealing with the circulation in enormous quantities of the report of the French commission in connection with alleged atrocities by Germans in the occupied districts. He cites two striking cases —after which he appears to have had enough of all these hopelessly unsubstantiable horror stories, unwitnessed and unverified. The Professor remarks: "And such things are accepted as authentic by the Committee of Investigation and presented to the Premier!"

Two points are made by Dr. Wernle at the close of his article. First, that the entire official report has merely a psychological and historical value in showing what the imagination of an excited people in times of war is capable of attributing to the enemy whose inroads it has been forced to endure, and how even educated men, entrusted with the duty of investigation, are liable to be infected by this excited state of mind. The most elementary sense of justice would decree that in every reliable and trustworthy examination, it would be necessary to listen to the other side, and to eliminate all passion prejudicial to a calm consideration of the facts or any other factors liable to influence the truth. But there is no trace of all this in the reports in question. There is, on the contrary, a distinct eagerness to attribute to the enemy all that is vile, and to augment the mass of monstrous charges by every means at one's disposal.

The second point is as follows: that all attempts to destroy the good name of the enemy and thus win the sympathies of the neutral countries by the circulation of atrocity stories alleged to be officially established, and the authenticity of which is so seriously open to question,—deserve to be characterized as "filthy propaganda."

"Filthy Propaganda." The term may be a little drastic but it is certainly an excellent designation for this populo-pathological literature of dirt. [1]

[1] A typical case is the essay of Pierre Nothomb on the "Martyrdom of Belgium" in the January number of the "Revue des deux Mondes." It deals with the alleged violation of a young girl by German soldiers in a minister's house. The two witnesses, the alleged victim and the minister, stated upon their oath that what really took place was as follows:

"Wilhelm," the First Lieutenant's orderly, came into the kitchen one day, and meeting the young lady, put his arm about her shoulders, and asked her if she would be his bride. Whereupon the girl laughingly answered: "After the war." Mademoiselle de Coninck concluded her sworn testimony with the words: "I certainly did not think any harm of this little incident: and on no occasion has a German soldier been guilty of any rudeness towards me." Out of this harmless scene Monsieur Nothomb builds up the drama of a violation; through his magnifying glass he sees seven men assaulting the innocent victim!

Still worse is the tale of a boy in Ternath, who had both hands chopped off. The Burgomaster declared on oath that there was not a word of truth in the whole story. "Everything is pure invention...." The Mayor was absolutely thunderstruck over the glowing imagination of Monsieur Nothomb.

One more example of the tricks which Monsieur Nothomb's inventive genius plays him: "The Duke of Gronau," says he, "plundered the Castle of Villers-Notre-Dame; all the silver has vanished." What, however, does the Curé O. S. Mazy, of Villers St. Amand, say in support of the German rule?—"that the silver treasures of the Castle were buried in a sand-heap in the cellars, and were delivered to his safe-keeping by the Germans."

So end nearly all the horror-stories of French, English, Russian and Belgian origin! But no sooner have they all been proved to be mere inventions, than they crop up again, months afterwards, like the tale of the 12 or 16 Italians who were obliged to dig their own graves. Truly, calumny is hydra-headed! Another such case is the tale in the "Indépendence Belge" of the 26th of March, 1915, of the Jordens Case in Sempft (violation of a 13 year old girl, and so on). The story is a lie from beginning to end. The Mayor, with many other witnesses, stated that the conduct of the German soldiers had been beyond reproach.

II. The Belgian report, *"Le Livre Rouge Belge"* upon *"Les Atrocités Allemandes en Belgique,"* published in Paris, is on a somewhat higher scale.

I say on a "higher" scale because at least in some instances names are given—names, which, to be sure, it is very difficult to investigate without a sufficient address. The alleged cases of the firing of houses, of looting, capture and killing which are therein related, reveal in the main nothing more than the terrible fury which had been engendered by the hate of the Belgians and their shameful methods in lawless *franc-tireur* warfare.

A people which conducts itself as the Belgians did during the first two months (see previous chapters), cannot complain if the other side carries on the war with all rigor. From this point of view no particular exception can be urged against the various public notices and proclamations (at least such as are genuine; see Chapter I); they are in full accordance with international law and freely admit the terrible fashion in which the war had been carried on by the Belgians. As to the rest, the German Government will not forego the opportunity of investigating in the most conscientious manner certain specific details mentioned in these papers.

III. The same thing applies to another interesting little brochure: *"Les crimes allemands"* by Joseph Bédier (*Études et documents sur la Guerre, Libr. Armand Colin, Paris*) "according to German evidence." These consist of fac-similes of original extracts taken from the letters of German soldiers and dealing with German cruelty. The compiler of these, of course, took no account of the hysteria of the trenches. He naturally assumed everything to be quite authentic. But even this book merely confirms what I have already maintained, that is to say, the raging fury with which the combats in the *franc-tireur* war were carried on by both sides during the first months. Bédier, as may be supposed, maintains an absolute and intentional silence regarding the *franc-tireurs*. The most important documents (as on page 29) are *not* given in fac-simile reproduction. These are obvious forgeries with which the author has been victimized. This is proven by the grotesque German, containing typical French errors, as well as by a number of military superficialities. The other documents (page 25, for example) are merely proofs of German discipline and sense of equity. The extracts are very interesting in themselves, but they do not establish the slightest case against the German conduct of the war.

So far as I am able to say, it was a Danish scholar, Professor Larsen (see his pamphlet, "Professor Bédier and the Diaries of German Soldiers," Georg Reimer's Verlag, Berlin) who first exposed the scientific weaknesses and the forgeries of Monsieur Bédier. He proved that the alleged scientific accuracy of Bédier has no basis in reality; that he either misinterprets or misreads the letters in question, that he tears separate sentences from their context, and even directly forges these. Another neutral, Professor P. Wernle of Basel, proves in the "Neuen Zürcher Zeitung," No. 461 (April 18, 1915) in the most exact, unimpeachable and scientific manner that Bédier had disgracefully flung all intellectual honesty to the winds when writing his pamphlet. By a number of examples he makes it clear that an investigator "commits a crime against scientific knowledge, when under circumstances such as these, he permits his patriotism to cause him to forget the most elementary decencies and exactitudes of research." He confronts Bédier with quotations and with proofs which irrefutably convict the latter of excessive ignorance, lack of information or deliberate falsification.

When a well-known French scientist and scholar makes a showing such as this, one may well imagine how lesser spirits and *ad hoc* fanatic officials serving on atrocity commissions, would render their verdicts. Still more annihilating for Monsieur Bédier is Dr. Max Kuttner's pamphlet, "Deutsche Verbrechen," published by Velhagen und Klasing, 1915. In this the author not only convicts Bédier in a number of instances of deliberate falsification and slander, but also publishes a series of *French* soldiers' letters in fac-simile—proving that everything which Bédier attempts to fasten upon the German soldiers, is here conclusively proved against the French *by their own witnesses.* In addition to this, and by means of unquestionable documents, he gives us the splendid testimonial vouchsafed by French wounded with regard to the German *"délicatesse de sentiments*" which they declare to be "*au-dessus de tous éloges.*" Furthermore Dr. Kuttner publishes many destructive criticisms by French commanders regarding the lack of discipline in the French army and the frequency of lootings.

In order that the author may not himself infringe the complete objectivity with which this book is written, he advises the German authorities and military courts to investigate the matter of the fac-simile letters and their alleged writers. I am firmly convinced that one of these letter-writers was voicing the sentiments of his comrades when he declares—commenting upon someone who had really attempted to assault a girl— "But *he* will certainly come in for his just punishment."

IV. The English Government has also created similar commissions, chiefly composed of prominent jurists. One of these, Mr. Theodore A. Cook, declares in the "Times" of December 26th, that the English publication will not give the name of a single informant—in order that the witnesses may be spared German revenge! This project seems to have been finally disposed of by the following communication from the anti-German New York "World." It bears the inscription: "Investigations in London Confirm no Violence to Belgian Refugees."

"Not one of all the thousands of Belgian refugees who are now staying in England has been subjected to cruelties on the part of the German soldiers. This fact is the most essential feature of a report which the Department of State has received from the American Embassy in London. The report confirms that the British Government had investigated thousands of reports as to whether German troops had been guilty of acts of violence towards Belgian refugees. *Agents of the British Government, according to the report of the American Embassy at London, have made a careful examination of all charges, have questioned the alleged victims and carefully sifted all evidence. As a result of these investigations the British Foreign Office notifies the American Embassy of the fact that the charges are based upon hysteria and natural prejudice.*" (*retranslation*)

The innumerable and contemptible slanders spread abroad by Sir Arthur Conan Doyle and others, seemed, so far as truth and logic were concerned, to have collapsed like a house of cards.

Then suddenly there appeared the report of the "Bryce Commission" upon the German atrocities in Belgium, concerning which the "Norddeutsche Allgemeine Zeitung," writes as follows:

"The atrocity stories which are being spread abroad concerning our army, grow like a hydra. When one head is struck off, two new ones spring forth in the same place, and cast their poison of calumny over everything.

It has been reserved for the English to achieve the masterpiece in this field. An English Commission was formed by the government to investigate German atrocities in Belgium, and has just published its report—with a special eye to America.

We have not yet seen the report itself, but the extracts from the newspapers contain the most unbelievable things that have ever been published in the way of atrocity lies.

The evidence contained in the report rests upon the testimony of witnesses, but it was necessary, as the "Times" observes, to promise these witnesses that their identity should not be revealed as they were afraid that otherwise they or their friends in Belgium might be made to suffer! In Germany and some other countries it is customary to throw anonymous letters into the waste-paper basket. Richelet said: "Les lettres anonymes marquent toujours de la part de celui qui les écrit un grand fonds de lâcheté et de bassesse." We are willing to grant the Belgian refugees the benefit of the doubt—that they have strained a point in the manufacture of such testimony as we find in the Report of the Commission, in order to ingratiate themselves with their hosts. We had expected, however, that a nation in which a spark of fair play and love of justice still existed would scorn to become a scavenger of such lies and rubbish as are accumulated in this report.

The stories that are dished up to a credulous or incredulous public surpass even the notorious tale of the English nurse, Grace Hume. The English Commission have at least the gratification of knowing that what they have written cannot possibly be surpassed. Women with breasts cut off, violated and mutilated babes, crucified children, German soldiers who triumphantly bear on their pikes through the streets of Belgian towns the decapitated heads of their enemies, German incendiary battalions who under the device "Gott mit uns," systematically reduce houses to ashes—these are some of the choice exhibits in this Chamber of Horrors.

Unfortunately the English do not follow the rule of the wax-works proprietor, who only admits to his Chamber of Horrors these sections of the public who have paid extra for the treat. They poison the souls of their own children and their own people with these perversities—they who still vividly remember the reports which these same English papers published at one time on the cruelties practised by the Belgians on the Congo. At that time it suited English policy to proclaim the cruelties of the Belgians and, if necessary, with eyes turned up in pious horror, to invent a few for the occasion.

Concerning various examples in the report one may observe that the Commission itself is a little nervous about its work. "It was with amazement and almost with incredulity that the Committee first read the depositions relating to such acts," it says in one place. We are not surprised that the Committee finally overcame its incredulity and its amazement. It is the British national virtue, cant, which in the final issue, has led to this result. Sir Roger Casement has annihilated the slanders of Lord Bryce with unanswerable logic and withering scorn.

What does Carlyle say of that most deadly of artifices—an artifice which slays them that practise it even unto their very souls, an artifice which transcends the degree of the conscious lie and leads to a belief in its own phantasms of the brain, dragging its devotees down into that most miserable of all conditions in which a man becomes honestly dishonest?

The Commission is not especially grieved over the gruesome facts which it reports: neither does it regret the bestial methods of warfare employed by the Belgian guerillas, whose conduct in hundreds of cases has been deposed to on oath by German soldiers who witnessed the acts which forced the German army to take measures against its will. But the Commission *does* very much regret that it should have found "obvious difficulty in proving intention." Swiftly and smoothly does it glide over the causes which constrained the German soldiers in certain places to take measures against Belgian civilians: "We have no reason to believe," we read in one place—"that the civil population of Dinant had threatened any provocative action,"—and again: "It is said that (in Aerschot) a German General or Colonel was murdered in the house of the Mayor. So far as the Commission could discover, the identity of this officer has never been established."

When one considers, on the contrary, that it is precisely in these two cases that the facts have been established absolutely beyond doubt, through the careful German Government investigation, which is just publishing the results of its work, we hope the English Commission will not take it ill if we venture to say, on our part: "Men have no reason to believe that the lies which you, with avowedly slanderous intent, are spreading abroad, have even a single grain of truth in them."

The "Norddeutsche Allgemeine Zeitung" concludes with these words: "We would like to call to the memory of the English Government, which does not scruple to send this sorry concoction abroad among the nations, that motto which says: "Let every man sweep before his own door." A government which permits hundreds of inoffensive and defenceless Germans to be robbed and plundered by a savage mob in its capital under the very eyes of its police, a government upon whose conscience rests the crushing guilt for the concentration camps in South Africa with all their horrors perpetrated upon women and children, has no right to reproach another nation,—and should refrain from constituting itself the attorney for a people for whose misfortunes it is itself chiefly to blame. It should cast a glance upon its own history—and keep silent."

CHAPTER XXII.

The Official German Refutation of the Charges Preferred by the French and Belgian Governments. Investigations by German Authorities of Violations of the Rules of War.

Through the courtesy of the Prussian Ministry of War I have been put into possession, as I have already indicated, of the enormous amount of material compiled for official purposes by the "Military Bureau for the Investigation of Violation of the Laws of War." After a careful study of this material, the mere volume of which runs to the extent of several books, I am only able once more to confirm upon my honor and conscience as a German judge, this one fact: that the investigations upon which this stupendous mass of data is based with regard to the lawless acts of the soldiery of the Triple Entente, have been made in the most conscientious, *painfully* conscientious manner and with real German thoroughness. The evidence is in the main established upon the utterances of witnesses sworn in the German field or civil courts.

A strong mixture of scepticism and of distrust of war-hysteria and trench-gossip prevailed in these military courts with respect to their own witnesses. Contrary to the practice of the French and Belgian authorities, these witnesses were not encouraged to spin atrocity tales, but were treated in a truly critical spirit, even when their evidence was entirely in our favor.

A comprehensive memorial contains the official evidence collected up to date (April 1915) with regard to the treatment of German prisoners in the hands of the French, treatment not in accord with the regulations of the Geneva Convention and the Hague Conference.

A very voluminous Memorial of 212 pages contains the refutation of the accusations which the French Government has so far made. The following extract is taken from the introduction to this work:

"The whole series of war atrocities of which the French Government has accused the German, constitute, so far as they have been made known, a single chain of the most degraded and unrestrained slanders, which merely engender hate and are intended to incite the population against the German invaders.

Since the Germans, without distinction and without any details as to place, time, victims or perpetrators, are accused of murder, looting, arson and the rape of women, the intention of spreading abroad the impression that the Germans are in the habit of committing such atrocities during their victorious marches, is made sufficiently plain.

Opposed to this is the fact that the German military leaders by the use of suitable measures have been able to maintain the discipline of the troops and the most rigorous observance of the rules of warfare with the greatest success in all the theatres of war. Therefore the stigma of falsehood attaches itself to the French Government and no less to the press which it leads and influences and which does not hesitate to depict the German commanders as the accomplices and the instigators of such outrages.

In so far as the French have troubled themselves to furnish us with specific instances, it goes without saying that the German Government at once ordered a strict and thorough investigation to be made. The results of this may be awaited in full confidence and with undiminished faith in the quality of the German character, as soon as the reports are made public.

One of these charges may, however, already be refuted today. This deals with the instance of Lunéville, in which city the German army has been accused of the wanton destruction by fire of some 70 buildings. Had the French Government taken the trouble to make a thorough investigation of the reasons why a court trial was held at Lunéville, it might have spared itself the reproach of having uttered a conscious untruth, —something of which it has repeatedly been proved guilty. The French Government might have discovered that the inhabitants of the town did not scruple, after its occupation by the Germans on August 25th, 1914, to open a sudden and treacherous fire upon the *hôpital militaire* from the windows and eaves of the neighboring houses. This took place about 5 o'clock in the afternoon. There were a great number of wounded in the hospital at the time. This attack lasted for over an hour and a half and was maintained entirely by civilians, since there were no uniformed Frenchmen in Lunéville at that time. On the following day in a similar fashion Bavarian troops were shot at from houses by civilians.

The circumstances of this event have been thoroughly and unquestionably established by the sworn testimony of numerous witnesses. (Appendices 1 to 4.)

Furthermore the attention of the French Government should be called to the manner in which the French soldiery conducted itself in its own land. It is they themselves who ventured upon robbery and plundering, and not the Germans whom the French Government so unjustly accuses. Authentic evidence has been given by the compatriots of the French themselves that chateaux and houses in France have been looted in the most ruthless manner by French troops and French civilians—at Fontaines near Belfort, at Rambervillers, Attigny, Villers devant Merrières, Vivaisse near Crépy, Thugny and Moy. The reproach for these crimes falls therefore, not upon the Germans, but upon the French. Opposed to such charges we find in many cases that most unimpeachable French witnesses have praised the excellent behavior, the seemliness and the strict discipline of the Germans. (Appendices 5 to 16.)

The absolutely unfounded charge of murder which has likewise been hurled at the heads of the German troops recoils with crushing weight upon those of their vilifiers. We would merely mention here that Frenchmen have in countless cases and in the most horrifying manner mutilated and butchered German wounded upon the field of battle. There have been innumerable cases treated in German hospitals, cases of helpless, wounded German soldiers who had been maltreated by French soldiers—through repeated bayonet stabs in the body, head and eyes, through blows from rifle-butts, through the cutting of the throat and other bestialities.

The incarceration of wounded men, tying them to trees or posts, the shooting of men incapable of fighting, the murder from ambuscades of kindly soldiers of the Medical Corps, the cutting-off of the genital parts, the ripping-up of the abdomen, the piercing of eyes, the cutting-off of ears, the transfixing of the wounded as they lay upon the ground, countless cases in which the wounded or the dead were robbed—all these things have been proved to have taken place wherever French troops have fought. They form an eloquent witness against these desecrators of civilization and of morals.

All these shameful deeds committed by the French troops have been confirmed by the most unimpeachable evidence of sworn and reputable persons and shall in good time be delivered to the public for criticism. (Appendices 17 to 114.)

But even in places far removed from the tumult of battle,—

even in the secrecy of prison cells, the tools of the French Government have made themselves guilty of murder in its basest forms. In August, 1914, German prisoners of war in the jail at Montbéliard were shockingly mutilated by French gendarmes and then beaten to death without the slightest reason. (Appendix 115.) Another case is furnished by the assault made by robber hordes of French soldiery upon the post-office at Niedersulzbach. They seized the members of the postmaster's family, dragged them off, maltreated them in a most cruel and outrageous manner, and finally threw the postmaster, an old and ailing man of 68 years, down a flight of steps into the street. In the prison at Belfort this poor man was abused so shockingly by his warder, so kicked and tortured and beaten, that he died a miserable death during the night of August 17th, 1914, (Appendix 116.) These cases are likewise substantiated by the sworn testimony of reputable eye-witnesses.

The statements in this memorial, as well as in the special publications so far issued, are all supported by sworn depositions of the most unassailable kind. My own material is also open to inspection by neutral committees at any time. It contains the most damning and abundant evidence against the methods of war sanctioned by the French Government and is full of the most shameful excesses as perpetrated upon German doctors, officers, and soldiers.

The "Norddeutsche Allgemeine Zeitung," of the 20th of May, 1915, published a "White Book" dealing with "the conduct of the Belgian guerilla warfare in violation of international law." The resumé contains the following:

"It would be easy for the Belgian Government to provide its organs with the requisite directions for quieting the impassioned and artificially engendered excitement of the people. They must therefore bear the entire responsibility for the monstrous blood-guilt which lies heavy upon Belgium. Their only purpose has been to escape this responsibility, so that the blame for the workings of the fury of destruction might fall upon the shoulders of the German troops, who would thus be shown to have committed causeless acts of violence. They have established a Committee of Investigation and have made the depositions of this Committee the subject of an official diplomatic protest. Their purpose,—that of representing the exact contrary of the real facts, has completely miscarried. The tales of the refugees, recorded as the result of painstaking and impartial investigation, bore in themselves the stamp of incredibility, and, at times, of obvious malicious intent. The accusations of the Commission against the German army are nothing more than petty calumnies, which are entirely nullified by the evidence on hand.

The fighting in Aerschot did not arise, as was stated by the English, from the fact that German officers had attacked the family honor of the Mayor, but on the contrary, from the fact that the populace made a deliberate attack from behind upon the Chief Officer in Command of the town, and murdered him. In Dinant it was not innocent, peaceful citizens who fell victims to the German sword, but assassins who had treacherously fallen upon the German soldiers. In Louvain the fight with the civil population was not begun by flying German troops who fired by mistake upon their own comrades, entering the town. On the contrary, the misled population, failing to comprehend the real conditions of affairs, imagined that the German troops were in retreat and could be easily and with immunity destroyed. In Louvain only that part of the city was destroyed, where the inhabitants had treacherously and murderously fallen upon the German soldiers. Indeed, it was the Germans themselves who took pains, not only in Louvain, but also in other cities, to ensure that the art treasures should, as far as possible, be rescued and preserved."

The memorial closes with the words: "The Imperial German Government believes that it has shown by the publication of the mass of evidence on hand, that the proceedings of the German troops against the civil population of Belgium were dictated by the necessities of war as a result of the lawless *franc-tireur* warfare. On the other hand it makes an emphatic and earnest protest against a population that by reprehensible means conducted a dishonorable warfare against the German troops, and still more earnestly impeaches a government that, in full knowledge of its duty towards the unreasoning passion of the populace, had allowed it unbridled license, and did not scruple to divert its own burden of guilt, by means of lying aspersions, on to the shoulders of the German army."

A most valuable and comprehensive memorial deals with the attack at Louvain. No man lives to-day who will not, after a judicial examination of this evidence, concede that it furnishes the most convincing proof of the base and cowardly *franc-tireur* attack made by the inhabitants of Louvain. A sketch plan accompanies the report and this shows that not even one-sixth of the town has been destroyed by fire.

The monstrous calumnies of which the so-called Belgian Committee of Investigation made itself guilty, are established by a variety of proofs.

The slight weight which the Commission itself places upon the tales dished up to it, tales which it circulated without exercising the slightest criticism, is made plain by the story of the execution of Bishop Coenraets and Father Schmidt—in the fifth report. The report itself speaks of the executions as "alleged"—and then proceeds to add the fable that the unwilling spectators of this (alleged!) scene were forced to express their approval by clapping their hands. It would be difficult to go to worse extremes than to serve up hastily-collected stuff of this sort for the mere sake of creating a sensation—and absolutely shutting one's eyes to all considerations of truth and justice. It must be known—and this is a fact of which the Belgian Government doubtlessly had a far better and earlier knowledge than the German—that M. Coenraets is at this very moment living in the best of health at the home of Dr. Toels at Tirlen in Holland.

The German Government, in all that refers to the case of Louvain, has been guided by the desire to serve two ends in its investigation of the facts—to defend its honor which has been aspersed by reckless accusations, and to serve the interests of common humanity which have been so grievously abused by the attitude of the Belgian Government and the people it succeeded in deluding.

Another memorial records the facts in connection with a very similar attack made at Aerschot in Belgium—as well as "fresh evidence of the untruthfulness of the French Government" with regard to the case of a non-commissioned officer named

Frank who revealed upon oath, confirmed by several other witnesses, the shameful behavior to which the French had subjected the German wounded—a particularly tragic case! It is a sad document of human civilization—and we recommend it with all our heart to all who shout most loudly in "neutral foreign countries." The entire official evidence is worthy of the closest study.

The enormous amount of evidence collected by the other commission—that for ascertaining instances of acts of violence towards German civilians in enemy countries—has, to be sure, a still more devastating effect, if that be possible, upon our conceptions of civilization. A complete, authorized transcript of this has also been placed at my disposal by the courtesy of the government.

How I long to spread the full knowledge of its contents through all the neutral lands! These pages shame the reader, they make him shudder to the very roots of his being. Such a vast access of cruelty, of breaches of international law, of heartless cynicism perpetrated upon unfortunate civilians who were guilty of no other fault than that they happened to be of German extraction, degrades the spirit of man, debases it to profundities of shame. Let modern civilization hide its face. The greatest, the most "cultured" nations commit abominations that would disgrace the negro hordes in the basin of the Congo. They trample underfoot compacts and fundamental rights of humanity—written and unwritten laws of old-established justice—*the beast that dwells in the peoples has been let loose!* And it is being goaded unto an added fury by the present governments of France and England—for they persist in lashing it to a maniacal frenzy—and in accusing the German people and its army of deeds which are committed wholesale by their own soldiery.

CHAPTER XXIII.

Art and War. The Case of Rheims Cathedral and Similar Instances. Louvain Once Again.

"Good nature cannot be accounted as humanity in a conquered country. If one is obsessed by humanity and again humanity, one should not attempt to conduct a war. You cannot make war with rose-water." Napoleon I.

Article 27 of the Rules and Regulations of Warfare by Land stipulates:

"In sieges and bombardments all necessary steps must be taken to spare, as far as possible, buildings dedicated to religion, art, science, or charitable purposes, historic monuments, hospitals, and places where the sick and wounded are collected, *provided they are not being used at the time for military purposes.*"

It is the duty of the besieged to indicate the presence of such buildings and places by distinctive and visible signs, which shall be notified to the enemy beforehand.

I. The German General Staff in this war used all endeavors to preserve historic monuments of art, precisely as in 1870. (See also chapter XXIV.) This cannot be said of the French who, to cite an instance, shot the cathedral of Dinant to pieces with their artillery. It should not be forgotten that it was entirely due to the self-sacrificing spirit of German officers and soldiers that the magnificent Town Hall at Louvain,—in the neighborhood of which a treacherous attack had been made by the population,—was preserved. Rheims, too, was twice entirely spared by the Germans. Only after it had been made the central point of the French position did the Germans do that to which the laws of war compelled them.

Even during the second bombardment of Rheims (at the close of September) all that was possible was done to protect the cathedral and save it from destruction.

Surely one must have had the most exalted notions as to the extent of German good-nature, in order to impute to the Germans that they would shoot *past* the cathedral *behind* which the French cannons thundered against them! Even the "Times" was forced to concede, on the 20th of September:

"Theoretically the bombardment of Rheims was provoked

by the French artillery, which was stationed in the city and was returning a vigorous answer to the German artillery fire. French soldiers were encamped in the streets, the artillery park was situated in the main street, behind this lay the infantry."[1] (*retranslation*)

I do not, to be sure, understand just what the "Times" means by a "theoretical provocation."

The subtle way in which the allied French and Belgians go to work in this matter, is clearly seen in the detailed description of the bombardment of Rheims in the Dutch journal "De Maasbode" of September 10th, 1914. It becomes evident from this that not only was this edifice used for military purposes out of military motives, but that its bombardment was *deliberately provoked*—in order to arouse indignation in foreign countries against German "Vandalism." In times of peace all these monuments are permitted to deteriorate in the most disgraceful manner, but in times of war you conceal yourself behind them and then invoke the howls of all the ignorant who come flocking in their droves whenever an opportunity offers to fulminate against the "Huns!"

The General Headquarters, under the date of September 22nd, p. m. writes thus in answer to this hue-and-cry:

"The French Government has declared that the bombardment of Rheims Cathedral was not an act of military necessity. In contradiction to this the following has been established:

"After the French had, by strong fortifications, made the city of Rheims a main point of support in their defences, they forced us to attack the town by all the means in their power. By order of the Commander-in-Chief, special care was to be taken to preserve the Cathedral, so long as the enemy refrained from using it to his own advantage. From the 20th of September on, the white flag was flown from the Cathedral and was respected by us.

"In spite of this we could observe with certainty that there was an observation post upon the tower, and this was further established by the successful effect of the enemy's artillery upon our attacking infantry. It was necessary to dislodge the observer.

[1] See "The Bombardment of Rheims Cathedral," published by Georg Reimer, Berlin, 1915.

This was effected by the field artillery, with shrapnel. The heavy artillery was not permitted to fire even now, and the firing was stopped as soon as the post had been dislodged.

"We were able to observe that the towers and exterior of the Cathedral remained undamaged. The framework of the roof was set on fire. The attacking forces, therefore, took no further measures than were absolutely necessary. The responsibility rests with the enemy who sought to make *an unlawful use of a venerable piece of architecture under the protection of the white flag.*"

The following day this communication was sent to the German Military authorities by the General in command of the troops fighting near Rheims:

"It was subsequently established that a shot from a mortar had been fired at Rheims Cathedral. According to a report of the . . . . Army Corps, this was necessary, as it was not possible, by the fire of the field artillery alone, to dislodge the post of observation which was known to be established upon the Cathedral."

So here we have a misuse of the white flag and the direct employment of the cathedral as a hostile post of observation. There is, accordingly, no basis for a charge against Germany, but the best of reasons for a drastic charge against France, which, in violation of an international agreement misused this splendid masterpiece of art for military purposes in order to prefer a false charge against Germany.

This contemptible trickery by which the cathedral was degraded to the purposes of a shield for bullets by the French army leaders, had scarcely taken place, when the German General Headquarters communicated under date of October 14th, the following facts to an astonished world. "Close by the Cathedral of Rheims two heavy French batteries were located. Light signals from a tower of the Cathedral were also observed. It goes without saying that all enemy measures and methods of war which are disadvantageous to our troops, will be contested, without regard to the preservation of the Cathedral. The French, therefore, now as formerly, must themselves assume the blame, if the venerable and noble building again becomes a sacrifice to the war."

On the 28th of October the vile game is once more enacted. The German Army Command thereupon communicated the fact that French batteries—including an artillery observation post upon the tower,—were stationed in front of the cathedral and that it was impossible to spare it any longer.

II. Ought we to reply to these hypocritical yells by pointing to the Chinese atrocities of Palikao's? Did not France in 1849 bombard Rome and destroy "masterpieces of art which can never be replaced"—as the official communiqué has it? Should we recall to the memory of mankind all the ghastly deeds of English warfare in South Africa—or bid the world remember the bombardment of Alexandria? Surely we have not forgotten the words of that excellent French patriot and famous historian of art, Viollet le Duc, who complained in 1870 that:

"The most furious enemy could not have made more havoc than our Garde Nationale."

It is not our intention in this place to enter more fully into the destruction of Louvain. The German official investigation has been made in the most honest manner and without regard to anything save the truth. The data that have been established lie before me in a printed record of some 115 pages. This confirms in the fullest degree that the people of Louvain had been equipped with arms with the knowledge and the approval of the Belgian Government, and that the murderous and cowardly attack upon wounded German troops was made under circumstances of the greatest cruelty. As already stated a map of the city with the burned portion marked annihilates the foul lie circulated through the world to the effect that "only the Town Hall and the railroad station were left." Is it necessary to repeat once more what all men may see for themselves—namely, that only one-sixth of the city went up in flames? And yet the lie of Rheims is repeated incessantly in the lie of Louvain.

We are able to establish upon the testimony of reliable eye-witnesses that these ruins in the neighborhood of the cathedral which the Belgians would represent as the results of German lust for destruction, are for the greater part due to explosions made in order to keep the flames from reaching the valuable old Town Hall. This, as is now known, was saved only through the heroic struggles of the German soldiers. Cunning photographs, "faked" so as to show certain ruins in the foreground as part of the walls of the Town Hall, have been used to deceive the public in other countries, as I see by certain illustrations in American periodicals.

An eye-witness reports thus:

"It was necessary to fire upon the Cathedral, since a murderous fire was directed against our soldiers from its towers during this treacherous attack. Of the art treasures in the Cathedral, there is only the loss of one Rubens to lament, according to the testimony of the second Mayor, who remained with us in the House of God.

"The destruction of the Library with all its manuscripts and old editions, is an irreparable loss, for many of the works had no duplicate in the world. The blame for this loss lies with those who placed machine-guns upon this famous and historical monument of learning, and shot down the unsuspecting Landsturm men. People in Louvain say that this deed was the work of Russian students."

An ex-member of Parliament writes thus to the "Westminster Gazette" during the early part of September, 1914:

"If the denizens of the city suddenly fired upon the Germans from the houses, then this insane act must bring about its just consequences. Field Marshal Lord Roberts ordered Boer farms to be laid in ashes for the same offense."

The best confirmation of the fact that the German soldiers were suddenly and treacherously fired upon from the houses, is found in the story of the Vice-Rector of the University of Louvain, Monsignore Dr. Coenrads, as published in the "Kölnische Volks-Zeitung." Even at this earlier period Dr. Coenrads confirmed all that has since been stated in the official inquiry. "There was no doubt that the German soldiers were fired upon in a most terrible manner. C'était une fusillade bien nourrie. . ." All attempts of the notable citizens of the town to restrain the people were useless.

"The firing was incessant," declares one of these gentlemen, surely an unimpeachable witness.

It has further been proved that in the serious fighting around Malines the heavy artillery of the Germans was expressly forbidden to fire upon the town, so that the cathedral might not be injured. As established by official investigation it was the Belgians themselves who threw shells from fort Walhem north of Malines, into the open city which the Germans occupied, and shot the cathedral to pieces.

A few days after this the "Daily Mail" laconically announced: "The Belgians were forced to bombard the cathedral of Termonde."

Wherever the rules of war were observed the German army used all the means within its power to prevent unnecessary damage. Wherever these rules were transgressed or abused the opponents were visited with the proper punishment.[1]

III. What Germany might have expected, especially what her Rhine Provinces might have expected, has been revealed by Monsieur Hanotaux in an indiscreet moment. Not a single stone of our great cathedrals would have been left standing, and not only that,—even private property, the immunity of which is ensured by national law,—all the districts of German industrial life would have been given over unto annihilation! Yet at Antwerp (despite the memory of indelible outrages upon German men, women and children) the Germans went to work with such extreme care that the press of the entire world—after certain hasty and preliminary attempts at blaring forth lies,—expressed itself as astonished that historic buildings and works of art should have suffered so very little damage. Even the "Morning Post" regarded it as a "wonder" that the Town Hall as well as the cathedral should have been spared. No, it was not a "wonder"—it was merely the solicitude, the discipline and the innate reverence for art in the breasts of the besiegers.

As to what was to happen to *our* temples and treasures of art—the unrestrained and unmartial loquaciousness of the French journalists and Maeceni of art left no doubt as to *that*.

[1] The "Times" of December 14th, published the letter of an officer of Field Artillery in which he writes as follows:

"It is nonsensical to complain of the destruction of large buildings, whether town halls, churches, or factories, when in the contested area. We do it as much as the Germans do, and observing officers of both sides use these same buildings to direct their artillery fire on those of the other. It happens to be in France now, but later on it may well be Cologne Cathedral. We had better not shout too loud now or we shall merit the epithet hypocrite later on."

We would like to place special emphasis upon the fact that an attempt made in the October issue of "Kunst und Künstler," a German art magazine, to introduce the subject of a German raid upon art treasures, was vigorously repudiated by Herr Bode, the General Director of the Berlin Museums.

Article 56 of the Rules and Regulations of Warfare by Land emphatically forbids the seizure of works of art and science. These are to be regarded as inviolate private property at all times.

The representatives of the *grande nation,* to be sure, proceed in an altogether different fashion in this matter.

The Napoleonic thefts of art in the year 1806, judging by the quoted opinions of our enemies, would have been mere child's play compared to the hauls of art treasures which our enemies would have fetched from Berlin—if that "*promenade à Berlin*" had really succeeded.

In short: we love and we reverence art—but we set the welfare of our Fatherland above that of art, that is to say, we would never permit our country to be injured or betrayed by a wanton *abuse* of the purposes of art.

The words of Theobald Ziegler have a great significance. "Art is made for man, not man for art." In this tremendous struggle against innumerable and ruthless enemies the lives of our brave and heroic soldiers are worth more to us than the most beautiful Gothic building.

CHAPTER XXIV.

The Bombardment of Towns and Villages from Aeroplanes. The Use of Shells that Develop Gas.

I. We have already proved that no legitimate protest on the part of international law can be made against the air bombardments of the Germans. The Hague Declaration with regard to the throwing of projectiles, etc., is no longer valid in its old form, having expired. The extension of the Conference of 1899 was not attended by Germany, as certain suggested conditions had not been fulfilled. Germany is therefore bound as little by this Declaration as are France and Russia.

The Hague Convention of 1907 paid no special attention to regulating the rules of warfare by air. But since the German aeroplanes and airships have been accused of bombarding cities and villages, we acknowledge that Article 25 of the Rules and Regulations of Warfare by Land expressly forbids that towns, villages, dwellings, or buildings which are undefended shall be attacked or bombarded "by whatever means." The phrase "by whatever means" is supposed to have a particular application to explosives thrown from above. It was inserted in the text of 1899 during the year 1907 owing to the great progress that had been made in the mechanics of flight.

As a matter of principle the Germans have thrown bombs only upon "defended places." No one would venture to assert that Paris is an undefended place; for the French themselves declare it to be the largest and strongest fortress in the world. And yet our enemies wax most furious over the bombardment of this city. London, the chief place of storage of war supplies, and the chief concentration centre of the military, must on the very face of it be considered as a "defended place." It is even said that London is defended by a series of outer earthwork forts, though these must have been built of late years. The determinative factor consists in this:—that the country is defended by the place in question, or that the city, by hindering hostile operations, becomes an element of defense. The place must therefore also lie within the zone of military operations. This zone, in view of the great radius in which the action of the German Zeppelins is exercised, is very extensive, that is to say, it is determined by the distance which the airships or the aircraft are able to cover.

"Undefended places"—*not* open places—are in any case places in which there are no troops or *franc-tireurs* and which are not used in any other way for hostile purposes, or whose population does not conduct itself in a hostile manner. As is obvious to some minds, shots fired at aircraft from a certain place plainly show this is *not* an "undefended" place. It is difficult to keep track of all the various items which appear in the press of the Entente and which, with a nauseating mixture of assumed horror, bathos and hypocrisy, harp upon what they designate as the "murder of women and children." Nor can the airman compute the exact spot in which he intends his missile to lodge. It is in accordance with the tragic essence of war that here too the innocent must suffer with the guilty.

Article 27 which stipulates that all attention is to be bestowed upon the care of historical or artistic monuments has been observed as conscientiously as possible by the German airmen. Even then it is possible that a bomb may strike a church or some other protected spot. This is something which cannot be avoided, and it must be included in the hazards of a war waged with such bitterness as this one. But the French and English since August 1st, have disregarded all these laws and protective measures and have indiscriminately flung their bombs upon the most peaceful places.

Churches and architectural masterpieces even in the land of the enemy were not spared by him. For an example, bombs were thrown upon Cambrai and its cathedral in the most reckless manner, resulting in considerable damage to both. Similar cases were constantly reported from Belgium and the north of France (even a funeral procession was bombarded at Dadigeele on November 5th). There are enough instances to prove that our antagonists have no reason to complain of German vandalism when the men of our flying corps pay a visit now and then to the French capital and leave their somewhat weighty visiting-cards there. We would merely ask one tentative question: How would things look in Germany—if the French airmen possessed the same dash and audacity as the German? Woe to the "Dom" at Cologne and the great Minster at Strassburg!

II. Germany has now begun the aerial war on a grand scale. No sooner had the first raids been made upon Great Yarmouth, Sheringham, Cromer and Sandringham, than frenetic voices of protest were raised in the English press. (January 19th).

The English flung bombs not only upon Freiburg, Friedrichshafen and Düsseldorf, all open cities, as well as that portion of Baden known as the Markgraveland with its peaceful villages far removed from the sphere of war operations, not to mention the entire district of South Baden, but they bombarded schools—whereby chiefly children were slain. They shelled open towns like Dar-es-Salaam, Victoria in the Cameroons and Swakopmund, and endeavored with the most incredible meanness to carry out their "starving-out policy." Nevertheless in this war of annihilation they adopt a tone of the most revolting cant and moral indignation. This may delude the foolish and the unknowing, but it remains without the slightest effect in Germany.

Lord Fisher has not only defined the limits of warfare in the air for England but also for us when he declared: "The chief thing is that the air-ships should prove their value and damage the enemy—nothing else matters."

The official German bulletin issued by the General Headquarters on the 25th of December, 1914, shows the proper German attitude. This states:

"On the afternoon of December 20th a French airman threw 9 bombs on the village of Inor, though only hospitals were established here, and these had been plainly marked so as to be visible even to aeroplanes. No great damage was done.

"As a reply to this act and also to those that involved recent bomb-throwing upon the open city of Freiburg, which lies outside the sphere of operations, certain villages which lie near the position of Nancy were bombarded today by our airmen with bombs of a medium calibre."

What we were to expect from the enemy airmen if these were able to carry out all their threats, may be seen by the bombastic recruiting phrases which led to the founding of the secret league "*France Aviateurs*" by Védrines and Garros.

"What is our purpose? We desire, in the first few hours after a declaration of war on the side of Germany, to strike a frightful blow by personal, swift and daring action. We will bombard the centres of German defence, overwhelm them with explosives and transform their palaces, their garrisons, their military buildings into heaps of rubbish. We will carry death and ruin into the very centres of the enemy's organization, for this will be a war of destruction, iron against iron, fire against fire, death against death."

The legitimate bombardment of the English coast cities is treated in a comprehensive fashion in the original edition.

A statement issued by the German War Ministry regarding the use of shells that develop gas was announced by the Great General Headquarters on April 22, 1915:

"In an announcement of April 21st, the English War Office complained that the Germans had violated all the laws of civilized warfare by the employment of shells which emit suffocating gases on explosion, during their recapture of Hill 60 east of Ypres. As established by the official German announcements, our enemies have been making use of this means of warfare for many months. So they apparently cherish the idea that what is permitted to them is not to be permitted to us. Of course this point of view, which is by no means accompanied by the charm of originality so far as this war is concerned, is perfectly comprehensible to us—especially when we consider that the developments of German chemical science naturally enable us to produce far more effective means of this sort than our enemies. We can hardly, however, expect them to share this point of view.

"Moreover there is no particular application of the law to the case in question. The German artillery uses no projectiles whose *one purpose* it is to develop suffocating or poisonous gases (Declaration at the Hague, July 29th, 1899). The gases of the German bombs generated upon explosion, though they may be far more obnoxious that those of the ordinary French, Russian or English bombs, are nevertheless not so dangerous as these. The system of generating clouds of smoke which we sometimes use during fighting at close quarters is also in no wise contrary to the rules of warfare. It means nothing more than a more efficient way of producing the effect formerly achieved by means of a burning bundle of straw or wood shavings. As the smoke is plainly visible even during the darkest night, it is left to the individual discretion of every man to withdraw from it in good time."

Inasmuch as both France and England, and above all Russia, had already made use of similar bombs against the Germans (see official bulletins of the German Headquarters of March and April, 1915), the German War Ministry would have been justified even from the viewpoint of mere reprisals in making use of such bombs, regrettable as their application may in general be held to be. The use otherwise made of burning missiles, the production of smoke, etc., does not come under the provisions of the Hague Declaration of July 29th, 1899.

With respect to the air-attack upon Karlsruhe the German Government reports officially as follows on the 17th of June, 1915:

In its official *communiqué* of June 15th, the French Army Headquarters boasts of the notorious air-attack upon Karlsruhe, and seeks to establish the point that this was a measure of retaliation for the bombardment of French and English open cities. This "justification" of the French attack must be challenged by the objection that only fortified points and places lying within the sphere of operations and having a close relation to the war, have been bombarded by the Germans. Wherever "open" cities were concerned, our attacks were in all cases reprisals for similar attacks made by our opponents. We have always expressly mentioned this fact in all our reports.

That the justification of the French action should be contrary to the truth, will surprise no one who has been in the habit of reading the reports of our opponents with a critical mind. But a new element is introduced by the brutal frankness with which the enemy acknowledges having indicated as a goal for his airmen a peaceful city, lying far distant from the scene of hostilities,—a city which had shown so much hospitality to the French just before the war.

Military measures cannot excuse this proceeding, for the only damage in a military sense inflicted upon our army, consists in the wounding of three soldiers in a hospital. The munition factory which lies beyond the city and whose military importance is not very great, was not damaged, beyond having a scaffold destroyed. Although furnishing an easily recognizable mark, only a few bombs were devoted to it.

It will be recalled that special attention was devoted to the *schloss* in which, in addition to the venerable Arch-duchess Louise, the Queen of Sweden had been staying for several weeks.

This particular air-attack, judged by its results as well as by the official instructions given the airmen regarding the objective of their attack, cannot be designated as a military enterprise, but merely as a crime, the brutality of which speaks eloquently of the real quality of the so much belauded civilization of the French.

What inroads this brutality has made upon the souls of the French, may be seen by glancing at the comments of the French press upon the air-attack made on Karlsruhe. The most violent of all journals, nearly all of which adopt an extreme tone, is the "Libre Parole," which writes:

"If we have murdered a few civilians in Karlsruhe, we have merely freed ourselves of people who carry on a dishonorable warfare against us in the economic field." The "Libre Parole" then demands that Pforzheim, the industrial centre of Baden, be bombarded, in order to avenge French industry. Every inhabitant of Pforzheim that was sent to the other world, meant one less active and hateful enemy of France.

Voilà! the civilized and polished French!

CHAPTER XXV.

English Business Morals and the Code of English Creditors. Deprivation of the Legal Rights of Germans in Russia and France.

"You may believe what I have told you of the English: They are total strangers to all magnanimity. As Paoli says: *Sono mercanti*—they are a nation of hucksters." Napoleon.

"No Englishman still ventures to believe the truth! For 200 years he has been lapped in lies of every sort. A delicate poison of falsehood penetrates society." Carlyle.

I. England is anxious not only to annihilate Germany in a military but in an *economic* sense. We have seen that the international grounds for her declaration of war were mere pretexts. From time immemorial it has been the custom of the English to make a great show of moral indignation in all questions concerning liberty and right. For England this war is nothing more than a business venture, an enterprise which, quite in accordance with ancient English tactics, the nations of the

Continent are to carry out for the benefit of the British state. Bismarck called this playing the game of the "Wolf and the Crane." Sir Edward Grey publicly and authoritatively acknowledged on the part of Great Britain that her participation in the war could not possibly increase the damage which she would suffer through non-participation.

The position assumed by the English State proves how right Heine was when he said of that country: "There is in all creation no being so hard-hearted as the huckster whose trade is at a standstill, whose customers have left him and whose wares no longer find a market." Bernard Shaw and Oscar Wilde have, each in his own way, expressed the same thought in still more drastic words.

As early as the year 1897 the "Saturday Review" wrote to the effect that nations have fought for years for a city or a right of succession—should they not fight for a commerce worth billions of pounds? If Germany were wiped to-morrow from the face of the world, there would be no Englishman who would not be the richer the day after.

A method of reasoning of such cold, calculating, material brutality as this, which would drive the French charger and the Russian bear as a tandem team, leaves no room for surprise at the mean and dishonorable methods adopted for damaging German industry and German trade. All these seem to be approved of by the English people of the present day.

That we once more find here a clear abuse and ignoring of the rules of international law, may be seen from the frequently-quoted Section II, Chapter I of the Second Peace Conference of October 18th, 1907. Herein, in Article 23, clause h, we find it stated that "it is specially forbidden:"

"*To declare* abolished, suspended, or inadmissible in a Court of law the *rights and actions of the nationals of the hostile party.*"

This law, as we have seen, is converted by England into something precisely opposite. And this in spite of its ratification by England and hence her agreement with it.

The proclamation published in the "London Gazette" on September 9th, 1914, and dealing with "Trading with the

Enemy," has the following contents, which in lieu of the original, we retranslate from the German version:[1]

"The Proclamation of August 5th, which refers to trading with the enemy, and paragraph 2 of the Proclamation of August 12th, as well as all official publications which serve as elucidation thereof, are hereby cancelled. In place of the former the following proclamation is to be regarded as in force. In this the term "enemy country" designates the territories of the German Empire and the Dual Monarchy of Austria-Hungary together with all their colonies and the dependencies thereof. In this proclamation the term "enemy" designates every person or society of every nationality which is situated in the enemy country or does business there. Not included in the above are persons of enemy nationality who do not reside in an enemy country nor carry on business there. With regard to corporations only those which happen to be incorporated in an enemy country will be regarded as of the enemy.

The following proscriptions enter into force:

1. To pay a sum of money to the enemy or for his use.
2. To pay a sum of money to an enemy for a debt or to give surety for his benefit.
3. To participate in drafting a cheque in favor of an enemy, or in accepting or paying same, or to present same for payment or to deal in any other way with negotiable papers.
4. To deal with a negotiable paper belonging to the enemy, to accept it or to pay it. This law will not be regarded as violated by those who in this case are able to prove their good faith.
5. To conclude any new business with the enemy in stocks, shares and other securities or to terminate current negotiations in such papers.
6. To conclude with the enemy or in his favor, any new marine, life, fire or other policies or insurance contracts, or to assume any insurance or other risk which by

[1] See in sequence the "Trading with the Enemy Acts" of September 18th, 1914, the 27th of November, 1914, the 11th of January, 1915, as well as the English Proclamation of March 15th, 1915, regarding measures to be taken with respect to German wares.

means of a policy or other insurance contract (inclusive of retro-active insurance) is calculated to render valid those entered into or agreed to before the war in favor of the enemy—it is forbidden to accept such or to permit them to be realized.

7. Directly or indirectly to import goods and wares to an enemy country or for an enemy's use or need, or to export them from the country—either by roundabout ways, or to deal with goods destined for an enemy or an enemy country or such as come from thence.
8. For British vessels to enter a port or other place in an enemy country or to enter into communication with same.
9. To make a mercantile, financial or other agreement with the enemy or in his favor.
10. To conclude business with an enemy against which the Crown Council has emitted a proscription, as proclaimed by a Secretary of the State,—even though this be permitted by law, or by a present proclamation or other decree.

Express attention is hereby called to the fact that whosoever, either directly or indirectly, trespasses against this law, is guilty of a crime and will be punished accordingly."

See further details in the original German edition, page 367.

What then, may be said to be law in England?

The answer to that may be comprised in a few words: Any agreements which have been concluded during the war between the nationals of belligerent states are, according to this law, absolutely invalid. Even after the restoration of peace no legal claims based upon these contracts can be made before an English court of law. In contrast to this it may be said that contracts concluded before the war remain valid, though no legal action respecting them may be taken during the war, and the obligations of Englishmen under these agreements may not be carried out during the course of the war. Should a British subject endeavor to do this, he would be guilty of treason.

This last regulation is to some degree suspended when the carrying-out of the contracts is possible only during the course of the war, either by the nature of the contract or by reason of special stipulations. The English theory, for instance, is that a freight contract is automatically dissolved in case the transportation was to have taken place during the period of war. This is of particular significance for all those branches of trade which import so-called products of the season from England. In case it proves impossible to make a timely delivery of the goods owing to the war, as has been stipulated, the purchaser is to be absolved from the duty of accepting the goods or paying for them.

On the other hand insurance contracts if concluded before the war become invalid, if the event that entitles the insured party to damages occurs during the course of the war.

The obligation of paying interest, since all claims are suspended during the war, is likewise abrogated by English law. A demand for interest can be made only after the conclusion of peace.

The German Imperial Government has naturally been forced to adopt corresponding economic measures in the shape of reprisals for those passed by Great Britain. We are concerned in this book only with the complete and ruthless disregard of signed compacts and agreements on the part of England.

II. It is an unfortunate fact, and emphatic reiteration of it may be made without committing the slightest injustice against England:—*there is no nation in all the world which so wantonly disregards the rights of other nations, or the sanctity of international treaties or the neutrality of other lands, as England herself.* This fact shouts from every page of English history. From Copenhagen to Alexandria, from Alexandria to Persia and the Boer Republics. *Once more England bases her principles upon wrong, in this case upon the unmoral aspects of the debtor's law.* But this too will be bound to have disastrous consequences for this nation of tradesmen. It is really nothing less than applying to ordinary commerce the rights of seizure at sea, the privilege of capturing prizes and booty. The purpose, the end is the same,—the ruthless annihilation of the opponent. And annihilation at any price! And yet England does not see that she is merely digging her own grave. "Business as usual," exclaimed the English papers and this variety of patriotism finds expression in England's every utterance.

While all the recent international agreements have been actuated by the principle that only the official armies are to wage war, and that citizens are to be kept as separate and immune as possible in their personal, economic, and financial relations from all the hostile proceedings, these singular English regulations, which might have applied to wars in the Middle Ages, are bent upon carrying war into the home, into the office, into the factory, into the most intimate family life, upon tearing asunder all those channels large and small, which modern intercourse has created between the citizens of the belligerent nations, all of whom stood so close to one another in relationship, amity, history and business life. All communication is to be prevented and interrupted, suspended by the ruthless hand of force. This is also the reason for the regrettable but excuseable hate which suddenly seized upon such wide circles of the German public, circles which had hitherto been inspired only by the friendliest feelings toward England and had in fact been altogether too much influenced by English traits and habits.

Such is England's desire. Without the slightest national impulse towards war, and from the standpoint of a mere business calculation, she proceeds in the blindest manner to stir up passion against herself through this ruthless measure, merely in the hope that other nations might again be foolish enough to enact the role of sacrificial victims. Through this method of waging war she arouses the spirit of the darkest Middle Ages and finds herself confronted by a great people, outraged in all that they hold dear, and ready to pick up the glove of challenge flung so frivolously at their feet. By acts such as these England ignores the development of hundreds of years of human intercourse, and endeavors artificially to create conditions the limits of whose operation she cannot foresee, and which must in their final results inevitably avenge themselves upon those who prepare them.

III. The British Bank of Northern Commerce sent an open communication to Ritzau's Bureau at Copenhagen at the end of August, 1914, in which it was openly stated that several German and Austrian Banks had made an attempt to cash their English checks and bills of exchange through the Scandinavian countries, or Holland, or Portugal. The banks of these countries were therefore to take note that English legal regulations now forbade all payments of money or other transactions that might favor the enemy. Austrian and German checks were neither accepted nor paid, even though presented with the endorsement of a firm in some neutral state. No inquiry was made as to the manner in which the Scandinavian banks had come into possession of the German checks; the payment was simply and flatly refused.

Acting upon this rule the French and English banks have refused to accept or discount checks that bore a German endorsement, even when such checks had been endorsed by German firms in neutral lands. As is self-evident the qualified German banks and banking interests were forced to proceed in a corresponding fashion in order to parry the stroke. The Reichsbank (Imperial Bank) has announced that after the 31st of January, 1915, it would buy, cash or negotiate no more drafts or checks that were couched in the French language. In the same way French remarks or notes upon checks or bills of exchange would exclude them from all circulation in the Imperial Bank. It is to be hoped that firms in Elsass-Lothringen may remember this.

A correspondent in the London "Financial News" raises the question as to whether he would be permitted to annul contracts which he had given to an English company the capital of which was, however, chiefly in German hands. The "Financial News" at once answers this affirmatively. It agrees—even though it might entail a suit at law:

"This newspaper is of the opinion that no English court of law would give the complainant the least assistance under such circumstances. If someone has made an agreement with A under the belief that he was B, he is justified, on discovering his error, in repudiating the contract. This is an ancient principle. Upon the same grounds an Englishman who has given orders to an English-German firm under the assumption that the German share-holders were civilized business people, would be justified in annulling these orders, when, as is now the case, he becomes aware that he is dealing, not with civilized people, but with a savage and barbaric nation." (*retranslation*)

The reader of the "Frankfurter Zeitung" who sends this cutting to that paper, observes with reason: "This is the serious opinion of a leading London financial paper which has been established in the City of London for over 31 years, and these are the people whose business classes were supposed to be the most respectable in the world—a people who because of their alleged strict adherence to good faith and sincerity, had possessed the confidence of business people all over the world! No matter what the result of the war may be England will never again be able to recover this confidence!"

That fanaticism which finds so unlovely an expression in this London organ of finance has about it something that is absolutely pathological, something which must cause even Englishmen to shake their heads. But such things are the black fruits of the thug-like policies of Grey and Churchill. The Parisian press also saw to it that similar unbridled frenzies aroused the laughter of all respectable folk. For it demanded that England should seize all those fabulous treasures which the German Emperor was alleged to have stored up in Vancouver, Canada, and in parts of British India in order that he might still have something left after his pensioning-off and flight to foreign countries! It would be interesting to learn what sheets such as these think of the mental calibre of their readers.

Economic War in the English Crown Colonies.

England's brutal actions at home, found a direct parallel in her Crown Colonies.

The policy of Great Britain stood in violent contrast to that of Japan in her interpretation of modern international law, especially when we consider the attitude of Japan after the capture of Kiao-Chau. We call attention to the following:

1. Immediately after the declaration of war by England, all male German and Austrian-Hungarian subjects in the Crown Colonies who were between the ages of 17 and 55 years, were led away into concentration camps. The only exceptions made were in the self-governing colonies of Australia, Canada, and New Zealand.

2. German and Austrian-Hungarian firms were forbdden to do new business. In the event of their not being over 55 years of age, the winding-up of aliens' businesses was to be entrusted to English or neutral employees. In certain instances the proprietors of large concerns were permitted to wind-up their businesses themselves on the condition that they gave their word of honor not to communicate with Germany either directly or indirectly.

3. In November came the incredible news, at first from Hong-Kong, and later from the other Crown Colonies, that all Germans had been interned there without further ado—and moreover in *Chinese* prisons. Their businesses had been placed in the hands of receivers and were to be sold at once, chiefly to English competitors of their firms, without any regard as to the consequences. There were punishments of 12 months imprisonment and $5000 fines.

4. The German men and women, including missionaries in the German colonies in West Africa which had been occupied by the French and English troops, were all arrested without notice and exposed to the ridicule of the negroes. The men were taken to concentration camps, the women and children were given over to the care of blacks and transported like cattle upon freight steamers for England under sanitary conditions that were a mockery of all human civilization.

5. The plantations and store-houses of the Germans were subjected to forced liquidation and disposed of outright for one-tenth to one-fifth of their value.

On December 7th the text of a new law was made public in the Straits Settlements and in Upper India. It was entitled: "Alien Enemies (Winding-up) Ordinance 1914." This law stipulates that all enemy firms are forthwith to be subjected to forced liquidation. Under enemy companies are included those which are inscribed in the colonies of Great Britain or elsewhere as stock companies, in case at least one-third of the capital stock or of the board of directors are German or Austrian-Hungarian.

The liquidator is authorized to sell all values and to dissolve the firm or stock company. For this he is to receive 2½% commission. He is then to send in his statement and to pay in the balance to some bank designated by the Governor. As soon as this has been done, all books, letters, vouchers, accounts and other documents which have been the property of an enemy or enemy company, *as well as the statement of the liquidator are to be destroyed.* ("Weserzeitung" of February 2nd, 1915.) This last regulation is characteristic of the spirit of all the rest. The properties entrusted to the tender mercies of the liquidator may be exploited by him in the most shameless manner without his incurring the least danger that he will be held responsible by the damaged party after the war. The proofs of his robberies have been annihilated according to law.

An announcement by the English Colonial Secretary in the "African Mail" of April 2nd, 1915, runs as follows:

"As announced in the press of February 17th, the business houses of German and Austrian firms have been closed upon command of the government, in Nigeria, the Gold Coast and Sierra Leone, and officials appointed to supervise the liquidation. The date up to which those who have claims against the firms may make them good has been postponed until the 30th of April. The firms in liquidation are the following: (Here the names of 17 firms in Nigeria, 22 on the Gold Coast, and 5 in Sierra Leone are given.)

"Persons or firms who have any claims whatsoever against the firms mentioned above can make these claims good until April 30th, by submitting all details, proofs and assurances under oath to the liquidators." (*retranslation*)

The original German edition contains many criticisms of similar happenings in France and especially in Russia, where the Germans and Austrians were deprived of even the slightest protection in law by measures passed during the course of the year.

The suspension of patents and trade-marks in the countries of the Triple Entente are fully described on page 386 *et seq.* of the original German edition.

The fact that Germany need have no fear of the future and that she is justified in regarding all these ruthless trade and financial war-measures as crass stupidity and short-sightedness which are bound to inflict fatal wounds upon English industry and English trade, is revealed in a very charateristic utterance of the "Times" at the end of September:

The quotation is from a review in the "Times" of a book by William Dawson:

"Regarding the development of modern Germany a great deal is now being said as to the opportunity offered by the war for a conquest of German trade and German markets. There is a great deal of foolish talk upon this subject. The trade-connections, which thanks to our fleet, we shall be able to obtain, will not long remain in our hands once normal conditions are restored.

How, then are we to draw out the capital invested in these ventures? *Germany has honestly assured herself of her trade through the knowledge, intelligence, industry and power of adaptation resident in her merchants and engineers. Only by the like qualities shall we be able to make conquest of these markets and retain them permanently.*"

Can he who has any knowledge of the difference in the moral and mental equipment of the two nations, have any doubt as to the issue?

The Violation of the Neutrality of Switzerland and other Neutral States by the Triple Entente.

A. It proved to be necessary to add a short chapter upon this subject to the first edition. And we are now forced to enlarge it.

From the very beginning of things France has been guilty of serious breaches of the neutrality of the Swiss Republic, especially by means of a continuous system of organized espionage directed from Basel. Likewise the attitude adopted toward Swiss citizens who, according to the undisputed reports of numerous Swiss newspapers, were confronted with the alternatives of "voluntary war services," "expulsion," or "enduring molestation by the authorities," appears most questionable from the point of view of the Second Peace Conference.

Brutal and violent actions committed against German-speaking Swiss subjects on the part of the French population were cited in numerous instances. Now the Italian mob follows the French example.

A clear and acute case of the violation of Swiss neutrality occurred when three English aeroplanes flew over Swiss territory in order to make an attack upon the Zeppelin wharves at Friedrichshafen on November 21st, 1914. This had evidently been preceded by a long and illegal espionage conducted from Switzerland.[1] The open manner in which a section of the Swiss frontier territory was crossed by the airmen put an end to the "harmlessness" of this entire procedure.

Flying over a neutral and, as such, inviolable territory according to the present development of the science of war, is, without doubt, a "moving of troops" in the meaning of Article 2 of the 5th Convention of the 2nd Hague Peace Conference, as cited.

According to Article 5 Switzerland was not privileged to suffer this action on the part of the airmen, and the protest she made was the minimum objection she could offer did she not wish to condone unforeseen and disastrous consequences. The very least we might have demanded would have been an equality of toleration, for this is the self-understood right of the opponent of that belligerent who first violates the said neutrality.

The success which attended the protest made by Switzerland was in itself a vindication of its justice.

The Swiss point of view which has been expressly recognized as correct by France, will doubtlessly also be acknowledged by the German and the Austrian-Hungarian Governments. It was precisely the aerial trespass upon the neutral territory of Belgium by French airmen before the beginning

[1] The unparalleled action with which the English Minister was charged with respect to an abuse of the Swiss wireless telegraphy station, is officially denied,—precisely like the flights across Swiss territory. One might also allude to that sojourn of an hour and a half on the church-steeple at Romanshorn on November 3rd, 1914.

Colonel Emerson, an American newspaper correspondent who is the informant of the "Frankfurter Zeitung," insists upon his version of this incident. It would naturally constitute one of the most impudent attacks upon the neutrality of the Swiss Republic and international law that has ever been recorded. (See Articles 1, 3, 5 and 9 of the 5th Hague Conference of 1907.)

of war which the German Government justly regarded as a crass instance of a breach of international law. Why should an action which in a military sense is infinitely more dangerous than the movement of a possibly small detachment of infantry or cavalry over a territory, be judged otherwise than this?

Any contrary decision would be illogical, untenable in a military sense; and indeed highly dangerous, and in contradiction to the letter and the significance of the 5th Conference which says: "Belligerents are forbidden to move troops or convoys of either munitions of war or supplies across the territory of a neutral power." Flight across territory in an airship or aeroplane is also a "moving across" of an apparatus of war, a mechanical fighting unit, of a "troop" across the territory in question, and is therefore strictly interdicted. The Swiss authorities would also have been justified, without being accused of any hostile attitude, (see Article X) in shooting down the airman.

There is no doubt that it is in accordance with universal modern conceptions of law that the tracts of air immediately above the territorial earth and water area as defined by the boundaries of a state, are to be reckoned as a part of that territory over which the State may exercise its rights of sovereignty. The British interpretation would reduce the value of neutrality to a mere minimum, and this would not be without a powerful influence upon the security of neutral states.

B. Other Cases of the Ignoring of Neutrality on the Part of the Triple Entente States.

In general one might say that the abuses of neutrality of nearly all neutral states were simply legion. We would merely call attention to the fact that at the beginning of the war the French and English fleet made use of Corfu and Zante in a most unabashed manner as a base of food supplies. Greece, whose sympathies for the Triple Entente were certainly at that time by no means negligible, was forced to beg that some restraint be placed upon these actions,—the transport of arms *en masse* over Saloniki, etc. During the bombardment of the Dardanelles the Triple Entente States again made use of two Greek islands, Lemnos and Tenedos, as a formal basis of long-continued operations.

As the "Osmanli Lloyd" reports from a reliable source: The English have brought two floating docks to Lemnos for the repairing of ships and have also begun to build coal bunkers for a coaling station, as well as a station for wireless telegraphy. So one may be entitled to say that the neutrality of Greece has actually for a long time been only a sham neutrality. The lengths to which England is prepared to go in her insolence toward a "neutral land" is shown in the following communication:

The "Kriegszeitung" has the following cablegram from Athens, dated May 16th: "The appearance of German submarines in the Mediterranean has caused great excitement in Athens. How greatly the German submarines are dreaded by the English navy people may be seen by the fact that the British Admiralty is not ashamed to attempt to bribe the citizens of a neutral state like Greece to commit acts which are not in agreement with the neutral attitude of their government and might lead to the most serious consequences. The British Minister in Athens, Mr. Eliot, was notified by the commander of the British Mediterranean Fleet of the presence of submarines. He at once proceeded to call upon the Greek people by means of their newspapers to help support the British Admiralty by means of espionage services and promised in the name of the government of Great Britain to pay for successful work of this sort, a reward of 12 500 drachmas."

An agreeable contrast to the attitude of so-called neutral lands, is the attitude of Sweden, which forbade the transport of all material of war, since she correctly recognized the fact that failure to pass such a law would really be a breach of neutrality on the part of a loyal government. This interpretation is one that is based on truth and good faith.

Let us compare with this the behavior of our enemies on the other side of the Canal, they who, according to the assurances of their statesmen, entered this war merely in the interests of the "sanctity of international treaties" and for the "protection of small nations." They have violated the neutrality of 1. China,—attack upon Tsingtau from Chinese territory; 2. of Denmark—the passage of an English submarine to the Baltic Sea; 3. of Holland—repeated flights over Dutch territory; 4. of

Switzerland,—flights across territory as already mentioned; 5. of Greece,—illegal use of Greek islands as naval bases; 6. of Chile,—attack upon the "Dresden" in Chilean waters; 7. of Brazil—(see the following); 8. of Spain,—in the case of the "Highflyer;" 9. of Turkey—in the matter of Egypt; 10. of Italy—seizing and holding back steamers; 11. of Sweden—bullying Swedish firms.

This does not pretend to be a complete list. On the contrary: the violations of the neutrality of the United States from the very beginning were so numerous that a special book might be written upon them. *A later day will bring the proof that there is scarcely a land under the sun whose neutrality has not been outraged by England in this war.*

PART TWO.

Questions of Legality in Naval Warfare.

CHAPTER XXVI.

England, the Laws of Naval Warfare, and Ourselves.

The chief fundamental laws in the matter of conducting war on land are sufficiently clearly defined from an international standpoint in the so-called "Rules and Regulations of War on Land." There are gaps, to be sure, such as are bound to ensue, considering the difficulties surrounding the entire matter and the recent attempts at regulation. But where the will exists to interpret them properly they form an excellent code for a humane conduct of war. But this is not the case in the matter of naval warfare. In this, England, under the sham halo of a concern for the liberty of Europe, had until the middle of the 19th century defended the principle or rather the privilege of capturing prizes at sea. All efforts made to attack this, especially at the Congress at Chatillon (1814) were frustrated. "Never," cried Lord Cathcart, in a manner truly English, "will Great Britain acknowledge any other law upon the seas —than the universal law of the nations." England regarded the seizure of merchant vessels as a universal law of the nations!

The original edition contains a thorough-going description of the evolution of international sea-law (see page 401 *et seq.*).

England has appended her signature to all conventions; she has ratified the 6th, 7th and 8th (with a reservation) the 9th and the 11th Conventions of the Hague Conference.

Her position with respect to international law is dictated solely by the chief dogma of her naval policy: Every power, whatsoever its name, that threatens her position as a great power, and that may imperil her safety in the Channel, becomes England's mortal enemy. This is the dominating thread in all the policies of England for over four hundred years. After Spain, Holland, France—comes Germany. And to this general military, nautical and economic idea England sacrifices every obligation of justice and civilization.

The London Declaration regarding naval laws of February 26th, 1909, was to be of immense importance in all matters pertaining to naval warfare. It was to produce a greater clarity and uniformity in the general principles of international sea-law, especially in the matter of blockades (Articles 1 to 21), of contraband of war (Articles 22 *et seq.* to 44), of non-neutral support (Articles 45 to 47), of the destruction of neutral prizes (Article 48) of transfers to neutral flags, (Articles 55, 56) of the enemy character of goods and ships (Article 57 *et seq.*) of convoys, resistance to search and the regulation of damages. These principles, to be sure, were signed by all the nations that were parties to the Conference, including the six great nations now at war, but owing to the opposition of the British House of Lords, they were not *ratified*. Thus, *formally*, things remained as they had been, that is, according to the Convention of 1907, which left much to be desired in the way of clearness and completeness.

The regulations of the London Declaration of Naval Law are nevertheless most valuable data for the *interpretation* of the customs that have hitherto been held to be valid in modern naval warfare. The German Imperial Government has set a good example in this respect and has adopted the clear and humane ordinances of the Declaration in its new Prize Law of September 30th, 1909 (R. G. Bl. 1914, Page 275) and declared it to be determinative for the German conduct of naval war. Neutral States in general conform in many ways to the Declaration and thus confirm its spirit.

The manner in which the English Prize Courts interpret law is revealed in a report in the "Mercantile and Shipping Gazette" of the proceedings and decisions in the case of several captured German ships.

In the case of the judgment delivered on the German

sailing-vessel "Möwe," the President of the Prize Court, Sir S. Evans, owned that the parties belonging to the hostile nation, under certain circumstances, were also permitted to appear before the Prize Court, and the more so if they believed themselves to have, on the basis of one of the Hague Agreements, a claim to protection, to a privilege, or to compensation. It is further necessary that the grounds upon which the claim is based should be set forth in a sworn declaration and laid before the Court, as is required by the Regulation of the Prize Courts Act of 1914. With this decision the Court departs from its earlier standpoint. The permission, in the case of the "Möwe," was rendered illusory, however, by the fact that the Court held the bringing forward of the German witnesses to be of no importance, and in an additional observation further amplified this by declaring that according to the evidence on hand, the German objections could not have held good, as they were disputed by an Englishman and the statements before the court were considered sufficiently determinative!

Another case concerns the German trawler "Berlin," which was captured by an English trading steamer. No evidence was brought to prove that the capture of the ship was a justifiable measure; no prize-crew, no entry in the ship's log; the confirmation of the moment of the capture was likewise impossible. Nevertheless the confiscation of the ship was decreed. The Court declared that it was on the whole, "fortunately," not bound to any rule of proof, and could pass judgment as it seemed good and proper to do. The Prize Court could not be compared to other courts, and was on that account free from the "narrow restrictions" of other tribunals. On these grounds the court presumed the legality of the capture of the ship, and that this took place after the outbreak of war. The result was the confiscation of the ship ("Frankfurter Zeitung" of the 7th of December, 1914). Such a hollow pretense as this is called "Law"—in England.

It is particularly necessary that the International Prize Court as discussed at the Second Hague Conference should be established to control such judges. But who controls England?

The opinion that England's stubborn adherence to the right of seizure at sea is one of the chief causes of the present war is not to be dispelled. For in consequence of this "right of piracy" Germany was in sheer self-defense forced to create a large fleet, which England on her part regarded as a threat against her vital interests.

From the very beginning of hostilities England ruthlessly carried out the ancient English principle: "The books of law are closed in times of war; England then determines Right and Law." She has in part simply ignored the conventions of 1907, briefly alluded to in the foregoing, and has made her own advantage and her chief goal—the annihilation of her rival upon the seas—the basic principle of her method of making war. And in this, as the world may see, Hate and Fear are her chief advisers. These, to be sure, have always been evil advisers.

These actions on England's part are the more to be deplored, since England, as may be seen from official Norwegian and Swedish communications of the 20th of August,—thus a considerable time after the declaration of war on Germany,—announced that she would judge the most important questions of sea-law, especially the law of contraband, according to the London Declaration of 1909. In complement of this announcement England issued orders in which she expressly declared that all the objects mentioned in Article 22 and 24 of the London Declaration would be considered as contraband in this war. But later on she greatly modified these declarations and finally altered them in a wise to make the whole appear little less than a complete nullification of all the advantages of the London Declaration. England through her Premier, Mr. Asquith, during the debate in the House of Commons in 1911, declared that after careful investigation it had been found that a great international agreement such as the London Declaration was a measure of the *greatest interest for the preservation of the peace of the world as well as for England's dominance on the seas*. The Premier added that the government would be guilty of gross negligence of duty should it not do all that lay in its power to help introduce this international guide to conduct. The Declaration was therefore passed by a large majority in the Commons. And to-day Great Britain imagines that she is able to dispense in her one-sided manner with all the moral and legal claims of this acknowledged code of ordinary law at sea? England, of course, could not more clearly show that "world peace" meant nothing to her, than through this rejection of the regulations of the London Declaration.[1]

The House of Lords on the 12th of December, 1911, rejected the Naval Prize Bill, although the opening proviso expressly states: "The signatory powers are unanimous in the conviction that these rules (of the London Declaration) are essentially in accordance with universally recognized principles of international law."

England cunningly follows two quite contrary systems in her abuses of the laws and usages of naval warfare. These often enable her to give an appearance of a certain justification to her trespasses in the face of the reproaches levelled at her. We have lived to see how a people who have so deep a regard for respectability and reliability in their private and commercial life in times of peace, are nevertheless capable in their politics or in the continuance of their politics by means of war, of carrying out the most brutal and inhumane ideas—ideas which in their revolting meanness and spitefulness are simply incomprehensible to the rest of us Europeans. They do not hesitate to instigate assassinations and foul betrayals, as in the case of Sir Roger Casement whose man-servant was approached by M. de C. Findlay, the British Minister to Norway, whit a bribe to slay his employer! These are low crimes against the fundamental laws of humanity and of nations. And with all this, the Englishman is extraordinarily formal in all affairs of business.

This formalism has begotten and perpetuated various

---

[1] In a sermon delivered on the 2nd of June, 1851, F. W. Robertson, thus characterizes his nation:

"....With other nations the traffic of commerce is to be deemed irregular, in fact diseased—thus it is with us English. This striving after wealth is the source of our greatness and our degradation, our fame and our shame; it is the cause of our trade, our sea-power, our enormous wealth, our inventions, but at the same time also the source of our quarrels and our party strife, of the dreadful poverty and the more than pagan brutalization and degeneration of great strata of our population.... *Therefore the roots of all our endeavors are greed and covetousness—not the wish to enjoy more, but to have more.*"

(*retranslation*)

bizarre and nondescript forms in the realm of English jurisprudence. The Englishman has no love for penetrating too closely into the inner nature of things. For this reason mere form is sufficient unto him and frequently serves him as an expedient for evading the actualities of the law. So long as appearances are maintained he feels that the underlying morality of the matter is sufficiently established for him to give it his approval. This point of view is very often of great convenience to him and helps him to ease his mind of conscientious scruples.

There is not the slightest doubt that the British jurist is well aware that all the laws written down in the different conventions of the Second Hague Conference of 1907, have long been accepted as the usual rules of procedure at sea. But to the mind of the Britisher it is sufficient that the mighty naval state of Montenegro or Servia did not ratify this convention in order to convince himself that this also releases England from her obligations. Laughable as this point of view may appear to him after a little consideration, he nevertheless will not hesitate to use it to his advantage whenever this is possible.

This merely formal interpretation of rules according to the letter, does not, of course, on the other hand, prevent British sea-power from basing its claim or its case precisely upon those very regulations the invalidity of which has permitted it to build up its brutal code of war, and to consider them as valid whenever this should redound to its momentary advantage. We are able to substantiate this in a number of instances.

Thus the mere utilitarian end in view is held to be the chief goal of English politics, as it is of English methods of war,—war in itself being only a continuance of politics. Ridiculous fanaticism as well as the most liberal interpretation are made to serve its purposes at one and the same time. It need merely have an opponent who is willing to concede all these things to mighty Great Britain in the most obliging and credulous fashion. And it is because this same lack of consideration did not actuate her opponents that England has in the past been able to do such good business in the matter of politics and to make easy conquest of a world. And inasmuch as England has always been able to find foolish nations willing, as at present, to support her wars of "trade and industry," and as she was an adept in making use of French vanity and thirst for revenge, and Russian lust for power, why her practices constantly met with renewed success.

But the greatest riddle of our day must remain this: that all humanity should be threatened today by the one common enemy and yet be unable to recognize him. The smaller states of Europe are uninterruptedly subjected to the violence of the English world power, their trade is destroyed and stolen, their honor trodden underfoot, the freedom of the seas, upon which the prosperity of all nations must needs be based, has become a figment of the imagination—and yet these maltreated peoples scarcely venture to indulge in a timid murmur of complaint!

"Rule Britannia, rule the waves!"—this motto of a nation which may as a whole be said to be obsessed with the insanity of Caesarism—*this is accepted as something self-evident.* But the fact that the German ventures to sing "Deutschland, Deutschland über alles" is regarded as a kind of national blasphemy—although he be merely defending his own skin.

The fact that we ventured to sow the entire English east coast as far as the Shetland Isles with mines a few days after the English declaration of war is considered as something very ruthless by the English mind. Was it not our duty to wait until the English had undertaken the same step upon our coasts? As in the case of "neutral" Belgium? But all this indignation will prove futile. The haughty Briton will have to unlearn many things—even if the war is to have a more favorable issue for him than we hold to be possible.

British "navalism" which is infinitely more dangerous for the peace of the world than so-called German "militarism," would not only like to "rule the waves," but also to "waive the rules"—as has been so truly and satirically said. It puts its hand upon the written laws of the nations and lo, these crumble to pieces. The "Morning Post" merely voiced the general English opinion when it declared, some time ago:

"Attempts to civilize warfare are attempts to tame the tiger, and lead to surprises and disillusions. The best method of conducting war is and must remain: to inflict the greatest amount of damage upon the enemy, so that he will surrender the more quickly." (*retranslation*)

Those famous words spoken by Lord Derby in the year 1867 are still valid today:

"We act in the most shameless manner towards foreign nations. We insist upon the full measure of international law, when this serves our purpose. In other cases we set ourselves without the least concern above the rights of others. The history of sea-law, which I would call sea lawlessness, is an inextinguishable testimony to the unbridled egoism and the greed of the English nation and its government." [1]

(*retranslation*)

Starvation as a Legitimate Weapon of Warfare.

The starving-out of a hostile civil population in war by land is unconditionally forbidden, since war operations may be conducted only against the official armies of a hostile state and not against private persons.

The starving-out of an enemy country may and must only

[1] Major Stewart Murray in his book, "The Future Peace of the Anglo-Saxons," utters these truly prophetic words: "For the people of this country to talk of the sanctity of international law is nothing but hypocrisy or ignorance."

And Carlyle was of the same opinion when he declared that there had been no English truth uttered since 200 years which was not composed half of untruth, that is to say, hypocrisy.

In a practical application of this sentiment, Keir Hardie recently published an article in the Manchester "Labour Leader"—in the early part of April, 1915, in which he expressed himself thus in relation to the war:

"Our entire military and naval policy works exclusively in the interests of millionaires and capitalists. What are the British interests in Persia, Egypt, India, Africa? Certainly not the welfare of the population, but merely the interests of the great financial enterprises, that is to say the moneyed classes... *Germany's terrible crime in the eyes of these people consisted in the great success of her international trade.* A shameful and unworthy fact in this war is the call of the press for a war to the knife against German trade. The results of this attempt, it is true, have had a more or less discouraging effect,—see the manufacture of aniline dyes as supported by the government,—in spite of which we are still to hope, after annihilating German skill and the German power of adaptation, without possessing these priceless qualities ourselves, to make a conquest of the rich German markets." (*retranslation*) See also an ironic essay in the "Nya Dagligt Allehanda" of Stockholm upon "England as a Mighty Phenomenon ofVirtue." (Norddeutsche Allgemeine Zeitung, No. 47/1915.)

take place in the sphere of naval warfare; and then only by means of the legitimate measures comprised in the cutting-off of imports, by blockade and by the right of seizure at sea.

In this sense and within these limits it is internationally recognized as one of the means of conducting war. Professor Lammasch writes as follows in the "Österreichischen Zeitschrift für öffentliches Recht" (1914, page 759):

"Even though the annihilation of trade as an end in war may not occupy the same prominence as in the trade wars between England and the Netherlands, the fact nevertheless remains that at present the interruption of imports and exports by sea, the interference with the trade in food supplies, raw materials and manufactured goods, the strangling of industry, the shattering of credit, the raising of prices and the scarcity of supplies necessary for the subsistence of life, are most effective measures for undermining the power of resistance of the enemy state. Unemployment and hunger are today, perhaps in a still greater measure than before, mighty allies, since they bring with them revolt and collapse."

The "right of blockade" is today practically negatived in view of the activity and the radius of action of the submarine, nor can England be said to be in a position to make a practical and effective blockade.

The right of seizure at sea may also be carried out only according to the limitations of international law, in especial with regard to the recognized principles of the Paris Declaration of Maritime Law as well as the accepted usages of the London Declaration. A special restriction is placed upon the seizure of neutral goods upon enemy ships as well as enemy goods upon neutral ships, provided that these are not comprised within the definition of what is legally declared as contraband. Wehberg, an authority upon these matters, is quite in the right in the position he assumes, namely, that the right of seizure at sea, *when carried out in accordance with international law*, is quite unable to produce a condition which would make it possible so completely to cut off a nation's supplies as to starve it out. The law of contraband, however, a law which the powers of the Triple Entente devote in reality to the starving-out of Germany, is under no circumstances permitted to serve the purpose of cutting-off the shipment of food supplies, but merely that of preventing the transport of war supplies. The great breach of international law of which England has made herself guilty, apart from her persistent laying of mines on the high seas, consists precisely in this abuse of the law of contraband.

This attempt to starve out the German nation, based as it is upon its present unjustifiable premiss, is and must remain a wanton sacrilege of a most atrocious nature against the spirit of the laws that all nations have agreed to observe, and it entitles Germany to retort with the severest reprisals of which she is capable by means of the submarine war.

In the event of a victorious issue in this war with England, one of the very first demands which must be made by the whole civilized world,—a demand for whose blessed consummation Germany is today battling with all her power, is this: *England's relinquishment of the right of seizure at sea.* Let us hope that the prophecy spoken by Dr. Oppenheimer may be fulfilled: "Pirates and filibusters like Francis Drake and Warren Hastings have created the British empire—and pirates and filibusters must the English remain—until such time as a stronger power overcome them."

May Germany prove to be this liberating power! [1]

The course of the war up to the present time has proved at least this much: *that so long as England remains the tyrant of the seas, all international law must be considered a sheer impossibility.* It is only in opposition to England that this condition of absolute lawlessness upon the "free seas" may be done

[1] An English periodical, "The Candid Review," which is a sort of mouthpiece of many leading members of the English Conservative Party, published an article in March 1915, entitled "Free the Fleet." This consisted of an extremely violent tirade against the London Declaration of 1909, the Hague Convention of 1907 and the Paris Declaration of 1856. Their complete abolition was demanded. We quote a few choice and quite delectable passages:

"All these conventions are, in reality, dead," we read here. "This is not the moment for political debates or party conflicts, this is not the moment for public differences of opinion between us, in the face of the enemy, but this is the moment for freeing the fleet. We must see how we are able to get rid of all this rubbish"—that is to say, the conventions! The Hague "Nieuwe Courant," commenting upon this, remarked: "Utterances of this sort in an influential political review are little disposed to induce a hopeful outlook for the future co-operation of Great Britain in abolishing the law of seizure at sea."

away with forever. *This war is above all things a war for the liberation of the seas!* [1]

For a clear-sighted and brilliant exposé of England as a rapacious pirate Empire, and the ancient bully with the big fleet, as well as the instigator of war among the Continental nations, Americans are recommended to read the famous work by Count zu Reventlow: "The Vampire of the Continent."

CHAPTER XXVII.

Breaches of Neutrality on the Seas by England and the Other States of the Triple Entente. Contraband of War. Blockades, etc.

I.

The mass of complaints, especially in relation to neutral sea traffic, grows from day to day. But as these complaints appear, for the greater part, in the foreign press and are very difficult to test as to their credibility, we are able to criticize them only to a very limited degree. The author confines himself in this book to the main charges against the English conduct of naval warfare and leaves it to neutral countries and to their newspapers to level their own charges against abuses by the English navy and violations of the XIII Convention of the Second Peace Conference.

But this much is established. England, pursuing an

[1] The decree of Napoleon I (21st of November, 1806) respecting the Continental Blockade, and his later observations in his reminiscences at St. Helena, suit the present English business methods as closely as though they had been coined for the occasion. "The behavior of England, which recalls that of the most ancient times of barbarism, has created for this power a monstrous advantage. . . . . One must use its own method of fighting when all ideas of justice, all liberal feelings, all the results of civilization, are trodden underfoot!"..... And in another place: "The reproach posterity makes against Pitt is the detestable political school which he bequeathed them: unabashed Machiavellianism, profound unmorality, cold self-interest, a contempt of human relations and of a just outlook on the world."

And to-day Charles Maurras ("Kiel et Tanger") writes of England as "Lord, exploiter and guardian of France!"—"One the leader, the other the led, the simple protégé" (page 191). Unhappy and deluded France!

analogous course to her ruthless procedure in the realm of civil rights, attempts to cut Germany off from all trade intercourse with the outer world, even with neutral states, and to create a "reversed continental blockade," simultaneously with a blockade by sea. This explains the continuous and unjustifiable complaints against Denmark, and other Scandinavian States, but especially against Holland, Italy (before the war), Spain and the United States of North America. But it is England, who on her own part, attempts to create breaches of neutrality on the part of these states by the acts of their subjects, and who complains bitterly of the "hostile" attitude of these countries when they insist upon maintaining their legitimate trade with Germany and Austria-Hungary according to the international regulations. The reader should consult a very objective, thorough-going and interesting description of the English attitude in the "Washington Post" of January 20th, 1915. This was likewise reprinted in No. 72, 1915, of the "Norddeutsche Allgemeine Zeitung."

The citizens of neutral states may of their own accord carry on trade in non-contraband goods with every country whether it be involved in the war or not, and may enter any port if it be not practically closed by the authorities of the country in question or effectively blockaded by the enemy. Should a belligerent power wish to prevent the exports of another power from leaving the country or to prevent its being supplied with other wares apart from war contraband, then the only way in which this may be legally carried out is to declare a blockade upon the ports of the respective country and to carry out an *effective* blockade, that is to say, it must cut off a stretch of hostile coast from all intercourse by sea in such a manner as to render it impossible for merchant vessels to penetrate the blockade.

It is self-evident that a neutral country in the pursuit of its rights must show the greatest and most friendly consideration to all sides so that it does not encroach too closely upon the interests of the warring nations. But no power has the right to demand the complete stoppage of that trade which flows from the ports of neutral countries, apart, of course, from contraband of war, since such a measure would be contrary to the law of nations and in the final result prejudicial to the interests of the belligerents themselves. The Norwegian periodical, "Norges Handel of Soefartstitende," has an excellent article upon this subject and makes a telling characterisation of the condition of international law at the beginning of the present war.

In the original there follows a penetrating exposition of the legislation concerning the International Law of Contraband (see original German edition, pages 421 *et seq.*).

There are three categories of goods that must be differentiated when investigating the question as to the presence of contraband:

1. Articles exclusively or chiefly used for war purposes (Articles 22, 23, 30, 31), that is, "*absolute contraband.*"

2. Articles susceptible of use for peaceful as well as warlike purposes,—"*relative contraband*" (Articles 24 *et seq.*, 33, 34, 35).

3. Articles which are not susceptible of use in war and may *never* be declared contraband of war (Articles 28, 29).

Articles 38—44 deal with the capture and condemnation of vessels. It is obviously impossible to enter upon all details in these pages. These may be looked up in the Declaration of London itself and other authorities, such as Sartorius, Pohl, etc.

The English list of contraband goods (Order in Council of August 4th, 1914) is based almost entirely upon the London conclusions. The regulations with regard to "absolute contraband" contain merely one alteration--namely, that "airships and flying-machines and their component parts" are declared as "absolute" contraband, though according to Article 24, clause 8 of the Declaration of London, these are declared as relative contraband. There is no doubt that this change was induced by fear of the superiority of the German air-service.

The regulations with regard to "relative contraband" were also at first in accord with the London provisions. The Order in Council of August 20th, 1914, which was the immediate basis for the treatment of contraband, opens by mentioning the fact that the French and Russian Governments intend "to act in accordance with the provisions of the Convention known as the Declaration of London so far as may be practicable."

But this is followed by a series (5) of "additions and modifications"—these, of course, being essentially altered and suspended by the later Order in Council of October 29th, 1914. The List of the 4th of August, 1914, and that of later issue were to be set up in place of Articles 22—24 of the Declaration of London. Modifying principles were applied to Articles 33, 34 and 35 of the Declaration and the "presumptions of the existence of the blockade." (Clause 4 and following.)

This recognizes a point which we would specially emphasize—the point that the law as laid down in the Declaration of London is the law of custom, something which was also recognized by the German Government in the lawful provisions of its Prize Law of the 30th of September, 1909:

"The General Report of the Drafting Committee on the said (London) Declaration presented to the Naval Conference, and adopted by the Conference at the II. plenary meeting of 25 February, 1909, shall be considered by all Prize Courts as an authoritative statement of the meaning and intention of the said Declaration and such Courts shall construe and interpret the provisions of the said Declaration by the light of the commentary given therein." Such is the literal text of the Order in Council of August 20th, 1914.

Four times in the course of three months and every time in the most one-sided manner did England alter her point of view. New English proclamations regarding contraband appeared on the 23rd of December, 1914 and the 12th of March, 1915. They all have the same purpose and end in view,—the suppression at all costs of the legitimate trade between Germany and the neutral states. There is no longer any thought of the immutability of law and principle. No man knows today what England may choose to regard as legal to-morrow.

All this is treated in a most thorough manner in the original work, upon the basis of the legal provisions of the Declaration of London, 1909, Articles 30, 32, 33, 34, 35, 65.

The basic principles of the Declaration of London, especially all the rules with regard to blockading, are merely swept aside by England. The alleged dependence upon the London Declaration is nothing less than "crass hypocrisy"—which, as might have been expected, France and Russia lost no time in imitating. A new and amazing stipulation is contained in the decision that according to English law a neutral vessel with papers made out for a neutral port of destination, may be captured when it proceeds to an enemy port, provided that it is seized before the *completion of its next voyage.* According to this it would suffice that a ship's papers were not in order to justify its being seized under the conditions of this presupposition. The London Declaration expressly states that after a vessel has completed its transportation of contraband, it may not be condemned, since the right of seizure on the part of the enemy does not represent a right, but a form of reprisal.

Further it is also presumed that an enemy destination is to be taken for granted when the wares are addressed to the agent of a hostile country or are intended for him. The London Declaration states that the agent must at least live in the enemy country.

Further the theory of a continuous voyage for goods that are relative contraband, which the London Conference had done away with, is, for the greater part, once more declared valid. Thus England in the event of an enemy country receiving goods for its fighting forces from a certain country, may order that the provisions of Article 35 of the London Declaration are not to apply to vessels destined for the ports of the neutral land in question, that is to say, the theory of continuous voyage will then be universally applied. In addition to this the theory of continuous voyage is to be applied to goods of relative contraband in case the goods are consigned to order or the ship's papers do not state the name of the recipient of the wares or goods, or when the recipient is living in territory that belongs to the enemy or is occupied by him. In such case the owners must provide proof of the neutral destination of the goods. Here, too, as we may observe, we have to do with most important changes in the London Declaration (see Wehberg, "Koloniale Rundschau," 1914, No. 11—12, Page 611). One might indeed say that this entirely obliterates the distinction between relative and absolute contraband in the practical execution of these measures.

4. Under no circumstances must articles and goods which are not susceptible of being used for warlike purposes be

declared as contraband (Article 27). Article 28 declares expressly that the following articles may *not* be declared as contraband, that is to say, *must* not be so declared, without committing a violation of international law.

1. Raw cotton, wool, silk, jute, flax, hemp, and other raw materials of the textile industries, and yarns of the same.

2. Oil seeds and nuts; copra.

3. Rubber, resins, gums and lacs; hops.

4. Raw hides and horns, bones and ivory.

5. Natural and artificial manures, including nitrates and phosphates for agricultural purposes.

6. Metallic ores.

7. Earths, clays, lime, chalk, stone, including marble, bricks, slates, and tiles.

8. Chinaware and glass.

9. Paper and papermaking materials.

10. Soap, paint and colors, including articles exclusively used in their manufacture, and varnish.

11. Bleaching-powder, soda ash, caustic soda, salt cake, ammonia, sulphate of ammonia and sulphate of copper.

12. Agricultural, mining, textile, and printing machinery.

13. Precious and semi-precious stones, pearls, mother-of-pearl, and coral.

14. Clocks and watches, other than chronometers.

15. Fashion and fancy goods.

16. Feathers of all kinds, hairs and bristles.

17. Articles of household furniture and decoration, office furniture and requisites.

According to this therefore, the declaration of cotton and iron ore as conditional contraband[1] as England has done and is still doing, is not permissible from the viewpoint of international law. *Such articles of non-contraband (see also Article 27 of the German Prize Rules) may at any time be taken into the unblockaded port of a belligerent and as a matter of course into any neutral port.* Numerous variations from these provisions, which England has determined upon in her Order of October

[1] Cotton has in the meantime been declared absolute contraband (August 1915).

29th, 1914, attest the fact that this power bases her point of view solely upon *brute force*, that is to say, mere piracy.

Of course, we must, not forget that the former First Sea Lord of the Admirality, Lord Fisher, expressed himself as follows in the "Times:" "The essence of war is violence; moderation in war is imbecility."

It is along these lines that England now proceeds in the question of contraband. By means of her Orders in Council of the 21st of September and the 29th of October, 1914, a new list of contraband wares, consisting of some 26 sub-divisions of unconditional (absolute) contraband, are created. Many new articles are included in this. Among these we find: sulphuric acid, hematite iron-ore, iron pyrites, crude hematite iron, nickel and nickel ore, ferrochromate, chromium ore, raw copper, lead, aluminium, silicious iron, barbed wire, and all apparatus for fastening and cutting-off of same; all kinds of motor-wagons as well as the parts thereof, rubber, petrol, as well as mineral oils, with the exception of lighting oil. The list of conditional contraband of the 21st of September 1914, in addition to the original list, contains also the following new articles: sulphur, glycerine, plates and tubes, leather, raw and tanned, and skins of all sorts.[1]

These are in part products which constitute non-contraband (as for instance; raw copper, nickel, nickel ore, sulphuric acid, lead, aluminium, silicious iron); others, such as barbed wire, are relative contraband. These should be declared absolute contraband as little as mineral oils and motor-spirit, since they are not utilized exclusively for the purposes of war.[2]

England up to the present has not been able to blockade

---

[1] A proclamation in the "London Gazette" of March 13th, 1915, declared raw wool, tin, petroleum, resinous oils, paraffin, wax, grease, hides, when suitable for military use, and ammonia, as absolute contraband.

There is a hideous amount of chicanery afoot just now with regard to the trade in rubber, wool and copper. The rubber trade is especially hard hit, in contravention of the American statutes (Sherman's Act, and the Act of the 12th of February 1913, Section 73). It is thoroughly dominated and tyrannized over by the English and subject to their acts of insolence although rubber cannot properly be declared contraband.

[2] Only now, by the statute of the 18th of April, 1915, have precise retaliatory measures been taken by the alteration of the German prize-law of the 30th of September, 1909, as well as the appendix added in 1914.

the German coast. But a blockade to which neutrals are also supposed to submit, can be recognized as valid, according to international law, only if it is proved to be *effective,* in other words it must be maintained by a fighting force that is sufficient to prevent all actual access to the enemy coast. The Paris Conference has established the law that a "fictive blockade" no longer exists. But England now attempts to make this "fictive blockade" valid everywhere.

According to undisputed reports, the British, as early as October, 1914, demanded a deposit from all neutral ships that left English ports,—this guaranty to be three times the value of the cargo. This sum is paid back only after the British consul in a neutral port has certified the arrival of the vessel. This was intended to prevent the neutral ship from proceeding to a German port. Surely this "paper blockade" in connection with neutral ships is something which must shortly become unendurable.

In other cases the English have determined that relative contraband was to be forwarded only upon a written declaration of the shipper's that this relative contraband was really destined for the needs of the neutral land in question. Here England returns to her theory and practice of the "continuous voyage." This was done away with in the London Declaration upon the proposal of Germany, as is clearly established in Articles 33 and 35. This is as much as to say that relative contraband, even though it be eventually destined for the enemy, is not subject to seizure even when it is to be unloaded in a neutral intermediate port. England on the contrary, seizes as contraband, or as that which she considers as contraband, all in violation of the most express provisions regarding positive contraband, wares upon neutral ships—even when these are under way to neutral ports.

II.

It appears to be the chief endeavor of England to antagonize all neutrals by the way in which she interprets the accepted customs of sea-law as laid down in the Declaration of London, and to reveal to them by drastic object-lessons the whole brutality embodied in the English tyranny of the seas. And all this is shown up the more glaringly when contrasted with the provisions of the German Prize Law. Who, we would ask, is the "barbarian" here?—who the "mad dog?" Apparently that power which strives in this day to maintain the old piracy laws of the freebooters—with some few modifications.

The question of food exports from the United States and other neutral countries is of the greatest importance. These are in themselves considered as "relative contraband." England, in gross violation of the laws of all civilized nations, proceeds to regard them without exception as "absolute" contraband, although they are not intrinsically meant exclusively for purposes of war. In this, England departs from her own customs as well as those of the entire world, which had always permitted the delivery of food-supplies to the civil populations of enemy countries.

The American Government has also assumed the same position (see the case of the "Wilhelmina" in February, 1915, also the note of December 28, 1914, in which the attitude of England during the Boer War as maintained by Lord Salisbury and as hitherto considered valid in English policy was made clear, —see also next Chapter upon American neutrality). It has always been recognized that a shipment of food-supplies from a neutral country to a neutral country must remain free from seizure. When the cargo of the "Wilhelmina," which represented a value of more than $200,000, and consisted of wheat, maize, oats, peas, and canned meats, was being shipped, the firm took the special precaution of obtaining from the German Ambassador Count Bernstorff, a certificate to the effect that the cargo was not destined for the German Government. This was a guaranty that the cargo of this vessel was solely for the use of the civil population. The German Government had also given its consent that an American consul should attend to the matter of the distribution. The British Government replied that inasmuch as the German Government had taken over the entire matter of provisioning the population of the land, no such distinction could be made. The "Wilhelmina" was captured by French ships. This action compelled Germany to resort to the stringent measure of waging war by means of her submarines,—as she has now done since the 18th of February, 1915.

The German Imperial Government has repeatedly declared its willingness to give up this drastic method of submarine warfare, if England were prepared to recognize the Declaration of London and permit the delivery of food supplies for the peaceful population as relative contraband, and would cease her practise of sailing under false colors. But England did not accept this offer—and thus the war of annihilation began!

Wheat and flour, according to the provisions of the London Conference, which sought merely to confirm the customary practise, is, as already declared, *relative* contraband. Thus the peaceful destination of the supplies being confirmed, their seizure must needs be held to be unjustifiable. But according to the reports of Louis Renault upon the Declaration of London, it is only the executive government offices depending upon the centralized power which are placed upon the same basis as the State and the military authorities in the matter of supplies. The district and municipal governments are not subject to this rule and that which is destined for their use, cannot be considered as contraband.

The chicaneries of Great Britain are legion. The neutrals accepted her decrees with hollow and scarcely serious protests. The Holland-American Line demanded written declarations certified by the British Consul, that the relative contraband aboard its ships was meant for use in Holland, that its transmission to other countries was not to take place before the end of the war, and that it was equally non-permissible to export an equal quantity of similar goods on hand. And such permits must be produced at Plymouth before goods may be transported to Rotterdam! What remains of the distinction between absolute and relative contraband under these circumstances? This extension of the term contraband is without parallel in the history of nations and justifies Germany—even without having the North Sea declared as "closed"—in resorting to the most rigorous counter-measures.

The "Manchester Guardian," one of the most reputable papers in England, published a long disquisition during March 1915 by Lord Courtney of Penwith, the well-known legal authority, in which he pointed out the vulnerable points of the proposed English measures for cutting-off the food-supplies from Germany. Lord Courtney proves that according to the Declaration of London only food supplies destined for the fighting forces of the enemy are subject to seizure. But as it is practically impossible to prove by examination whether the supplies in question are eventually used by soldiers or by civilians, the entire provisions of the Declaration of London would indicate *that food can never be declared as contraband.* As soon as deliveries were permitted to be made to the civilian population, a simultaneous relief must necessarily take place in favor of the army or the navy. For instance, a government might pledge itself to give out the imported supplies of wheat only to its citizens in strict conformity with the Declaration of London, since the wheat grown within its own territory would suffice for the needs of its soldiers.

Pursuing still further the question of the illegality of these intended measures on the part of England, Lord Courtney remarks:

"It will be asked what purpose is served by these wearisome representations? Now, when, as we hope, we are able to vanquish Germany by means of hunger, we are loath to devote ourselves to juristic considerations. Let the conduct of war grow more cruel, if it must. That will not matter, we say, so long as it will bring about an early peace."

He replies to that argument as follows:

"Our hopes in this connection are unfounded. Apart from this, wars have never been shortened through brutality. One may, of course, have one's own opinion as to this. But the chief point to consider is that our government should not, for the sake of its good name, succumb to a transient temptation and really enter upon so disgraceful an undertaking as is now contemplated." [1] [2] (*retranslation*)

[1] The following shows how weak the policy of the United States Government is even in this connection. With reference to the transmission of postal packets containing food-stuffs for civilians in Germany and Austria-Hungary, the German-American Chamber of Commerce upon its enquiry as to how far these consignments would enjoy the protection of the American postal service, received the following answer from the U. S. Post-Office Department:

"Provisions and other goods which are delivered at post-offices in the United States for transportation to belligerent countries, are to be accepted, but are forwarded only at the risk of the sender. With regard to the eventual

III.

The illegal capture of German and Austrian-Hungarian citizens upon enemy and neutral ships is thoroughly treated of and confirmed in the original German edition (pages 435 to 440). The author shows that England offered free passage to Germans liable to military service, thus luring them once more aboard the ships, and he closes his statement with these words:

Here we have to deal with the grave suspicion that not only was international law violated but that the Germans liable for military service were *mala fide* purposely lured aboard the enemy steamers in order to be made prisoners. What were the words of England's king, he who lately declared that his realm regards the absolute respecting of a word once pledged

---

procedure of the belligerent countries, these postal packets are subject to the same regulations which apply to provisions and other wares which are forwarded as ordinary freight or express. In accepting food supplies or merchandise which are to be sent by parcel post, the postmaster must give heed that these are kept separate from other articles, so that any action on the part of the belligerents with regard to them, may not result in any delay or disturbance of the regular postal traffic." (*retranslation*)

The German-American Chamber of Commerce rightly protested against this interpretation and pointed out in what an unworthy fashion the United States Government allowed itself to be dictated to by the English Ambassador, and controlled upon its own American soil. He for his part decided at his own pleasure the admissibility or otherwise of every export from the United States.

[1] England is now harassing the neutral states, especially the Scandinavian states, with a view to putting an end to their legitimate trade with Germany. A scandalous system of trade-espionage plays a great part here. Leading Swedish newspapers, such as the "Stockholmer Dagblad," and the "Svenks Tidsskrift," emphasize earnestly their opinion that England's trade measures are designed to impair the neutrality and independence of Sweden. As the "Svensk Tidsskrift," declares, the English system of trade-espionage endeavors, by means as energetic as they are cunning, to discover, by examination and enquiry, the names of such Swedish firms as "dare" to continue their old business relations with Germany, or even to open up quite new enterprises with Great Britain's enemy. They are especially concerned as to the kinds of goods with which Germany, according to the authoritative principles of the starving-out policy, "must" not be supplied. The names of these Swedish firms are then with "the greatest conscientiousness" inscribed on the "Black List," and the members of these firms are looked upon as "suspicious personages." They were the first to be hit by the severe yet elastic provisions of the English blockade regulations of the 11th of March, 1915, when ships containing consignments to these firms were brought into an English port of control.

in a treaty as a "common heritage?" Bernard Shaw writes of English hypocrisy as being a national disease. Here, in a clash of ideals, treaties were shattered, ancient sea-law throttled and the law of England itself bróken and outraged.

IV.

England, moreover, began to act more and more as though other nations no longer existed upon the high-seas of the world, and as though she had the right of unlimited power over these. And all this without any blockade, which, as already indicated, must form the basis for all measures of closure. According to Article I of the Declaration of London, the blockade must confine itself to enemy coasts or ports or to coasts or ports occupied by the enemy, and Article 18 stipulates that the blockading forces must not impede passage to neutral coasts and harbors. It is small wonder that a growing sense of irritation is making itself felt in the smaller neutral nations such as Norway, Holland and Denmark, as well as in the United States of North America.

Sweden entered an energetic protest against iron ore being declared contraband and this was acceded to under certain reservations. On the other hand cotton, though also declared non-contraband according to Article 28, clause 1, was in a number of instances, judged to be contraband. These reservations were afterwards supposed to be removed upon the insistence of the United States, until cotton was finally declared absolute contraband under the dishonest cry of "Cotton and Death!" All manner of illegal steps were also taken against the petroleum steamers of the Standard Oil Company—petroleum being relative contraband—and a number of American ships, laden with oil for neutral ports, were seized in a most arbitrary manner and taken into English ports.

On another occasion England held up Nuremberg toys which a Dutch vessel was to transport from Rotterdam to New York. The endless annoyances which Dutch,[1] Danish, Norwegian and

[1] England has forced Holland to institute an "Overseas Trust," so that she may have an exact control over goods coming into Holland. All consignments which are not addressed to this "Overseas Trust" are liable to be treated by the French and English warships as suspicious consignments. (See above, the Holland-America Line.)

above all Swedish vessels were forced to endure, are simply legion. As has been confirmed in numberless public reports and private letters, these vessels are often repeatedly stopped at intervals of a few hours in one day, in order that they may again and again be subjected to examination and to the searching of their passengers and their freight, and to interminable questions. It is little less than a wonder that all these nations should so patiently endure these insolent liberties on the part of England. One would imagine that they were dependent upon her not only in a political but also in a moral sense.

It is not difficult to comprehend that the export trade of the United States which consists chiefly of cotton (some $ 12 500 000 per annum),[1] copper, wood, lard, petroleum, wheat, cotton-seed and tobacco, must suffer to an appreciable extent under these knavish tricks, whose chief purpose is the disruption of trade with and between neutral lands In a cablegram of October 29th, 1914, from Washington *via* London, "Reuter" reports that the British Ambassador had delivered two notes to the American Department of State, in which it was stated that cargoes of cotton would not be condemned. It was not the intention of the British Government to place cotton as contraband upon the list that was then in course of preparation. So far as mineral oils and other wares listed as contraband were concerned, England would condemn no shipment when the ship's papers made it clear that the port of destination was neutral. Only when goods were consigned "to order" would England undertake an examination (see the foregoing). The American shippers are at the same time recommended to direct their shipments to neutral governments or to other certified consignees.[2]

---

[1] The agricultural paper, "Farmers' Fireside and Bulletin," of the 27th of January, 1915, calculated that the American farmer has already lost half a milliard of dollars through England's proceedings. It remarks drastically: "When we pray for peace and send out millions of dollars' worth of war-material, we are either fools or hypocrites,—perhaps both."

[2] An estimate of English naval policy by the well-known French exponent of international law, M. Bonfils, is interesting. He says: "The principal source of the strength and well-being of England is her trade by sea. All means, *even illegal means*, seem good to her when it is a question of safeguarding the basis of her greatness. Her only motive in action is her *self-seeking*

V. The Declaration of the North Sea as a War Zone.

At last England,—to use a distinctly English phrase,—decided to "go the whole hog." The English Admiralty issued the following proclamation under the date of November 3rd, 1914:

"In view of the indiscriminate laying of mines by German ships under neutral flags, the whole North Sea must be regarded as a war zone. From the 5th of November on, all ships which sail from the northern point of the Hebrides through the Faroe Islands to Iceland, do so at their own risk, unless they observe the directions of the Admiralty. The merchant vessels of all nations for Norway, the Baltic, Denmark and the Netherlands are advised to go by way of the Channel to Dover. There a safe way will be indicated to them from Great Britain to Farne Island, from which the safest route possible to the light-ship "Lindesnäs" will be indicated to them, towards the Norwegian coast. From here on it will be necessary to sail as close as possible along the coast." (*retranslation.*)

Through this measure, which England now endeavored to put into forcible operation, the rights of neutrals, according to which contraband upon neutral ships must be proved to have at least an enemy destination, were absolutely disregarded. *A fictive traffic blockade of the export trade of neutral foreign countries was hereby declared.* Pursuant to Article 18 of the Declaration of London which corresponds entirely to the view maintained in the Declaration of Paris of 1856, "it is absolutely forbidden for the blockading forces to bar access to neutral ports or coasts." This action on the part of Great Britain is the more unheard-of since it is not one single neutral harbor, nor the harbors of one single neutral state which are closed by this measure, but almost *all* the ports of *all* the neutral European states.

---

material interest. Her presumption grows with her power. If she felt herself strong enough to allow free play to all her daring plans, it would plainly appear that her care for her position as a naval power was the foundation of her naval law. In order to enlarge her trade she feels herself constrained to proclaim unjust ordinances against neutral peoples." A severe but just judgment from the mouth of a brother-in-arms!

This procedure is also in complete contradiction to the principles of the free export rights of the neutral states, as set down and guaranteed in Article 1 of the 13th Convention of the Second Hague Conference. Furthermore the right of laying mines in accordance with the 8th Convention has been grossly abused by the sowing of vast quantities of contact mines upon the high seas, that is in international waters—regions which had been respected by the Germans. The area of the mine-field laid by England comprises some 5000 square kilometers. England, that "respecter" of treaties has outdone even herself, and by declaring the North Sea as a closed war area she has sinned against three separate treaties at once and has in fact declared war upon neutral trade. Captain Holmstroem, the Chairman of the Swedish Shipper's Union, hits the nail on the head when he declares that "this step on the part of Britain in analogous to a death sentence upon neutral maritime commerce."

Equally to the point is the German protest of November 14th, 1914:

"Peaceful commerce in the eyes of England, is confined, apparently, to those neutral vessels which are engaged in carrying goods to England, and does not include those which carry, or attempt to carry goods to her enemies. The German Government on its part is convinced that the endangering or damaging of neutral sea-traffic rendered necessary by military measures, has been confined within the smallest possible limits, and that it has strictly adhered to the rules which have hitherto prevailed among all civilized people for the control of naval warfare. On the other hand, the damage inflicted upon the vital interests of neutral shipping by the English side cannot be justified by any military necessity, because it does not form a necessary measure of warfare. It seeks only to strike at the economic life of the enemy through the medium of legitimate neutral trade. This disregard for the principles of the liberty of the seas to which it makes appeal, nullifies the entire claim of the British Government to act as the attorney of the neutrals in the far less dangerous matter of laying mines."

The Channel is practically closed for neutral traffic because of the reckless scattering of English mines, and despite the attempts of England to direct the ships of all neutral nations through the Straits. This has already been given out as the official opinion of the Swedish Government. It had been an accepted rule that these straits were not to be considered as territorial waters. It will be necessary to recall the reply made by General Den Beer Portugael, the well-known representative of Holland at the Second Peace Conference, in answer to the assertion, "almost bordering upon lunacy," as the press universally described it,—of Vice-Admiral Germinet, that the narrows between Dover and Calais were territorial waters which could be closed entirely to all sea-traffic: The views of the Dutch deputy were expressed some time during September, 1912:

"The straits of Dover, at the point Dover-Calais, are 35 kilometers broad. Although there is no fixed measure in international law for the breadth of territorial waters, it has formerly been reckoned as the distance of a cannon shot, that is to say, about 4000 m. Now the general decision to regard it as a breadth of 3 sea-miles, that is 5556 metres, has been arrived at. The English "Jurisdiction Act" of 1898 expressly defines it as 3 miles. The assumption that the Straits of Dover are territorial waters is therefore invalid, and rests upon an unjustifiable presumption. The French authorities in this field, Gérard de Reyneval, Ortolan and Pradier Fodéré, hold exactly the same opinion, and Cabro, an American authority, is also in accord with them. It therefore appears to me that the French Admiral's knowledge of sea-law is as defective as the powder of the French navy. One should remember that in every war the neutral states must be in the majority, and it is unthinkable that this majority should allow itself to be dictated to in matters of law by the minority. Such a gross breach of justice would suffice to drag them into the war!"

The *principle of the freedom of the open sea*, which has been lamentably left in the lurch by the neutral nations, is to today championed only by Germany. (See Chapter with regard to those further developments which arise as a matter of course from the English procedure in the North Sea.)

"We may await with tense expectancy the answer of the

neutral states,—especially that of the United States of North America and of Holland." Such were the words of the author in the first original edition of this work. The answer, unfortunately, consisted only of a general declamation which England completely ignored. Germany was therefore forced to ACT!

In Sub-division VII the author treats of the illegal interference by England and France with the postal rights of neutrals. (See the original, pages 450 to 452.)

CHAPTER XXVIII.

American "Neutrality." Unfair Deliveries of Munitions to the Triple Entente. The Shipments of Food Supplies to Germany and their Stoppage. Other Breaches of Neutrality.

I.

Despite various suspicious manifestations even during the first months of the war, the author, when compiling the original edition of this book, still clung to his belief in the good faith of the government of the United States. But he is now, in conjunction with the overwhelming majority of the German people, forced to give up this untenable supposition.

During the past months the government of the United States, far from pursuing an independent American policy, has pursued a dependent English one. There is no doubt that this will within a short time lead to bitter disillusion and regret. In this chapter and the following it will be clearly seen that the government which maintained such a sensitive and haughty attitude towards Germany, adopted towards England a policy of the most incomprehensible servility. Every unfriendly act, every blow directed against neutral commerce upon the seas, seemed to find its reward in a still greater devotion to British arrogance.[1] Mr. Wilson and Mr. Bryan, according to a

[1] I need only recall, for example, the scandalous and illegal conduct of England in the case of the American steamer "Greenbriar," on the 30th of

logical conception of things, acted more like British governmental agents in the question of deliveries of arms and munitions, than as representatives of a great, free and proud country and people. The nation, as such, may, of course, have made no deliveries to the Triple Entente—(in so far as that is capable of being proved here—the very opposite having been asserted in the press of neutral countries). It may also be acknowledged that a neutral power is not *pledged* but only *justified* in forbidding the export of weapons, munitions and all other supplies for the use of the army or the navy of one or the other belligerent. (See Article 7 of the 5th and 13th Convention of the 18th of October, 1907, 1st edition, page 337).[1]

But the spirit and the significance of the two conventions proves,—and this is in no sense nullified by Articles 17b and 18, since these are concerned only with the rights and duties of individual manufacturers,—that a country violates its neutrality when it permits a condition to arise, and in fact favors and supports it, in which as a matter of fact only one of the belligerents is able to receive war supplies from the neutral country in question, while it remains impossible for practical reasons for the other belligerent to take advantage of that "equality" according to which the United States is con-

December, 1914. This steamer was commanded to haul down the American flag and run up the English. This provocation was swallowed as calmly by the Americans as was the complete interruption of the shipping of provisions through the illegal misuse of the conception of absolute and relative contraband by England (see above). There is, further, the ignominious throttling of the entire American copper, wool and rubber trade (see "Münchner-Augsburger Zeitung," No. 101, 1915). See also below a whole series of instances of scandalous trickery which the United States Government patiently endured from England. The protests made were the merest formalities, which raised a smile among the prophets of both sides.

[1] One may compare the statement of Mr. Bryan that by a prohibition of the export of weapons, the United States would violate her neutrality, with the splendid example set by the Swiss form of neutrality. Switzerland, has, in regard to Article y of the 5th Agreement of the 18th of October, 1907, as already cited, through Article 8 of its proclamation of the 4th of August, 1914, forbidden all export of weapons and munitions. Who has been so foolish as to proclaim that through this prohibition it has violated its neutrality? Not a single soul!

stantly justifying itself upon paper. A neutrality of that kind is only a paper neutrality, since the United States has, as a matter of fact, recognized the breach of international law committed by England (complete ignoring of the Paris and London Declarations with respect to blockade and contraband), a breach which was essentially responsible for the ensuing conditions, and to which the United States bowed its head to the great detriment of the Central Powers, after having uttered nothing more effective than another paper protest. This breach of the law of nations by England converted the *right* of the United States to hinder the export of ammunition, into a simple *duty*.

As has been publicly acknowledged even by the American Ambassador to Germany, Mr. Gerard, on the 13th of February, 1915, "there are wide circles among the population of the United States who do not consider it fair to proceed with the export of ammunitions because, owing to the condition of things, this means a one-sided advantage in favor of Germany's enemies." This conception, according to Mr. Gerard, has steadily gained ground in the United States during the past few months, "and much that was favorable to Germany might be hoped from its development." This hope was doomed to bitter disappointment: No serious step was undertaken. An expert Rehm rightly declares that: "The right *not* to forbid such exports ceases when the act of non-forbidding develops into support of one of the belligerents."

England rests its case upon the 13th Convention of 1907, which it did not sign, whereas it was ratified by the United States. By an *analogous application* of Articles 8 and 25, the government of the United States is morally *pledged* to use all the means within its power not only to prevent the equipment of a vessel within its territorial jurisdiction, but also to exercise all vigilance to prevent one of the belligerent parties from receiving support through the delivery within United States ports or waters, of war supplies subject to the same rules. Any opposite course is unfair, nay more, it is a material breach of neutrality.

The action of the United States would, of course, constitute a grave violation of neutrality if the assertion of the Swiss press (for instance, the "St. Galler Tageblatt") should be correct—namely, that the United States had a law dating from the year 1818, which forbids the export of weapons, etc., to warring powers with which the United States is on terms of peace.

This law was put into very stringent operation some three years ago, during the Mexican rebellion—and *that against* the legal President of Mexico—whilst the rebels were plentifully supplied with arms that were smuggled across the borders with the knowledge and connivance of the government. These charges of gross and de plorable injustice have since then been verified in every particular. We recommend the reader to contrast President Wilson's words on that occasion with his subsequent position in the case of Germany.[1]

The attitude of the American Republic abuses not only the spirit of neutrality according to the law of nations, but also the spirit of the "treaties of friendship" which still exist to this day between Prussia,—now the German empire—and the United States. Even in international law all outrages against morality, all acts perpetrated upon "that sense of decency which actuates all fair and right-thinking men"—to use the words of a lofty tribunal, the German Imperial Court, must eventually succumb to the great law of compensation.

The attitude of the president and of the government was from the very beginning characterized by no particular friendliness and gave rise to serious doubts as to its correctness

---

[1] The "Daily News" of London, reports as follows from New York under date of May 3rd, 1915:

"The Boer General Pearson filed a suit in the United States Court in Milwaukee, against the Allis-Chalmers Company, which in conjunction with the Bethlehem Steel Company, he accused of conspiracy against the State Laws of Wisconsin by manufacturing shrapnel for delivery to the Allies. Pearson also intends to institute similar charges in states that have similar laws." (*retranslation.*)

Reuter remarks upon this from Washington that President Wilson had requested the Attorney-General of the United States to investigate this charge of Pearson's. The American Government, to be sure, quite openly condones the violation of the law by the English—(the Passenger Act) in the case of the "Lusitania."

according to international law. When the German wireless telegraphy station was objected to and even closed down, to be re-opened only after the repeated urging of the German Embassy and then only when subjected to the most rigorous censorship, it was difficult to perceive upon what grounds of international obligations the president's action was based. According to Article 3 of the 5th Convention of the Second Hague Conference, the belligerent powers are "likewise forbidden to erect on the territory of a neutral Power a wireless telegraphy station or other apparatus for the purpose of communicating with belligerent forces on land or sea," or to "use any installation of this kind established by them before the war on the territory of a neutral Power for purely military purposes, which has not been opened for the service of public messages."

Here too the unconditional and necessary "equal" application of all these provisions of the 5th and 13th Conventions with regard to Germany and Germany's antagonists is completely ignored.

No one ever spoke of a censorship of the telegraphic communication between Canada, England and France. The "Allies" were permitted to send despatches to their heart's content. Never had England's monopoly of an international news service possessed so vast a value for England, never did it embody so great a danger for the rest of the world, especially with regard to the sentiments of the United States, as precisely in this war (see "The Examiner"). The pressure of the censorship was *de facto* turned only upon Germany, and there is no doubt that a well-established case of military favoritism of England, therefore a breach of neutrality, had been committed by the United States (see, in addition, Rehm in a lecture of November 28th, 1914, page 100). The interning of the little cruiser "Geier" was also more than an unfriendly act on the part of the United States, and was occasioned by a breach of neutrality on the part of a British Marconi Station.

But the most dubious aspect of the whole matter, as has already been said, is the attitude of the United States in the question of deliveries of war supplies. The facts and figures of to-day prove that not only Britain but all the states of the Triple (now Quadruple) Entente have purchased and still purchase enormous quantities amounting to hundreds, yes, to thousands of millions of dollars worth of war supplies, munitions, arms, etc., from American firms.[1]

German as well as other newspapers, have repeatedly published from American sources lengthy lists of the firms, the shipments, the value, etc., that were represented in this murderous business. The amounts run into billions. There is scarcely a single article used in war which has not been delivered to the foes of Germany. And these deliveries increase progressively in quantity from month to month.[2]

The loan through the firm of Morgan and Co., and other American banking concerns to all the members of the Triple Entente need merely be alluded to here.

The toleration of these deliveries by a government which simply turned facts upside down in sophistical expositions in its attempts to prove that the permission granted for these shipments was in itself an act of honest and loyal neutrality—a government which prays for peace, and pretends to be actuated by an earnest desire for peace, ***while it bears the chief guilt***

[1] The "New Yorker Staatszeitung" had already stated in January, on exact statistical grounds, that but for America's help, the war would long since have been over. It proves the gigantic danger for American production (apart from the profits of a few multi-millionaires) which lies, for instance, in the export of gold to Canada, and in the arbitrary despotism of English domination in naval and business matters.

[2] The "Vossische Zeitung" has raised the question whether the partisan position assumed by America to the detriment of Germany might not be explained by the existence of certain agreements between England and the United States? In its evening edition of the 31st of May, 1915, the same paper gave space to an article by Admiral Kalaü vom Hofe upon a speech by Joseph Chamberlain to the effect that an agreement existed with the United States, "an understanding or a compact, as one may say." The author alludes further to the outspoken anti-German attitude of Roosevelt in an article in the weekly "Fatherland" of the 15th of May, which also refers to a "secret treaty" with England, and lastly to the work of a Washingtonian journalist and professor of history, Roland G. Usher, in the year 1913. According to him there has existed since 1897 a secret understanding between America, England and Russia, in which it was provided that in case of a war brought about by Germany, the United States must support the other allies. Is America still "free?"

for the prolongation of this fearful slaughter of peoples, in order that a small clique of industrial magnates may be guaranteed millions in profits from this butchery of the nations, must surely in time arouse the greatest excitement not only in Germany but also in the United States.

The chief American argument is a sophism which will not bear investigation. It separates the government and the people in a manner that would immediately have been rejected as untenable by the American Government had it been confronted with the question as to what its attitude would be in case *its* enemies had been supplied with materials that render it possible to carry on a long war. It is very likely that in this case Mr. Bryan would have argued that the government of the state that supplied the tools of destruction had no right to assume so cool and indifferent a position in a question in which the woe and welfare of the government and the people were concerned, not *separately,* but *as a whole.* A problem which is so deeply concerned with matters of life and death and in which the factors of people and government cannot be separated, is not to be solved by any such hollow pretexts as this.

The entire treatment in Congress of the bills and legal measures connected with this question prove that this policy is not maintained and supported by the American *people* but by a small clique of industrial magnates who pursue it simply for their own profit. This fact is most conspicuous in the fate of the Bill which was to empower the President to forbid the export of such materials of war—a Bill opposed with all his energy by the Presidential apostle of peace:

The point of view held by the German Government is clearly and strikingly expressed by the "Norddeutsche Allgemeine Zeitung" of January 21st, 1915, as follows:

It is reported from London, that at a Committee meeting of representative American export firms, Chairman Flood, appealing for a memorial to the German Government, conveyed the impression that in the matter of the American deliveries of contraband of war, Germany had made no further objections. This is a great mistake. The memorial sent by Mr. Flood merely declared that with regard to the prevailing basis of international law, Germany possessed no right to enter a formal legal protest against the delivery of munitions of war by neutral private persons to its enemies. Therefore, as it is stated at the close of the memorial, the United States must depend upon its own initiative with regard to such deliveries of munitions.

It goes without saying, however, that on a basis of international law, the United States is likewise empowered, by the passing of a prohibitive law against the export of munitions of war, to suppress the entire traffic in contraband with all belligerent states; especially as the international illicit trade in weapons to England and France has taken on such dimensions that the neutrality, not only of the American Government, but of the whole American people has thereby been called into question.

This interpretation is made the more applicable by the fact that England will by no means allow the *legal* international trade between America and Germany, to take its course, and further, seizes the goods designed for the use of the economic life of Germany in the most ruthless manner. We see that the whole traffic with the belligerent nations resolves itself into a one-sided transaction, benefiting only our opponents. Further —and this weighs heaviest of all upon us—the providing of our opponents with American weapons is the chief reason for the lengthening of the war. This fact is in flagrant contradiction to the repeated asseverations of the United States that they wish to see the speedy re-establishment of peace, and to work for that end. [1]

---

[1] Not only German-Americans, but also genuine "real" Americans suspect the short-sightedness of the policy which the United States Government is to-day pursuing. The learned statistician, Roger W. Bobson. in the "New York Sun," a sheet which is anything but pro-German, rightly brands this mean hypocrisy as follows:

"What implacable hatred must the Germans shortly feel against us, when they hear that our government day after day permits munitions and arms to be transported from America to England, Russia and France, whereas Germany cannot even obtain from us the mere necessities of life! This is sheer hypocrisy on our part, and the day will come when we shall dearly have to pay for it. Even if we are not hurt in a worse place, we have at least lost a good friend and customer in Germany."

The German-Americans rightly demand an "embargo" upon these deliveries.

An embargo is an excellent measure of retaliation for the violations of law on the part of an alien state.

There can be no doubt of the fact that England has committed the grossest violations of the law. This is conceded even by Wilson in his answer to the German protest. When England seizes food-supplies on neutral ships, when it extends the list of contraband far beyond the limits of the Declaration of London, when it decrees that everything that does not suit England is to be considered as contraband, when it carries off Germans as prisoners from neutral ships, when it captures American oil-steamers, when it prevents the increase by purchase of the American merchant marine, when it presumes to fly the American flag, when by every possible trickery it interferes ruthlessly with the legitimate trade in provisions, copper, rubber, wool and cotton, either wholly or in part—then the state whose sovereignity is thereby abused—in this case the neutral United States,—has the right, even if it do not directly wish to declare war against the law-breaking state,—to exercise the privilege of an embargo.

Senator Stone, the Chairman of the Senate Committee for Foreign Affairs, recently uttered his opinion:

"The government of the United States will uphold its neutrality now as heretofore; but other nations must be convinced that we shall not be disposed to overlook injuries to the right of our own government or people."

But these manly words should at last be followed by deeds.

President Wilson, so far as Mexico was concerned, had the pride and the courage to impose an embargo upon arms, in addition to his policy of "watchful waiting." Without declaring war upon Huerta, he was able to bring him to terms. But England, to be sure, is not Mexico! And "right" and "right" are just as you may be pleased to interpret them: though this must necessarily apply only to a dependent vassal state, whose interpretation of "right" is forced upon it by a stronger power.[1]

[1] E. J. Hexamer, the President of the German-American League, spoke in terse and biting terms of a country such as his, which "on Sunday prays

We are, to be sure, aware that the United States sent a Note of Protest to England on the 28th of December, 1914. In this they spoke of the

"Growing concern with which they observe the great number of vessels with American goods destined for neutral ports, which are seized by England and taken into British ports."

(In the original edition the author enters more fully into the question of the American Note.)

The Note very properly points out that to claim that a consignment of wares proclaimed as conditional contraband and destined for a neutral port, may permit of a legal assumption that the final destination may be that of an enemy, appears to be in direct contradiction to the principles formerly maintained as correct by Great Britain, and formulated as follows by Lord Salisbury during the South African War:

"*Food supplies*, even though they may have an enemy destination, can only be considered as contraband of war,

---

for peace, and on all other week days supplies England and her allies with weapons, ammunition and every conceivable variety of contraband of war."

. . . . "I must admit, that I, as a born American, who dearly loves this land of freedom, cannot but feel disgust at the lickspittle policy of my native land, which allows England to punch us on the nose and bat us about the head, and then licks the hand that strikes us." That this judgment is not too severe is demonstrated, apart from the question of the export of provisions, by the complete throttling of the American copper, wool and rubber trade. In this case the government has permitted the plain violation of Section 73 of the statute of the 12th of February, 1913, which establishes that every kind of combination or trust which attempts to restrict the legal trade of free competition in the imports from abroad to the United States of America is illegal and invalid. In the matter of the export of cotton, there has also been great trickery, in spite of all promises.

Many ships with American goods aboard were taken by the English into the tiny harbor of Kirkwall in the Orkney Islands, to be searched. The United States Government sought permission to send a Consular officer to Kirkwall, which England flatly refused to allow. On the other hand the American agents of neutral shipping firms objected to take freights, unless the bill of lading was accompanied by a guarantee from the British ambassador, Sir Cecil Spring-Rice, in which all British officials were charged to let the vessel pass unmolested. "The British ambassador has, so to speak, erected the Great Wall of China about the United States, and plays the part of a Dictator of American commerce," is the justifiable exclamation of the German-American Chamber of Commerce in New York and many othor institutions.

when they are destined for the enemy forces. *It must be proved, that such is in fact their destination at that moment in which they are seized."* (*retranslation*)

The Note even musters up enough courage to declare that "there exists a growing belief in the United States, which without doubt is not unjustified, that the present British policy with respect to American trade is responsible for the depression in certain industries which are dependent upon European markets. The attention of the British Government is directed to the possible consequences of its present policy, in order to show how far-reaching is the damage inflicted upon the industrial life of the United States and to lay emphasis upon the importance of obviating the causes of the complaints."

But the *entire energy* of the big republic seemed to be consumed in the making of this paper protest which occupied itself chiefly with commercial considerations in connection with the damage inflicted. The answer of the English Government not only showed not the slightest trace of conciliation, but even displayed a stiff-necked intention to adhere to the entire illegal practise. The orders of the 21st of September, the 29th of October, and the 3rd of November remained in force as before. The lack of regard for others shown by the English sea authorities became day by day more unendurable, until it reached its culminating point, at the beginning of February 1915, through the open misuse of flags and false colors—acts which may be considered the acme of contempt for the rights of neutrals.

Then, when the German Government demanded the application of the rules of the Declaration of London with respect to the delivery of provisions to the peaceful population of a country, a demand made not only in the interests of neutrals and especially of the United States—which, in the event of its rejection would be followed by submarine warfare as a reprisal for the order of November 1914—then the United States protested *not* against the unheard-of measure of closing the North Sea, an act which in its effects was directed against the Union as well as Germany,—but against this defensive measure of necessity on the part of Germany!

Finally, when in order to justify in some small measure

its weak-kneed and ridiculous attitude in the face of the steadily-growing indignation of the German-American and Irish-American population, the government once more ventured to protest to England against its dishonest use of other flags—the real cause for Germany's procedure—a protest couched in that tame and timid tone which offers so marked a contrast to the language adopted towards Germany—then the United States showed that it was determined to maintain its one-sided attitude to the last. For this injustice it is likely that Japan in China may be the first indirectly to avenge the wrong done the German people. (See the Note of the United States of February 12, 1915.)

The answer which England returned to this Note on the 18th of February was nothing less than a contemptuous rejection of all the justifiable American claims of neutrality. Its crowning insolence was the citing of Bismarck as testimony for the attitude maintained by Sir Edward Grey. The righteousness of the English Government towards all "neutrals" was revealed as in a glory of Bengal lights.

The answer of England to the United States, dated February 18th, 1915, lays stress upon the point that the difference between food supplies for the civil population and the military-forces ceases to exist as soon as the difference between the civil population and the military force itself ceases to exist,—as was the case with Germany. No matter what was imported for the consumption of the civil population, this would nevertheless be used by the military, whenever the necessities of the situation required this to be done,—especially at a time when the German Government had assumed all control over the supplies of provisions. While England was concerned in avoiding all damage to neutrals, Germany's intention to sink all merchant ships and their cargoes without ascertaining their nationality and character, and without providing for the safety of their crews, made it necessary for the British Government to consider the taking of steps which would shield their interests. It would be impossible for one belligerent to remain bound by the customs of war in the event of the other belligerent departing from the observation of these.

Concerning the right of declaring as contraband of war

food supplies not meant for the use of the military forces, Grey refers to the measures undertaken by France in the Franco-Chinese war of 1885, in which rice was declared as contraband, and further cites Bismarck's answer to the representatives of the Kiel Chamber of Commerce in this matter. Bismarck declared: "Every war is bound to have evil results for neutral nations, and it is possible that these evils in the event of a neutral power interfering in the conduct of the war, may easily multiply themselves to the disadvantage of the nation that ventures upon such a course. By such means German commerce might be subjected to far greater losses than would ensue from a temporary embargo on the rice trade in Chinese waters. The measures in question have the purpose of shortening the war by increasing the difficulties for the enemy, and this is an excusable measure when impartially applied to all neutral vessels." Grey places special emphasis upon the last sentence and remarks: "His Majesty's Government are disposed to think that the same view is still maintained by the German Government. The measures of His Majesty's Government take into consideration, as far as possible, the rights of neutrals."

Grey closes with the words:

"It will still be our endeavor to avoid injury and loss to neutrals, but the announcement by the German Government of their intention to sink merchant vessels and their cargoes without verification of their nationality or character, and without making any provision for the safety of non-combatant crews or giving them a chance of saving their lives, has made it necessary for his Majesty's Government to consider what measures they should adopt to protect their interests. It is impossible for one belligerent to depart from rules and precedents and for the other to remain bound by them."

We have already controverted the legality of these contentions (see, also next chapter). The chief point for Sir Edward Grey—and possibly for those gentlemen in whose hands the destinies of the Union lie—is the alleged statistical proof that so far the United States of North America have done an excellent stroke of business with the Triple Entente on the basis of their so-called neutrality.

II.

1. The government of the United States has also broken its neutrality in other ways than those mentioned. In one instance the United States made themselves guilty of a grievous outrage against not only neutrality but humanity in that they permitted—and, as we declare, knowingly permitted—cruel and illegal Dum-Dum-bullets to be delivered in great quantities by American factories to *one* of the belligerents, primarily England. (See also chapter X.) Through this the United States, a country to which the Kaiser appealed in August, 1914, thus giving it the opportunity of acting, to a certain extent, as arbiter in the use of these inhuman projectiles,—has made itself guilty of the same shameful violation of the law of nations as England and France themselves. For there can be no question that since America tolerated the act, it must share the guilt.

The "Kölnische Zeitung" at the beginning of January, 1915, gave as proof the following statement from Washington:

"At the beginning of December the German Ambassador in Washington sent to the Department of State a declaration in which the attention of the Department was directed to the fact that England persistently allowed her troops to use projectiles which were in contravention of International Law. The Ambassador alluded to the soft-nosed bullets, made by the firm of Gley Bros., 254 Gray's Inn Road, London, which had been found upon English soldiers; further he referred to an order for 20,000 rifles and 50 million buckshot cartridges, which the English Government had given to the Winchester Co., and the use of which was forbidden in civilized warfare. In addition he reported that the Union Metallic Cartridge Co. in Bridgeport, State of Connecticut, on the 20th of October, had, through Frank D. Hoagland, taken out a patent for mushroom-shaped cartridges, and according to reliable information, 8 million cartridges of this kind had found their way to Canada and would be used in the English army. The patent which the government of the United States bestowed upon Mr. Hoagland on October 20th, 1914, bears the number 1,114,356. In a description of his fiendish device, the inventor remarks: "I have invented an improvement in Mushroom Bullets. This invention applies to all fully covered and jacketted bullets in which the cover of the lead core and that of the point may be manufactured separately. This invention enables one to produce a bullet which, while retaining all the peculiarities of an ordinary jacketted bullet, assumes a mushroom form upon striking, that is to say, it spreads itself, and flattens out.... Apart from the grooves, the bullet retains all the *appearance* of an ordinary jacketted bullet...."

This patent was applied for on February 24, 1914, but granted only on October 20th, that is to say at a time when the European war was already in full progress and the first German complaints regarding Dum-Dum bullets had been presented to the President through the telegram of Kaiser Wilhelm!

After the attention of the Department of State had been called to this patent, and after it might have been assumed in all reliability that England had expressed itself as having no intention of making use of such an invention, one might have expected that Mr. Bryan, the expectant candidate for the Nobel Prize, would have given some consideration to the decisive representations made by the German Ambassador. But what did Mr. Bryan do? He sent an announcement to the press which is supposed to be an answer to Count Bernstorff, and in which he flatly rejects the idea of taking up the German charges, since—"this government in its endeavors to preserve a strict neutrality is obliged to forego any examination of the credibility of these complaints and declarations or any expression of opinion regarding them." (!) (*retranslation*)
(See Kölnische Zeitung, February, 1915.)

It would have been an easy matter, had Mr. Bryan displayed the slightest willingness, for him to have examined the projectiles in question. The shell of the cartridge is impressed with two letters which indicate that it is meant for use in the English military rifle.

The "Nieuwe Rotterdamsche Courant" writes: "'The armies of the Allies, fed upon American meat, protected by American barbed-wire, are bombarding the Germans with American shells,' as an American recently remarked, and everybody knows that not half has been told by far. Silence is desirable—for the government of the United States, in criminal violation of all neutrality, must bear upon its conscience the guilt for the prolongation of this terrible slaughter, and a thousand-fold curse must fall upon it for establishing its right to do this upon a scrap of paper which it tears to tatters day by day." [1]

2. With respect to the delivery of submarines and parts of submarines to England, see the 1st edition, page 337 and 338. Articles 6 and 8 of the 13th Hague Convention clearly indicate that a neutral government is *pledged* to make all efforts in its power to prevent the arming within its territorial waters of any vessel against which there are grounds of suspicion that it may participate in hostile operations against a power with which the neutral power is at peace. During December, 1914, things were presented in such a manner as to lead to the belief that the American ship-building firms in question had refused to deliver the submarines at the request of the President. During the spring of 1915 rumors from American sources became constantly more persistent to the effect that this too had been merely a blind. The New York "Tribune," for instance, declared that the delivery of submarines was proceeding despite the declarations of Secretary Bryan. The contracts of the Bethlehem Steel Company at first called for the delivery of complete submarines. Then, when this was declared to be a breach of neutrality, the submarines were taken in parts to Canada, there to be assembled and transported to England. Thus England was able to secure her submarines despite Mr. Bryan's protestations. It was the usual refuge behind a technicality, the customary evasion of the "criminaloid."

All further negotiations between the German Ambassador

---

[1] The "Continental Times," in an article by a famous publicist, wrote, on the 21st of April, 1915:

"It is common knowledge that the Cunarder "Lusitania," when she entered Liverpool on 8th February last, flying the Stars and Stripes, had in her hold two submarines, built in America, and sold to the British Government in open breach of the President's injunctions. This gross breach of international law was consummated under the neutral flag of the chief neutral power in the world." It is noteworthy that this was written nearly a month before the torpedoing of the Lusitania.

and the American Government in connection with the export of arms led in all cases to nothing more than a repetition of the two opposed points of view. The government of the United States stubbornly maintained its standpoint of a purely formal paper neutrality, yes, it even went so far as to assert that the forbidding of munition exports would cause a change in the provisions of neutrality and thereby involve an alteration in the principles of strict neutrality!

3. The "New Yorker Staatszeitung" in April, 1915, published the news that the National Reserve Commission of the United States had granted to National Reserve Banks which have the right of issuing notes, the privilege of accepting as negotiable drafts such as were made out in Paris and London for arms and munitions delivered, and accepted by American bankers.

As early as the beginning of the 19th century it was an accepted principle in international law and one that had not been violated during the course of the century, that no neutral state might, as such, offer a loan to a belligerent power. Formally, of course, the measure adopted by the National Reserve Commission of the United States is not a loan, but its effect, as Professor Hatschek of Göttingen explains in the "National Liberal Beiträgen," (National Liberal Essays) is precisely the same. The National Reserve Commission is one of the central organs of the National Reserve Banks. The Secretary of the Treasury of the United States is the Chairman of this Commission. The functions of this body in certain ways resemble those of the "Kuratorium" of the German Reichsbank. The bank-notes issued by the National Reserve Banks are valid as obligatory notes of the United States. In addition to the bank itself, the republic vouches for the security of these notes.

Since a neutral state is obliged by virtue of the law of nations to grant no loan to a belligerent, it must needs follow that it cannot accept any national debts in favor of a belligerent. But it is precisely this which has been done by the United States. Since the London or Paris deposits are regarded as acceptable "cover" by the National Reserve Banks, they receive money and create obligatory notes of the Union in order to assist one of the parties at war.

III.

In marked contrast to the dilatoriness and the patience of the government of the United States in all its relations with England, is the promptness and the energy with which this government presents the German Government with alleged claims for damages. As a proof of this the exchange of notes in the case of the "William P. Frye" might be cited. We reproduce these notes with the omission of certain unessential passages, for the entire legal question regarding especially the seizure, the sinking of ships and the claim for damages, is discussed in a most unassailable manner by the German Government:

The American sailing-ship "William P. Frye," was sunk in the Atlantic Ocean by the German auxiliary cruiser "Prinz Eitel Friedrich. An exchange of notes took place between the governments of the United States and Germany regarding this matter, and these were published in the "Norddeutsche Allgemeine Zeitung" on the 18th of April, 1915. In the original edition the author publishes the text of the American Note as taken from the American newspapers,—subdivision III, page 467.

The answer of the Secretary of State of the German Foreign Office to the Ambassador of the United States, was as follows:

Berlin, 4th of April, 1915.

"According to the reports which have reached the German Government, the Commander of the "Prinz Eitel Friedrich" stopped and searched the ship "William P. Frye" upon the high seas on January 27th. He found on board a cargo of wheat which was consigned by order to Queenstown, Falmouth or Plymouth. After an attempt to remove the cargo of the "William P. Frye," he finally took the crew and the ship's papers aboard and sank the vessel.

It may be seen from these facts that the German Commander acted in full accordance with the principles of international law as laid down in the Declaration of London and the German Prize Court laws. The ports of Queenstown, Falmouth and Plymouth, to which the seized vessel was consigned, are strongly fortified English ports which, moreover, serve as supply bases for the British fighting forces.

The cargo of wheat in accordance with Article 24, No. I

of the London Declaration was therefore to be considered as relative contraband under the head of food supplies, and in accordance with clauses 32 and 33 of the German Prize Regulations as destined for a hostile belligerent power and thus to be treated as contraband until proof to the contrary had been furnished. This proof, was however, not forthcoming after the vessel had been stopped, for the ship's manifest was made out in the form of an order. The necessary conditions for the sinking of the vessel were therefore given—pursuant to Article 49 of the Declaration of London and clause 113 of the German Prize Regulations, — since the auxiliary cruiser possessed no opportunity of taking the prize into a German port without endangering its own safety or decreasing the success of its operations. The obligations imposed by Article 50 of the Declaration of London and clause 116 of the German Prize Court Rules were duly observed in that the persons on board the ship as well as the ship's papers were removed to the auxiliary cruiser before the ship was destroyed.

The legality of the measures taken by the German Commander is moreover to be tested in accordance with Article 51 of the Declaration of London, as well as Paragraph 1, No. 2 of the German Prize Regulations by the German Prize Court. This procedure will take place immediately after the delivery of the ship's papers to the Prize Court at Hamburg and will resolve itself upon a decision of the questions as to whether the destruction of the cargo and the ship was necessary in the sense of Article 49 of the London Declaration, and as to whether the sunken property was liable to seizure, or in the event of damages being payable, what sum is to be paid the owners. In this action the owners of ship and cargo would be required to prove, according to Article 34 of the Declaration of London, that the shipment of wheat had a peaceful destination and was not therefore in the nature of contraband. Should this proof not be forthcoming, then, according to the general principles of international law, the German Government would be under no obligation to pay damages.

According to the special regulations applying to the relations between Germany and the United States the laws in question are to a certain extent modified by Article 13 of the

Prussian-American treaty of friendship and commerce of July 11th, 1799 in connection with Article 12 of the Prussian-American merchant marine treaty of May 1st, 1828, according to which contraband belonging to one party may not be seized by the other party, but merely detained or taken over upon payment of the value. Based upon these terms of the compact, which are naturally determinative for the German Prize Court, the American owners of ship and cargo would receive damages even if the lading of wheat were to be declared contraband. The foregoing procedure is however not to be assumed as conclusive since the regular Prize Court must first investigate the legality of the seizure and the sinking as well as the proofs furnished by the claimants, and the amount of damages to be awarded.

(signed) von Jagow.

The "treaty of friendship" of 1799, be it observed! A peculiar "friendship"—which delivers billions of dollars worth of murderous implements to one's enemies!—an act which is above all things responsible for the prolongation of the present butchery.[1]

---

[1] The "Rotterdamsche Courant" reports from London that the "Daily Telegraph" in a cablegram from New York declared that the strikes in the eastern states are increasing in extent, a fact which occasions great anxiety to the government officials. *They were afraid that these labor disturbances which are supposed to be the work of German agitators may be regarded as a violation of neutrality, since the delivery of ammunition might thereby be interfered with!*

"According to this the American Government would be nothing more than a business branch of the Triple Entente," remarks the Dutch paper. It would, in fact, be an actual ally of England against Germany.

The following is also worthy of note. The New York "Herold" of March 23rd contains the following:

"Under the "pressure" of several shots from the guns of the American fort El Morro at Porto Rico, the Hamburg-American steamer "Odenwald," which attempted to leave the port without clearance papers, returned to the harbor. It appears that the captain of the steamer had demanded his clearance papers but that these had been refused him—"in the interests of maintaining American neutrality"—for there was "a grave suspicion that the "Odenwald" was intending either to supply provisions to German warships or to damage enemy merchant vessels.

"This is indeed the most remarkable neutrality mortal man could imagine.

Is there anyone who imagines that the German people are so naive as really to believe any longer in a "neutrality" such as this? All the declarations of Mr. Woodrow Wilson will go to wreck upon the justifiable distrust of the entire German people, who will have nothing to do with the "peace mediation" of a government which has shown itself so hostile towards a nation which has felt nothing but friendship for the American people. Yet the German people are just enough to make a distinction between a government controlled by "interests," Wall Street, and English machinations, and certain great sections of the American people, especially in the west. Ignorance of the real, the modern Germany, as well as the baneful effect of the British press and cable monopoly, are largely responsible for the lack of understanding shown, and this in turn for the lack of sympathy. But truth, like falsehood, will out.

The last representations of the German Ambassador (April 1915) with regard to the deliveries of arms was met by the same cynical and stereotyped remark of Mr. Bryan's in his official capacity—that any change in the policy of the government would mean a breach of neutrality.

The "Morning Post" at the same time published an interesting contribution to the conception of neutrality entertained by America:

"Great Britain has arrived at an agreement with the Amalgamated Copper Co., the greatest copper producers of the United States, which would have the result of placing the entire copper production of the United States under English control. A similar arrangement has been made with other copper com-

---

This is a case more curious than all those curious cases of a one-sided neutrality as it has hitherto been indicated and carried out according to the interpretation of our Secretary of State! Day after day British, French and American steamers leave the various ports of our country laden from keel to deck with contraband of war of all sorts and without the slightest difficulty they obtain their clearance papers from the proper authorities; that is to say, the government authorities openly convert themselves into auxiliaries and participants in the trade with contraband of war—which is carried on to the advantage of England and its allies. And the German vessel "Odenwald" is driven back into port by the guns of a fortress, because it is "suspected" of intentions of taking provisions or munitions to the "Kronprinz Wilhelm!"

Such is the drastic, unanswerable logic of this New York newspaper.

panies. The blockade of Germany will be complete, as soon as it is no longer possible for Germany to obtain copper. England is from now on master of the copper supplies of the world."

If this news be correct then the rumors of a secret compact or treaty between England and the United States might well be considered as proved.

To sum up: the "neutral" United States of North America permit the blockade of Germany in favor of England. They have wantonly sown in the souls of a great people a deep and righteous hatred against a gross and hostile policy which is bound to have disastrous results in many ways, politically, historically and economically upon the position and good name of the republic.

IV. The Americans and Ourselves.

All unfriendly acts which America has perpetrated against Germany we lay at the door of the government or rather of certain responsible persons at the head of the government. We desire to live on terms of peace and friendship with the American people and we have given them no cause for any unfriendliness—much less for their destructive and hostile material breach of neutrality.

How do we stand towards the American people?

We are in a position to prove—and have already proved in the foregoing—that never in the history of the world has a people been more systematically, more shamelessly fed with lies, more thoroughly "fooled" for months, indeed for years, than the American people by the press (foreign and domestic) of the Triple Entente. And not only by the printed word but by the printed picture. If may prove worth while to cite a few particular instances. In place of the Rominter House they are gulled with a picture of St. Bartholomew on the Königssee. Old pictures of Russian pogroms are palmed off on them as those of alleged German atrocities. There is nothing so base, stupid or clumsy but it will serve as a means of propaganda to be carried on month after month.

Germans cannot be indifferent as to what a great and kindred nation of the future, permeated with the fruits of German civilization, may think in days to come of Germany's position in this war, of the moral and military attitude of its army of the people, and especially of the lofty ideals of culture and citizenship which pervade Young Germany. Every educated American, conversant with conditions in Germany, knows what tremendous havoc is committed in the ranks of truth by means of a world-wide press organized to perfection for the purposes of propaganda, and what a horrible and distorted picture of German views and conditions, of the causes leading to the war, and of the way the war is conducted, such a press is capable of spreading through out the world.[1]

We must insist upon a proper conception of the realities, not only for the sake of the past but also for the sake of the future.

From the time of Frederick the Great during the war of Independence up to the War of the Rebellion and the present day, the rise of the United States to a world power has been followed with the most sincere interest and sympathy by the German nation. The German Emperor has been able to see,

---

[1] See the protest addressed by the Central Committee of Americans living in Europe to the Department of State at Washington. It culminates in these fine and ringing words:

"We protest against the destruction of America's integrity, America's business interests, America's security, which must result from such a one-sided "neutrality." We also protest in the name of humanity against this horrible war being prolonged through our country."

Also see the "American Notes in Munich," issued by Dr. Leslie Bissell in the Bavarian capital. The Americans in that city have repeatedly expressed themselves in these words: "Whoever knows Germany as it really is, loves it."

According to a communication of the "Daily Telegraph," a regular campaign for the boycott of American goods is supposed to be taking place in Germany. The Committee of the German-American Association of Commerce emphatically refutes this charge of the "Daily Telegraph." That the impossibility up to the present time of the United States continuing its neutral trade has aroused considerable surprise, and that the delivery of munitions to the enemies of Germany has created a strong feeling of bitterness among the German people is certainly true. Nevertheless nothing is known in Germany of a campaign for the boycott of American goods. If the United States are at present practically cut off from the German markets, then this is to be attributed to the measures taken by the English. It is nothing less than a stupid distortion of the facts to pretend that a condition created by England and passively submitted to by the United States, is to be attributed to an alleged boycott on the part of Germany!

with a sure and almost prophetic vision, the many points upon which the interests and the ideals of the Germans and the Americans are one, and for the support of which they must mutually depend upon one another. Germany has voiced her resolution to carry on this war against England, a war thrust upon Germany by England herself, by all the means within her power, and to a successful issue. It is a war which, though on an infinitely vaster scale, bears, nevertheless, a strong resemblance to that which for all time liberated the young Union from the domination of England.

There is no need for us to plead "mitigating circumstances." *We give voice merely to the sacred conviction of our right to develop, of our right of free movement, of our right to exist.*

Without self-praise or nationalistic exaggeration we would merely point to what the German people has accomplished during the last months in the greatest war that the world has ever seen and against overwhelming odds such as no other nation ever faced. It has asserted itself in a spirit of just defense and with consideration for the laws of nations—in so far as its enemies themselves respected these. We are able to prove that all this embecile talk about the imperialistic tendencies of the German nation towards the conquest of the world is something that is directly opposed to the spirit of the German people, but that the entire country as a united whole is ready to sacrifice its blood and its treasure for the sake of maintaining its place in the council of the nations. Surely wisdom decrees that the just hatred of so great and powerful a civilized nation ought not to be invoked by a one-sided favoritism displayed towards its mortal enemies,—enemies, moreover, which are in part America's own enemies, some of them immediate, like Japan; others, like England, the enemies of a not too distant future. The wisdom of avoiding the permanency of such a feeling must become plainly apparent to America in the light of the vast sacrifices made by the German people and the great goal it has before its eyes.

We expect, we trust, that the common sense of Americans and their love of justice will finally disclose to them how shamefully they have been deceived by an infamous and lying press, and how monstrous was the picture of Germany held up before their hypnotized eyes. We hope that they will realize how little ideas of conquest or chauvinistic policies have to do with true German feeling, and how little the real thoughts and ambitions of the German Kaiser, that much-misunderstood and grossly-abused man, have to do with the caricatures and insults and calumnies spread through foreign countries.

The Americans are the people who are supposed to act as mediators in the matter of peace, for the position as well as the constituent elements of their country would render this rôle a natural one for the United States. But it is to be feared that the short-sighted policy of the government will make all American claims to this important post absolutely untenable. The universal disappointment of the German nation with regard to the attitude hitherto assumed by the American Government may make the negotiations for peace all the more difficult.

V. Regarding the Monroe Doctrine and Neutrality in General.

The steadily growing entanglement of the American continent in the European war, especially the participation of Canada, the breaches of neutrality by the United States, etc., have brought important international questions to the fore, which are also related to the so-called Monroe Doctrine; and to other problems to which we have already referred in the 1st edition.

According to the Monroe Doctrine, the entire western hemisphere is regarded as one single unit so far as its economic territory is concerned;—this territory is supposed to have common political interests. If this interpretation is accepted, it must appear that any act undertaken by a single member of this united America is to be regarded as an action for which the whole of this unified American sphere of interests is responsible, and in especial the United States. If European states are not to have the right of interfering in domestic American or "Pan-American" affairs, even when these affect their interests, be it in a commercial, be it in a political sense, it must naturally be understood on the other hand that all the separate states belonging to this assumed American complexus must refrain from all interference in the domestic politics or conflicts of

Europe. As soon as an organized state, situate upon the American continents, ventures to interfere in a European struggle by sending troops to the Old World, it throws down a challenge which demands the taking of military measures which must naturally extend themselves to the American continent.

This dictum, which is almost in the nature of a political axiom, has been further elucidated by Judge Dr. Paul Alexander Katz in the "Vossische Zeitung" of October 3rd, 1914.

The German Government has so far maintained a most exemplary attitude towards this purely arbitrary Monroe Doctrine, and it has sacrificed much merely for the sake of maintaining friendly relations with the United States. Whether this will be possible in the future, considering the *hostile* attitude of the *American* Government is a difficult and momentous question which extends beyond the purpose or scope of this work. In any case the attitude of the government of the United States is such that this great question of the future can hardly be said to appear in a particularly favorable light—in the sense of real Americanism. That nation which frivolously discards its real neutrality and ventures to interfere in European contingencies, possesses no right from the point of view of international law, to consider itself in any degree *ex lex* so far as European interpretations are concerned. Is it Japan who must persuade the United States of the foolish ishness of its past and present policy of provocation towards Germany?

Not only has the Monroe Doctrine been shaken to its very foundations by the position assumed by the United States, but also by the numerous violations of neutrality of which England has been guilty in connection with South American states, especially Brazil and Chile.[1]

[1] 1. A notorious breach of neutrality, for example, according to a Brazilian paper, was the part played by the English cruiser "Glasgow" in the *sea-fight* off the Malvina Islands. After the battle of Coronel, off the Chilean coast, the "Glasgow" was obliged to put into Rio de Janeiro for repairs. This is permitted to belligerent powers. Warships in such cases are allowed to remain in a neutral harbor, until the necessary repairs are effected, and are under no obligation to be dismantled.

They are supposed, however, to make only such repairs as will ensure the safety of the ship's homeward voyage. The "Glasgow," apparently, was completely refitted, and that in the dockyard of the Ministry of Marine. Then

Even the courteous policy of the United States towards Japan in the matter of the Turtle Bay question in April 1915, offers a glaring contrast to the attitude of Washington in 1901-2 when Germany's quarrel with Venezuela brought up the mere ghost of a suspicion that the Monroe Doctrine might be violated by Germany. Although Germany at that time demanded nothing more from Venezuela than some security

---

openly, instead of making for England, she proceeded to a naval station which the English maintained in Brazilian waters, as has been established, off the Abrolhos Isles near the coast of Bahia. Here she took aboard men and ammunition, and proceeding southward, joined the strong English squadron, which lay there in wait for the German ships.

2. The "Kölnische Zeitung" reports: According to the Chilean military paper, "Gazette Militaire," which appears in Santiago, Admiral Cradock, on the day before the naval battle off Coronel, caused a lieutenant and four men from the "Good Hope" to erect a wireless station upon the island of Mocha. After the destruction of the greater part of the Cradock squadron on the Ist of November, this station still remained in communication with the remaining ships. The five men were taken off six weeks later by the armored cruiser, "Canopus." The Chilean paper calls special attention to the fact that Admiral Cradock ordered the erection of this station upon the island, so that he might have exact information as to the movements of the enemy squadron.

3. A particularly grave case of the violation of Chilean neutrality attended the sinking of the "Dresden," in Cumberland Bay, part of the island of Juan Fernandez. The ship lay, damaged and without coal, only 400 metres from the shore. In spite of the protests of the German commander, three English ships opened fire. The English commander replied, in true English fashion, that he had orders to destroy the "Dresden" wherever he found her. He left the rest for the diplomats to settle. Thereupon the Germans themselves blew up the ship, which was lying in Chilean waters. A Chilean trading vessel lying near was hit by the shot from the English ships. Such is English regard for neutrality. England offered an excuse since Chile proved that the German ship was already interned. Chile was again to blame in the matter of the "Glasgow," which she illegally allowed to go free, whereas the German ship was treated in the strictest manner. Chile was rewarded by the mockery of the English press. "We apologize, and the "Dresden" remains sunk." (See the exact description of this scandalous breach of neutrality in the Chilean newspaper, "El Mercurio" in Valparaiso and "La Union," which, although friendly to the Triple Entente, laid bare the scandalous trick. ("Münchener-Augsburger Zeitung," No. 126, 1915).

The procedure in the question of the Panama Canal is also very serious. The Union supports the Triple Entente by forbidding the import of contraband and damages Germany by the one-sided way in which it creates difficulties in coaling in Central America.

for the payment of twenty million dollars owing to citizens of the German Empire, and in order to obtain this security, sent a squadron to levy upon the Venezuelan customs, its procedure was violently attacked by a considerable section of the press of the United States. The jingoes of the republic forthwith declared that Germany was striving for the acquisition of territory in Central or in South America, and made use of this shallow pretense in order to make rash and unfounded attacks upon Germany in the name of the injured Doctrine of President James Monroe. English diplomacy, as usual, pulled the strings.

It might also be observed that gradually, even though tentatively, some of the larger Chilean and Argentine newspapers, such as "La Prensa" in Buenos Aires, "El Mercurio" and "La Union" in Valparaiso, etc., are beginning to assert themselves against English insolence and breaches of neutrality, some energetically, others with more or less timidity.

CHAPTER XXIX.

The Declaration of the North Sea as a Zone of War (the So-called "Submarine Blockade") and its Consequences.

I.

In its issue of February 2nd, 1915, the "Reichs- und Staatsanzeiger" ("Bulletin of the Empire and the States") published the following official notifications:

Berlin, February 1st, 1915.

PROCLAMATION.

England is about to transport great bodies of troops and large quantities of war materials to France. All available military measures will be put into operation in order to proceed against these transports. Peaceful merchant ships are hereby urgently warned against approaching too closely to the north and west coasts of France, since they may incur serious danger through being mistaken for vessels that are serving the purposes of war.

Merchant vessels on their way to the North Sea are recommended to take the route around Scotland.

The Chief of the Admiralty Staff of the German Navy.
von Pohl.

PROCLAMATION.

1. The waters around Great Britain and Ireland, including the entire English Channel are hereby declared to be a war zone.

From the 18th of February on, every enemy merchant vessel encountered in this zone of war will be destroyed, nor will it always be possible to avoid the danger which crews and passengers may thereby incur.

2. Neutral vessels are also liable to incur danger in the zone of war, since in view of the misuse of neutral flags sanctioned by the British Government on the 31st of January, and the accidents of war at sea, it may not always be possible to avoid the possibility of justifiable attacks upon enemy vessels from involving such as may be neutral.

3. Navigation north of the Shetland Islands, in the eastern part of the North Sea and a strip of at least 30 sea-miles along the Dutch coast may be considered as free from danger.

Berlin, February 4th, 1915.

(signed) Chief of the Admiralty Staff of the German Navy.
von Pohl.

As an amplification of this Proclamation the following memorial of the German Government respecting the measures of retaliation taken against the lawless methods of England for suppressing neutral commerce with Germany, was communicated to all allied, neutral and hostile powers:

"Since the beginning of the present war Great Britain has been carrying on a commercial war against Germany in a manner which is nothing less than a mockery of all the precepts of international law.

It is true that the British Government has designated in several orders that it intended to abide by the rules and regulations regarding naval warfare as laid down by the Declaration of London, but so far as the essential points were concerned it has radically departed from these, despite the fact that its own representatives at the London Conference had recognized these provisions as valid in international law. The British Government places upon its list of contraband a number of articles which are not used or are only indirectly used for purposes of war, and which are therefore, by virtue of said Declaration of London, as well as by all the acknowledged laws of nations, *not* to be declared as contraband. The British Government has, moreover, actually obliterated the difference between *absolute* and *relative* contraband, in that all articles of relative contraband destined for Germany have been seized by it without regard to the port at which these goods were to be disembarked, and without regard to their peaceful or warlike use. It does not even scruple to violate the Declaration of Paris, since its naval forces have ventured to seize German non-contraband property even upon neutral ships.

Exceeding its own regulations as embodied in the Declaration of London, the British Government seized German citizens liable for military duty and made them prisoners of war despite the fact that they were travelling on neutral ships. Finally it has declared the entire North Sea to be a zone of war, and if it has not made the free sea-passage of neutral vessels between Scotland and Norway impossible, it has made it endlessly difficult and dangerous. To a certain extent it has introduced a blockade of neutral coasts and neutral ports in contravention of all international law.

All these measures have but one purpose—which is illegally to paralyze legitimate and neutral trade,—and to strike not only at the military operations but also at the commercial life of Germany, and finally by means of starvation to devote the entire German people to destruction.

In the greater as well as the lesser issues of this question the neutral powers have submitted entirely to the measures undertaken by England. These powers have in particular failed in securing the release of German citizens and German goods taken from their vessels in contravention of the law. In certain directions they even accepted the dictates of England, irreconciliable as these are with the freedom of the seas, since under the open pressure of England they themselves agreed to institute regulations forbidding the export of wares destined for peaceful purposes and to set up laws forbidding the transit of goods through their own territory.

It was in vain that the German Government called the attention of the neutral powers to the fact that they would be forced to consider the question whether they could still be entitled to have recourse to the provisions of the Declaration of London, hitherto scrupulously observed by Germany, if Great Britain was to continue in the course she had adopted and all these breaches of international law to the disadvantage of Germany be accepted by them without protest. Great Britain appeals to her vital interests in order to justify her lawless actions, the interests of the British empire which are supposed to be jeopardized, and the neutral powers seem to content themselves with theoretical protests, and, in fact, to accept the life interests of the belligerents as a sufficient excuse for tolerating every possible method of waging war.

Germany too must make appeal to these vital interests on her own behalf.

She is therefore to her regret forced to adopt military countermeasures against England as a retaliation for the English procedure. Just as England has designated as a war-zone the waters lying between Scotland and Norway, so Germany now designates the waters surrounding Great Britain and Ireland, including the entire English Channel, as a war-zone; and will proceed by all the warlike means within her power against all enemy vessels within the proscribed area.

To further this end she will endeavor from the 18th of February, 1915, on, to destroy every enemy merchant vessel that enters the war-zone, nor will it always be possible to avoid the dangers that thereby threaten both persons and goods.

The neutral nations are therefore warned against entrusting crews, passengers, and wares to such vessels in the future. Their attention is also called to the fact that it is to the interests of their own ships to avoid entering the proscribed area. For even though the German navy is under orders to avoid all acts of violence against neutral vessels, in so far as these are recognizable, yet in view of the misuse of neutral flags ordered by the British Government and the accidents of war, it may not always be possible to prevent such ships falling victims to attacks directed justly against enemy vessels. It is expressly declared that navigation north of the Shetland Islands, in the eastern parts of the North Sea and in a strip of at least 30 sea-miles breadth along the coast of Holland, is free of danger.

The German Government gives this timely notice of its intentions in order that the enemy as well as the neutral ships may have time to make their arrangements with regard to reaching the harbors that lie within the war-zone. It ventures to expect that the neutral powers will show consideration for the vital interests of Germany in no less a degree than that shown for England's, and will do their share in keeping their citizens and their property away from the theatre of war. This is the more to be expected since it must also be to the interests of the neutral powers that the present destructive war should be ended as soon as possible."

This announcement of the German Admiralty is the immediate and logical result of the proclamations issued by the Imperial Government on the 2nd and 3rd of February—the warning addressed to neutral shipping and the notice given as to the secret English order in respect to masking English merchant vessels under neutral flags. In a wider sense it is also the consequence naturally resulting from the entire procedure of England upon the seas, which has from the very beginning of the war torn the principles established by the nations into shreds as though these were some frail gossamer. And from month to month the contempt she has shown for other nations and for accepted laws has steadily increased. For over half a year Germany hesitated in the face of a ruthless and unscrupulous England, ere proceeding on her part to make a drastic application of the forcible measures that lay within her power.

England has in the most arbitrary manner, to the detriment of Germany—(and no less to the detriment of the neutrals) extended the definition of absolute contraband and the right of search with respect to neutral ships. The commercial life of the entire world suffers under this arbitrary domination. So far the neutrals have ventured to expostulate only in unsuccessful diplomatic protests. Especially in America huge supplies of all sorts are accumulating and none of these can be transported because of the English procedure. Only the exportation of weapons and war supplies, that is to say, the most unqualified kind of absolute contraband—in favor, of course, of England and her allies—is permitted to the neutrals in contradiction to the very spirit of all true neutrality.

Thus England has succeeded in turning the most elementary laws of international rights concerning neutral shipping simply topsy-turvey, and as though this were not enough, in lieu of a legitimate blockade of the German coast, she has declared the entire North Sea to be closed as a zone of war. In connection with this England has forced neutral ships to pick their way through a narrow trough, so to speak, between the English east coast and the French and English mine-fields. The loss of a great number of neutral vessels has been the result.

But her most arrogant piece of work consisted in her order to the British merchant marine to hide itself under the protection of neutral flags,—as made known in the German bulletin.

Germany's injunction of February 4th, 1915, caused a tremendous sensation throughout the world. It was received by the neutral press as an historic act,—Germany took up the gauntlet of challenge which had been flung at her feet—and this acceptance meant nothing less than the starving-out of the greatest sea-power in the world.

As might have been expected, the neutral nations took advantage of the fourteen days' grace to organize a campaign of protest against these measures.

The United States issued a Note on February 12th in which in polite but decisive terms it declared that ..."if the commanders of German vessels of war should act upon the presumption that the flag of the United States was not being used in good faith and should destroy on the high seas an American vessel or the lives of American citizens it would be difficult for the Government of the United States to view the act in any other light than as an indefensible violation of neutral rights........If such a deplorable situation should arise the Imperial German Government can readily appreciate that the Government of the United States would be constrained to hold the Imperial German Government to a strict accountability for such acts of their naval authorities and to take any steps it may be necessary to take to safeguard American lives and property, and to secure to American citizens the full enjoyment of their acknowledged rights on the high seas."

There is then talk of a "cloud upon the intercourse of the two Governments" and Germany is called upon to declare "that American citizens and their vessels will not be molested by the naval forces of Germany otherwise than by visit and search, though their vessels may be traversing the sea area delimited in the Proclamation of the German Admiralty."

The tone of this "Droh-Note" (Note of Threats, as the Germans called it) a note which is conceived in the most superficial fashion, with no doubt an intentional mis-reading of "all" in place of the "enemy" vessels, as distinctly set down in the announcement of the German Admiralty issued on the 4th of February, 1915,—offers a characteristic contrast to the modest "representations" to the majesty of Britain. The United States are once more prepared to carry out a "paper neutrality."

Privy-Councillor Dr. Wach-Leipzig has very accurately designated the American Note as a "remarkable product of faulty logic and an imperfect sense of justice." It assumes that we would be willing to respect the American flag at our own expense until we were absolutely reassured as to the abuse of this emblem of neutrality. But Mr. Wilson forgot that the American flag had lost its property of being accounted such an emblem from that very moment in which England proclaimed the very acme of its misuse by flying it upon her own ships. Surely it must be acknowledged as a law of logic and justice that the responsible protector of the neutrality of his own state must be the very first to see that the sign or symbol by which a ship is known to belong to his state is not abused or deprived of this differentiating property? Or in case it cannot or will not do this, should it not undertake other measures to secure the safety of American merchant vessels by making their nationality easily recognizable? If this is not done it must needs follow that the right to demand consideration for the flag under these circumstances is forfeited, and the responsible executive of the country thereby makes *himself guilty of complicity in the deceitful procedure of England.*

This is still more the case when this executive has offered *no protest* against the illegal British declaration of the 3rd of November, 1914, the consequences of which we are now resisting, for this deprives him from the very beginning of any right to make a protest against the corresponding measures of defence —unless this governmental head regards his "neutrality" purely as a form of demonstration, or as a mere "paper-neutrality." Had the American Government fulfilled its duty after the order of the 3rd of November and again in the matter of the misuse of its flag, the entire order of the German Government of the 4th of February, 1915, would have been unnecessary. Yes, the German Government had expressly declared that it would refrain from the right of search, if England would respect the Declaration of London, and make redress for the misuse of neutral flags. This, as all the world knows, England refused to do.

II.

The German answer of the 16th of February, 1915, was dignified and decisive. In spite of its length we must reproduce it word for word (as translated) since it will be certain to rank as an historic document:

"The Imperial Government has examined the communication from the United States Government in the same spirit of good-will and friendship by which the communication appears to have been dictated. The Imperial Government is in accord with the United States Government that for both parties it is in a high degree desirable to avoid misunderstandings which might arise from measures announced by the German Admiralty and to provide against the occurrence of incidents which might trouble the friendly relations which so far happily exist between the two Governments.

With regard to the assuring of these friendly relations, the German Government believes that it may all the more reckon on a full understanding with the United States, as the procedure anounced by the German Admiralty, which was fully explained in the note in the 4th inst., is in no way directed against legitimate commerce and legitimate shipping of neutrals, but represents solely a measure of self-defense, imposed on Germany by her vital interests, against England's method of warfare, which is contrary to international law, and which so far no protest by neutrals has succeeded in bringing back to the generally recognized principles of law as existing before the outbreak of war.

In order to exclude all doubt regarding these cardinal points, the German Government once more begs leave to state how things stand. Until now Germany has scrupulously observed valid international rules regarding naval warfare. At the very beginning of the war Germany immediately agreed to the proposal of the American Government to ratify the new Declaration of London, and took over its contents unaltered, and without formal obligation, into her prize law.

The German Government has obeyed these rules, even when they were diametrically opposed to her military interests. For instance, Germany allowed the transportation of provisions to England from Denmark until today, though she was well able, by her sea forces, to prevent it. In contradistinction to this attitude, England has not even hesitated at a second infringement of international law, if by such means she could paralyze the peaceful commerce of Germany with neutrals. The German Government will be the less obliged to enter into details, as these are put down sufficiently, though not exhaustively, in the American note to the British Government dated Dec. 29, as a result of five months' experience.

All these encroachments have been made, as has been admitted, in order to cut off all supplies from Germany and thereby starve her peaceful civil population—a procedure contrary to all humanitarian principles. Neutrals have been unable to prevent the interruption of their commerce with Germany, which is contrary to international laws.

The American Government, as Germany readily acknowledges, has protested against the British procedure. In spite of these protests and those from other neutral States, Great Britain could not be induced to depart from the course of action she had decided upon. Thus, for instance, the American ship Wilhelmina recently was stopped by the British, although her cargo was destined solely for the German civil population, and, according to the express declaration of the German Government, was to be employed only for this purpose.

Germany is as good as cut off from her overseas supply by the silent or protesting toleration of neutrals, not only in regard to such goods as are absolute contraband, but also in regard to such as, according to acknowledged law before the war, are only conditional contraband or not contraband at all. Great Britain, on the other hand, is, with the toleration of neutral Governments, not only supplied with such goods as are not contraband or only conditional contraband, but with goods which are regarded by Great Britain, if sent to Germany, as absolute contraband; namely, provisions, industrial raw materials, &c., and even with goods which have always indubitably been regarded as absolute contraband.

The German Government feels itself obliged to point out with the greatest emphasis that a traffic in arms, estimated at many hundreds of millions, is being carried on between American firms and Germany's enemies. Germany fully comprehends that the practice of right and the toleration of wrong on the part of neutrals are matters absolutely at the discretion of neutrals, and involve no formal violation of neutrality. Germany, therefore, did not complain of any formal violation of neutrality, but the German Government, in view of complete evidence before it, cannot help pointing out that it, together with the entire public opinion of Germany, feels itself to be severely prejudiced by the fact that neutrals, in safeguarding their rights in legitimate commerce with Germany according to international law, have up to the present achieved no, or only insignificant, results, while they are making unlimited use of their right by carrying on contraband traffic with Great Britain and our other enemies.

If it is a formal right of neutrals to take no steps to protect their legitimate trade with Germany, and even to allow themselves to be influenced in the direction of the conscious and willful restriction of their trade, they have on the other hand, the perfect right, which they unfortunately do not exercise, to cease contraband trade, especially in arms, with Germany's enemies.

In view of this situation, Germany, after six months of patient waiting, sees herself obliged to answer Great Britain's murderous method of naval warfare with sharp counter-measures. If Great Britain in her fight against Germany summons hunger as an ally, for the purpose of imposing upon a civilized people of 70,000,000 the choice between destitution and starvation or submission to Great Britain's commercial will, then Germany today is determined to take up the gauntlet and appeal to similar allies.

Germany trusts that the neutrals, who so far have submitted to the disadvantageous consequences of Great Britain's hunger war in silence, or merely in registering a protest, will display toward Germany no smaller measure of toleration, even if German measures, like those of Great Britain, present new terrors of naval warfare.

Moreover, the German Government is resolved to suppress with all the means at its disposal the importation of war material to Great Britain and her allies, and she takes it for granted that neutral Governments, which so far have taken no steps against the traffic in arms with Germany's enemies, will not oppose forcible suppression by Germany of this trade.

Acting from this point of view, the German Admiralty proclaimed a naval war zone, whose limits it exactly defined. Germany, so far as possible, will seek to close this war zone with mines, and will also endeavor to destroy hostile merchant vessels in every other way. While the German Government, in taking action based upon this overpowering point of view, keeps itself far removed from all international destruction of neutral lives and property, on the other hand, it does not fail to recognize that from the action to be taken against Great Britain dangers arise which threaten all trade within the war zone, without distinction. This is a natural result of mine warfare, which, even under the strictest observance of the limits of international law, endangers every ship approaching the mine area. The German Government considers itself entitled to hope that all neutrals will acquiesce in these measures, as they have done in the case of the grievous damages inflicted upon them by British measures, all the more so as Germany is resolved, for the protection of neutral shipping even in the naval war zone, to do everything which is at all compatible with the attainment of this object.

In view of the fact that Germany gave the first proof of her good-will in fixing a time limit of not less than fourteen days before the execution of said measures, so that neutral shipping might have an opportunity of making arrangements to avoid threatening danger, this can most surely be achieved by remaining away from the naval war zone. Neutral vessels which, despite this ample notice, which greatly affects the achievement of our aims in our war against Great Britain, enter these closed waters will themselves bear the responsibility for any unfortunate accidents that may occur. Germany disclaims all responsibility for such accidents and their consequences.

Germany has further expressly announced the destruction of all enemy merchant vessels found within the war zone, but not the destruction of all merchant vessels, as the United States seems erroneously to have understood. This restriction which Germany imposes upon itself in prejudicial to the aim of our warfare, especially as in the application of the conception of contraband practiced by Great Britain toward Germany—which conception will now also be similarly interpreted by Germany—the presumption will be that neutral ships have contraband aboard. Germany naturally is unwilling to renounce its rights to ascertain the presence of contraband in neutral vessels, and in certain cases to draw conclusions therefrom.

Germany is ready, finally, to deliberate with the United States concerning any measures which might secure the safety of legitimate shipping of neutrals in the war zone. Germany cannot, however, forbear to point out that all its efforts in this direction may be rendered very difficult by two circumstances: First, the misuse of neutral flags by British merchant vessels, which is indubitably known to the United States; second, the contraband trade already mentioned, especially in war materials, on neutral vessels.

Regarding the latter point, Germany would fain hope that

the United States, after further consideration, will come to a conclusion corresponding to the spirit of real neutrality. Regarding the first point, the secret order of the British Admiralty, recommending to British merchant ships the use of neutral flags, has been communicated by Germany to the United States and confirmed by communication with the British Foreign Office, which designates this procedure as entirely unobjectionable and in accordance with British law. British merchant shipping immediately followed this advice, as doubtless is known to the American Government from the incidents of the Lusitania and the Laertes.

Moreover, the British Government has supplied arms to British merchant ships and instructed them forcibly to resist German submarines. In these circumstances, it would be very difficult for submarines to recognize neutral merchant ships, for search in most cases cannot be undertaken, seeing that in the case of a disguised British ship from which an attack may be expected, the searching party and the submarine would be exposed to destruction.

Great Britain, then, was in a position to make the German measures illusory if the British merchant fleet persisted in the misuse of neutral flags and neutral ships could not otherwise be recognized beyond doubt. Germany, however, being in a state of necessity, wherein she was placed by violation of law, must render effective her measures in all circumstances, in order thereby to compel her adversary to adopt methods of warfare corresponding with international law, and so to restore the freedom of the seas, of which Germany at all times is the defender and for which she today is fighting.

Germany therefore rejoices that the United States has made representations to Great Britain concerning the illegal use of their flag, and expresses the expectation that this procedure will force Great Britain to respect the American flag in the future. In this expectation, commanders of German submarines have been instructed, as already mentioned in the note of Feb. 4, to refrain from violent action against American merchant vessels, so far as these can be recognized.

In order to prevent in the surest manner the consequences of confusion—though naturally not so far as mines are concerned—Germany recommends that the United States make its ships which are conveying peaceful cargoes through the British war zone discernible by means of convoys.

Germany believes it may act on the supposition that only such ships would be convoyed as carried goods not regarded as contraband according to the British interpretation made in the case of Germany.

How the method of convoy can be carried out is a question concerning which Germany is ready to open negotiations with the United States as soon as possible. Germany would be particularly grateful, however, if the United States would urgently recommend to its merchant vessels to avoid the British naval war zone, in any case until the settlement of the flag question. Germany is inclined to the confident hope that the United States will be able to appreciate in its entire significance the heavy battle which Germany is waging for existence, and that from the foregoing explanations and promises it will acquire full understanding of the motives and the aims of the measures announced by Germany.

Germany repeats that it has now resolved upon the projected measures only under the strongest necessity of national self-defense, such measures having been deferred out of consideration for neutrals.

If the United States, in view of the weight which it is justified in throwing and able to throw into the scales of the fate of peoples, should succeed at the last moment in removing the grounds which make that procedure an obligatory duty for Germany, and if the American Government, in particular, should find a way to make the Declaration of London respected—on behalf, also, of those powers which are fighting on Germany's side—and thereby make possible for Germany legitimate importation of the necessaries of life and industrial raw material, then the German Government could not too highly appreciate such a service, rendered in the interests of humane methods of warfare, and would gladly draw conclusions from the new situation." *(Official Translation by U. S. Embassy.)*

Every fair-minded, logical reader will acknowledge that this Note offers every possible expedient for averting damage to American ships. It is willing to recognize as legitimately accredited all merchant ships flying the stars and stripes and convoyed by American men-of war, and to permit their cargoes to pass without examination as non-contraband. It expresses a willingness to change its entire method of procedure as well as its intentions if England will adhere to the provisions of the Declaration of London and refrain from the use of false colors. But all these attempts at conciliation were in vain. England insisted upon carrying out her plan of starving Germany, and rejected every suggestion for making the question of food supplies less stringent. She refused to give up the cheating with neutral flags. It is worthy of remark that only in her misuse of neutral flags and in her attempts to deceive with them does England show any regard for neutral flags, but not in their justifiable use by the nations entitled to them! Such are the peculiar conceptions of right and morality held by "civilized and law-abiding" Albion!

The procedure of the German Government is, according to the foregoing, nothing more than a measure of retaliation, of necessity and defense, and the natural result of the British order of November 3rd, 1914,—to which it forms the inevitable answer.

The force of arms and the rights of destruction may be employed, according to German Prize Court Law:

1. When the ship attempts to resist capture by using forcible means, or when it refuses to obey the order of the submarine, as provided for in Article 50 of the London Declaration.

2. After seizure, when through the removal of the captured vessel to a home port or an allied port, the war-vessel, or the crew, or the success of the immediate military enterprise of the warship may be endangered. The ship may be destroyed only under the condition of paying damages for the neutral cargo.

A blockade by submarine is something entirely new, something which had not been foreseen by the Declaration of London. The submarine, or "U boat," has completely wrecked all previous and customary conceptions of a blockade. For the essence of its nature is that of invisibility. The following appears to be certain:

1. When the safety of the submarine permits of it, then the persons aboard the vessel under seizure are to be granted time to leave the ship (analogous application of Articles 49 and 54 of the Declaration of London).

2. A previous declaration is not necessary. The ship liable to capture need not be notified—in contradistinction to a mine-blockade.

3. The immediate torpedoing of enemy merchant vessels is likewise permissible, when a condition of reprisals prevails, that is to say, when international law has been violated by the other combatant.

4. When the neutral states do not insist upon their just rights according to international law, especially when they assist one country by means of special favors and deliveries in contravention of the law. In such cases reprisals against them must also be considered as valid, without damages for loss of or injury to neutral wares. The same holds good when they permit international law to be interpreted in favor of one belligerent to the disadvantage of the other, above all by the misuse of neutral flags. In other cases the owner of the neutral goods will be entitled to compensation.

5. An enemy vessel that carries neutral goods may be destroyed without any further preliminaries.

6. It appears to be debatable whether the express notification of the danger to which neutral ships are subject, does not also deprive them of the right to compensation. There is no doubt a gap in international sea-law as to this point—but it must nevertheless be assumed that, analogous to the law relating to mines, when one belligerent declares navigation in certain waters to be dangerous and a neutral ship, despite this warning, persists in entering this area, then no compensation is due to it for neutral goods or bottom, since the entire blame for a negligence which borders on felony, lies with the neutral. Confirmation that the cargo is neutral is almost impossible in view of the conditions of submarine warfare. Even the confirmation of the neutrality of the ship itself is extraordinarily difficult. But as soon as one of the belligerents enters upon a systematic misuse of the neutral flag, this becomes absolutely impossible, and under no conditions could there be any question

of compensation on the part of the state effecting the capture. If damage ensues the damaged nation or person must apply to that state which by its illegal actions, in especial by its misuse of neutral flags, has been really responsible for the damage.

This point of view is essentially more correct in that, according to the English press, it must be infallibly assumed that English merchant-ships (sailing under neutral flags!) are armed with artillery, that they have been instructed to ram submarines, to hurl bombs at them, to voyage in groups, and to do all within their power to destroy submarines. Thus, English merchant ships can, in principle, no longer be regarded as undefended. (See the special warning issued to Holland by the German Government, and delivered to the Rotterdam Chamber of Commerce on February 16, 1915.)

But a "defended" merchant vessel is no longer a merchant-vessel. It must be recognized as a warship or more correctly still, as a pirate ship.[1]

III.

Another English principle in this war, as established in the "Times" of November 12th, is the following: "All international law is valid only in so far as it is backed up by force."

[1] According to a dispatch to the "Central News," the "Shipping Gazette" offers a reward of £ 500 for the crew of the merchant vessel which first succeeds in sinking a German submarine.

As early as February 2nd the "Times" had advised merchant vessels to do battle with submarines instead of obeying their injunctions to stop. Rewards in money were also offered by French societies. And action was taken along the lines of this piratical procedure. It may be recalled that no details were given as to the sinking of the "U 29," the submarine commanded by the heroic young Captain, Otto Weddigen. It was affirmed, however, that his vessel had been sunk by an act of treachery by an English merchant vessel or trawler disguised under a neutral flag. The truth will yet out.

[1] The "Times" comments on this order as follows: "The purpose of this announcement is to close the greater part of the northern channel and to limit traffic to the day-time, in order to facilitate the examination of the ships which enter the Irish Sea from the west and at the same time to make things difficult for the enemy ships operating in this region. Through this measure the larger part of the traffic will very likely be diverted by the route around the south of Ireland. It may be assumed that there are mines and other dangers in the forbidden districts which render the passage of vessels dangerous."

And it is upon this that England bases her acts, now as heretofore.

The English Admiralty made the following announcement on Feb. 23rd, 1915:

"The navigation of the sea between the northwesterly line from 55 degrees 22½ minutes north latitude and 6 degrees, 17 minutes west longitude to 55 degrees, 31 minutes north latitude and 6 degrees, 2 minutes west latitude and 5 degrees, 24½ minutes west longitude, to 55 degrees, 2 minutes north latitude and 5 degrees, 40½ minutes west longitude, as well as the southwesterly line from a to d and the northeasterly line from b to c is absolutely forbidden to ships of all dimensions and nationality from the 23rd of February on. All sea traffic which desires to go by way of the northern Irish Channel, must navigate south of Rathlin Island between sunrise and sunset. No vessel must be found at night within four miles of Rathlin Island." (*retranslation*)

On the 2nd of March the American Ambassador in the name of his government delivered the well-known note of February 22nd to the Imperial German Government. (See German text of this note in the original edition, pages 491 to 493.)

This note of the American Government was answered as follows by the German Government under the date of February 28th, 1915:

Foreign Office. *(Official Translation by U. S. Embassy.)*

Berlin, February, 28th, 1915.

"The Imperial German Government have taken note with great interest of the suggestion of the American Government, that certain principles for the conduct of maritime war on the part of Germany and England be agreed upon for the protection of neutral shipping. They see therein new evidence of the friendly feelings of the American Government toward the German Government, which are fully reciprocated by Germany.

"It is in accordance with Germany's wishes also to have maritime war conducted according to rules which, without discriminately restricting one or the other of the belligerent powers in the use of their means of warfare, are equally considerate of the interests of neutrals and the dictates of humanity.

"Consequently, it was intimated in the German note of the 16th instant that observation of the Declaration of London on the part of Germany's adversaries would create a new situation, from which the German Government would gladly draw the proper conclusions.

"Proceeding from this view, the German Government have carefully examined the suggestion of the American Government, and believe that they can actually see in it a suitable basis for the practical solution of the questions which have arisen.

"With regard to the various points of the American note, they beg to make the following remarks.

"1. With regard to the sowing of mines the German Government would be willing to agree, as suggested, not to use floating mines, and to have anchored mines constructed as indicated. Moreover, they agree to put the stamp of the Government on all mines to be planted. On the other hand, it does not appear to them to be feasable for the belligerents wholly to forego the use of anchored mines for offensive purposes.

"2. The German Government would undertake not to use their submarines to attack mercantile vessels of any flag, except when necessary to enforce the right of visit and search. Should the enemy nationality of the vessel, or the presence of contraband be ascertained, submarines would proceed in accordance with the general rules of international law.

"3. As provided in the American note, this restriction of the use of the submarines is contingent on the fact that enemy mercantile vessels abstain from the use of the neutral flag and other neutral distinctive marks. It would appear to be a matter of course that such mercantile vessels also abstain from arming themselves and from all resistance by force, since such procedure, contrary to international law, would render impossible any action of the submarines in accordance with international law.

"4. The regulation of legitimate importations of food into Germany suggested by the American Government appears to be in general acceptable. Such regulation would, of course, be confined to importations by sea, but that would, on the other hand, include indirect importations by way of neutral ports. The German Government would, therefore, be willing to make the declarations of the nature provided in the American note, so that the use of the imported food and foodstuffs solely by the non-combatant population would be guaranteed.

"The Imperial Government must, however, in addition, have the importation of other raw material used by the economic system of non-combatants, including forage, permitted. To that end, the enemy Governments would have to permit the free entry into Germany of the raw material mentioned in the free list of the Declaration of London and to treat materials included in the list of conditional contraband according to the same principles as food and foodstuffs.

"The German Government venture to hope that the agreement for which the American Government have paved the way may be reached, after due consideration of the remarks made above, and that, in this way, peaceable neutral shipping and trade will not have to suffer any more than is absolutely necessary from the unavoidable effects of maritime war.

"These effects could be still further reduced if, as was pointed out in the German note of the 16th instant, some way could be found to exclude the shipping of munitions of war from neutral countries to belligerents on ships of any nationality.

"The German Government must, of course, reserve a definite statement of their position until such time as they may receive further information from the American Government, enabling them to see what obligations the British Government are, on their part, willing to assume."

The following proclamation of France and Great Britain in answer to the suggestions of the United States, suggestions which, as has been repeatedly shown, met with the fullest consideration and reciprocity on the part of Germany,—as was duly acknowledged in all neutral lands,—may be regarded as the official answer of the two Entente powers.

"The governments of France and Great Britain have communicated the following declaration to the governments of the neutral states:

"Germany has declared the Channel and the North Coast of France as well as the waters surrounding the British Isles to be a zone of war. It has officially announced that "every enemy vessel encountered in this zone of war will be destroyed" and that neutral vessels "may incur serious danger" there. This at the first glance indicates that every merchant vessel without regard to the flag under which it sails, or the safety of the passengers and crew is to be torpedoed. Since the German Admiralty is not in a position to hold up a single ship sailing upon the surface, these attacks can be executed only by means of submarines.

"International law and international usages of war with regard to attacks upon commerce have always proceeded from the postulate that the first duty of those who seized a merchant vessel was to bring the vessel before a Prize Court by whom the case was to be judged and the justice of the seizure determined, and by verdict of which neutrals might recover their cargoes. The sinking of a captured vessel is in itself a debatable point, which may be resorted to only under extraordinary circumstances and only after measures have been taken to bring the entire crew and passengers into security.

"The responsibility of distinguishing between an enemy vessel and a neutral vessel and an enemy or neutral cargo rests indisputably with the attacking vessel, whose duty it is to ascertain the nature and the character of the ship and its cargo and to secure the safety of the ship's papers before the ship is seized and sunk. It is also the duty of a belligerent to provide for the safety of the crew of an enemy as well as of a neutral vessel. All previous discussions regarding the laws which are to set up regulations for warfare at sea, are based upon this principle. But the German submarine is not in a position to act in accordance with these obligations. It does not take the captured vessels before a Prize Court and has no Prize Crew aboard to place aboard a captured ship. It applies no sufficient means to make a distinction between a neutral and an enemy vessel; it does not take the crew and the passengers of the vessel to be sunk aboard in order to secure their safety.

These methods of conducting war according to this, are

therefore quite beyond the limits of those international regulations which prescribe the warlike measures to be taken against commerce in time of war. The German Government sets indiscriminate destruction in place of the regular seizure. Germany applies these methods against peaceful merchants and crews that are not participants in war, with the intention of preventing wares of all sorts, among them provisions for the support of the civil population, from entering the British waters or from being imported or exported from the north of France.

"Germany's opponents are therefore forced to take refuge in measures of retaliation, in order on their part to prevent the import or export of goods to Germany or from Germany. Nevertheless these measures are to be carried out by England and France without endangering the ships or lives of neutrals and non-combatants in strict accordance with the principles of humanity. The English and French Governments therefore consider themselves justified in seizing wares, which are presumably destined for the enemy, which belong to him or are of enemy origin, and in taking these into their ports. These ships and cargoes shall not be declared as confiscated unless they are subject to this by verdict of the Prize Court. The treatment of vessels, which have put forth before this date, is to undergo no change." (*retranslated*)

A more untrustworthy document than this Anglo-French Note has surely never seen the light of day. The increased severity of the war waged against English sea traffic is not the *cause* but the *consequence* of England's monstrous, inhumane and lawless attempt to wage a war of starvation against the German people. Even the French press has acknowledged this in its self-satisfied argumentations regarding the alleged "besieged Fortress of Germany." in which no difference could be made between the military and the civil population.

As to its facts this Anglo-French note has scarcely a leg to stand on. Enemy ships—as is conceded by all maritime principles of law— may be destroyed when their capture and their taking into port is impossible owing to the dangers that may befall the vessel that makes the capture. It is true that the duty of caring for the lives of the crew is one that by virtue of international law falls to the vessel that effects the capture, but only so long as the antagonists themselves adhere to the rules of international law—a condition which, so far as England is concerned, is lacking. Moreover, as we have already proved, the German submarines had up to a certain time, coincident with further aggressive moves on the part of England in arming her merchant vessels and trawlers, always given ample time to the crews of the sunk ships to save themselves and had even displayed the most gracious and knightly courtesy toward them.

Since the English merchant ships, in contravention of international agreements, had been equipped with cannon, and had sought to escape examination by the commanders of the submarines, which is again in violation of Article 63 of the Declaration of London, the German submarines were forced, in case they did not wish to commit hara-kiri, to adopt a less considerate method of warfare, something for which England alone must bear the blame. There were numerous cases in which ships that could not be classed as war vessels in the regular sense of the term, shot at submarines,—for instance, when in March, 1915, the steam-yacht "Vanduba" fired at a German "U-boat" without showing a flag.

Finally in their regulations regarding the German export of goods of German origin England and France have destroyed the last vestiges of the provisions of the Declaration of London and begun a warfare of pure piracy. This has justified Germany in suspending all customary consideration in her war operations, since the entire law of contraband has been simply wiped off the slate by her enemies. The note therefore contains a complete rejection of all the American proposals,—a fact which, as may be imagined, caused a great deal of unpleasant surprise on the part of neutral nations throughout the world.

The quintessence of the English procedure, which by its declaration of a closed war-zone directly provoked all further counter-measures, is this: it demands the privileges of a blockade, without wishing to undergo the naval disadvantages and dangers of an effective blockade, for which it substitutes a so-called "paper blockade." The British by their present actions have completely abrogated all the provisions of the Parisian Conference. They have set aside the entire structure of the law of nations. Their procedure in the matter of non-military vessels[1] is nothing less than direct piracy. According to Oppenheim, a Cambridge authority, "every unauthorised act of violence against persons or goods committed on the Open Sea either by a private vessel against another vessel or by the mutinous crew or passengers against their own vessel" is to be so designated.

A *franc-tireur* naval war of this kind (carried on by vessels which, consonant or not with the orders of the British Admiralty, have been equipped with guns and ammunition for the purposes of defence) was fittingly characterized by the order of von Pohl, the Chief of the Admiralty Staff of the German Navy on June 22nd, 1914, that is to say, before the war. And it is against this kind of warfare that the German Prize Court Law is aimed.

If an armed enemy merchant vessel offers armed resistance against legitimate prize-taking measures, then this resistance is to be broken by any and every means. The responsibility for all damage done to ship, cargo and passengers must be borne by the enemy government. The crews are to be treated as prisoners of war.[2]

---

[1] The intentional grouping of vessels for the purposes of ramming submarines as well as the offer of prizes for such acts of piracy also belong to this category. Consult chapter 38 with reference to the misuse of merchant ships.

[2] The German Government behaved with perfect correctness even according to the conception of law held by the Naval War College of the United States.

The "Norddeutsche Allgemeine Zeitung," No. 63, of the 3rd of March 1915, writes:

"Should the Imperial Ministry of War no longer allow Germany to be injured through permitting an exception in the case of neutral ships, but should forbid these ships to pass through the war-zone, such a measure would be absolutely along the natural line of development of international law, which has not previously had to reckon with the possibilities of submarine warfare. How far such a prohibition would suit the English and American conception of law, and how the present mild form of limitation of the war zone agrees with the ideas of their legal experts, may be seen by a letter of Dr. A. Pearce Higgins in the "Times" of October 21st, 1914. His statement was designed to establish the legality of England's declaration of a war zone, and he had perhaps not reckoned with the fact that Germany would be able to appropriate

IV.

There are various other points which might be emphasized in the interchange of notes between the United States and other neutrals and the Triple Entente. See, for instance, the interchange of letters between the Ambassador of the United States in Paris and M. Delcassé, the Minister of Foreign Affairs, page 99, of the original edition.

But the very acme of the piratical measures which have been discussed in the foregoing were achieved by the states of the Triple Entente some time in March, 1915.

The official organ of the French Government under the date of March 17th, published a "decret" upon the "measures of retaliation" to be undertaken by the Allies against the German trans-oceanic trade. This decree is preceded by a report directed by the French Ministers of Foreign Affairs, of Finance, of War and the Navy, to the President of the Republic. This report is supposed to furnish the reasons for the new regulations.[1]

---

part of his arguments. These are the more interesting for us to-day, as they are grounded upon the principles of war according to the Naval War College of the United States. Nor do Dr. Pearce Higgins and the Naval War College stand alone in their opinions. The naval correspondent of the "Times"—which frequently represents the views and standpoint of the Government—comments upon Dr. Higgins' letter in the issue of November 12th, 1914, and says that the Law of Warfare therein discussed, the right to remove neutral ships which disturb or interfere with military operations, had not yet been employed by England. But the time might come, when it would be necessary." See further Dr. Higgins' letter to the "Times."

[1] The announcement of the measures to be taken by England for preventing the export and the import of goods to and from Germany is, according to Reuter, introduced with the following declaration: "In consideration of the fact that the German Government has published certain conclusions, wherein in contradiction to the usages of war, the waters around Great Britain are declared as a zone of war, within the limits of which all the merchant vessels of England and its allies are to be destroyed without consideration for the lives of the passengers and the crews; in consideration of the fact that in an explanatory memorandum to these determinations it is declared that neutrals are warned against entrusting crews, passengers and goods to the vessels of England and its allies; in consideration of the fact that such an attitude on the part of the enemy, gives his Majesty the indisputable right of retaliation—His Majesty has determined to take other measures in order to prevent all articles of commerce from either leaving or reaching Germany." (*retranslation*)

The "decret" itself declares:

"All goods belonging to Germans, coming from Germany, or going to Germany, which have left port after the 13th of March, are to be detained. Territory occupied by Germans is to be considered the same as German territory.

All those goods which bear German trade-marks, or are produced or harvested in Germany, or whose port of embarkation is German territory, are to be regarded as goods emanating from Germany.

This rule, however, does not apply to goods concerning which a neutral is able to prove that he imported them into a neutral country before the 13th of March, or that he has acquired them in good faith as property before the 13th of March.

Wares will be considered as destined for Germany when the accompanying papers do not prove the final conclusive destination to be a neutral land.

Neutral ships on which the goods described above are found are to be taken into French or allied ports, and the wares unloaded, unless the contrary is deemed expedient. The ship is then to be discharged as free and all wares which are recognized as German property, are to be sold or seized, the proceeds to be paid to the owner only after the conclusion of peace. Goods belonging to neutrals and coming from Germany remain at the disposition of the neutral owner, in order to be returned to the port of origin, within a certain period, after the expiration of which they are to be sold for the account of the owner.[1] The same procedure is to be followed with goods that belong to neutrals and are consigned to Germany. The Minister of Marine may, as an exception, grant the transit of goods which are consigned to a particular neutral country

[1] The "Kölnische Zeitung" received the following from Christiania: "The Foreign Office here learns officially from London: The Christiania steamer "Bravo," bound from Norway to San Francisco, put into Cardiff to coal, and was there compelled to unload 1192 gallons of fruit-juice, which had been taken aboard at Bremen. That is the first case in which England has seized German export goods which were not contraband. In England, however, a great outcry was raised because a German U-boat had sunk a Dutch steamer which carried a cargo of oranges for England!"

or which originate in this country. The provisions with regard to contraband remain in force. The Prize Court will decide the question as to whether the captured goods belong to Germans, are consigned to Germany or originate in Germany."[1, 2]

---

[1] The "Daily Telegraph" reports as follows from Washington under date of the 8th of March:

"Sir Cecil Spring-Rice states that the British Government has arrived at the following conclusions with regard to cotton destined for neutral ports:

1. Cotton, which has been sold before the 2nd of March and meant for export is to be allowed to pass, or in case of seizure is to be purchased at the selling price, in case the vessels have not left port after the 31st of March.

2. The same holds good for cotton which has been insured before the 3rd of March, in case it has not been embarked after the 16th of March.

3. All cotton freights, which desire to avail themselves of the regulations above, must be notified before their departure and provided with certificates by consular authorities and by other officials provided therefor by the government. Shipments to enemy ports will not be allowed to pass."

The last provision is an open breach of the law of nations and a flagrant outrage upon the sovereign rights of the Union.

[2] It is best, when considering the entire disregard of universal naval laws by the Triple Entente, to note what a contrast the behavior of another neutral state offers to that of the United States: On the 22nd of March, 1915, the Minister for Foreign Affairs gave out to the Second Chamber the contents of the Dutch Note of the 19th of March. It ran in part as follows:

"The government of the Netherlands will pass no judgment as to the legality of the measures adopted by the warring powers. But it is the duty of the Netherlands, as a neutral power, to raise its voice against these measures, in so far as they violate the recognized principles of the rights of neutrals. Already at the beginning of the war, the Dutch Government protested in the interests of its rights as a neutral power and in the interests of international law against every curtailment of the rights of neutrals by the warring powers. It cannot alter its position in respect to the present measures, since these ignore the great principle of the Declaration of Paris of 1856, whereby neutral and enemy goods, with the exception of contraband, are not subject to seizure, so long as they are under the protection of a neutral flag. With the setting-aside of this principle the British ordinance intended that the British fleet should be empowered to enforce measures of compulsion, not only against the private property of the enemy, even when not contraband, but also against the goods of neutrals, when it was conjectured that these were of enemy origin or were intended for the enemy. The definition of the British order guarantees a liberal interpretation of the measure with respect to neutral goods, but without any fixed rule which could serve to protect the interests of sea-going ships and commerce. Article 8 allows the possibility of a relaxation of the

The Parisian edition of the "Herald" reports from London on the 29th of March that in the matter of the representations of the United States in regard to the English blockade war carried on against Germany and Austria-Hungary, a negative answer had been given to the Ambassador of the United States on the 24th of March.

This news was undoubtedly authentic. Thus, while Germany was exerting her utmost endeavors in order to arrive at an understanding, England, the ancient arch-enemy of all law, exercised her sea-tyranny to the full, indifferent alike to American sympathies and American protests. This is a point which, in view of the increasingly unfriendly attitude of the United States—not towards England—but towards a yielding Germany,—cannot be sufficiently emphasized.

V.

On the 7th of April, 1915, a new American Note was submitted to England. In this the following passage occurs:

"The government of the United States has given careful consideration to the subjects treated in the British notes of March 13 and March 15, and to the British Order in Council of the latter date.

These communications contain matters of grave importance to neutral nations. They appear to menace their rights of trade and intercourse not only with belligerents but also with one another. They call for frank comment in order that

---

provisions of the ordinance as regard ships of all countries which give an undertaking to carry no goods to or from Germany, or German-owned goods, under their flag. I believe I must say, however, that in such a case as the foregoing, the government of the Netherlands would not be able to give an undertaking of this kind. According to their view, the exact fulfilment of the duties of neutrality forbids the undertaking of any such obligation. Before the publication of the British ordinance Your Excellency had already given me to understand that the interests of the Netherlands in their oversea possessions would not suffer, but however moderate the working of the ordinance might prove, the government of the Netherlands could not acquiesce in silence in such a grave violation of the fundamental principles of an international law which has been guaranteed by all the powers for more than half a century.

misunderstandings may be avoided. The government of the United States deems it its duty, therefore, speaking in the sincerest spirit of friendship, to make its own view and position with regard to them unmistakably clear.

The Order in Council of the 15th of March would constitute, were its provisions to be actually carried into effect as they stand, a practical assertion of unlimited belligerent rights over neutral commerce within the whole European area, and an almost unqualified denial of the sovereign rights of the nations now at peace."

The Note hereupon defines the standpoint of international law, and says further that it is confidently expected, that the British Government will not deny that even when a blockade exists and the laws of contraband are strongly enforced in regions unaffected by the blockade, harmless cargoes plying in neutral regions can be carried freely between the United States and the warring areas, without incurring punishment for contraband trading and blockade-running. It continues thus: "When the British Government proceeds to speak of measures of reprisals that may become necessary through the proceedings of the enemy, the United States believe that hereby only an increased activity in naval forces is justified, and not any illegal proceeding. If the proceedings of Great Britain's enemies prove to be illegal and in disregard of the principles according to which enlightened nations make war, the United States Government does not for a moment suppose that the British Government could wish that its conduct should be open to a like reproach, nor would the government of the United States regard this as a justification for similar acts, in so far as the rights of neutrals were affected.

The United States confidently hopes that the British Government, which by the holding-up of cargoes to and from enemy territory is making use of an unusual method, will bring its practise into harmony with international law, especially as the blockaded territory lies in such a position that ships must necessarily pass the blockading forces, in order to reach important neutral harbors."

The American note then makes allusion to the circumstance that the Scandinavian and Danish harbors are free for American trade, although in fact nothing prevents these harbors from trading with the German Baltic ports. The principal condition of a blockade is that all neutrals must be uniformly affected. An exact interpretation of the Cabinet's order would do immense damage to neutral trade and place a heavy responsibility upon the British Government. The British Government must give full compensation for all offensive measures which are contrary to international law. The government of the United States adheres firmly to the point that the rights and duties of its citizens, through the established statutes of international law and the agreements of the United States, have certain bounds, and it stipulates in every case, that if the aforesaid rights and duties be violated, or their free exercise hindered by the British Government, it shall have the right to make a protest and to demand compensation.

The concluding sentence of this Washington Note recalls to mind by its context the representations made by Ambassador Gerard to the German Government at the time the latter announced the opening of its submarine warfare. The only difference consists in the fact that the exchange of notes which had in the meantime taken place between Germany and the United States had unmasked England even to the eyes of the American observer as the country responsible for the increased bitterness of sea warfare. If the continuance of the mercantile war between Germany and England should entail damage and inconvenience to American shipping, Germany may with a quiet conscience observe whether the efforts of the United States to procure consideration for their rights from Great Britain will also be rewarded by success.

Paper protests and the threat of levying claims for the subsequent damages must, of course, be looked upon as hopelessly futile! Such puny measures are regarded not only by a vast section of the German public but also by the public of all neutral states as a mere cloak or mask to hide the incomprehensible weakness of a great sovereign state which allows itself to be treated by the English sea-tyrant as though it were some petty little opera-bouffe republic.

VI.

It is a fact that the production of munitions by the American factories has increased to the proportion of a regular avalanche, and the most prejudiced observer is forced to admit that the American manufacturers are *alone* responsible for the continuance of this slaughter of the peoples. Russia, as we know from various authentic sources, would long ago have been vanquished but for American supplies of ammunition, and this would in turn have brought about the end of the war on the western front. In consequence of America's activities in directly supporting Germany's enemies, the Imperial Government made new representations regarding these deliveries of arms and their direct furtherance and protection by the government of the United States.

The great guilt that rests upon the United States, a guilt which all sophistry and appeals to alleged international laws, —laws which have never been recognized by England and which cannot therefore apply in this war—cannot wipe away, consists in the fact that it upholds the *illegitimate* trade in arms of its citizens, that is to say, in *absolute* contraband,—but makes a mere pretense of defending its *legitimate* trade in food supplies and raw products with Germany. Its paper protests and empty phrases cannot be conceived as real actions against England, the despiser of all the laws of the nations, England that knows how to strike the most deadly blows at the vital interests of the United States,—empty bluffs which England and its satellite France regard as nothing more than "evidences of friendship,"—since there is no sign of any intention to back them up with deeds. Words! words! words!

In Chapter XXXVII of the original the author treats of various other questions of maritime law, and of outrages against German merchant vessels, such as the destruction of the "Gneisenau" at Antwerp, as well as the dishonest and tricky capture by the English of the German Hospital Ship, the "Ophelia." See pages 506 to 514.

CHAPTER XXX.

Sailing under False Colors. Ruses of War? Misuse of Merchant Vessels for War-Like Undertakings. Ruses of War Employed by German Ships. Flying the Flag.

I. In the first part of this book we have discussed the "Ruses of War" according to the provisions of the two Hague Conferences (Article 2 g of the Rules and Regulations of Warfare by Land). In naval warfare this subterfuge is still more permissible. All naval powers have made the most liberal use of this expedient. A typical example is the change made in the appearance of the little German cruiser "Emden" by the addition of a fourth smoke-stack, etc. It is also permissible to fly an enemy flag up to the point at which hostilities are opened. Even the London "Times" declares this to be fair in every way. A war vessel which is desirous of remaining unknown in certain coastal waters or is anxious to conceal its identity, is allowed to use a false flag for this purpose—in accordance with the common acceptance of the law upon this point. It is also permissible for a war or a merchant vessel to attempt to avoid attack or capture by hoisting false colors, in face of a superior enemy,—a rule which is acknowledged by English maritime circles as being quite fair. On the other hand it is not permitted that a more powerful ship lure a weaker out of neutral waters or from a safe distance by flying false colors in order thereupon to attack it.

According to the recognized rules of naval usage, which are also followed by German ships, this uncertainty regarding the nationality of a ship must be quickly cleared up as soon as the battle is opened. The first shot fired from a vessel obliges that vessel to fulfil the law in showing its true colors—and this holds good whether the shot be blank or one with solid ball. This shot, "the affirming gun," *le canon affirmatif*, is thus to be conceived as an honorable assurance that the flag flying from the vessel is the true flag. But this shot also represents an official challenge to the other vessel to confirm the honorable authenticity of its own flag by firing a shot in return. When this challenge or demand is not fulfilled—a further deception must certainly be regarded as excluded—then the challenging vessel is entitled to proceed to offensive measures without further delay.

In all these cases we have to deal with certain details of this exchange of flags--details which in their execution are by no means above suspicion.

It is of course self-evident that the systematic deception by means of false flags as practised by a state,—a deception which England has suddenly converted into a principle for her own convenience,—is quite a different matter. It is a contemptible act from the point of view of international law, morals and politics. In order to form a correct estimate of this pusillanimous act it is not merely necessary to recall to mind the pride of the Union Jack and the boast that it ruled the seas, whereas now it slinks miserably in abject cowardice behind the flags of little neutral nations for protection, but it must also be recalled that it was precisely the British Government which, without the shadow of a proof, levelled gross accusations against the German torpedo-boats in August and September 1914, to the effect that they had made an illegal use of the flags of neutral countries. It was also spread throughout the world with that show of virtuous indignation of which England is such a master, that German trawlers had dared to fly neutral colors.

II. And this is the England, which after insolently defending the use of neutral flags for more than six months of war, now issued, in her fear of the German submarines, the following secret order:

"On account of the appearance of German submarines in the English and Irish Channels, all English merchant vessels are at once to hoist neutral flags and to conceal all marks of identification, such as the marks of shipping companies, name, etc. House flags are not to be hoisted. This order is to be kept secret." (*retranslation*)

The tremendous sensation which this order, which fell into German hands, created in all quarters, compelled the British Government to issue the following public order. Reuter, under date of February 8th, 1915, announces: The British Foreign Office publishes the following declaration:

"The use of the neutral flag is, with certain limitations, well established in practice as a ruse de guerre. The only effect in the case of a merchantman of wearing a flag other than her national flag is to compel the enemy to follow the ordinary obligations of naval warfare, and to satisfy himself as to the nationality of the vessel and of the character of her cargo by examination before capturing her and taking her into a Prize Court for adjudication.

The British Government has always considered the use of British colors by a foreign vessel legitimate for the purpose of escaping capture. Such a practice not only involves no breach of international law, but is specifically recognized by the law of this country."

In the Merchant Shipping Act, 1894, it is enacted (Sec. 69) (1) as follows:

"If a person uses the British flag and assumes the British national character on board a ship owned in whole or in part by any persons not qualified to own a British ship, for the purpose of making the ship appear to be a British ship, the ship shall be subject to forfeiture under this Act, unless the assumption has been made for the purpose of escaping capture by an enemy or by a foreign ship of war in the exercise of some belligerent right."

And in the instructions to British Consuls 1914, it is stated: "A ship is liable to capture if its British character be improperly assumed except for the purpose of escaping capture. As we have in practice not objected to foreign merchant vessels using the British merchant flag as a ruse for the purpose of evading capture at sea at the hands of a belligerent, so we should maintain that in the converse case a British merchant vessel committed no breach of international law in assuming neutral colors for a similar purpose, if she thought fit to do so.

By the rules of international law, the customs of war, and the dictates of humanity, it is obligatory upon a belligerent to ascertain the character of a merchant vessel and of her cargo before capture. Germany has no right to disregard this obligation. To destroy ship, non-combatant crew, and cargo, as Germany has announced her intention of doing, is nothing less than an act of piracy on the high seas."

The British Government acknowledges the misuse of neutral flags as ordered to protect the British merchant marine from attacks by German submarines. The justification advanced for the secret Admiralty order by the Foreign Office in London furnishes a conspicuous example of an awkward excuse, and is as inept as it is dishonest.

There are only two codifications of international maritime law, dealing with the substitution of flags during times of war. The London Declaration of Sea Law of 1909, determines thus in Article 56:

"The transfer of an enemy vessel to a neutral flag, effected after the outbreak of hostilities, is void unless it is proved that such transfer was not made in order to evade the consequences to which an enemy vessel, as such, is exposed. However, there is an absolute presumption that a transfer is void:—if the transfer has been made during a voyage or in a blockaded port."

This applies to the case under consideration. England did not ratify the Declaration of London and is therefore averse to subscribing to its provisions whenever these may be deemed disadvantageous to her. Yet the English representatives at the London Conference *voted in favor of all these rules and acknowledged them as customary and as valid.*

The second compilation of sea-law which treats of the substitution of flags, is the draft of a Hand Book upon the laws of naval warfare published under the auspices of "The Institute for International Law" during its session at Oxford in the year 1913. According to Article 15 of this Hand Book, the use of false flags is forbidden and is designated as "*moyen perfide et barbarois*" (a base and barbarous expedient). The delegate who expressed this view at Oxford was M. Fauchille of Paris. This Oxford Conference was attended by many of the most distinguished jurists of international law from all countries—among them U. S. Senator Elihu Root—and Professor Holland of Oxford, as well as Sir Thomas Barclay of London. The collaboration of these gentlemen, however, was not able to prevent this expedient "perfide et barbarois," from being made use of as one of the most important features of British naval tactics. "The instance of the British liner "Lusitania" (American flag) and that of the steamer "Laertes" (Dutch flag) prove that the system of flag deception was put into practical operation at once. Scandinavian skippers report that after the 18th of February the English flag had entirely disappeared from the North Sea.[1]

Domenico Gnoli writes to the "Giornale d'Italia," that when he reads the legal statements about the blockade of the English coast, he is obliged to think of the tale of the man who called out to a soldier of the Swiss Guard, who had fallen into a well in the Vatican: "Drown very quietly! the Pope is asleep." For Germany it is a matter of life and death. England wants to starve 70 million Germans into surrender. They use every means to protect themselves...... There is no nation that would do otherwise under like circumstances."

The well-known Conservative sheet, "Berlingske Tidende," writes: "This latest step of English naval policy begins to

---

[1] The voice of the neutral press on the misuse of neutral flags:—

The Danish paper "Extrabladet" writes in a leading article: "One must do the Germans justice. If Germany has the power to starve out England it is not only her task to do so, *but it would be a shame if she did not make the attempt*..... Now that England defines the misuse of flags as a permissible military stratagem, one perceives that war sets no bounds to what is permissible, and that there is no wickedness which will not in war-time find some pretty explanation and excuse."

"Aftonbladet" writes: "By an action such as this the English rob the genuine neutral ships of the protection of their own flag..... To sail under a false flag is as dishonorable as if one produced a false passport or a stolen visiting-card to avoid some threatened peril by means of such a legitimation."

"Dagens Nyheter," which until now favored the Triple Entente, writes that the English method of procedure was strongly to be condemned; in the first place it betokened cowardice, which was something painful to observe in the great English nation; in the second place it endangered the rights of the small nations.... This paper had designated the German report of the English secret order as an official German false report and an uncommonly mean trick! Altogether the press considers this new war-device of England's to be, as the "Wys Dagligt Allehande," styles the English proclamation, something incredibly mean and scurvy.

open the eyes of even the most credulous in Denmark, as to who is the real ruthless and selfish enemy of the neutrals. The acknowledged fact that this alleged world-empire finds it expedient to shelter itself behind the flag of little Denmark, has seriously injured the position of England with the public here, as one may hear every day."

Holland couches its note to England in language sharp as that employed by English naval law authorities or those of the United States. The letter sent by the Dutch Minister of Foreign Affairs to the British Envoy, Mr. Johnstone, reads in part as follows:

"The act of using the flag of another state without its consent is always to be regarded as an abuse, and in times of war this abuse assumes a character the seriousness of which no power which has been a signatory to the Declaration of Paris can afford to ignore. An act of this kind compromises the neutral flag and creates doubt as to the neutrality of those ships which fly their own flags. It exposes them to the possibility of being themselves regarded as enemy vessels and thus incurring serious consequences.

"Your Excellency was good enough to remind me of the provisions of the "Merchant Shipping Act" which punishes the misuse of the British flag, save in cases when a merchant vessel of a belligerent power makes use of this flag in order to evade capture. The government of the Netherlands cannot agree that this provision is sufficient to serve as an acknowledgment of the right of British merchant-ships to use the flag of the Netherlands for this purpose. The law of the Netherlands likewise forbids the misuse of the flag of the Netherlands, but does not treat an exception in a sense analogous to the "Merchant Shipping Act"—that is to say, the misuse of a flag as a means of evading capture by an enemy. Lacking all international regulations in reference to this point, every State is forced of itself to set up the conditions under which its flag may or may not be used. It is certain that the British Government will not always be in a position to prevent the use of a neutral flag by British merchant vessels, but the government of the Netherlands thinks it may reasonably expect that the British Government will sanction no misuse which would expose the merchant marine of the Netherlands to the dangers of a war."[1]

We refer the reader to the developments in the question of deception by misuse of flags as given in the two preceding chapters.

One may justly declare that there is scarcely one great maritime power in the world to-day whose neutrality in this war has not been outraged by England either by the abuse of its flag or by other means.[2]

---

[1] Flagrant violations of neutrality and a shameless misuse of flags have been shown by the English in the following cases (March, 1915):

Captain Wilson, who was taking a Swedish cargo from Spain to Karlskrona, was held up at Dover. A number of English soldiers came aboard and their commander said to the Captain: "I have orders to accompany neutral ships for a certain distance, so that my men can let fly at any German submarine that shows itself." Although the Captain made a formal protest and characterized the conduct of the Englishmen in strong language as in the highest degree outrageous and dishonorable, the English crew remained on board.

In the same fashion the English forced Captain John L. Duffy of the American ship "Brynhilda," to receive one officer and ten men aboard, for the purpose of attacking German submarines. When the submarine officer ascended the turret to ascertain the nationality of the ship, he would be shot. In spite of protests, the ship was brought into Aberdeen. What of the American Government? Could there be a greater or more wanton outrage against neutrality?

What German U-boats have to expect from ships under neutral flags, under certain circumstances, is shown by the following statements of neutral ships' officers.

Captain Hanssen and First Officer Jannssen, both American citizens, of the American steamer "Oliver J. Olson," made coinciding statements to the following effect: "We put out from Savannah via Scotland for Bremen. Off the Island of Foula, west of Scotland a lieutenant, a cadet, and six seamen came on board from the English auxiliary cruiser "Celtic," and brought us into Kirkwall. During this voyage the lieutenant, who had taken command of the ship, declared that if a German submarine appeared, he would endeavor to ram her with the "Oliver J. Olson." And even self-subsisting, independent states apparently condone these piratical methods without protest. In connection with such practices, which knock all conceptions of law on the head, the methods of warfare of the German navy are quite justifiable and logical, even against those states which suffer, allow and give countenance to such actions without taking the most rigorous measures against them.

[2] Holland has in her Statute Book of the State registered a severe

The enemy press has repeatedly announced that the arming of merchant-vessels with guns as had been planned by Mr. Churchill as early as 1913, was soon to be put into execution not only by England but also by France.

The German Prize Court law of 1909 was given a special appendix on June 22, 1914, that is before the beginning of the war, in which it was plainly stated that all hostile acts on the part of an armed merchant vessel would be regarded as piracy and that the crews were to be treated as freebooters and pirates, and not as regular troops, "in accordance with the regulations appertaining to extraordinary acts of war."

III. England, enraged by the heavy losses which she suffers, now advises her merchant vessels to ram war-vessels, that is to say, our "U-boats"—to refuse to obey their signals to stop, to attack them, and offers premiums and equips merchant vessels for this purpose. It has always been recognized as a law among nations that a vessel which resists a warship is subject to seizure without further consideration. Thus the emission of this general order to English merchantmen and the arming of these with cannon, renders every English vessel liable to be treated as an enemy vessel of war without further formality. Whosoever, without being a part of the regular armed forces of a country, or being recognized as such, undertakes hostile actions against the armed forces of another country —"U-boats" in this instance—must be considered as a freebooter—a guerilla— and by virtue of the prevailing penalties deserves death upon the gallows for piracy.

And when English ships sail under an alien flag with hostile intent, they must, according to the law of nations, be held to be guilty of so-called indirect piracy and must be placed upon the same basis as pirate craft, even though they may receive their official orders from the British Government. Not even this government has the right to give a legal sanction to freebooters. The recognition of such arbitrary insolence

---

punishment against such of her own people as shall misuse the Dutch flag; but no more than Sweden, Denmark, Norway, the United States, etc., can she prevent the misuse of her flag by England.

would be tantamount to the recognition of English tyranny at sea.[1,2]

The provision of the German Prize Law cited in the foregoing is based upon sea customs and laws which have been considered valid for hundreds of years by all nations and duly recognized by them.

In Chapter XXXIX of the original work, the author discusses the bombardment of the English coasts by warships and airships, and proves that the German fighting forces, despite the falsehood, fury, and sophistry of the Allied press, had kept well within the bounds of what is provided for by international law.

---

[1] The "Shipping Gazette" of March 26th, 1915 writes:

"The Steamer "Thordis" entered the docks on the 18th of March. Upon arrival of the vessel, representatives of the company handed the Captain a letter of the Admiralty which ran us follows: 'I am requested by the Chiefs of the Admiralty to communicate that they have appointed J. M. Bell, the Captain of the "Thordis" to the rank of a lieutenant in the Royal Navy.... I am further to inform you that the King has decided to reward Lieutenant Bell for his services —the ramming of a German submarine—with the Distinguished Service Medal." *(retranslation)*

Thus we have the King himself as the rewarder of one of the most shameful breaches of the laws of nations and of military decency.

[2] It may be plainly seen from the publications of the English Admiralty Staff that all the English trawlers are now armed and turned into patrol vessels and vessels of war. See, for example, the official publication of May 3rd, 1915.

The news that the German submarine U 29, commanded by the gallant Otto Weddigen, had been rammed by an English tank steamer sailing *under the Swedish flag,* was received shortly after writing the above. The U 14 met the same fate in the same treacherous manner. Day after day reports are being received which tell of attempts at ramming made by English trawlers which either fly no flags or false ones. But the neutral press is loud in its protests and its reproaches whenever an occasional really neutral steamer happens to fall a victim to this cowardly and treacherous English action!

CHAPTER XXXI.

Aggravation of the Strained Relations Between Germany and America. The Case of the "Lusitania."

I. The tremendous sensation occasioned by the torpedoing of the Cunarder "Lusitania" on May 7th, 1915, and the consequences that followed this, call for a brief and yet fairly comprehensive discussion of this "case"—which both from the viewpoint of common law and international law, is one of uncommon clarity. But a purchased and unscrupulous press in the Old World as well as in the New immediately seized upon it as another opportunity for a raging campaign against German "barbarism."

The facts of the case are clear. The "Lusitania" was sunk in broad daylight on the 7th of May, 1915, on the South coast of Ireland by a German submarine in the very spot where shortly before two English steamers had been torpedoed by a German "craft." On May 11th, 1915, the following communication was made to the government of the United States of North America and the governments of all neutral powers in Europe by the accredited representatives of the Imperial Government:

"The German Government desires to express its deepest sympathy at the loss of American lives on board the steamship "Lusitania." Responsibility rests, however, with the British Government which through its plan of preventing importation of foodstuffs and raw materials for the civilian population forced Germany to resort to retaliatory measures and answered the German offer to stop submarine war in case this plan be given up by even more stringent blockade measures. British merchant vessels being generally armed with guns and having repeatedly tried to ram German submarines so that previous search became impossible, cannot be treated as ordinary merchant vessels. A recent declaration in the British Parliament by the parliamentary Secretary answering a question of Lord Beresford's, stated that at present practically all British merchant vessels are armed and provided with hand grenades.

It is, moreover, openly admitted by the English press that the "Lusitania" was armed. The German Government knows that the "Lusitania" on previous voyages repeatedly carried large quantities of war material. On the present voyage the "Lusitania" carried five thousand four hundred cases of ammunition, the rest of the cargo was also chiefly contraband. **If England, after repeated official and unofficial German warnings, considered herself able to declare that the ship ran no risk and thus light-heartedly assumed responsibility for human lives on board a steamer which, owing to armament and cargo, was liable to destruction, the German Government, in spite of its heartfelt sympathy for loss of American lives, cannot but regret that Americans felt more inclined to trust English promises rather than pay attention to warnings from the German side."**

So we have, in the first instance; an English auxiliary cruiser; in the second, a vessel engaged regularly for several months in transporting munitions and material of war; in the third instance a vessel transporting vast quantities of war materials of absolute contraband; in the fourth instance, a ship guilty of deliberately flying false colors. In addition to all these iniquities which concentrated themselves upon this one particular vessel, we must add that of an insolent and hare-brained frivolity which manifested itself in idiotic ridicule of those express, considerate and courteous warnings, public and private, issued by the highest German authorities—warnings which showed, indeed, a more than remarkable solicitude for the lives of the deceived and deluded passengers.

The notice issued by the German Embassy, was published extensively throughout the United States and reads as follows:

NOTICE.

"Travellers intending to embark on the Atlantic voyage are reminded that a state of war exists between Germany and her allies and Great Britain and her allies; that the zone of war includes the waters adjacent to the British Isles; that, in accordance with formal notice given by the Imperial German Government, vessels flying the flag of Great Britain, or any of her allies, are liable to destruction in these waters and that travellers sailing in the war zone on ships of Great Britain or her allies, do so at their own risk.

IMPERIAL GERMAN EMBASSY.

Washington, D. C. April 21, 1915.

The English answer to this was given by the "Daily Mail" of May 3rd, 1915. Under the heading of "Count Bernstorff's Warning—Transatlantic Danger Proclaimed—The Latest Bluff for America" this paper published the following cablegram from its New York correspondent under date of

Saturday, May 1st:

"The "Lusitania" left to-day two and a half hours late, under circumstances of considerable excitement, arising out of the latest evidence afforded by the German Embassy of its misapprehension of the spirit of American neutrality.

At the pier the passengers received numerous telegrams advising them not to leave, as the ship was to be torpedoed by German submarines. The messages were apparently signed by fictitious names. Mr. Alfred G. Vanderbilt also received one, but he tore it up without remark. The sending of these messages is undoubtedly a part of the German Embassy's pre-conceived plan for the intimidation of intending travellers. The Embassy caused a warning to passengers by ships under the British flag to appear in all the principal newspapers this morning, with the statement that these vessels were doomed to destruction. So far as is known, not a single passenger abandoned the voyage."

The "Daily Mail" concludes with the following communication by Reuter:

"Washington, Saturday, May 1st.

The British and the French Ambassadors called the attention of the Department of State to the notice and to its prospective effect upon travel. They also directed attention to the most unusual method pursued by Count Bernstorff in turning directly to the public, instead of through the medium of the Department of State. Count Bernstorff was not at the Embassy, but other officials there declared that the notice had followed upon general advices from Berlin." (*retranslation*)

This is quite true. This *warning*, after the actions of the British Government, its starving-out tactics, the declaring of the North Sea as a closed war zone, the treatment accorded German grain imports and similar things, might well be conceived as a most extraordinary act of German mildness and consideration. England would never have thought of attacking it in principle had she herself been forced to wage war by means of the submarine through the action of her enemy. It must also be acknowledged that a heavy burden of guilt rests upon the American Government which, in a manner inexcusably criminal, permitted passengers to be embarked upon a vessel carrying absolute contraband of war and explosives in violation of its own laws. These passengers were used simply for the purpose of protecting the dangerous and death-dealing cargo.

But all this cannot obscure the fact that not only is the German Government free of all blame in the light of international law, but that, compared to the sorry experiences the world has had of British brutality and arrogance, it acted in the most magnanimous manner and even exceeded its duty in this respect. The chief responsibility lodges upon the head of English unscrupulousness which in this case dared to juggle with the lives of many hundreds of human beings. Despite this fact it did not consider it worth while to have a warship convoy the liner, although both the British Government and the steamship line had received due warning, and both in addition were well aware that the "Lusitania" had put to sea on February 26th as well as April 4th, 1915, and the beginning of May, laden with vast quantities of war supplies of all sorts. Inasmuch as the poor, deluded victims of British cold-bloodedness and calculation were lured aboard by means of false representations regarding the "absolute safety" of this vessel and imbecile sneers at a so-called "German bluff," the Cunard Line, as

[1] The "Times," "Daily Telegraph," *e tutti quanti*, talked in the same mocking fashion. The General Manager of the Cunard Line, Charles Sumner, declared: "It is a fact that the "Lusitania" is the safest ship on the seas. She is too fast for any submarine. No German warship will have a chance at her." And further, the braggart tone of the "Daily Mail" of the 3rd of May, 1915: "This demonstration affords a number of American citizens an opportunity of showing their contempt for Germany's submarine threats."

well as the English Government which tolerated these things, must be branded with infamy for all time. They alone must be held accountable for all claims of damages for the lives of their victims—who were first of all their dupes.[1]

It would naturally have been the duty of the United States to issue this warning officially and to do all in its power to call attention to the danger. The question must still be cleared up as to how far, if at all, the American Government took steps to fulfil its duty in this respect. The unusual method taken by the German Ambassador to warn the people of the United States justifies the conjecture of a grave neglect of duty on the part of the United States Government, strenuously as it may at present dispute this.

II. One of the best things so far written upon the subject is published in an objective and neutral paper, the "Basler Anzeiger." The article concludes its summary thus:

"It must be granted that the warning as given on the German side was so express that corresponding precautions on the part of the British fleet might very possibly have prevented the torpedoing. The warning was in fact so explicit, that the German Navy thereby put the success of the whole enterprise in jeopardy. Further, it must be pointed out that it was precisely the Cunard Line which particularly proclaimed the

---

[1] The English Magistrate's Court in Kinsale has once more done honor to the furious demand of Lord Beresford that our submarine crews be declared murderers. That is to say, it "solemnly" brought in a verdict of murder against the officers of the submarine that sank the "Lusitania." It made no "solemn" accusation against the crew of the submarine, for this worthy Court of Justice kept itself free of this one absurdity, when it extended its accusation to the German Government, which had issued orders for committing this deed to the officers. One recognizes in this insane conduct of a royal English court of law, what devastation a state of impotent fury can wreak upon the sense of justice of a so-called civilized people.

The verdict of the Magistrate's Court of Kinsale is, however, also a monument of the most disgusting English hypocrisy. If the Court of Kinsale was seeking the "murderers" of the "Lusitania," it should have turned its attention to the English Government, which allowed an auxiliary cruiser of the English fleet to take passengers aboard, in spite of the fact that she was laden with contraband, without troubling about the German declaration of a war zone and the warning of the Ambassador, Count Bernstorff. The real "murderers" of the "Lusitania" sit in the English Cabinet. (See Chapter XLI.)

security of its ships on the ground that they were all armed, which is in direct contradiction to the dementi afterwards issued in the case of the "Lusitania." If one assumes it to be correct, however, that the ship was not armed, there still remains her character as an auxiliary cruiser of the English war fleet, in consideration of which the owners of the ship received every year a large subsidy from the English Government. This gives the vessel the character of a warship. It is entirely irrelevant whether at the moment of her destruction she carried guns or not. This character of the ship, even though she were only incidentally capable of being used as an auxiliary cruiser, justifies the action of the German submarine without further consideration. All reproaches regarding the destruction of so many human lives must be directed against the Company, which in spite of the ship's rating as an auxiliary cruiser, allowed her to carry passengers. *The guilt lies with that spirit of commercialism, which puts profit before responsibility. Nor are the passengers, who put their faith in such a ship, entirely blameless. Their position is very much like that of people who should choose a fortress in the actual theatre of war amongst the contending armies, and use it as a summer resort.*[1]

III. The Naval correspondent of the "Daily Telegraph," Mr. Archibald Hurd, an English expert, contradicts the assertions of the English Admiralty and those of the American Government at one and the same time. He writes thus:

---

[1] See also in particular the very characteristic terms of the agreement between the English Government and the Cunard Line, published in the "Hamburger Correspondent" (quoted by "Münchener Neueste Nachrichten" of the 12th of May, 1915), which prove that the "Lusitania" as an English auxiliary cruiser, stood entirely under the authority of the English Government, and therefore must be considered as a warship and a Government vessel.

It is absolutely idiotie to demand that the German submarine should have given one last warning. The giant would have rammed the dwarf, or shot him to pieces, on the spot. Such naïveté only shows what is expected of German good-nature! However, the "Huns" are certainly not quite so simple! Needless to say, had England behaved in a similar manner, the whole neutral world would have been filled with wonder at the prowess of the great and dominating sea-power! But it was only the "*Boches*" who are fighting for the freedom of the seas, and for the benefit of these same servile neutrals. This great World-War has truly far, far too much of the element of unconscious irony to show!

"There were only two ships in the British merchant marine which by reason of their guns and their speed did not require any special protection in time of war—the "Lusitania" and the "Mauretania." They were subsidized by the Admiralty as "Reserve Mercantile Cruisers," but after all were not put into commission. The "Lusitania" was heavily armed with rapid-fire guns and had Naval Reserve Men aboard to serve these. The ship was not to seek battle, but on meeting with hostile cruisers was to make off at full speed, worrying the enemy with gun-fire and causing him as much damage as possible. It is nevertheless astonishing that the "Lusitania" approached Liverpool in full daylight—since it must have been assumed after the issue of the German warning that the enemy would do all in his power to carry out his threats..... It is doubtful whether the British Admiralty will consent to a formal investigation, since the naval authorities are not prepared to do this when warships are lost." (*retranslation*)

The "Times" further states that the liner had on board some hundreds of enlisted Canadians. In addition to these, there were some 5400 cases of ammunition aboard. The existence of this cargo of ammunition has now been confirmed from many sources. An official note issued by the German Ministry at Bern declares as follows:

"The British Ministry in Bern publishes a communication to the effect that the English auxiliary cruiser "Lusitania" was not armed during any period of the war, though the vessel, to be sure, carried war supplies for the use of the English troops during its last voyage..... It must now be obvious that the British Government thus officially acknowledges that it had endeavored to protect its transportation of war materials by carrying as passengers neutral civilians, women and children, on the identical steamer. This subterfuge is the more detestable since, on the one hand, the passengers in the very face of the German warning, were assured that no danger threatened them, and on the other hand, not a single common-sense measure of protection was taken by the British Government in order to preserve the civilians travelling under the protection of its flag against dangers of which the English were only too well aware.

The open confession that passengers and arms had been transported upon one and the same steamer is characteristic of that cynical disregard with which England disposes of the lives of neutrals. If the British Admiralty does not arm the ships which are described as auxiliary cruisers in its official lists, that is a matter which concerns no one but itself. Since there are no means by which the Imperial Government may inform itself as to the present state of the armament of an enemy auxiliary cruiser, it will be forced to regard as heretofore all auxiliary cruisers mentioned in the lists as enemy ships of war."

This point of view is unassailable from every legal principle, and in itself contradicts the note which the United States—with a promptness and an energy that were more than remarkable—sent to the German Government on the 17th of May with regard to the affair of the "Lusitania."

To which the following must be added:

IV. In the legal ordinances of the United States (Passenger Act of August 2nd, 1882, Section 8, and certain appendices) it is declared that all vessels engaged in transporting persons to and from the United States, are subject to this regulation:

"That it shall not be lawful to take, carry, or have on board of any such steamship or other vessel any nitro-glycerine, dynamite, or any other explosive article or compound, nor any vitriol or like acids, nor gun-powder, except for the ship's use, nor any article or number of articles, whether as cargo or ballast, which, by reason of the nature or quantity or mode of storage thereof, shall either singly or collectively, be likely to endanger the health or the lives of the passengers or the safety of the vessel.... For every violation of any of the provisions of this section the master of the vessel shall be deemed guilty of misdemeanor, and shall be fined not exceeding one thousand dollars, and be imprisoned for a period not exceeding one year."

It is further declared in these laws that:

"It shall not be lawful to transport, carry, or convey, ship, deliver on board, or cause to be delivered on board, the substance or article known or designated as nitro-glycerine, or glynoin oil, nitroleum or blasting oil, or nitrated oil, or powder mixed with any such oil, or fiber saturated with any such article or substance, upon or in any vessel or vehicle used or employed in transporting passengers by land or water between a place in any foreign country and a place within the limits of any State, Territory, or district of the United States, or between a place in one State, Territory, or district of the United States, and a place in any other State, Territory, or district thereof."

According to this the "Lusitania," or more correctly the British Government, in whose service the liner was listed as an auxiliary cruiser, was beyond all doubt guilty of a grave infraction of American law. It is something almost inconceivable how the American Government, in view of conditions such as these prevailing in the execution of its own laws, could venture to send so iron-clad a note of protest to the German Government because of the "Lusitania," instead of taking drastic measures against that despiser of American law, Great Britain.

V. The obligation of paying damages to the owners of neutral wares or on behalf of the neutrals who lost their lives can in no wise be fastened upon Germany, since the chief blame must be attributed to the criminal negligence of the British Government, after the German warning had been given. The following consideration also comes into play: In accordance with Article 48 of the Declaration of London and Article 112 of German Prize Court Law, the "Lusitania" was legally liable to being sunk, since she carried absolute contraband and it was under the circumstances impossible to take her into a German port. There is therefore no just basis for any claims for damages. This also applies to neutral wares. All means of destruction are permitted against the fighting forces or instruments of the enemy be it by land or by sea, and that without any obligation to pay damages. The "Lusitania" was a war-vessel—properly, an auxiliary cruiser. Nor need any state suffer the transportation of vessels of war or of war supplies to its enemies. The same decision is arrived at when we take into consideration the literature dealing with the laws of nations, especially that of England, and analyze certain cases of precedent.

Hall, the author of "A Treatise on International Law"

(1910) declares that although neutral goods on enemy vessels may not be taken away, this means merely that these must be returned, and in case of sale, the proceeds be given to the owner—but that in the event of their being destroyed, no restitution need be made: so long as this destruction was conditioned by an act of military necessity. Such was also the decision given by a French Prize Court in 1872 in the case of two German ships, the "Ludwig" and the "Vorwärts," sunk by a French warship in the war of 1870—71. This case was also cited by Calvo, "Le Droit International théorétique et pratique, V.," page 279, and approved by him. The "Lusitania" carried enormous quantities of contraband of war, including 5400 cases of munitions, by means of which many German soldiers might have met their death.[1] To prevent the delivery of these was an act of military necessity, which act, under the circumstances, could be carried out only by sinking the ship. There is no question of judicial or moral guilt in this act. Those who choose to travel upon a war-vessel or a military transport must bear the consequences of their acts. (See article by Prof. Arndt in the "Berliner Tageblatt" of May 18th, 1915.)

It is a principle, a basic principle, of international law that

---

[1] Several sensible American voices are raised in protest against the gross injustice of the American Government. Thus, Professor Yandell Henderson, a well-known physiologist at Yale University, writes as follows in the Teutophobe "New York Times:"

"The sinking of the "Lusitania" was horrible chiefly because it was dramatic. *It probably saved ten times as many lives as it cost.* The ammunition which the "Lusitania" carried would have slaughtered thousands. *Have not those who may be made widows and orphans in Germany a right to expect of their Government that, if in any way possible, it will prevent that ammunition from reaching their enemies?*

"Around Germany is a ring of millions of enemies mad with hatred. Suppose that American ammunition enables them to break in, *how will German women fare at the hands of such savages with a veneer of discipline as Cossacks, Ghurkas, Sikhs, Turcos, and Senegambians? Would not our forefathers have been justified in any act which would have kept arms out of the hands of the Indians who ravaged Northern New York under Burgoyne?*

"Above all, let us not be hypocrites in condemning the atrocities of people on both sides who are half crazy with fear and hate, when we Americans, looked at through German eyes, are calmly fattening on blood money."

the question as to whether ships and their cargoes have been justly seized or not, or whether damages are to be paid or not, is always decided by the courts of the country effecting the capture. It is only in the special case of a vessel being taken into neutral waters, that the question is to be solved by the application of international law (Article 3, clause 2 b of the Convention concerning the establishment of an international Prize Law Court, which hitherto has not been ratified). The demand of the United States that differences of this sort be settled by diplomatic means must therefore be rejected, and the point maintained that these can be decided only by the German Prize Law Courts, precisely in accordance with the precedent established in the case of the "Ludwig" and the "Vorwärts" by the French Prize Law Courts.

VI. The German-American Notes in the "Lusitania" Affair.

The American Ambassador in Berlin handed to the Secretary of State for Foreign Affairs the well-known note of the 17th of May. The text of this has been published in all American papers. It is also given in translation in the original version of this book, Pages 539 to 542.

The answer of the German Government was delivered to the American Ambassador on the 29th of May, 1915. Its contents stands in close relation to the international points of law already cited in the foregoing. It reads as follows in the official translation by the American Embassy:

Berlin, May 29th, 1915.

"The undersigned has the honor to submit to Ambassador Gerard the following answer to the communication of May 15 regarding the injury to American interests through German submarine warfare. The Imperial Government has subjected the communication of the American Government to a thorough investigation. It entertains, also, a keen wish to co-operate in a frank and friendly way in clearing up a possible misunderstanding which may have arisen in the relations between the two governments through the events mentioned by the American Government.

"Regarding, firstly, the cases of the American steamers Cushing and Gulflight. The American embassy has already been informed that the German Government has no intention of subjecting neutral ships in the war zone, which are guilty of no hostile acts, to attacks by a submarine or submarines or aviators. On the contrary, the German forces have repeatedly been instructed most specifically to avoid attacks on such ships.

"If neutral ships in recent months have suffered through a German submarine warfare owing to mistakes in identification, it is a question only of quite isolated and exceptional cases, which can be attributed to the British Government's abuse of flags, together with the suspicious or culpable behavior of the masters of the ships. The German Government, in all cases in which it has been shown by its investigations that a neutral ship not itself at fault was damaged by German submarines or aviators, has expressed regret over the unfortunate accident, and, if justified by conditions, has offered indemnification.

"The cases of the Cushing and the Gulflight will be treated on the same principles. An investigation of both cases is in progress, the result of which will presently be communicated to the embassy. The investigation can, if necessary, be supplemented by an international call on the international commission of inquiry as provided by article III of the Hague agreement of October 18, 1907.

"When sinking the British steamer Falaba the commander of the German submarine had the intention of allowing the passengers and crew a full opportunity for a safe escape. Only when the master did not obey the order to heave-to, but fled and summoned help by rocket signals did the German commander order the crew and passengers by signals and megaphone to leave the ship within 10 minutes. He actually allowed them 23 minutes' time and fired the torpedo only when suspicious craft were hastening to the assistance of the Falaba.

"Regarding the loss of life by the sinking of the British passenger steamer Lusitania, the German Government has already expressed to the neutral governments concerned its keen regret that citizens of their states lost their lives. On this occasion the Imperial Government, however, cannot escape the impression that certain important facts having a direct bearing on the sinking of the Lusitania may have escaped the attention of the American Government.

"In the interest of that clear and complete understanding which is the aim of both governments, the Imperial Government considers it first necessary to convince itself that the information accessible to both governments about the facts of the case is complete and in accord. The Government of the United States proceeds on the assumption that the Lusitania could be regarded as an ordinary unarmed merchantman. The Imperial Government allows itself in this connection to point out that the Lusitania was one of the largest and fastest British merchant ships, built with government funds as an auxiliary cruiser and carried expressly as such in the 'navy list' issued by the British Admiralty.

"It is further known to the Imperial Government from trustworthy reports from its agents and neutral passengers that for a considerable time practically all the more valuable British merchantmen have been equipped with cannon and ammunition and other weapons and manned with persons who have been specially trained in serving guns. The Lusitania, too, according to information received here, had cannon aboard which were mounted and concealed below decks.

"The Imperial Government, further, has the honor to direct the particular attention of the American Government to the fact that the British Admiralty in a confidential instruction issued in February, 1915, recommended its mercantile shipping not only to seek protection under neutral flags and distinguishing marks, but also, while thus disguised, to attack German submarines by ramming. As a special incitation to merchantmen to destroy submarines, the British Government also offered high prizes and has already paid such rewards.

"The Imperial Government, in view of these facts, indubitably known to it, is unable to regard British merchantmen in the zone of naval operations specified by the Admiralty staff of the German navy as 'undefended!' German commanders consequently are no longer able to observe the customary regulations of the prizc law, which they before always followed.

"Finally, the Imperial Government must point out particularly that the Lusitania on its last trip, as on earlier occasions, carried Canadian troops and war material, including no less than 5400 cases of ammunition intended for the destruction of the brave German soldiers who are fulfilling their duty with self-sacrifice and devotion in the Fatherland's service. The German Government believes that it was acting in justifiable self-defense in seeking with all the means of warfare at its disposition to protect the lives of its soldiers by destroying ammunition intended for the enemy.

"The British shipping company must have been aware of the danger to which the passengers aboard the Lusitania were exposed under these conditions. The company in embarking them, notwithstanding this, attempted deliberately to use the lives of American citizens as protection for the ammunition aboard and acted against the clear provisions of the American law, which expressly prohibits the forwarding of passengers on ships carrying ammunition and provides a penalty therefor. The company therefore is wantonly guilty of the death of so many passengers.

"There can be no doubt, according to the definite report of the submarine's commander, which is further confirmed by other information, that the quick sinking of the Lusitania is primarily attributable to the explosion of the ammunition caused by a torpedo. The Lusitania's passengers would otherwise, in all human probability, have been saved.

"The Imperial Government considers the above-mentioned facts important enough to recommend them to the attentive examination of the American Government.

"The Imperial Government, while withholding its final decision on the demands advanced in connection with the sinking of the Lusitania until receipt of an answer from the American Government, feels impelled in conclusion to recall here and now that it took cognizance with satisfaction of the mediatory proposals submitted by the United States Government to Berlin and London as a basis for a modus vivendi for conducting the maritime warfare between Germany and Great Britain. The Imperial Government, by its readiness to enter upon a discussion of these proposals then demonstrated its good intentions in ample fashion. The realization of these proposals was defeated, as is well known, by the declinatory attitude of the British government. The undersigned takes occasion, etc., etc.

von Jagow."

It is almost inconceivable that the American Government did not of its *own* accord proceed to establish these facts through its *own* authorities,—facts which were and are of the utmost consequence for a correct judgment of the case—even though it may have incurred the danger of being constantly confronted by the fact that the reproaches of the American Government had been directed to the wrong quarter.

Or are principles of law, diametrically opposed to those held valid for England, to be applied to Germany? It is seldom that the justice of a case is so simple and so clear as in the case of the "Lusitania." *And the law, as well as the justice are entirely on the side of Germany.*[1,2]

The following facts in connection with the affair of the "Lusitania" are of great importance and still further justify the action of the German "U-Boats."

1. The correspondent of the "St. Galler Tagblatt" wrote to his paper as follows under date of May 31st, 1915: "Congressman Hobson has made the following sensational declaration concerning the affair of the "Lusitania:"

"A widowed cousin of mine went to the offices of the Cunard Line and wished to secure a ticket for the "Lusitania,"

---

[1] Also see the "Norddeutsche Allgemeine Zeitung" of May 12th, 1915, regarding naval judgments on the "Lusitania" episode, as well as the Note of the German Government to neutral governments, issued May 12th, 1915.

[2] The leading English technical journal "Engineering," allowed a perfectly fatal blunder to escape its notice. In one of its issues about the end of May, 1915, the author of the leading article completely omitted to study the drawings by which it was accompanied. These were not drawings from imagination, but 10 plans from a professional hand. The leader-writer wrote: "The ship was an unarmed steamer, which was fulfilling her accustomed duties, as in time of peace" —whereas design No. 5 showed a ground plan of the promenade deck with drawings of two 15-centimetre cannon near the bow of the ship, and, in design No. 6 (Shelter-deck) there are a further eight guns to be seen (amidships and astern) so that here the ship's engineers, with remarkable candor, have disclosed the existence and the position of twelve 15-centimetre quick-firing guns on the auxiliary cruiser "Lusitania." Design No. 10 (Plan of the Hold) betrays where room is made in the ship for the necessary ammunition for the guns to be stored. This "Shell Room" is situated in the narrow fore-part of the "Lusitania," and must not be confounded with the big store-room in which the 5400 cases of ammunition exploded, causing the death of 1500 persons.

when she was told by one of the officials, an old friend, that she should not take the steamer, as he had orders from the British Admiralty. My cousin was made to promise that she would not speak of this warning until the "Lusitania" had reached her destination. This fact necessitates the urgent question: Why, in the name of humanity, did not the Cunard Line issue the same warning to all passengers?"

(*retranslation*)

2. The superintendent of the passenger department of the Cunard Line in New York, Mr. Herman Winter, stated to a representative of the "Düsseldorfer Generalanzeiger," that there were 4200 cases of rifle-cartridges aboard the "Lusitania," as well as 1250 empty shrapnel shell-cases, which were to be filled in England. A chemist at Pittsburg, Dr. Braun, likewise testifies that 250 000 pounds of chlorine were shipped on the "Lusitania,"—this to be used in France in the manufacture of gas bombs. These revelations throw light upon the complaint of many of the passengers, who spoke of the suffocating smoke that arose, and which up to now was attributed to the explosion of the torpedo.

3. A prominent American professional journal, "The Journal of Commerce," of the 18th of May, publishes an authentic record of the lading of the "Lusitania," which furnishes such a perfect justification of the German action, that nothing further is necessary. This record is the "Lusitania's" bill of lading, as laid before the Customs. According to this list, the "Lusitania" had 200 000 dollars' worth of ammunition, 112 000 dollars' worth of copper, brass and iron, and 67 000 dollars' worth of military sundries on board. As this well-known paper points out, the greater part of the lading consisted of copper, copper wire, brass plates and other metals, which, as the paper states, "were obviously intended for use in the manufacture of ammunitions."

4. The "Daily News" on the 5th of June, 1915, reported from Washington that Count Bernstorff had submitted the sworn declaration of four German reservists to Secretary of State Bryan. These men had visited the "Lusitania" before her departure and had discovered guns which had been concealed by Collector of Customs Malone during the examination in

New York harbor. It was, of course, to have been expected that these witnesses would be denounced as being "perjured." That is eminently characteristic. Another "German plot."

The full text of the next American note delivered by the Berlin representative of the United States to the German Foreign Office on June 10th, 1915, is given in translation in the original work on pages 546 *et seq.*

This American Note, must, like the others, be adjudged as remarkably superficial from the standpoint of international law. The refutation of such arguments as it contains has already been made in the foregoing. The entire document may be fairly characterized as a "moral preachment," swarming with glittering generalities about "humanity." Mr. Wilson might well have spared the German people this sermon, the impressiveness of which he no doubt vastly over-estimated. Its effect in Germany was by no means so serious as its tone—because of the simple fact that a country which by reason of *its material and systematic violation* of neutrality permitted hundreds of thousands of German warriors to be either endangered or sacrificed, has no right to charge another with a lack of humanity towards a few dozen American citizens.[1]

That the German nation wishes to live on the best terms with the American people has already been proved in many places and on many occasions by the unmistakeable voice of the people themselves. But America has no right to add to the one great *wrong*—the toleration of a gross breach of neutrality—a second folly—the demand that Germany give up her "U-boat" warfare—merely because England is at present

---

[1] Stockholm, June 10, 1915. The "Svenska Morgenbladet," speaking of the breach between Secretary of State Bryan and President Wilson, writes: "Spiteful language levelled against Germany because of the "Lusitania" affair is scarcely in keeping with a country which, by permitting American citizens to embark as a protection for a cargo of munitions, is itself in part guilty for the sinking of the ship. America, through this, loses from a moral standpoint all right to levy accusations. By levying war upon Germany America could harm Germany in no greater degree than it has already done by its neutral delivery of munitions. Wilson's attitude is influenced by a vigorous partisanship of England as against Germany. Wilson has done nothing to hinder England's attempt to starve out Germany, although he knew that the cessation of the starving-out policy would also mean an end to the submarine war."

placed at a disadvantage by it—England which meanly and sneeringly rejected all proposals of mediation made by the United States.

England, by reason of her mode of conducting her mercantile war and by reason of her proclaiming the North Sea as a zone of war, is alone responsible for all the consequences that have ensued. Germany, as we have seen in the foregoing, has expressed her willingness to give up this method of warfare if England would consent to give up her illegal "paper blockade" and contraband campaign. Here again the United States made application to the wrong party with their proffers of mediation. So far these have availed nothing and it is not likely that they will ever avail anything. England can be forced to budge only by *force*, by the "old system"—to adopt Mr. Bryan's phrase, and not by *argument*—or the "new system." Therefore, if the government of the United States would procure for its citizens the right of travelling freely upon the merchant ships of all nations without endangering their lives, let it first resort to force in order to prevent England from committing the most outrageous of all breaches of neutrality—the misuse of other nations' flags—or from resorting to the use of auxiliary cruisers for the transportation of passengers.

Precisely at the psychological moment Dr. Wehberg properly reminds us in the "Kölnische Zeitung," of the following disquisition of the English delegate to the Hague Conference of 1907.

"The English representative, Lord Reay, a member of the Privy Council and former President of the Institute of International Law, declared as follows;—his opinions constitute an important justification on the part of England for our entire procedure:

"Ships which render such services, bestow a hostile support upon the belligerent, which his opponent cannot consider as permissible. They are through this subject to all the consequences entailed by the position of a regular belligerent. It is not a simple mercantile enterprise which is here in question, but an interference in the operations of war. The ships which undertake this supply service are unconditionally subject to the orders of the regular authorities of the belligerents. Their warlike character is indisputable, since they participate actively in the operations of war. The shipping companies which in this manner place their vessels at the disposal of one of the belligerents, thereby expose themselves to all the dangers which threaten the warships of that belligerent to whom they give hostile support.

Were one to regard their action as legal, it would merely result in a prolongation of the war and an extension of the field of operations. The acceptance of the English proposal would on the contrary lead to an increased protection for the neutrals and a limitation of the fighting forces to the means commanded by the belligerents themselves."

(Protocol of the Conference, Volume II, page 847 *et seq.*)
(*retranslation*)

To sum up: Germany, in view of the British procedure, could not act otherwise than she did—and she stands thereby upon the basis of international law.

The chief question contained in the note may be stated as the following:—whether it is reconciliable with the principles of humanity to torpedo a passenger ship when this offers no resistance or when it seeks to evade search and inquiry through flight?

This is, without doubt, the crux of the note, for it is a question which closely touches the very essence of warfare by submarine. The justification of submarine warfare is thereby attacked in its very principles. In other words nothing less is demanded than that the old principles of cruiser warfare should be applied to the new forms of warfare of the submersible boat. This, as is well-known, is impossible, without completely paralyzing submarine action, since the submarine lacks the means whereby it would be able to carry on an examination of a suspicious vessel—such as is possible to a cruiser with heavy guns and a crew of many hundreds of men. It is difficult to say at present just how Germany could answer this question save by declining to accede to its postulates—unless England likewise definitely suspends her provocative system of freebooting. Germany cannot afford to forego her right of insisting that this question be not answered in a just and impartial manner.[1]

It is significant that even the "Daily Telegraph" reports from New York on June 1st, 1915:

"The proposal of the German answer to the American note is precisely the same method of procedure the application of which has been urgently recommended by Bryan in all American proposals and treaties of settlement."

In spite of this, President Wilson, the Apostle of Peace, almost brought Germany and the United States to the verge of war—even though the most primitive rules of justice would have made it necessary to fulfil the duty of at least investigating, however late in the day, those charges which clearly proved England's breach of common as well as international law.[2]

In another note the American Government assumes as its own standpoint the one-sided and illegal *English* contention, so strenuously combated at the Hague and London Conferences,—that "merchant vessels may be armed for their

---

[1] If the news reported by the N. Y. "Fatherland" regarding the closing down of the wireless stations at Sayville and Tuckerton be correct, we should really be justified in assuming that the pacifistic Wilson has in mind a policy of sheer provocation similar to that of Signor Salandra—and is deliberately forcing a war. Bryan's honorable resignation would in this case, appear in a still more favorable light.

[1] Wilson, in his note of the 23rd of July, 1915, likewise obstinately refuses in any way to consider the decisive facts. He persistently doctrinizes like a professor, declaring that an American may remain at his pleasure within the theatres of war. Why does not Wilson make the same representations to that really scientifically-minded press of America which rejected as ridiculous these very contentions when applied in the case of Belgium, Northern France and Russia? He will not acknowledge that in view of England's lawless misuse of flags and the ramming of submarines by merchant-ships, it would be suicidal for the German U-boats to conduct the preliminary examination which he demands.

Where there is a flare-up, a peaceful man goes out of his way to avoid it: a hot-headed brawler, the chip on his shoulder, sticks his hands in his pockets and shouts: "I have a right to go walking here; whoever opposes me is my mortal enemy." That is Wilson's policy. And instead of at least shaking his fist against the incendiary in present case (England) he threatens the fireman (Germany) who is trying to protect his own property and that of the brawler himself!

own defense"—in order thus to circumvent, under the plea of "self-defense," laws which have been recognized by all nations. An organized belligerent power does not act contrary to law when it makes use of the force of arms by means of its warships—so that the term "self-defense" cannot be said to apply in the case of merchant vessels. Were it otherwise, one might permit every mail steamer full of passengers to be equipped with "guns for the purpose of defense"—guns which naturally might at any time be employed for the purpose of attacking submarines. This is as nonsensical as is the demand that every auxiliary cruiser, carrying vast stores of ammunition, is to be considered as immune from attack merely because an American happened to be aboard her! The fate that would befall Germany should she subscribe to theories of that sort is proved by the treacherous running down of the German submarine "U 29," commanded by the heroic Captain Weddigen, by means of an English tank-steamer flying the Swedish flag, as well as the "U 14," and the attempts to ram others—in June, 1915.

The answer of the German Government to the American note of June 10th, 1915, is dated Berlin, July 8th, 1915, and the text is as follows in the official Embassy translation:

"The Undersigned has the honor to make the following reply to the Note of His Excellency, Mr. James W. Gerard, Ambassador of the United States of America, dated the 10th ult., on the subject of the impairment of American interests by the German submarine war.

The Imperial Government has learned with satisfaction from the Note how earnestly the Government of the United States is concerned in seeing the principles of humanity realized in the present war also. This appeal finds a ready echo in Germany and the Imperial Government is quite willing to permit its statements and decisions in the case under consideration to be governed by the principles of humanity just as it has done always.

The Imperial Government welcomed it with gratitude when the American Government in its Note of May 15, 1915, itself recalled that Germany had always permitted itself to be governed by the principles of progress and humanity in dealing with the law of maritime war. Since the time when Frederick the Great negotiated with John Adams, Benjamin Franklin and Thomas Jefferson the Treaty of Friendship and Commerce of September 10, 1785, between Prussia and the Republic of the West, German and American statesmen have in fact always stood together in the struggle for the freedom of the seas and for the protection of peaceable trade. In the international proceedings which have since been conducted for the regulation of the right of maritime war, Germany and America have jointly advocated progressive principles, especially the abolishment of the right of capture at sea and the protection of the interests of neutrals. Even at the beginning of the present war the German Government immediately declared its willingness, in response to the proposal of the American Government, to ratify the Declaration of London and thereby to subject itself, in the use of its naval forces, to all the restrictions provided therein in favor of neutrals. Germany has likewise been always tenacious of the principle that war should be conducted against the armed and organized forces of the enemy country, but that the civilian population of the enemy must be spared as far as possible from the measures of war. The Imperial Government cherishes the definite hope that some way will be found when peace is concluded, or perhaps earlier, to regulate the law of maritime war in a manner guaranteeing the freedom of the seas, and will welcome it with gratitude and satisfaction if it can work hand in hand with the American Government on that occasion.

If in the present war the principles which should be the ideal of the future have been traversed more and more the longer its duration the German Government has no guilt therein.

It is known to the American Government how Germany's adversaries, by completely paralyzing peaceable traffic between Germany and the neutral countries, have aimed from the very beginning, and with increasing lack of consideration, at the destruction not so much of the armed forces as the life of the German nation, repudiating in so doing all the rules of international law and disregarding all the rights of neutrals. On November 3, 1914, England declared the North Sea to be a war area and by planting poorly-anchored mines and the stoppage and capture of vessels, made passage extremely dangerous and difficult for neutral shipping, so that it is actually blockading neutral coasts and ports contrary to all international law. Long before the beginning of the submarine war England practically completely intercepted legitimate neutral navigation to Germany also. Thus Germany was driven to submarine war on trade. On November 16, 1914, the English Prime Minister declared in the House of Commons that it was one of England's principal tasks to prevent food for the German population from reaching Germany by way of neutral ports. Since March first of this year England has been taking from neutral ships without further formality all merchandise proceeding to Germany as well as all merchandise coming from Germany even when neutral property. Just as was the case with the Boers, the German people is now to be given the choice of perishing from starvation with its women and children or of relinquishing its independence.

While our enemies thus loudly and openly have proclaimed war without mercy until our utter destruction, we are conducting war in self-defence for our national existence and for the sake of a peace of assured permanency. We have been obliged to adapt submarine warfare to meet the declared intentions of our enemies and the method of warfare adopted by them in contravention of international law.

With all its efforts in principle to protect neutral life and property from damage as much as possible, the German Government recognized unreservedly in its Memorandum of February 4th that the interests of neutrals might suffer from submarine warfare. However, the American Government will also understand and appreciate that in the fight for existence which has been forced upon Germany by its adversaries and announced by them it is the sacred duty of the Imperial Government to do all within its power to protect and to save the lives of German subjects. If the Imperial Government were derelict in these its duties it would be guilty before God and History of the violation of those principles of the highest humanity which are the foundation of every national existence.

The case of the "Lusitania" shows with horrible clearness to what jeopardizing of human lives the manner of conducting war employed by our adversaries leads. In most direct contradiction of international law all distinctions between merchantmen and war vessels have been obliterated by the order to British merchantmen to arm themselves and to ram submarines, and the promise of rewards therefor; and neutrals who use merchantmen as travellers have thereby been exposed in an increasing degree to all the dangers of war. If the commander of the German submarine which destroyed the "Lusitania" had caused the crew and travellers to put out in boats before firing the torpedo, this would have meant the sure destruction of his own vessel. After the experiences in the sinking of much smaller and less seaworthy vessels it was to be expected that a mighty ship like the "Lusitania" would remain above water long enough even after the torpedoing to permit the passengers to enter the ship's boats. Circumstances of a very peculiar kind, especially the presence on board of large quantities of highly explosive materials, defeated this expectation. In addition it may be pointed out that if the "Lusitania" had been spared thousands of cases of ammunition would have been sent to Germany's enemies and thereby thousands of German mothers and children robbed of their supporters.

In the spirit of friendship with which the German nation has been imbued towards the Union and its inhabitants since the earliest days of its existence, the Imperial Government will always be ready to do all it can, during the present war also, to prevent the jeopardizing of the lives of American citizens.

The Imperial Government therefore repeats the assurances that American ships will not be hindered in the prosecution of legitimate shipping and the lives of American citizens on neutral vessels shall not be placed in jeopardy.

In order to exclude any unforeseen dangers to American passenger steamers made possible in view of the conduct of maritime war on the part of Germany's adversaries, the German submarines will be instructed to permit the free and safe passage of such passenger steamers when made recognizable by special markings and notified a reasonable time in advance. The Imperial Government however confidently hopes that the American Government will assume the guarantee that these vessels have no contraband on board. The details of the arrangements for the unhampered passage of these vessels would have to be agreed upon by the naval authorities of both sides.

In order to furnish adequate facilities for travel across the Atlantic Ocean for American citizens, the German Government submits for consideration the proposal to increase the number of available steamers by installing in the passenger service a reasonable number of neutral steamers under the American flag, the exact number to be agreed upon, under the same conditions as the American steamers mentioned above.

The Imperial Government believes that it can assume that in this manner adequate facilities for travel across the Atlantic Ocean be afforded American citizens. There would therefore appear to be no compelling necessity for American citizens to travel to Europe in time of war on ships carrying an enemy flag. In particular the Imperial Government is unable to admit that American citizens can protect an enemy ship through the mere fact of their presence on board. Germany merely followed England's example when it declared part of the high seas an area of war. Consequently accidents suffered by neutrals on enemy ships in this area of war cannot well be judged differently from accidents to which neutrals are at all times exposed at the seat of war on land when they betake themselves into dangerous localities in spite of previous warning.

If however it should not be possible for the American Government to acquire an adequate number of neutral passenger steamers, the Imperial Government is prepared to interpose no objections to the placing under the American flag by the American Government of four enemy passenger steamers for the passenger traffic between North America and England. The assurances of "free and safe" passage for American passenger steamers would then be extended to apply under the identical preconditions to these formerly hostile passenger steamers.

The President of the United States has declared his readiness, in a way deserving of thanks, to communicate and suggest proposals to the Government of Great Britain with particular reference to the alteration of maritime war. The Imperial Government will always be glad to make use of the good offices of the President and hopes that his efforts in the present case as well as in the direction of the lofty ideal of the freedom of the seas will lead to an understanding.

The Undersigned requests the Ambassador to bring the above to the knowledge of the American Government and avails himself of the opportunity to renew to His Excellency the assurance of his most distinguished consideration."

(signed) von Jagow.

To His Excellency, the Ambassador of the United States of America, Mr. James W. Gerard.

Moreover the German Government had made a very simple proposal in the best of faith to the American Government, since the latter had expressed a desire to "mediate." Germany merely requested that she be given the same control over American exports as had already been granted to the English. If the American Government had agreed to this in an honest and truly neutral spirit all quarrels would have come to an end! Then the disgraceful traffic in munitions would also have ceased. And the American Government would have had an opportunity for doing something for the high and holy rights of humanity. Up to the present it has merely preached humanity, and acted in direct, violent and monumental opposition to it.

The American eagle, in travesty of the republic's own coat of arms, held in one claw an olive branch *for* England, in the other guns and bayonets *against* Germany. The magnitude of this gigantic historical wrong, or rather crime, is in effect, quadruple, both in extent and intensity, in view of the fact that America had always been shown nothing but good-will and friendship by Germany, whereas every move that England has made, both in the past as well as the present, has been to the detriment of the republic.

In the original the author treats of the English and South African atrocities perpetrated against Germans. He shows how these cover the name of England with ineradicable blots of shame. These English pogroms are a blow in the face of all the decencies of civilized peoples. The contrast between the care, protection and consideration afforded enemy subjects and enemy property in orderly and dignified Germany is glaringly apparent. The horrible excesses committed by bestial mobs in

Moscow and other Russian cities against harmless German civilians and their businesses attests the true spirit of barbarism.

The damage done by these outbursts of brutality, and lust for looting is calculated to amount to about a half billion of roubles. (Pages 554 to 556.)

Italy's Betrayal of her Allies. The Basest Act of Perfidy in all History.

Chapter XLIII of the original work treats more fully of Italy's betrayal of her Allies and her breach of neutrality under a motto taken from "The Temptation of Pescara," by Konrad Ferdinand Meyer:

"Thou art a son of Italy and therefore above all faith and all conscience!"

The author proves that the treaty between Austria-Hungary and Italy (the text of which is given in full in the original), could not have applied, even by the most wilful misinterpretation, to the war with Servia, but only to Turkish contingencies, and that Italy had made demands for "compensations" immediately, on the 5th of July, 1914, thus even before the war. It had spoken of "advantages" which the Dual Monarchy had obtained for itself and claimed "damages" for these. See page 561, *et seq.* in the original work.

In summing up his indictment of Italy's conduct the author remarks: It must be acknowledged that Italy's base betrayal of its former allies is to be condemned more from the standpoint of ordinary morals, being a foul violation of all the ethical concepts of faith and belief in the sanctity of solemn compacts. But even from the viewpoint of international law this country deserves the severest condemnation on the part of mankind. For, in direct abuse of still valid agreements and compacts, it made new agreements with the enemies of its allies, and in breach of its own solemn promises, broke faith with its partners behind their backs. It is an act which for low and degraded faithlessness and vile greed for the possessions of others, stands forth in infamous isolation in the history of the world.

The horrible picture is completed by the monstrous cynicism

of a state which under the threat of attack seeks vilely to extort from its hard-beset brother ally lands to which it has no right and then stabs him in the back and prates of a "breach" of treaty on the other side—a breach of which it spoke no word while engaged in auctioning itself off to the highest bidder! Moreover Italy had broken mere neutrality towards its partners in the Alliance during many months, in that it permitted the French enemy of its ally to withdraw hundreds of thousands of troops from the Italian frontiers. In fact, instead of exercising the "benevolent neutrality" this Judas of the nations boasted of, its "neutrality" was from the very beginning of things not only hostile but despicable. It was for this reason that Italy permitted England to treat it as she pleased.

Turati, a Deputy of the Italian Parliament, justly declared in his speech of the 21st of May, that Italy had long before outraged all the postulates of true neutrality.

The verdict of the Swiss press is incontrovertible: "*Whoever protests against the violation of Belgian neutrality, must also protest against the violation of the treaty of the Triple Alliance.*"

The whole of this *perfidia Italica* is revealed in the telegram sent by King Victor Emanuel on August 2nd, 1914, in answer to a despatch by Emperor Franz Josef in which the King declared that he need not assure his ally that Italy would do all that lay in its power to bring about the restoration of peace as soon as possible, and that it would preserve towards its allies a cordial and friendly attitude in accordance with the treaty of the Triple Alliance, its own sincere feelings and the great interests which it must guard. (Austrian Red Book, II, Page 22 and 24.) Immediately upon the report of Count Berchtold the Italian Government announced on July 25th, that it intended in the event of an armed conflict, to "preserve a friendly attitude, in keeping with its duties as an ally!"

The publication of this despatch utterly damns the action of the king of Italy. Here, after dashing to bits all fidelity to the Alliance of which it was a member, Italy once more solemnly assures its allies of its "friendly" and its "benevolent neutrality." This is without doubt the most shameful example of Latin treachery and perfidy known to the history of the world!

Even the neutral press, especially that of Switzerland and Sweden, is convinced of this, and has openly proclaimed its disgust.

The policy of the camorra, that is to say, of breach of faith and betrayal on a wholesale scale, has in the case of Italy been made an *official and leading principle of the state.*

Even Italy's refusal to intervene on behalf of its Allies in August, 1914, was nothing less than a breach of contract. (See Austrian Red Book, II, page 5.) At the time at which Austria is alleged to have committed a breach of treaty, the declaration of neutrality by Italy was couched in these terms: "Italy will consider what means it is to take in order to be of friendly use to its allies." That is to say: "benevolent neutrality!"

The annulment of the alliance by Italy on May 3rd, 1915, the terms of which were not to expire until the year 1920 and were subject to one year's notice being given, and the hostile manifestations of its so-called neutrality, constitute therefore not only a breach of faith so far as a compact is concerned, but a wanton outrage upon the law of nations. The grounds for this monstrous act, based upon a tardy notification of the Austrian-Hungarian ultimatum of July 22nd, 1914, were the more grotesque, since Italy itself had violated the terms of the Triple Alliance in the most contemptible fashion. (See original edition, page 564.)

The fact remains that Austria-Hungary had notified Italy of this ultimatum as early as all the other Great Powers The reader is referred to the original German version for a detailed presentation of the facts based upon the official documents, page 565 *et seq.*

The "Esercito," the official organ of the Italian Ministry of War, published an article in September 1914, in which these words occur: "*Should Italy now attack the Monarchy (Austria-Hungary) the government would be guilty of an act of felony and of suicide in the eyes of history.*"

The King of Italy spoke thus to the Cardinal-Archbishop of Vienna, Monsignor Piffl, during the winter of 1914: "Let no one be disquieted. I should be the first of the House of Savoy that had ever broken his word." And then he broke it out of fear of the howling hooligans of the street. "Only I and the canaille would have been capable of acting thus," this weak puppet of a king under the dominance of the mob, is said to have exclaimed. But his actions were as ruthless as those of his ministers,—those gentry who had so recently been loud in their praises of "benevolent neutrality," without giving a thought to any subsequent and shifty interpretation of old agreements of 1901 and 1912.[1]

In the universal orgy and delirium of war all honest policies were bound to be smothered and submerged. "The Angler with the Artificial Fly," (the life work of King Edward and the title of the only book Sir Edward Grey ever wrote) hooked a new fish—which now writhes and flounders on its gory hook—all for the benefit of England.[2]

---

[1] Italy's evil conscience is very clearly seen in its anti-German press ("Corriere della Sera," "Secolo," and so on), which pretends to find a necessity for the war by saying that Germany and Austria-Hungary are really pursuing a policy of revenge on account of Italy's betrayal and breach of faith in August, 1914. Italy was consequently thrown into the arms of the Triple Entente! This is real Italian brigand thought, which, out of fear and an evil conscience, endeavors thus to impute its own motives to the Central Powers!

[2] Against the will of the saner politicians, the original majority in the Senate, the House of Representatives, and almost all the former ministers, —the King, the street mob and the bribed press, have made this war.

Here is a picture of the latest "Cousin of His Majesty," the War-fomenter-in-chief, Gabriele d'Annunzio, which is at the same time a picture of the whole shameful nation of degenerates which follows him:

The Socialist organ "Avanti" writes in the issue of the 16th of May: "What signs of corruption and moral degradation! In Milan the rejected of all men and the renegades are carried about in triumph by the beardless youth. In Rome the hired mob, which has been fed from the troughs of the bureaucracy, has been getting drunk on the blatant speeches of Gabriele d'Annunzio. And what speeches! The singer of all kinds of criminal decadence has incited a grateful audience in the Theatre Costanzi to betake themselves on Thursday to Montecitorio, and to force the deputies, who were there to decide Italy's political position, to declare for war and assume the offensive. Here is an incitement to open treachery. D'Annunzio as leader and inspirer of the national conscience! This brings a flush of shame to one's cheeks. This fellow, a public example of abhorrent indecency, who always showed the greatest contempt for all the laws which rule the lives of ordinary decent citizens, who made

The translated text of the various notes is given in the original, page 572 *et seq.*

The madness of the spy-fever seized upon Italy in its turn and led to the most degraded forms of brutal excess, such as the demolition of the furnishings of the Hotel Metropole in Milan. These organized outbursts of sheer animalism in Milan, a town in which the mob raged and ruled in its anarchistic fury and looted and devastated some eighty German and Austrian shops in a single day, took place with the open assent and toleration of the police and the military. It was only after it was too late that the latter intervened in an energetic way. The same conditions prevailed at Turin and at Ancona. The "Avanti" of Milan declares that the new Prefect had ascertained that 980 dwellings had been looted, 672 business quarters destroyed and a great number of valuable goods stolen from the houses of Italians during these riots of the mob.

Apart from all this there were other acts and outrages which were quite Russian in their character. The German Consulate in Milan was stormed by the mob on the afternoon of May 28th, 1915, without the slightest effort being made by

---

a disgusting traffic of his talent, added new and shameful pages to the Italian "Chroniques Scandaleuses," whose name dishonors even the List of Bankrupts, who, in conclusion, on account of his unbridled excesses, sought refuge in France, from whence for some years he used to hurl his spite and his reproaches against Italy and the Italians,—this D'Annunzio it is who suddenly appears in the character of a leader and counsellor of the nation, and as a prophet of war! Such triumphs cannot pain us. When that class which declares that it moulds the destinies of the nation furnishes an example of moral paralysis such as this it must certainly make every effort to withstand the severest tests. Nevertheless the most terrible disillusions are in store for it. The orgy of patriotism, of which D'Annunzio is a symbol, is only the outward sign of an approaching decay. And when the war comes, when affliction, want and agony descend upon our country, and the unhappy situation of our people is rendered still worse by the oppression of the wretched working classes, then, as always, the people alone will have to endure these consequences. For the poet will once more have crossed the Alps, to revel in his heathenish pleasures among strangers, there to enjoy in comfort the fruits of these heroic labors of his which have plunged the Italian people in a bath of blood...."

What can be the worth of a people that will follow a leadership such as this?

the police to hinder it. The furniture and the archives were flung into the streets and everything was burnt.

Herr Wahl, a German Consular Agent at Bologna, as well as the Chief Clerk of the Austrian-Hungarian Consulate at the same place, have described the brutality of Italians in official positions. The vile calumny that Italians had been murdered in Germany was supposed to serve as an excuse.

All this madness and depravity was received in Germany with the most high-minded reserve and magnanimous serenity. Scarcely a single Italian was molested. On the contrary hundreds of Italians living in Germany demanded certificates of naturalization, and cursed the foul betrayal of their Fatherland. Thousands declared that they would prefer to remain in Germany, since they did not wish to join in the criminal war which had been unloosed by their former Fatherland, and would rather suffer arrest and internment than fight against that country which had shown constant kindness not only to them but to their own country.

It is to some degree gratifying to think that even a nation of base Black-handers still possesses sane and worthy elements which are capable of shame.

Italy must in the future be utterly despised, and the consequences of its reptilian conduct forced home and carried out to the utmost economic degree. Germany's other enemies acted at least in accordance with their treaties and alliances, even though in opposition to Germany, and, though criminal in their aims, may be recognized as open adversaries. But for Italy, through all the records of time, there can be only contempt. No German who has the least self-respect will ever again have anything in common with Italian cowardice and Italian treachery.[1]

[1] In the Original work the author discusses in an appendix, the barbarous treatment to which the German civil prisoners were subjected by the French in Dahomey and North Africa. The tragic situation of these poor people, transported to an infernal climate where their health suffered under the most unbearable conditions, is only one more instance of that pogromish and sadistic spirit of cruelty which seems to live in the hearts of Germany's enemies.

CHAPTER XXXII.

A Final Political Survey.

I.

We accuse the French, Belgian, English and Russian army authorities of the following: that under their very eyes, by their sufferance and even by their orders, all international laws, both by water and by land, have been violated not only by the civil population which these laws decree must be kept apart from the fight, but also by the official armies of the various powers. They have disregarded all the customs that have hitherto prevailed among civilized peoples, all the laws of humanity and all the demands of public conscience.

We charge the governments of the Triple Entente with a systematic deception of other countries from the very beginning of the war, a deception intended to conceal their own wanton outrages and by means of falsehoods to throw the onus of blame upon those who, because of the degradation of warfare by the Entente, were forced to make use of reprisals,—reprisals of which they had given due and urgent warning before the war and for which they must now justly disclaim all responsibility.

We charge these governments with building up artificial barriers of hate by means of these tissues of lies,—barriers between our children and children's children and those of the enemy, and that by this they perpetrate a crime against the future of humanity!

We charge above all the government of Great Britain with the fact that for sordid reasons, out of lust of power and out of envy of the fruits of German industry and German energy, it has abused its influence in order to loose this world-conflagration which it alone could have prevented. We charge it with double-dealing in its alleged policy of peace, of a corrupting dependence upon the despotism of Russia, of craft and cunning against its own people, and of inner dishonesty toward both friend and foe.

We charge it with attempting in its inconceivable blindness to "starve out" a great civilized kindred nation, by annulling all the ethics of the commercial world, an enterprise more dastardly and more barbaric than laying the torch of war against the homes of the peoples—and an act far more foolish than one might have attributed to an enemy so cunning and so calculating.

We accuse all those who with eyes turned to Heaven in their unutterable hypocrisy and with their right hands clutching the printed Word of God, practise a lip service of Christianity, yet do not scruple to send against our cultivated homesteads their heathen negro hordes, their yellow Jap robbers, their Indian and Africanish beasts as well as the scum of their prisons and their slums, or, with a besotted mania that verges on the suicidal, to hound on Kaffirs and Hereros against white civilized people in the African colonies—an act so abysmally atrocious that most of the Boer population of South Africa, not yet corrupted by English ways, refused to participate in the dastardly act, and arose in revolt.

We accuse them of treating sacred compacts and the rights of nations and all the customs of war sanctioned by the peoples, as though they were merely so many conventional lies.

We charge England with exercising a tyranny of the seas which renders all real international law an utter impossibility and brings about a condition of perpetual wrong upon the "free seas." Will the neutral nations, especially those of Germanic and Scandinavian peoples, not see whither this must lead? Will the League of Central European States, will the Union of the Germanic nations and those of the Western Slavs and of Islam, form a bulwark for the future against Muscovite megalomania and British tyranny? We have no means of knowing this today. The future of Europe is darker than it has ever been before.

History shall yet drag the unholy perpetrators of all these horrors before the tribunal of the world. And may the wretched democracies never forget the monstrous game by means of which some dozens of unscrupulous, so-called statesmen, and demagogues and gutter journalists of the Harmsworth stripe, hounded them into the ruinous carnage,—may they remember this and arrange their policies in the future in accordance with their bitter experience. That species of insanity which is known as Chauvinism will have a terrible awakening. And may all this result finally in a triumph for the reason of all the peoples!

This book is likewise dedicated to the high and honorable traditions of the German army. It is not that the German army requires defense at the hands of its own people. They who know the soul of Germany know this all too well. They know that the titanic strength of this towering young Siegfried is qualified by properties of intellect and soul which turn that base and monstrous caricature created by a criminal press into the abortion of a festering imagination.

A clean conscience and the knowledge of the moral force and power inherent in our just cause,—that cause so heroically defended by our army of the people,—might suffice us, were it not necessary to collect and coordinate all the available material in order that at a later day it may be presented for the consideration of those neutral lands whose credulity has been so shamefully abused.

Another purpose which this work endeavors to fulfil is that by the nature of its contents—to which it is hoped more or less historical value attaches,—it may serve as a terrible warning to the coming generations, proving to them how hatred and envy, wickedness and falsehood were able in the twentieth century to drag the so-called civilized nations down to a conception of warfare long since held impossible, a warfare that is nothing but a negation of all that had hitherto been known to civilization. The future of the German people rests only in our own forces. And so does the future of international law. Such is the lesson taught by these arduous times.

II.

We have been forced to reveal hideous pictures of cruelty, brutality and the lust to slay, of hate and unutterable baseness. The written laws of the nations lie trampled and torn in the dust. Those laws, those customs which rest upon morality and reason and ancient and venerable tradition,—laws which had never before been disputed and which were meant to render war between the nations less terrible and more humane, —these have been ignored,—nay, in many instances, despised! The wise labors and endeavors of generations, achievements which marked the proud progress of true civilization more than all technical or other triumphs, have been spat upon and made a mockery.

And yet, despite all this, there is no State that ventures to deny the validity, the sanctity of these laws! No State but is convinced that it abides by them, and swears to that effect. In the bare maintenance of the principle and in the direct appeal to it by that belligerent power which has most betrayed it—does not this attest the vitality of the principle itself and of the thought, and offer a hope for the future? There is no State that dares to say: "I laugh at these laws which you so cunningly devise. Your right is simply my might." There are States that act thus—but there is none that ventures to say so. On the contrary they call Heaven and earth to witness that they regard the laws of nations with the deepest reverence. *What would be the condition of things if there were no international law at all?*

In spite of all that we have lived through, this ideal, this concept of international law and that "world-opinion" which is so closely bound up with it—still live and will continue to live. Perhaps they may become reinvigorated and more powerful than ever before. Many a nation, most of all the German, will discover that it has paid all too little attention to this "world-opinion," and that this has led to its being so hopelessly misunderstood. No less will the great victory achieved by the victory of the idea of the State, a victory over even the viewpoints of race and nation,—a victory which is the most characteristic element in this gigantic struggle,—tend to show the tremendous forces that abide in the power of right and in its organization.

"To remember the principles of international law, is to preserve the common inheritance of civilized nations, and to prevent that progress which mankind owes to centuries of labor, from falling into decay." Such was the just pronouncement of the three Scandinavian nations in their protests against "certain belligerents."

For that reason we need not and cannot close this work with a vision too dark or pessimistic. It would mean nothing less than to despair of the sane reason of the nations, of every advance of humanity—a tendency cherished today by millions in view of the action of our enemies,—were the prospect towards the future as dismal as that of the present. Hate can create nothing that is permanent, it can but poison and destroy. Its gradual diminution will be the chief task and demand of the day, however great one's love for one's homeland and Fatherland may be. A better understanding, a policy of civilization embodied in the "open door and the open eye" must succeed to this most tragic of all the epochs of history. A feeling of stupendous and fathomless shame must make itself felt in the hearts of the people, who have now helplessly succumbed to the hysteria of their "spiritual leaders" and partly to the lures of their political charlatans and mountebanks.

The aspect offered by the German people forces one to a most hopeful optimism. The German people has truly found itself, in a sublime exaltation, and like some stalwart young hero it has purged its body of all traces of national, social, political and religious decadence. It is not in lust of land, not in dreams of conquest that we must seek the German ideal, but in the organization of the vital life of the state developed inwardly and outwardly to its highest degree. Even today there is no other land in which the idea of justice is so closely interwoven with the ideà of the state as in Germany.

Furthermore, it is also in the life of nations that the principle of the conservation of energy holds good. Paradoxical as it may at present appear, all the blood that now flows on every side, all those gigantic sacrifices which all the civilized nations now make upon the battle-field, will nevertheless operate in helping to build up a great and enduring common law in order to shield those common interests of all civilized nations—interests which exist, however cruelly they may at present be disturbed by the war. War will be made upon the horrors of war in a manner which few can now foresee. The "collapse of international law" which has become almost a stock phrase in Germany, a collapse which resulted under the blows of the mace wielded by the god of war, is merely temporary, even though many may regard it as amounting to the practical death of all such law hitherto existent. Purer, clearer, and mightier than ever before will the code of laws that binds the nations of the world lift itself out of the ruins, when the historic mission of Germany has been achieved, when the freedom of the "right to work" has been attained by a German victory by land and sea. The future will prove this,—and living men shall yet hail it as a blessed reality.

For our German people and our German Fatherland this exalted hour shall be a period of purgation, of instruction for the errors of the past, a time of testing and of probation.

The unparalleled, free and heroic devotion of the whole nation to the service of the Fatherland proves that the spirit of its great democratic army has seized upon all levels of the people. A common necessity creates a vast and profound confidence and a common spring of action.

Carlyle declared that Germany had since ancient times, been the most peace-loving and the strongest of all nations—and one that inspired the most reverence. He held the view that it should become the spiritual leader of Europe and that according to all appearances this office would be conferred upon it for five centuries to come.[1]

Today we merely know that the first part of this opinion of Thomas Carlyle's is correct. Germany's victorious resistance against a world of enemies has furnished the historical evidence thereof. Whether the second of these prophetic utterances is to find its fulfilment only the future can show.

At all events war for Germany will not mean only the Great Destroyer, but also the Great Regulator and the Great Master-Builder of the entire inner and outer structure of the land. The War of Liberation of 1813 gave us our German freedom from without, the war of 1870 our inner unity. Whether the war of 1914/15 will bring us social peace, as so many declare, I do not know. But I doubt it. Yet surely it ought to bring us Germans the tremendous testing and firm establishment of all that we have achieved during the last century in a political, a military, an economic and a cultural sense.

This heroic people has already withstood this ordeal in the most marvellous manner. May its policy be a continuance of these lofty deeds and successes. May our entire domestic policy in the future be actuated by the conviction that the triumph and the position and the future of a nation depend upon the moral and the physical power of a people filled with the spirit of a joyous pride in that state. This is the first lesson taught by the war.

Do not forget, O German People, all that your heroic sons have fought for. Never forget, you Princes of Germany, that this great hour must also give birth to years of unlimited trust in the nation, if the great, newly-created national values, the newly-found and immense moral and ideal treasures are not once more to sink miserably into ruin. From such an end may the good Genius of the United German People protect them to the end of time!

FSC
www.fsc.org
MIX
Papier | Fördert gute Waldnutzung
FSC® C083411

Kolibri 360 GmbH
Ferdinand-Jühlke-Straße 7
99095 Erfurt, Deutschland
produktsicherheit@kolibri360.de